BEING BENEVOLENCE

Topics in Contemporary Buddhism
GEORGE G. TANABE, JR., EDITOR

Establishing a Pure Land on Earth: The Foguang Buddhist Perspective on Modernization and Globalization
STUART CHANDLER

Buddhist Missionaries in the Era of Globalization
LINDA LEARMAN, EDITOR

Being Benevolence: The Social Ethics of Engaged Buddhism
SALLIE B. KING

TOPICS IN
CONTEMPORARY
BUDDHISM

BEING BENEVOLENCE

The Social Ethics of Engaged Buddhism

SALLIE B. KING

University of Hawai'i Press
Honolulu

**Library of Congress Cataloging-in-
Publication Data**
King, Sallie B.
Being benevolence: the social ethics
of engaged Buddhism / Sallie B. King.
p. cm. — (Topics in contemporary Buddhism)
Includes bibliographical references and index.
ISBN-13: 978-0-8248-2864-6 (hardcover : alk. paper)
ISBN-10: 0-8248-2864-X (hardcover : alk. paper)
ISBN-13: 978-0-8248-2935-3 (pbk : alk. paper)
ISBN-10: 0-8248-2935-2 (pbk : alk. paper)
1. Buddhism—Doctrines. 2. Buddhist ethics.
3. Buddhism—Social aspects. I. Title. II. Series.
BQ4160.K56 2005
294.3'37—dc22   2005006988

Designed by Elsa Carl, Clarence Lee Design
Printed by The Maple-Vail Book Manufacturing Group

For Steve, Leslie, and Sarah

Contents

Series Editor's Preface

One of the most significant developments in contemporary Buddhism in Asia and the West has been the development of Engaged Buddhism. This is a particularly important and difficult challenge for a religion that values detachment as a central ideal. Whereas Buddhists throughout the ages have been involved with society, their development of a social and political philosophy has not been as advanced as their teachings on inner spirituality. Engaged Buddhism arises from and responds to this vacuum and is committed to the production of a viable social philosophy that remains true to Buddhist teachings.

Engaged Buddhism distinguishes itself from contemporary Buddhist fashions centered primarily on personal faith, enlightened disengagement, or, as a popular phrase puts it, a radical acceptance of everything. Engaged Buddhism promotes judgment, critique, and action against social maladies and political injustice, and it confronts the world even at the risk of compromising its spiritual ideals.

In this study of Engaged Buddhism, Sallie King provides a comprehensive survey and critical evaluation of the major Asian exponents of Engaged Buddhism in our time. She also gives her own philosophical analyses, which attempt to resolve some of the thorny problems of applying Buddhist teachings to social and political realities. By her own estimation, Engaged Buddhism is a work in progress, and this volume tracks its growth in Asia and contributes to its advancement as a religion capable of dealing with economic and political realities of the contemporary world.

George J. Tanabe, Jr.

Preface

In recent years, a welcome and growing body of information on Engaged Buddhism has begun to appear. Christopher S. Queen's and my *Engaged Buddhism: Buddhist Liberation Movements in Practice* (State University of New York Press, 1996) was the first major academic study. Since then, other compilations have appeared, including David W. Chappell's *Buddhist Peacework: Creating Cultures of Peace* (Wisdom, 1999); Christopher S. Queen's *Engaged Buddhism in the West* (Wisdom, 2000); and Christopher S. Queen, Charles Prebish, and Damien Keown's *Action Dharma: New Studies in Engaged Buddhism* (RoutledgeCurzon, 2003). All of these works have been multiauthored volumes making available multiple Engaged Buddhist stories and analyzing them primarily as individual cases. Of course, many of the Engaged Buddhist leaders themselves have made their own work directly available via traditional and electronic publishing.

With this information at hand, I believe that it is now possible to take a different approach. It seems that there now is enough information to study Engaged Buddhism, as such, as a whole. Thus, in this study, I have worked from the data presented by the many instances of Asian Engaged Buddhism and examined it altogether, as a single body of material. In addition, for some time, I have been intensely curious to understand the thinking that underlies, or serves as the foundation of, Engaged Buddhist actions. Engaged Buddhist actions seem to have a certain character. How would I articulate what that character is? And what is it that makes Engaged Buddhism have that character? Following this line of questioning has led me to write this volume, the primary purpose of which is to articulate and analyze the social ethics underlying the practice of Engaged Buddhism.

A few words on the parameters of this study are in order before beginning.

In the course of my analysis of Engaged Buddhist social ethics, because of the nature of Engaged Buddhism, questions arose concerning the relationship between Buddhist and Western ways of thought in Engaged Buddhism. This is particularly true in the second half of the book, which focuses on issues of political theory, human rights, nonviolence, and social justice. Engaged Buddhists address both their own countrymen and a global audience. Because they are in dialogue with people around the world and address a global audience, their language on sociopolitical issues, while fundamentally Buddhist, has imported not a few elements from the Western social and political thought that dominates international discourse. Interesting questions arise in this way about the response of the Engaged Buddhists to Western ideas concerning such concepts as individualism, liberalism, human rights, and social justice. As I wrote this book, the issue of the Buddhist response to Western sociopolitical thought emerged as an important secondary focus. For this reason, I decided to limit the present investigation to the Asian Engaged Buddhists, leaving aside the Western Engaged Buddhists. It is obviously an entirely different matter if one queries an Asian Buddhist whether the idea of social justice, for example, fits into a Buddhist worldview than if one asks an American Buddhist the same question. I wanted to preserve the focus on the encounter between Asian Buddhism and Western thought and avoid muddying the water by including Western Buddhist voices. Moreover, although I see Western Engaged Buddhists as wonderfully creative in terms of innovations in practice, I also see them as still the students of Asian Buddhists in the area of religious and ethical thought—appropriately so, in view of any Westerner's need to overcome cultural habits of thinking to clearly perceive the otherness of Buddhism and what it has to offer.

There are no established standards for the use of diacriticals in Sanskrit and Pali words appearing in English language works on Buddhism. I have made decisions on the use of diacriticals and italics in this volume according to the following principles, which I developed as I proceeded. First, words in widespread use in the English language are considered to be English-language words. Which words should be so considered is the question. The list of such words in this book is based purely upon my judgment. The present list is much shorter than the list of English language words culled from *Webster's Third New International Dictionary* proffered in the *Journal of the International Association of Buddhist Studies* 5:2 (1982): 141–142. I consider that list to be far too inclusive; for example, I am not convinced that words such as *pratyekabuddha* and *nirmāṇakāya* can be considered to be English-language words, despite their appearing on that list. Some words that do not appear on that list but that I nevertheless judge to be very familiar to the reader familiar with Buddhism are written without diacriticals, however, such as the names of the Buddha (for example, Shakyamuni) and the sect name Theravada. Second, there are only two categories of words: words that are English-language words and foreign words. English-language words need neither diacritical marks nor italics, but foreign words require both. There is no category of words requiring diacriticals but not italics. Third, the Engaged Buddhists routinely write for a global audience. In their English-language work, they generally do not use diacriticals. I decided that it would be orientalistic to introduce diacriticals where the Buddhist writers do not use them, even outside of quotations. Therefore, the names of the Engaged Buddhists and their organizations and some of the key terms that they repeatedly use without diacriticals or italics are consistently rendered here without diacriticals or italics. Finally, of course, none of this holds for quoted material, which is reproduced as originally written.

I am rich in debts. I am deeply grateful to Dr. A. T. Ariyaratne, Venerable Dhammananda (Chatsumarn Kabilsingh), Venerable Somdech Preah Maha Ghosananda, Samdhong Rinpoche, Sulak Sivaraksa, and Geshe Sopa for multiple interviews and for permission to publish their remarks. Much of my insight into the social ethics of Engaged Buddhism has come from my having had the opportunity to converse with, listen to, and observe these leaders in action. Without their support, this book would not have been possible, and I am greatly appreciative.

My thanks also to Patricia Crosby, executive editor of the University of Hawai'i Press, for her enthusiasm and meticulous support of this project from our first conversation, and to George Tanabe, the editor of the series of which this book is a part, for helping me to think through substantive issues concerning the parameters and structure of this book. My thanks also to the anonymous reviewers of the manuscript, who asked a number of helpful questions that resulted in improvements in the book. Of course, I take full responsibility for the book as it has finally taken shape. Thanks, finally, to my husband, Steve Keffer, who brought me meals and did all the work to keep our family functioning throughout a summer during which I sat at the computer, sixteen hours a day, writing this book. Many men receive this kind of support from their wives, but very few women, indeed, receive such support from their husbands. Without Steve's help, I could not have completed this project.

Portions of this book appeared elsewhere in earlier versions. I gratefully acknowledge the University of Virginia Press for permission to use excerpts from my chapter, "The Genesis and Decay of Responsibility in Buddhism," in *Taking Responsibility*, edited by Winston Davis (Charlottesville: Virginia, 2001); the Sathirakoses-Nagapradipa Foundation for permission to use excerpts from my chapter, "Buddhism and War," in *Socially Engaged Spirituality: Essays in Honor of Sulak Sivaraksa on His 70th Birthday*, edited by David W. Chappell (Bangkok: Sathirakoses-Nagapradipa Foundation, 2003); the University of Hawai'i Press and *Buddhist-Christian Studies*, for permission to use a portion of my article, "They Who Burned Themselves for Peace: Quaker and Buddhist Self-Immolators During the Vietnam War" (*Buddhist-Christian Studies* 20, 2000): 127–150; and the *Journal of Religious Ethics* for permission to use my article, "From Is to Ought: Natural Law in Buddhadasa Bhikkhu and Phra Prayudh Payutto" (30.2): 273–291.

1   Introduction

In the Buddhist Compassion Relief General Hospital in Hwalien, Taiwan, a large mosaic in the lobby greets visitors. The mosaic depicts Shakyamuni Buddha treating the illness of a sick monk, an event recorded in Buddhist scripture. Visitors to this Buddhist hospital are told that this image "represents the policy of this hospital. Besides treating the illness, the staff must, as Buddha did in the mural, also show compassion towards the individual." The founder, Master Cheng Yen, states that "illness is one of the many unavoidable sufferings between birth and death, and that we should do all we can to help the sick feel less miserable — if it is at all possible." [1]

When I read this passage, I was strongly struck by the juxtaposition of three things: the words, "illness is one of the many unavoidable sufferings between birth and death," calling to mind the first of the Four Signs that led Siddhartha Gautama, the future Buddha, to renounce his life of wealth and ease to seek answers to the problem of the human condition; the image in the mural of the same man, now Shakyamuni Buddha, treating with compassion and skill the sickness of an ailing monk; and, finally, the existence of the Buddhist Compassion Relief General Hospital, founded by the nun Master Cheng Yen. In the juxtaposition of these words and images is a response to those who feel that Engaged Buddhism is somehow inappropriate or un-Buddhist, the product of Western influence.

It is often pointed out that the kind of suffering that Shakyamuni Buddha was concerned to eliminate is the kind that is intrinsic to the human condition, inherent and ineliminable; the paradigm of this kind of suffering, in fact, is represented by the first three of the Four Signs: illness, old age, and death. As Master Cheng Yen says, illness is one of the "unavoidable" forms of suffering. There will always be illness, just as there will always be birth and death, as long as there are human beings. But to those who say that the Buddha, in response to his dismay over the human condition and the first three of the Four Signs, sought and discovered a way to end the human condition as such and that this and only this is the end of Buddhism, one may point to Master Cheng Yen who, in turn, points to the Buddha as not only the Great Physician, the one who shows the way to cure the inherent ills of humankind, the human condition as such, but also the one who, in the meantime, bends to help a sick man here and now with his skill and compassion. One does not preclude the other. Indeed, for Engaged Buddhists, each necessarily encompasses the other. In short, to those who say that Buddhism's cure for *ill*, for suffering, for *duḥkha,* is to leave the world of samsara altogether, to leave behind a condition of being that is unfixable, one may point to the example of the Buddha, who did indeed teach a way of leaving samsara altogether, but who also, as the record shows, was concerned to heal that part of the suffering of samsara that could be healed within samsara.

As for Western influence, the Buddhist Compassion Relief General Hospital is again instructive. The hospital was fundamentally born out of the dedicated compassion of Master Cheng Yen. This compassion was guided by two events. The first occurred when Master Cheng Yen visited a friend in a hospital. While leaving the hospital, she saw a pool of blood on the floor of the entrance hall. When she inquired about it, she was told that the blood was from an aborigine woman suffering from a miscarriage who had been refused admittance to the hospital because she was unable to pay the required entrance fee (at the time such fees were required by all hospitals in Taiwan). The second event came from the visit of three Catholic nuns to Cheng Yen. They pointed out to her that "there are all sorts of Catholic hospitals and schools and charity organizations, but never any Buddhist ones. They told the Master that, in the eyes of the world, the Buddhists are but a passive group of people contributing nothing to society."[2] The combination of these two events determined Cheng Yen to found a hospital that would care for everyone with compassion and skill, regardless of whether they could pay.

Is this Western influence? There is no doubt that the Catholic nuns' words served as a goading irritant. Cheng Yen writes, "I left home because the teachings of kindness, compassion, joy and unselfish giving in the sutras touched me deeply. However, for the last two thousand years, from India to China, there is little concrete evidence of Buddhist contributions to society. While other religions such as Christianity and Catholicism have acted to improve public welfare, I felt ashamed about being a nun who could not implement the Buddhist teachings of compassion and wisdom in society."[3] As she was hatching the idea for the hospital, Cheng Yen said to her followers, "We will become Kwan-yin's [Kuan-yin's] watchful eyes and hands, and the world can never call us Buddhists a passive group again!"[4]

But let us be careful of one thing. I gather that many of those who want to dismiss Engaged Buddhism as "merely" the product of Western influence, and thus not truly Buddhist, are concerned about Western cultural imperialism. They want Buddhism to be preserved as Buddhism and not to be overrun and transformed into some distorted, Westernized quasi-Buddhism by the tidal wave of Western culture that is sweeping the world. This concern, with which I very much sympathize, overlooks something important. Ironically, it diminishes the very thing it is trying to protect: the agency of individual Buddhist leaders.

Buddhism today, like all religions, exists in a dynamic world of constant encounter among the world's religions. Buddhist leaders and followers are regularly exposed to a barrage of Western culture. The leadership of Engaged Buddhism, in particular, is highly subject to such influence. Many of them sought out Western education and spent formative years in the West, and almost all of them regularly engage in discussions and exchanges with Western leaders, religious and secular. The heart of the question is this: does this extensive exposure to Western culture, religion, ideas, and ways of thinking—which I by no means want to minimize— mean that Engaged Buddhism is the *product* of Western influence? To assume so is to deny the subjectivity and agency of the Engaged Buddhist leaders themselves.

Those who think that Engaged Buddhism is the product of Western influence have in mind a model of cross-cultural encounter that assumes the overwhelming power of Western ideas and culture and minimizes or negates the power of Buddhist ideas and culture. It assumes that Buddhist ideas and values are helpless before the onslaught of the conquering culture. But this set of assumptions negates precisely those things that it is most concerned to protect: the alterity and agency of the Buddhist leadership. Of course, there are good historical reasons for conceiving of cross-cultural and interreligious encounter in terms of this model (for example, the joint offensive of British imperialist and Christian missionary forces in colonial India). I believe, however, that it would be much more accurate in the case of Engaged Buddhism to take as our model for cross-cultural encounter the model of dialogue.

In the dialogue model, representatives of the two cultural/religious groups meet as equals, each side represents itself in its own words to the other side, and each listens respectfully to the other and then does whatever it wants (or nothing) with what it has heard. In dialogue, ideally all participants are aware that everyone always speaks from a particular point of view, based in each case upon the person's cultural background and personal experience. Thus, in this model, the image of the tidal wave of cultural imperialism, obliterating everything in its path, may be replaced by the image of a less overpowering wave, depositing all kinds of detritus— sand, shells, and garbage—from a distant shore on one's beach. Dialogue gives one more material upon which one may draw, but one is by no means forced to accept anything. One responds as one will and, it is important to note, always from the cultural and religious place where one is situated. Thus, if an Engaged Buddhist, in the course of learning about Western culture, hears an idea that sparks interest, it is *as a Buddhist* and *from a Buddhist perspective* that that idea sparks interest and from that perspective, again, that he or she responds to the idea and chooses what to do with it.

I believe this model fits the case of Engaged Buddhism very well. It respects the agency, the subjectivity, and ability to choose of both parties to the discussion. The Engaged Buddhist leadership is constituted by highly intelligent, very well educated men and women who are not of a nature to be pushed around, intellectually or otherwise. Think, for example, of the Dalai Lama, Thich Nhat Hanh, Buddhadasa Bhikkhu, Sulak Sivaraksa, Aung San Suu Kyi, and A. T. Ariyaratne. Intellectually, these leaders are quite capable of holding their own. The first three have even written books in which they articulate their own Buddhist perspectives on Christianity! In their lives of social and political engagement, moreover, they have all made a career, on the one hand, of resisting force and, on the other, of fashioning and holding up creative visions of new possibilities. Asia is no longer the world of the British Raj. All the evidence indicates that, although the Engaged Buddhist leadership is thoroughly familiar with Western religious and socio-economic-political ideas, they are more than capable, in dialogical fashion, of selecting particular ideas of interest from the Western world (for example, human rights) and responding to them in a Buddhistically trained and educated manner, incorporating them into their views, when they so choose, by finding parallels or sympathetic values in the Buddhist tradition that have perhaps received little attention in the past. Ideas or values that are dissonant with their own they let pass.

The other thing missing from the tidal wave image is the fact of the two directions in which cultural exchange flows. It is not the case that the Engaged Buddhist side is doing all the receiving. The Dalai Lama's and Thich Nhat Hanh's books are published in English and can be found in most American bookstores; some of the Dalai Lama's books have even made the *New York Times* bestseller list. The Dalai Lama and Thich Nhat Hanh speak regularly to large audiences throughout the West. The nonviolent struggle of Tibet has made a great impression upon many. Thich Nhat Hanh's idea of "being peace" has begun to alter the fundamental thinking of many Christian pacifists about how one approaches social activism. It is no doubt fair to say that there has been greater influence from the West on Engaged Buddhism than the reverse, but we should not forget that this is a two-directional exchange.

It may fairly be asked whether such a thing as "Engaged Buddhism" exists. Or, to speak more carefully, is there a form of Buddhism with sufficient unity among its various examples and sufficient difference from other forms of Buddhism to go by the single name, "Engaged Buddhism"? Engaged Buddhism is not defined by geographic location. There are Engaged Buddhists throughout the Buddhist world—

in South Asia, Southeast Asia, East Asia, and the West—wherever there is sufficient freedom for Buddhists to engage the problems of society as conscience and Buddhist principles dictate. Nor is Engaged Buddhism defined by sect—there are Theravada, Mahayana, Vajrayana, and nonsectarian forms of Engaged Buddhism. Engaged Buddhism is defined and unified by the intention to apply the values and teachings of Buddhism to the problems of society in a nonviolent way, motivated by concern for the welfare of others, and as an expression of one's own practice of the Buddhist Way.

Engaged Buddhism did not begin from a single point and spread. On the contrary, it arose in different locations throughout the Buddhist world in response to the crises faced in each place in the twentieth century, a century that was in many respects disastrous for Buddhism in Asia, but also propitious in seeing the spread of Buddhism to the West and the development of many reform movements, of which Engaged Buddhism is one. Today, a loose network among Engaged Buddhists exists in the International Network of Engaged Buddhists, founded by the Engaged Buddhist leader Sulak Sivaraksa, and, more important, in the many personal relationships among Engaged Buddhist leaders and activists. This networking is a way for Engaged Buddhists to share ideas but no more than that. There are no institutional or ecclesial structures formalizing Engaged Buddhism as a sect or as a sociopolitical movement, nor are any such structures likely to develop. They would serve no purpose. Engaged Buddhism exists as an intention and a practice within existing forms of Buddhism.

Naturally, with the geographic and sectarian diversity that exists among Engaged Buddhists, there will be differences among them. There are differences as well based upon individual character and individual interpretations of Buddhism. Engaged Buddhism is unified the way a philosophical school is unified. In the latter, there is a set of issues of particular interest, a set of ideas and values that all thinkers assume, and a characteristic way of approaching issues, but each individual thinker takes a somewhat different approach and indeed makes his or her contribution to the formation of the school of thought by virtue of those individual variations on the common theme. In the case of Engaged Buddhism, there are two categories of variation on a theme. First, there are differences in idiom in which the forms of expression, images, and language of the individual thinkers and movements differ to some extent. Second, there are cases of more substantive difference in which the fundamental values remain the same, but those values are interpreted or applied differently or in different degree.

An example of the first kind of difference concerns one of the most important values of Engaged Buddhism, universal benevolence. A Mahayana idiom for expressing this value uses the bodhisattva Kuan-yin, beloved throughout East Asia as the Bodhisattva of Compassion. Cheng Yen takes the familiar image of Kuan-yin, whose many eyes and arms in one of the traditional forms is traditionally understood to represent Kuan-yin's ability to perceive and respond to trouble everywhere, and transforms it in Engaged Buddhist style:

> [T]he Master looked at the crowd, met their pleading eyes, and saw their beseeching hands with palms touching. Suddenly she realized that by joining all these eyes and hands a force could be formed—a force with enough eyes to locate the suffering ones and enough hands to grant them help.
>
> The Master smiled when she thought of Kwan-yin, the Goddess of Mercy and the Protector of All in Distress, who, according to legend, has a thousand observing eyes and a thousand helping hands. The Master then said, "We will become Kwan-yin's watchful eyes and useful hands, and the world can never call us Buddhists a passive group again!"[5]

In a masterful way, Cheng Yen simultaneously demythologizes Kuan-yin while using the traditional meaning and devotion accorded her to inspire a large group of Buddhist faithful to translate their ideals and devotion into practical, hands-on action.

Of course, the image of Kuan-yin would not work in a Theravada country. Though Theravadins do speak of compassion, they more frequently speak of *mettā*, loving kindness, than of compassion, as their idiom for expressing beneficence. A little reflection makes clear that, when compassion (concern that others not suffer) and loving kindness (wish for others to be well and happy) are translated into action, they come to the same thing: benevolence, concern for the welfare of others, and action to enhance others' welfare. Thus, Theravada language and images of loving kindness are used in fashion similar to Mahayana compassion language to inspire action to enhance the well-being of others.

For example, in Sri Lanka, A. T. Ariyaratne, founder of the Sarvodaya Shramadana and leader of an important movement to end the violence in that country, organizes mass peace meditations. At those mass meditations, hundreds of thousands of people are taught not only to meditate on *mettā*, but also to use those meditations to dismantle attitudes and actions of hostility supporting the violence in Sri Lanka and to inspire action to bring the violence to an end. Like Cheng Yen referring to Kuan-yin in the Mahayana case, here Ariyaratne refers to a central icon of the Theravada Buddhist tradition and uses it to inspire beneficent action. This seems to me a difference in idiom.

More significant differences, it seems to me, are those that involve differences in interpretation and application of common values. We will see in chapter 6, that, although all Engaged Buddhists strongly espouse nonviolence, some do so as principled pacifists and some as pragmatic pacifists. Some recognize potential limits to nonviolence, and others would give up all else before they gave up pacifism. These are significant differences, but they are not great enough to break the coherence of Engaged Buddhism, because all remain committed to living by nonviolence, often under the most difficult conditions. It is important to bear in mind these individual differences among Engaged Buddhists. Although there is general agreement among them, they do not as a rule speak for each other.

A book like this cannot be exhaustive—it cannot survey each of the Engaged Buddhists on each issue—they do not all write on each issue!—nor can it compare and contrast their variations and differences in all combinations on all issues. As a result, I have concentrated upon the views of those who have commented most extensively or thought most deeply or with most innovation on an issue and selected the most significant differences to explore.

I do not wish in this volume to repeat the information already available in *Engaged Buddhism: Buddhist Liberation Movements in Asia.*[6] I refer the reader to that volume for much fuller descriptions of the Asian Engaged Buddhist movements than I will provide here. The intention of this work is to dig more deeply into the philosophical substructure beneath the Engaged Buddhist movement as a whole, to examine Engaged Buddhist thinking, its roots in traditional Buddhist thought, and its creative development of tradition; to identify its strengths and probe its implications; and to raise questions, opening doors for further thought and investigation where there is thinking yet to be done. I have the greatest respect for all the Engaged Buddhists. When I challenge them, it is in a spirit of taking their ideas seriously and with the hope that such challenges may in a small way assist the ongoing development of an important contribution to Buddhism and the world.

Although I do not wish to go into detail here, I do want to introduce briefly the thinkers and activists whose words will appear most frequently in these pages. Others will appear occasionally, but these are the thinkers on whom we will focus. Not all Engaged Buddhist leaders will be found in these pages. Because of the nature of this volume, I have been most interested in those who have made the most important and/or most creative contributions to Engaged Buddhist *thought* per se.

A. T. Ariyaratne is a Sri Lankan Buddhist layperson and, since 1958, the founding director of Sarvodaya Shramadana, a development and peace organization that is the largest nongovernmental organization in Asia. He has pioneered the discovery of Buddhist economics as an alternative to capitalist and communist economics and invented a Buddhist self-help development process (Sarvodaya Shramadana) that has revitalized village life in more than half the villages of Sri Lanka. This is a development process that is concerned not only with economic development, but also takes a holistic approach to the well-being of both the individual and the village in their economic, cultural, social, political, psychological, and spiritual dimensions, ultimately seeking the "awakening" or enlightenment of both individual and community. In recent years, Ariyaratne's attention has turned more and more to the effort to end the violence between Tamils and Sinhalese in Sri Lanka. Ariyaratne has won the Niwano Peace Award and the Gandhi Peace Prize.

Aung San Suu Kyi is the leader of Burma's National League for Democracy, which since 1988 has worked for the emancipation of Burma from its brutal military regime and the institution of democracy and human rights in Burma. She and her party won a landslide victory in 1990, winning more than 80 percent of the constituencies, after which the military regime refused to transfer power and instead placed her under house arrest, where she remained for six years. Separated from her family as her sons grew from childhood to adulthood and even as her husband was dying, she has remained a steadfast and courageous example of the nonviolent struggle of a people for self-determination and decency. She was awarded the Nobel Peace Prize in 1991. At this writing, she is once again under arrest.

Buddhadasa Bhikkhu (1906–1993) was a Thai Buddhist monk, exceptionally skilled in interpreting the Dhamma of the Buddha for the modern era. A rebel against the Buddhist institutional system, he broke from the Buddhist establishment, educated himself in a new way of approaching Buddhist thought, and established himself independently in his own monastery. He was not an activist, but a Pali scholar and creative thinker intent on reforming Thai Buddhism and challenging Thai Buddhists lulled by traditional interpretations to look at the teachings of the Buddha more deeply and to see them with fresh eyes. He articulated a fresh and powerful spirituality that gave many people renewed interest in Buddhism. More than a thousand people a year, including many foreigners, came to his monastery, Suan Mokh—itself a creative approach to Buddhist spirituality—for training.[7] Buddhadasa also made very original and even deliberately provocative contributions to Buddhist social and political thought, always with the intention of stimulating thought and discussion. In this sense he has been instrumental in communicating the idea that Buddhism *should* have an application for the life of society. His talks and writings have been of great interest in intellectual and socially progressive circles in Thailand and beyond, and through them his influence on Thai society has been considerable.

Venerable Master Cheng Yen is a Taiwanese Buddhist nun who in 1966 founded the Tzu Chi Foundation, a huge charitable organization with more than four million members based in Taiwan but with branches in twenty-eight countries where expatriate Taiwanese and Chinese are found. The four missions of Tzu Chi are charity, medical care, education, and culture. It has made particularly significant contributions in establishing free medical care in Taiwan and elsewhere, in providing international disaster relief, and in establishing the world's third-largest bone marrow data bank. With her tremendous charisma and exalted moral standards, Master Cheng Yen is the object of deep devotion to her followers. She has been nominated for the Nobel Peace Prize and has won the Philippine Magsaysay Award, the Eisenhower Medallion, and the Noel Foundation Life Award.[8]

In the company of the other Engaged Buddhist leaders, Venerable Cheng Yen stands out as the only one who is firmly apolitical. Whereas, of the present company, only Aung San Suu Kyi has sought political power, all the other Engaged Buddhist leaders have made extensive comments on political matters, and most of them have been directly involved in political struggles. Cheng Yen is the only one who never comments on political matters or in any way engages them. In addition, she requires that her many followers have nothing to do with politics. It would be possible to argue that Cheng Yen is not an Engaged Buddhist leader but a Buddhist reformer and leader of a huge Buddhist charitable organization. She has, however, galvanized millions of Buddhists to take concrete action to relieve the suffering of others by convincing them that their identity as Buddhists requires this active expression. Thus, I believe that it is best to see her as an Engaged Buddhist, though somewhat anomalous with respect to her strict abstention from politics.

His Holiness, the Fourteenth Dalai Lama, Tenzin Gyatso is the spiritual and temporal leader of the Tibetan people. Born in Tibet, he was identified as the Dalai Lama at the age of two and taken at four for training to the Potala Palace in Lhasa. Following the Chinese invasion of Tibet, he fled Tibet in 1959. Since that time, from his home in Dharamsala, India, he has led the Tibetan government in exile— overseeing its transformation from a medieval institution into the beginnings of a modern democracy. He has also headed the Tibetan liberation movement and overseen the well-being of the Tibetan people in exile. He has continually reached out for dialogue with the Chinese and offered many peace plans, to no avail. He has popularized his core beliefs of nonviolence and universal responsibility to a global audience. The Dalai Lama has won the Wallenberg Award, the Albert Schweitzer Award, and the Nobel Peace Prize. His courage and cheerfulness in the face of adversity and his unique personality, sense of humor, and principled pacifism have all combined to make him the most popular and influential Buddhist teacher in the world, indeed a spiritual teacher to many non-Buddhists, and a beloved figure and inspiration to countless more.

The Cambodian monk Venerable Somdech Preah Maha Ghosananda spent the years of the Khmer Rouge era in a Thai monastery, where he had been in training since 1965. He returned to Cambodia in 1978, shortly before the fall of the Khmer Rouge and immediately entered the refugee camps, where he worked tirelessly to heal wounds and prevent acts of revenge. Since that time, he has worked for reconciliation among the still mutually hostile camps in Cambodia and attained fame through instituting the Dhammayietra. The latter have been a series of annual peace walks that have had a tremendous impact on the healing of Cambodia. These walks have, in various years, accompanied refugees returning home, helped to ensure peaceful elections, brought a taste of peace to areas still experiencing hostilities, and drawn attention to the problems of land mines, domestic violence, and deforestation. Maha Ghosananda travels the world, looking after the Cambodian people in diaspora and attending meetings for peacemaking. He is the Supreme Patriarch of Cambodian Buddhism and is often called the "Gandhi of Cambodia." A nominee several times for the Nobel Peace Prize, Maha Ghosananda was awarded the prestigious Niwano Peace Prize. Despite having lost his entire family in the Cambodian Holocaust, Maha Ghosananda always radiates infectious joy.

Venerable P. A. Payutto (Phra Dhammapitaka) is a leading Thai Buddhist scholar. His masterpiece, *Buddhadhamma*, is considered the most important work of Theravada Buddhist scholarship of the modern era. Like Buddhadasa, he has written extensively on the application of Buddhism to contemporary social issues. Payutto decries the paucity of social applications of modern Thai Buddhism as one of its deficits.[9] "In fact, one of the hallmarks of Venerable Prayudh's presentation of the Buddha's teachings is his emphasis on Buddhism as a religion of action and effort . . . not one of inaction as it is commonly pictured."[10] In addition to his works of Buddhist scholarship, Payutto has written books on economics, political theory, science, the environment, and education. These writings have made a considerable impact and "helped bring Buddhism out of the monastery to a much more active involvement in social issues."[11] Phra Payutto has won the UNESCO Prize for Peace Education, in recognition of his efforts to promote world peace.

Sulak Sivaraksa is a Thai Buddhist layman and social activist. Himself of aristocratic descent, he champions the causes of the poor and the oppressed. He is a prominent social and political critic in Thailand and has been twice arraigned, and once imprisoned, on charges of lese majesty for his words critical of the government. His concerns are wide ranging. He is an outspoken critic of corruption, militarism, consumerism, injustice, and globalization. He consistently promotes, with both words and creative actions, protection of the environment, gender equality, nonviolence, human rights, protection of local culture, and the application of Buddhist values to social reform. He has founded numerous publications and nongovernmental organizations, including the International Network of Engaged Buddhists. Sulak has been nominated for the Nobel Peace Prize and has won the Right Livelihood Award.

Thich Nhat Hanh is a Vietnamese Zen monk, trained in Theravada as well as the Zen tradition. He coined the term "Engaged Buddhism" to refer to the kind of Buddhism that he wanted to see develop: one that would actively and directly concern itself with the welfare of the people. He cofounded the School of Youth for Social Service to train young Buddhists in applying their Buddhist values to serve the needs of the Vietnamese people. When the war broke out, he became one of the leaders of the "Struggle Movement" or "Third Way" that tried to bring the war to an end without taking sides with either North or South. He traveled the West as a spokesperson for the Buddhist antiwar perspective, after which he was unable to return home. He became the chair of the Vietnamese Buddhist Peace Delegation that tried to bring the Buddhist message to the Paris Peace Talks. Martin Luther King, Jr., nominated him for the Nobel Peace Prize. Since the war years, he has lived in exile in France, traveling the world giving talks and training on nonviolent social activism. He is a prolific writer and has published many books of prose and poetry on Buddhism, peacemaking, and Buddhist-Christian dialogue.

The structure of this volume is as follows. I begin in chapter 2 by examining the roots in Buddhist tradition of Engaged Buddhist social ethics. In that chapter, I survey the traditional Buddhist concepts and practices that come up most consistently in Engaged Buddhist discourse—interdependence, compassion, meditation, and so forth—and begin to look at how the Engaged Buddhists apply them to their particular concerns. Chapter 3 constructs a theory of Engaged Buddhist social ethics using an inductive method—that is, building the theory from its elements. Chapter 4 is a transitional chapter. It begins with Engaged Buddhist metaphysical views on the individual, society, and the relationship between the two and moves from there into a consideration of questions in political theory concerning the proper balance between the individual and society. The second half of the book focuses on applied social-political issues, chapter 5 on human rights, chapter 6 on nonviolence, and chapter 7 on social justice. In chapter 8, I summarize the major achievements of the Engaged Buddhists and then offer my own views on the issues that I have examined in the second half of the book.

2   Building from Tradition

Engaged Buddhism is a modern, reformist movement found throughout the Buddhist world. As a reformist movement, it by no means breaks from or is discontinuous with the preceding tradition. On the contrary, Engaged Buddhism draws extensively from tradition, key texts, and well-established concepts, values, and practices of the tradition, interpreting them and applying them in accordance with the challenges and demands of modernity and with its own ethos of response to the immediate needs of sentient beings.

Although Engaged Buddhism differs from country to country, certain key ideas and practices drawn from tradition turn up again and again in the speeches of its leaders and theorizers. Reference to these ideas and practices both legitimizes Engaged Buddhism, by placing it within the continuum of orthodoxy and tradition, and establishes the foundational concepts and approaches upon which Engaged Buddhists build. The fact that these ideas and practices turn up again and again throughout the distinct Engaged Buddhist movements also has the consequence of establishing a degree of unity in both discourse and practice among Engaged Buddhists. It will be useful, therefore, to introduce these foundational ideas and practices at this early stage of our inquiry.

In this chapter, we will briefly examine how Engaged Buddhists think about key concepts, teachings, and practices drawn from tradition. These themes will be further developed throughout the book.

INTERDEPENDENCE AND CAUSALITY/CONDITIONALITY

Buddhist teaching on interdependence and causality is at the root of many Engaged Buddhists' way of thinking. A. T. Ariyaratne writes,

> One of the unique teachings of the Buddha is the theory of dependent arising. Everything is related to every other thing. If there is no peace in a society, there should be a variety of interdependent and interrelated causes that bring about such a situation. All these causes have to be attacked simultaneously and removed to make a reversal of the processes that have

brought about a loss of peace in our society so that we can rebuild a culture of peace.

The Sarvodaya Shramadana Movement of Sri Lanka has evolved during the last 41 years an integrated self-development approach to counteract the causes that bring about conflicts, crimes, and war.[1]

Here we see a typical application of both interdependence and causality to a concrete problem by an Engaged Buddhist. In fact, Ariyaratne was one of the pioneers of seeing and putting to use such applications. If "everything is related to every other thing," as the Buddha taught, and if everything comes into being through causes and conditions outside itself, as the Buddha also taught, then in a given society there will indeed be a multiplicity of "interdependent and interrelated causes" that make that society what it is. Again, as the Buddha taught, if there is something that is unpleasant and is a source of suffering, and if one wants to be free of it, one should identify its causes and eliminate them. Thus, if a society, like Sri Lanka, is experiencing "conflicts, crimes and war," one should identify the "interdependent and interrelated causes" of those things and eliminate them.

Every step of this thinking is directly based upon the teachings of the Buddha. The only thing that one might consider to be new is the application of those teachings to the problems of society—but even that is not entirely new, as Ariyaratne and others correctly point out. There is advice to laymen and to rulers in the Buddhist canon, though certainly the development of this applied thinking among the Engaged Buddhists has gone far beyond what Shakyamuni ever said and did. Thus, in its roots the thinking is not new, and even the application of this thinking to society's problems is not new; it is the extent of the application that is new.

One of the key points that Engaged Buddhists return to again and again in their thinking is the fact that human beings are social beings—that is, each one of us lives in a condition of interdependence within society. The Dalai Lama says that that interdependence is so profound that "our every action, our every deed, word and thought" has implications for others. He points out that our interests are inextricably linked because we all depend on both the social web and the web of the natural environment in order to survive. Moreover, we all want to be happy, and we all have an equal right to be happy. Our happiness can only exist within a shared matrix—I need certain things from you for my happiness, and vice versa. Therefore, he says, it is clearly essential that we work out ethical social and political systems that will promote the happiness of all.[2]

One of His Holiness's great themes is the insight that the bonds of our inter-dependence, while always a fact, have grown more plentiful and more inexorable with modernity.

> In the past, families and small communities could exist more or less inde-pendently of one another. . . . Today's reality is so complex and, on the material level at least, so clearly interconnected that a different outlook is needed. Modern economics is a case in point. A stock-market crash on one side of the globe can have a direct effect on the economies of countries on the other. Similarly, our technological achievements are now such that our activities have an unambiguous effect on the natural environment. And the very size of our population means that we cannot any longer af-ford to ignore others' interests. . . . In view of this, I am convinced that it is essential that we cultivate a sense of what I call universal responsibility.[3]

In the modern world, our interconnectedness is intensified by the growth and power of the international market, our ongoing serious harming of the natural en-vironment, and the growth in human population, which puts us in ever greater physical contact with each other and exacerbates all our other problems. All of this makes more urgent the necessity described above of developing ethical relation-ships. For His Holiness, because our happiness is interdependent, the best founda-tion for ethics is what he calls "universal responsibility," each one of us caring for the welfare of each other.

A Mahayana Variant: Emptiness

As we have seen, Engaged Buddhists of both Theravada and Mahayana traditions draw upon the idea of interdependence to guide their thinking about social issues. Mahayana Buddhists also draw in the same way upon the idea of emptiness, which of course is itself a somewhat more developed form of the idea of interdependence. Thich Nhat Hanh, who has a gift for putting complex ideas into simple, compre-hensible words, has particularly drawn upon the idea of emptiness to express his Engaged Buddhist ideas.

> When we go to a meditation center, we may have the impression that we leave everything behind—family, society, and all the complications in-volved in them—and come as an individual in order to practice and to

search for peace. This is already an illusion, because in Buddhism there is no such thing as an individual.

Just as a piece of paper is the fruit, the combination of many elements that can be called non-paper elements, the individual is made of non-individual elements. If you are a poet, you will see clearly that there is a cloud floating in this sheet of paper. Without a cloud there will be no water; without water, the trees cannot grow; and without trees, you cannot make paper. So the cloud is in here. . . .

The paper is made of all the non-paper elements to the extent that if we return the non-paper elements to their sources, the cloud to the sky, the sunshine to the sun, the logger to his father, the paper is empty. Empty of what? Empty of a separate self. . . . Empty, in this sense, means that the paper is full of everything, the entire cosmos. . . .

· In the same way, the individual is made of non-individual elements. How do you expect to leave everything behind when you enter a meditation center? The kind of suffering that you carry in your heart, that is society itself. You bring that with you, you bring society with you. You bring all of us with you. When you meditate, it is not just for yourself, you do it for the whole society.[4]

Here Nhat Hanh is making a case for Engaged Buddhism itself on the basis of emptiness. To be empty is to be empty of a separate self and full of the nonself components that have come together to constitute what is called "self." The individual is not a separate entity. The individual is made up of nonindividual parts; each one of us carries society within us. Therefore, the idea of meditation as an escape from society is wrong-headed. We can never escape society; it is within us; it *is* us. Therefore when we meditate, we meditate for ourselves, but also for all others. We will return to society transformed, and what we offer to society in our daily interactions and behavior will be transformed as well.

KARMA

Karma is cause and effect as it applies to human action and its consequences. Individuals who commit negative acts reap negative consequences in this or a future life. Positive acts result in positive consequences for those who do them.

Engaged Buddhists point out that the law of karma also applies to human societies. Many Engaged Buddhists refer to the first chapter of the *Dhammapada* in this connection. Maha Ghosananda of Cambodia has composed a "Prayer for Peace" incorporating these words from the *Dhammapada*. "In those who harbor thoughts of blame and vengeance toward others, hatred will never cease. In those who do not harbor blame and vengeance, hatred will surely cease. For hatred is never appeased by hatred. Hatred is appeased by love. This is an eternal law."[5] In a society such as post–Khmer Rouge Cambodia, to which Maha Ghosananda repeatedly spoke these words, this quotation reminds the audience that it is in their own interest to refrain from acts of retaliation or revenge no matter how overwhelmed by anger they may be with those who caused them and their families so much suffering. If they take revenge, they will simply plant another karmic seed that will inevitably result in future suffering. This way of thinking seems to have been widespread among the Cambodian people. When I asked Dith Pran, the subject of "The Killing Fields," why it was that there had not been widespread acts of revenge after the fall of the Khmer Rouge, he replied, "They don't want to suffer any more. They know that if they try to take revenge they are only going to suffer more, in the future. They don't want to suffer any more."[6] Thus, without having to assume that Cambodia is a society made up of saints, we can see that the teaching of karma, known and understood by almost everyone, counseled restraint for one's own sake and thereby helped prevent further violence and chaos post–Khmer Rouge, helping to pacify the society at large.

A second implication of the *Dhammapada* passage cited above is a message to nations in combat: violence cannot achieve your ends. Think of the Middle East. One side, say the Palestinians, attacks the Israelis. The Israelis angrily retaliate militarily. This further angers the Palestinians, who attack again. In response, the Israelis retaliate again. There is no way to resolve the situation with this approach. Hatred cannot be appeased by hatred, violence cannot be appeased by violence; this is an eternal law. What law? The law of karma, cause and effect, action and reaction. How can one get past this cycle of cause and effect? By introducing something radically new into the situation, something Maha Ghosananda calls "love" and the *Dhammapada* itself calls only "nonhatred" or "nonenmity." In other words, if a country is able to have sufficient self-mastery to avoid reactivity and to introduce some constructive proposal in an effort to resolve the conflict that underlies and has caused the violence, it may be possible to move forward. Thus, the Dalai Lama replies to those who say that his devotion to nonviolence is praiseworthy but impractical, "Actually, it is far more naive to suppose that the human-created problems which lead to violence can ever be solved through conflict."[7] A simple statement, but it turns our ordinary ideas of realism and common sense on their heads. If we want to end violence, he suggests, is it not more practical to identify the cause of the violence and resolve that, rather than to react to the symptom, violence, with more violence, adding fuel to the fire?

Sulak Sivaraksa introduces the idea of social karma: "The world in which we live includes cultural, socioeconomic, and military structures as well as psychological realities. It follows that karma is simultaneously individual and social. Merely tinkering with one link in the complex circle of causation does not stop the process that leads to violence and warfare. Rather, the practice of Buddhism strives to address each aspect of the process in a holistic way. This requires not just a counter-psychology, but also a counter-culture, a counter-economy, and counter-policies."[8] Sulak is one of the Engaged Buddhists well known for advocating that we should work for a better world not only through the psychospiritual approach of changing ourselves—eliminating our anger, and so forth, so that the part of the world we create will be more peaceful—but also by changing institutional structures. These too are agents that cause and condition subsequent reality, agents whose actions can be harmful or beneficial. Just as we transform our unskillful (harmful) behaviors, we should also transform the unskillful (harmful) behaviors of the institutions we have created. For Sulak, if we do not take into account both individual and social karma, we will not be able to create the peaceful society that we seek.

THE FOUR NOBLE TRUTHS AND *DUḤKHA*

In the core teaching of the Four Noble Truths, the Buddha taught (1) there is *duḥkha*; (2) the cause of *duḥkha* is craving and ignorance; (3) it is possible for *duḥkha* to cease altogether in the state of nirvana; and (4) the way to end *duḥkha* is the Noble Eightfold Path, consisting of ethical discipline, mental discipline, and wisdom. *Duḥkha* (Pali *dukkha*), ordinarily translated into English as "suffering," means something like dis-ease or dis-satisfaction. It refers to the structural misfit between human desires (for happiness and security) and what life is able to give us (a mix of happiness and sorrow and constant change).

The Four Noble Truths have been very fruitful for Engaged Buddhists, but they have also required some interpretation. One very popular traditional understanding has been that samsara is laced with *duḥkha* in such an unsalvageable way that the only cure for human dis-satisfaction with life as we know it is to remove oneself entirely from samsara by cutting oneself off from it and attaining nirvana. Because Engaged Buddhism wants to cure the problems of the world, not turn away from them, this interpretation will not do for its exponents. Here is how Buddhadasa handles this matter:

Having not fully appreciated or examined the Buddha's teaching regarding *dukkha*, many people have misunderstood it. They have taken it to mean that birth, old age, sickness, death, and so on are themselves *dukkha*. In fact, those are just its characteristic vehicles. The Buddha summarized his explanation of *dukkha* by saying ... anything that clings or is clung to as "I" or "mine" is *dukkha*. ... Therefore birth, old age, sickness, death, and so on, if they are not clung to as "I" or "mine," cannot be *dukkha*. ... The body and mind are the same. Don't think that *dukkha* is inherent in the body and mind. Only when there is clinging to "I" or "mine" do they become *dukkha*. With the pure and undefiled body and mind, that of the Arahant, there is no *dukkha* at all.[9]

Thus, for Buddhadasa, samsara or *duhkha* is found in the realm of attitude and behavior, not in the world as such. Buddhism therefore does not require world rejection in order to reject samsara. It requires transformation of the person in such a way that she or he stops generating samsara—which is a state of being, not the world—in his or her state of mind and behavior.

This is a key point, because Engaged Buddhists, by and large, want to have it both ways. Sometimes it may seem as if Engaged Buddhists only are concerned about curing mundane suffering, but that is not the case. They want to cure both mundane suffering *and* the human condition, *duhkha* in its larger sense. These two are held together, both valid. Ariyaratne, for example, speaks of the goal of his movement as awakening both the individual (that is, enlightenment) and society (that is, curing society's ills). "In the Buddhist perspective, development is an awakening process. ... It is a sustained effort to awaken in all aspects, spiritual and ethical as well as social and economic, the individual, the family, the community, rural as well as urban groups, nations and the world community."[10]

Ariyaratne has been particularly creative in his treatment of the Four Noble Truths. We can see in his work in the field of development two ways in which the Four Noble Truths are taken up and applied by Engaged Buddhists. First, the Four Noble Truths are used as a form of analysis or template to structure problem solving. That is, the first Noble Truth states the problem; the second analyzes the problem and identifies its root causes; the third expresses the hope and faith that the problem can be resolved; and the fourth states what must be done to attain the goal. Thus, for Ariyaratne's purposes in developing Sri Lankan villages toward awakening, Noble Truth 1 states the problem: there is a decadent village (characterized by conflict, disease, poverty, and so forth); Noble Truth 2 identifies the causes of the village's decadence (egoism, ill-will, disunity, and the like); Noble

Truth 3 describes the hope (a village characterized by cooperation, constructive activity, and equality); and Noble Truth 4 lays out the way to attain the goal (by means of spiritual development, education, and economic development).[11]

The second way Ariyaratne appropriates this teaching of the Buddha is the dual focus described above: he identifies both mundane suffering and the human condition of duḥkha as the problem and sets out to create conditions that support the elimination of both. For Ariyaratne, the problem is both egoism *and* poverty; the cure is both spiritual development *and* economic development. Moreover, as the opening quotation reveals, these factors are all interdependent. Entrenched poverty, with its accompanying characteristics of hopelessness, self-loathing, and passivity, is not supportive of striving for spiritual awakening.

An interesting variation on this theme can be found in the thought of the early Indian Engaged Buddhist leader B. R. Ambedkar (1891–1956).[12] Ambedkar, himself a former Untouchable, championed the ex-Untouchables' cause and led millions to convert from Hinduism to Buddhism as a political act of rejecting the Hindu caste system. Ambedkar believed, however, that the second and third Noble Truths, as recorded and explained in the Pali *Suttas*, seemed to indicate that one was oneself to blame for one's sufferings (negative karma from past lives having caused one to be born in a condition of suffering in this life). This was unacceptable to him, in light of his keen awareness of the role played by unjust social institutions in causing the Untouchables' suffering. He therefore rejected this aspect of the Buddha's teaching altogether and produced an interpretation of the Four Noble Truths that looked only to social causes of suffering. In this respect, he differs from an Engaged Buddhist like Ariyaratne who looks to both social and individual causation of suffering. Yet even though Ambedkar did denounce the idea of the ex-Untouchables having caused their own suffering by earning negative karma in past lives, he strongly encouraged the ex-Untouchables to take responsibility for their condition *now* and to work hard to improve themselves. In this way, Ambedkar's understanding of the Fourth Noble Truth, at least, came to be much like Ariyaratne's: the path to freedom from suffering embraces both individual and social transformation.

ANĀTMAN

The Buddhist idea of *anātman*, no self, is a basic tenet of Engaged Buddhists and plays an important role in their ethics. Nhat Hanh expresses this in a particularly clear way in his remarks about a cloud floating in a sheet of paper. His principle, "the individual is made of non-individual elements," applies to humans as well.

"Just as a piece of paper is the fruit, the combination of many elements that can be called non-paper elements, the individual is made of non-individual elements. If you are a poet, you will see clearly that there is a cloud floating in this sheet of paper. Without a cloud there will be no water; without water, the trees cannot grow; and without trees, you cannot make paper. So the cloud is in here. . . . In the same way, the individual is made of non-individual elements."[13] That is, the individual is made up of such nonindividual elements as the food we eat, the air we breathe, the lessons our parents and teachers have taught us, our society, our culture, and the natural world. Thus, the individual is not really an individual; he or she is continuous with the social and natural world around.

For Maha Ghosananda, the lack of self frees us of the necessity to struggle with others or with ourselves. "There is no self," he writes. "There are only causes and conditions. Therefore, to struggle with others and ourselves is useless. The wise ones know that the root causes and conditions of all conflicts are in the mind."[14] In other words, because there is no self, to achieve social change we need to think in terms of the reasons, or causes and conditions, that make people do things. We do not need to waste any time focusing on blame and guilt. This is one of the roots of the nonadversarial element in Engaged Buddhist ethics: there is no reason for hostility toward others even if one opposes what others are doing. One must simply identify the cause(s) behind persons' causing harm and try to eliminate or change those causes.

Aung San Suu Kyi draws another implication from the same point. "To forgive," she says, "basically means the ability to see the person apart from the deed and to recognize that although he has done that deed, it does not mean that he is irredeemable. There are aspects of him that are acceptable."[15] Here we see that the Buddhist *anātman* teaching results in the same position that Gandhi expressed so well: hate the deed, not the doer. If we separate deed from doer, we can relate well to those whose actions we oppose, and this may work toward finding a mutually acceptable resolution in the end. Suu Kyi herself has stated many times that she has felt no hostility toward those who have kept her under house arrest in difficult circumstances and looks forward to dialogue with them, to resolve the issues between them.[16]

ENLIGHTENABILITY

Theravada Buddhism does not have a formal doctrine stating that all human beings can and will attain enlightenment, as Mahayana Buddhism does. Theravada does, however, have doctrines and a record of the Buddha's words and deeds that amount to almost the same thing as far as the Engaged Buddhists are concerned. Theravada has the important teaching that a human birth is the precious birth, because only a human can attain enlightenment. There is also the record of Shakyamuni Buddha: he rejected the Hindu caste system; was willing without reservation to teach persons of all castes, both genders and any background whatsoever; and confirmed during his lifetime that persons of all backgrounds had attained enlightenment. All of this not only affirms human equality, in the Engaged Buddhist view, but also gives a special status to humankind as a very precious form of life with the potential for enlightenment.

Even though traditional Theravada has no explicit doctrine of universal enlightenability, some contemporary Theravada Engaged Buddhist thinkers have taken the traditional doctrines pointing in that direction and, perhaps under Mahayana influence, come to an explicit understanding of universal enlightenability. Sulak writes simply, "Buddhism teaches that all sentient beings have the capacity for enlightenment."[17]

Introducing his development movement, Sarvodaya Shramadana, Ariyaratne writes, "All human beings have the potential to awaken one's personality to the fullest by practicing 'Dana'—which means giving, beneficence or righteous sharing, 'Sila' or moral principles, and 'Bhavana' or cultivating right-mindfulness. . . . The well-being, the happiness and the awakening of all is the objective of the Buddhist approach to social, economic and political development."[18] For Ariyaratne, the goal of a Buddhist development program for an impoverished country should not be only economic well-being. Because "all human beings have the potential to awaken one's personality to the fullest," the goal of a *Buddhist* development program should include spiritual development toward enlightenment as well. The belief in the human potential for Buddhahood, then, establishes the goal for Sarvodaya Shramadana and shapes the means of reaching that goal: economic development must follow Buddhist moral guidelines, it must not harm the environment, and it must empower people and awaken them to their potential; it must also include opportunities for giving, for cooperation, for growing in responsibility and developing mindfulness. These are all things that simultaneously help the economy develop in a sound and sustainable way, help the community develop toward peace and harmony, and help the individual develop toward awakening.

Mahayana Variant: Buddha Nature

Mahayana Buddhism, of course, has made it a central principle of its teachings that all human beings have the potential to attain Buddhahood. Not only do we have the potential, we all have within us already present Buddhahood, our innate wisdom, and compassion. It is in effect sleeping, waiting to be awakened by our activating it.

Nhat Hanh writes,

> Children understand very well that in each woman, in each man, there is a capacity of waking up, of understanding, and of loving. Many children have told me that they cannot show me anyone who does not have this capacity. Some people allow it to develop, and some do not, but everyone has it. This capacity of waking up, of being aware of what is going on in your feelings, in your body, in your perceptions, in the world, is called Buddha Nature, the capacity of understanding and loving. Since the baby of that Buddha is in us, we should give him or her a chance.[19]

In many ways, the Buddha nature is the key principle of Nhat Hanh's approach to Engaged Buddhism. His entire approach to developing inner and outer peace is based upon developing our innate understanding and love.

COMPASSION, LOVING KINDNESS, AND GIVING

Compassion (*karuṇā*), loving kindness (*mettā*), and giving (*dāna*) are rich sources in tradition for Engaged Buddhists.

Sulak draws on these three related values to challenge a traditional understanding of karma. It is common, he writes, for a landowner to require 70 percent of the harvest from those who work his land. Surely, he says, it is clear that this is morally wrong. Establishment Buddhism, though, "explains this oppression as the working of *karma*, saying that both peasants and the landlord are reaping the results of their actions in former lives; the peasants of bad deeds and the landlord of merit achieved by building temples and images of the Buddha." In place of this understanding, he proposes that "if the landlord understands and practices *dana* he will know that it is wrong to take 70 percent of the harvest when the workers do not have enough to sustain them." In an ideal world, and following Buddhadasa's Dhammic Socialism, "out of *metta* and compassion people will share whatever extra they have."[20]

Here we can see that karma is not only an important resource for Engaged Buddhist thinking, but also something of a problem for Engaged Buddhists. Engaged Buddhists do want to emphasize cause and effect both as a tool of analysis and in such a way as to encourage people to make wise choices. They do not, however, accept what they consider popular misunderstandings of the teaching of karma that encourage passivity with regard to the status quo. We will see in subsequent chapters that this is a conscious concern for other Engaged Buddhists as well. Suu Kyi finds such popular understandings of karma to be a major obstacle for her work in Burma. Phra Payutto makes a careful, scholarly case refuting such understandings by extracting from the Pali Canon quotations from the Buddha that he believes demonstrate a different understanding. Here Sulak refutes such understandings indirectly by pointing out their moral bankruptcy in light of the central values of giving, loving kindness, and compassion.

Mettā, a value that has long been fundamental to the layperson's practice of Buddhism, is central to contemporary Engaged Buddhism as well. Thus, when asked how she visualizez a democratic Burma, Suu Kyi responds, "When we visualize a democratic Burma . . . we see it in terms of less suffering for the people. . . . We don't think of it in terms of abstract institutions but in terms of what it can do to contribute towards the happiness and well-being of the people. . . . That is why I would say that metta is the core of our movement—a desire to bring relief to human beings."[21]

In this remarkable passage, given the opportunity to speak on the essence of a future democratic Burma, Suu Kyi describes it as a manifestation of mettā, loving kindness. That is, she and her colleagues see it as the form of government best able to promote the well-being of the people, and it is for that reason that they choose it. As a self-identified Engaged Buddhist—"I do believe in 'engaged Buddhism,' to use a modern term"[22]—it goes without saying that the government she would represent would endeavor to embody such a core Buddhist value as mettā.

Suu Kyi says elsewhere, "As Burmese Buddhists, we put a great emphasis on metta."[23] But she would very much like to see the Burmese make their mettā more active:

Engaged Buddhism is active compassion or active metta. It's not just sitting there passively saying, "I feel sorry for them." It means doing something about the situation by bringing whatever relief you can to those who need it the most, by caring for them, by doing what you can to help others. . . .

In Burma today, many people are afraid to visit families of political prisoners in case they too are called in by the authorities and harassed. Now, you could show active compassion by coming to the families of political prisoners and offering them practical help and by surrounding them with love, compassion and moral support. This is what we are encouraging.[24]

Suu Kyi imagines an immediate practical application of *mettā* that could have tremendous political impact if many people did it: standing in friendship (that is, solidarity) with families of political prisoners. In a country like Burma, even a traditional act of *mettā* such as bringing food to such people can be a dangerous political act. As she well knows, though, if people stood in solidarity (that is, in friendship) with people being harassed by the government, it would greatly alter the political dynamic in Burma.

For many years, the Dalai Lama has been interested in articulating an ethic for humankind that is not dependent upon any particular religious view, but is based upon universal humanistic values. These universal human values turn out to be in the family of values Buddhists recognize as compassion and loving kindness, that is, benevolence, caring about the welfare of others. He distinguishes between religion and spirituality, taking the former as referring to faith in specific claims to salvation and the latter "to be concerned with those qualities of the human spirit—such as love and compassion, patience, tolerance, forgiveness, contentment, a sense of responsibility, a sense of harmony—which bring happiness to both self and others." The unifying factor in spirituality he takes to be "some level of concern for others' well-being. . . . To speak of spiritual practice in any terms other than these is meaningless."[25] Thus, as far as the Dalai Lama is concerned, growth in caring about others is the universal and only valid spirituality, spirituality that has no necessary relationship to religion per se.

It is important for the Dalai Lama's effort to articulate a universal, humanistic ethic that all people potentially could embrace, to make the point that human beings are caring and empathetic by nature.

> When I speak of basic human feeling . . . I refer to the capacity we all have to empathize with one another, which . . . we call . . . "the inability to bear the sight of another's suffering." Given that this is what enables us to enter into, and to some extent participate, in others' pain, it is one of our most significant characteristics. It is what causes us to start at the sound of a cry for help, to recoil at the sight of harm done to another, to suffer when confronted with other's suffering. . . . That we all, excepting perhaps only the most disturbed, appreciate being shown kindness, suggest that however hardened we may become, the capacity for empathy remains.
>
> . . . [A]longside our natural ability to empathize with others, we also have a need for others' kindness, which runs like a thread throughout our whole life. . . . [The] instinctual care of mother for child—shared it seems with many animals—is crucial because it suggests that alongside the baby's

fundamental need of love in order to survive, there exists an innate capacity on the part of the mother to give love. . . . [T]his need and capacity for love suggest that we are, in fact, loving by nature.[26]

Here we see that our capacity for empathy is innate and that we are by nature beings who care and who need caring. On this depends not only our biological survival, but also our ability to live together, that is, our ethics. Since, for His Holiness, "ethical conduct consists in not harming others," in order to be ethical, we need to take others' feelings into consideration, and the basis for this is "our innate capacity for empathy."[27] Thus, ethics for His Holiness is based in empathy. Our success as human beings, then, whether in realizing Buddhahood or in managing to live together in peace and cooperation, depends upon our developing our inborn capacity of caring.

MAHAYANA VARIANT: BUDDHA NATURE AND THE BODHISATTVA IDEAL

In passages above from the Dalai Lama we can see him drawing upon the idea of Buddha nature. Although he refrains, in his work intended for non-Buddhist audiences, from using specifically Buddhist terminology, the idea that humans are by nature not only wise, but also innately caring and compassionate, is one of the central themes of Buddha nature thought. Whereas elsewhere in this chapter we looked at Buddha nature in the context of enlightenability, here we focus on Buddha nature as innate caring and compassion and on its expression in the bodhisattva ideal.

Reflecting upon the phenomenal growth of her charitable organization, the Tzu Chi Foundation, Venerable Cheng Yen writes, "For more than 30 years, millions of people have enthusiastically responded and joined in the good work, without complaint or regret. I deeply believe that in every heart there exists priceless great love."[28] For Cheng Yen, the growth of the Tzu Chi Foundation from a handful of people to millions in just thirty years is confirmation of our inborn capacity—even eagerness—to love, our Buddha nature. She built her organization on faith in that Buddha nature. Thus, when Cheng Yen found herself seriously underfunded while trying to build a hospital and a wealthy donor offered sufficient funds to more than complete the project, Cheng Yen turned him down, declaring that she relied upon her "faith in others, that within the heart of every person lies love that is only waiting to be awakened."[29] This is a faith in Buddha nature.

Appealing to an audience of faithful Buddhists rather than a mixed international audience, as do many other Engaged Buddhists, Cheng Yen perhaps refers directly to the bodhisattva ideal more frequently and explicitly than any other Engaged Buddhist.

> Is the "Thousand-handed and thousand-eyed Bodhisattva" a figure of speech in Buddhism, or is there really a Bodhisattva with a thousand hands and eyes? . . . The timing was perfect when three Catholic nuns . . . correctly mentioned that even though the philosophy of Buddhism is beneficial spiritually, it has not accomplished much that actually supports the physical well-being of society.
>
> Their words motivated my aspirations. Everyone could be the Bodhisattva's eyes to look at all beings with benevolence. Everyone could be the Bodhisattva's hands to save all beings with mercy.[30]

Cheng Yen concluded that everyone in her organization could be a bodhisattva. "Tzu Chi is different from many charitable organizations. The spiritual belief, the footing on which Tzu Chi stands, has created an extraordinary organization of bodhisattvas."[31]

The Soka Gakkai International (SGI) is another organization that refers to its membership and work in terms of the bodhisattva. SGI president Daisaku Ikeda writes that he likes to promote the idea of "world citizens" competing among themselves in humanitarianism. "World citizens," in his mind, are not chauvinistic about their culture but work for world peace on behalf of all humankind. Such people, he says, are bodhisattvas. "The bodhisattva, as a world citizen, is someone who is constantly challenging egotism and is engaged in the race to transform . . . deluded impulses . . . into enlightenment. Bodhisattvas, refusing to be engulfed in the consumerism and materialism of contemporary society, embrace a noble spirit of serving others, and pledge to make this their mission in life. This process sets in motion a fundamental change in life orientation—from egotism to the desire to create happiness for oneself and others."[32] For Ikeda, the bodhisattva is the world citizen, working on his or her own enlightenment through service to the world, the one who dedicates his or her life to making the world a better place.

The Dalai Lama seems to agree with Ikeda that the bodhisattva ideal, in a secularized form shorn of ideas of rebirth and miraculous power, is an ideal that can be appropriate across cultures. His Holiness closes his ethics book written for the global audience with a bodhisattva prayer (though without using the term):

> May I become at all times, both now and forever,
> A protector for those without protection

A guide for those who have lost their way
A ship for those with oceans to cross
A bridge for those with rivers to cross
A sanctuary for those in danger
A lamp for those without light
A place of refuge for those who lack shelter
And a servant to all in need.[33]

SELF-TRANSFORMATIVE PRACTICES (BHĀVANĀ)

Traditional Buddhism emphasizes spiritual practices intended to deeply transform the individual practitioner. Engaged Buddhism continues to emphasize such practices, often the very same practices, but with a shift in intention: one transforms oneself not only as an aspect of personal spiritual development, which remains central, but also in order to be more capable of effectively serving all sentient beings.

Nhat Hanh has probably done more than any other Engaged Buddhist to make clear the link between spiritual practice and social activism. He puts it succinctly in his book, *Being Peace:* "Smiling is very important. If we are not able to smile, then the world will not have peace. It is not by going out for a demonstration against nuclear missiles that we can bring about peace. It is with our capacity of smiling, breathing, and being peace that we can make peace."[34] Nhat Hanh teaches a simple mindfulness meditation based upon conscious relaxation ("smiling") and mindfulness of breathing. Such practices, he believes, generate personal peacefulness without which any effort to generate community or world peace is useless. He has often spoken of the anger he saw in American "peace protestors" during the war in Vietnam and how inappropriate he thought anger was in people trying to "make peace." In short, one needs to "be peace" in order to "make peace." To help people to "be peace," he has popularized simplified Buddhist mindfulness practices.

Buddhism has traditionally emphasized individual psychospiritual transformation through Buddhist practice. Contemporary Engaged Buddhists have discovered that many of the same practices play an important role in transforming individuals in ways that are very useful for those individuals' roles as agents of social change and humanitarian work. Nhat Hanh writes of the role of meditation and mindfulness practice during a period of crisis in his group's effort to rescue Vietnamese boat people. "The suffering we touched doing this kind of work was so deep that if we did not have a reservoir of spiritual strength, we would not have

been able to continue. During those days, we practiced sitting and walking meditation, and eating our meals in silence in a very concentrated way. We knew that
without this kind of discipline, we would fail in our work. The lives of many people
depended on our mindfulness."[35] In the context of social activism, such spiritual
practice plays a very useful role in helping to sustain the activist: preventing dis-
couragement and feelings of being overwhelmed, taking the mind off its worries
and ruminations, keeping the person focused and steadfast, and physically ener-
gizing the person.

In the case of the Dalai Lama, even when addressing a global audience and
articulating a nonreligious, universal humanistic ethic, he indicates that spiritual
practice for self-transformation is essential. For His Holiness, because ethical behavior is defined as loving and compassionate behavior, we need to engage in intentional practices that remove those attitudes, habits, and so forth within ourselves that impede the development and expression of such love and compassion
for others. The first step in doing so is self-discipline. A second is the intentional
cultivation of compassion. Thus, he writes, "I have suggested that developing . . .
compassion . . . demands a two-pronged approach. On the one hand, we need to
restrain those factors which inhibit compassion. On the other, we need to cultivate
those which are conducive to it."[36] For the Dalai Lama, the compassion that is innate to us nonetheless requires considerable spiritual practice to remove obstacles
to its expression and cultivate its further development.

All the Engaged Buddhists agree on the necessity of individual spiritual practice as a prerequisite for engaging in the kind of social activism that constructs the
kind of world that humankind and other species need and want. Between them,
they draw on many kinds of spiritual practice to serve the dual purposes of self-
development and social service.

PRECEPTS AND VOWS

Working with precepts and vows plays a role in the work of most of the Engaged
Buddhists. In light of the variety of sectarian affiliation among them, there are
naturally several versions of such precepts and vows upon which they draw.

Five Lay Precepts
The Five Lay Precepts play major roles in the work of Ariyaratne, Nhat Hanh,
and Sulak. The Five Lay Precepts are the assumed moral ground for Ariyaratne's

movement. When asked how violence such as that between Tamils and Sinhalese in Sri Lanka can occur in a Buddhist country, he replied,

> I venture to say that though we have a majority of people who are categorized as Buddhists, still we do not have a Buddhist society as such.
>
> One can call a society a Buddhist society if two basic conditions are satisfied. First, as citizens that majority of people . . . should follow the basic tenets of Buddhism. They should accept and respect Buddha . . . , follow the Dhamma . . . , and emulate and take care of the Sangha. . . . Then the basic minimum, the ethical code against killing, thieving, sexual misconduct, lying and intoxication, should be the guiding foundation for the personal conduct of human beings. As citizens we do not sufficiently satisfy this first condition of respecting the Triple Gem and following the Five Precepts.
>
> Secondly, the guiding principles of the State should be formulated in such a way that the above code of moral conduct is facilitated. The State should abstain from doing anything that would encourage people to break the Five Precepts.[37]

For Ariyaratne, without the Five Precepts, there is really no Buddhism. To him, they are essential for a society that works.

Nhat Hanh has rewritten the Five Lay Precepts as the Five Mindfulness Trainings. They are considerably expanded in both length and meaning. The traditional Five Lay Precepts state, "I undertake to observe the precept (1) to abstain from the taking of life; (2) not to take that which is not given; (3) to abstain from misconduct in sensual actions; (4) to abstain from false speech; (5) to abstain from liquor that causes intoxication and indolence."[38] Nhat Hanh's version reads, in part,

1. Aware of the suffering caused by the destruction of life, I am committed to cultivate compassion and learn ways to protect the lives of people, animals, plants, and minerals. I am determined not to kill, not to let others kill, and not to condone any act of killing in the world, in my thinking, and in my way of life.
2. Aware of the suffering caused by exploitation, social injustice, stealing, and oppression, I am committed to cultivate loving kindness and learn ways to work for the well-being of people, animals, plants, and minerals.

I am committed to practice generosity by sharing my time, energy, and material resources with those who are in real need. I am determined not to steal and not to possess anything that should belong to others. I will respect the property of others, but I will prevent others from profiting from human suffering or the suffering of other species on Earth.[39]

These rewritten precepts clearly take the traditional Five Lay Precepts and transform them from purely negative precepts ("I will not kill") to precepts that are both negative and positive ("I will not kill" and "I will prevent others from killing"), from purely personal precepts, or training guides, to precepts that are both personal and social. They are concerned not only with what the individual will and will not do, but also with actively transforming society. Nhat Hanh makes these Five Mindfulness Trainings major foci of the retreats he offers as he travels around the world. He continually urges those who look to him as a teacher to take these on as personal disciplines.

For his part, Sulak thinks through the five precepts, examining their implications for ethical behavior in the modern world. He does not rewrite them as Nhat Hanh does, but attempts to open up their implications, inviting reflections upon those implications and suggesting applications of them. Here is an example: "The third precept repudiates improper sexuality. In contemporary terms, Buddhist sexual ethics must address the global structures that facilitate male domination and the exploitation of women. . . . Rape, pornography, and prostitution are the inevitable outcome of systems that objectify women's bodies, which are reduced to commodities on the market. . . . In contrast, Buddhist practice seeks to develop full human beings, free from socially learned 'masculine' and 'feminine' patterns of thought, speech, and behavior."[40] Again the precepts are transformed into vehicles for a proactive engagement with society and its problems. Here, Sulak unabashedly applies the third precept to contemporary issues of rape, pornography, and prostitution, with a very contemporary interpretation.

New Precepts
Some Engaged Buddhist leaders compose new sets of precepts for their followers. Master Cheng Yen asks her followers to observe the "Tzu Chi Ten Precepts," which are the Five Lay Precepts plus another five, both negatively and positively stated, "no smoking, no drugs, no betel nuts; no gambling, no opportunistic investments [especially in the stock market]; must show filial piety, be soft spoken, have a gentle expression; must abide by traffic regulations; and [must] not participate in political activities, protests or demonstrations."[41] In this list, the sixth precept could be

understood as an expansion of the traditional fifth precept, against intoxication, and the seventh as an expansion of the second, against stealing (understood as taking something that one had not earned by one's own work). The eighth makes explicit the incorporation of filial piety into the Buddhist ethical code, an incorporation of a Confucian value into Chinese Buddhism that occurred in ancient times. The gentleness to which this eighth precept also refers is, however, a value found throughout the Buddhist world. The ninth precept, to abide by traffic regulations, is simply a matter of common sense and necessity, but the tenth precept, not to participate in political activities, protests, or demonstrations, shows how much Tzu Chi differs from many other Engaged Buddhist organizations. Tzu Chi is the least political of the major Engaged Buddhist organizations, a fact that no doubt contributes to its ability to work in the People's Republic of China. Cheng Yen stresses that change comes from within and emphasizes the development of compassion in her followers, avoiding calls for structural, institutional changes in society.

Nhat Hanh has worked a great deal with precepts. In addition to his rewriting of the Five Lay Precepts, he has developed at least two new sets: the Tiep Hien Precepts of the Order of Interbeing, composed during the war as guidance for the early community of Vietnamese Engaged Buddhists and now rewritten as the "Fourteen Mindfulness Trainings of the Order of Interbeing," and a set of precepts for children. The children's precepts, or promises, state:

> I vow to develop my compassion in order to love and protect the life of people, animals, and plants.
>
> I vow to develop understanding in order to be able to love and to live in harmony with people, animals, and plants.[42]

These promises focus on the two main Mahayana virtues of compassion and wisdom. Nhat Hanh has been particularly innovative in experimenting with ways to bring the teachings of Buddhism to children. Here he trains children the same way he trains adults, shaping their outlook with frequent repetitions of promises in the spirit of the adults' precepts, but in a language the children can understand.

Bodhisattva Vows

In the Mahayana tradition it is usual for practitioners to take bodhisattva vows, dedicating their practice for the sake of all sentient beings.[43] Engaged Buddhists who belong to the Mahayana follow this traditional practice. There are also some new variations on this tradition. Tzu Chi founder Master Cheng Yen has founded her life of service upon three bodhisattva-like vows of her own devising: "Purify minds; Harmonize society; Free the world from disasters."[44]

MEDITATION

Meditation is a key Buddhist practice for self-transformation, and Engaged Buddhists make ample use of it. In their hands, it becomes a tool both for self-transformation and for the transformation of society. Again, as with precepts and vows, Engaged Buddhists use a variety of meditation practices, with the choice depending largely on sectarian identity.

Mindfulness

For Nhat Hanh, the practice of mindfulness is the key meditation practice. "With 50,000 atomic bombs, humankind has become the most dangerous species on earth. We were never so dangerous as we are now. We should be aware. The most basic precept of all is to be aware of what we do, what we are, each minute. Every other precept will follow from that."[45] Nhat Hanh has written of the importance for him personally of meditative mindfulness practice in the midst of a crisis. This crisis occurred during the efforts of Nhat Hanh and his associates to rescue Vietnamese boat people who were at sea in highly dangerous conditions, off the shores of countries that refused to take them in. When the government of Singapore discovered their effort, Nhat Hanh's travel documents were seized and he was ordered to leave the country within twenty-four hours, despite the fact that two large boats full of people remained adrift, waiting to be brought to shore.

> What could we do in such a situation? We had to breathe deeply and consciously. Otherwise we might panic, or fight with the police, or do something to express our anger at their lack of humanity. . . .
> I decided to practice the meditation topic, "If you want peace, peace is with you immediately," and I was surprised to find myself quite calm, not afraid or worried about anything. I was not just being careless. This was truly a peaceful state of mind, and in that state, I was able to overcome this difficult situation.[46]

For Nhat Hanh, then, mindfulness is particularly important for social activists, enabling them to respond appropriately and effectively in the midst of crisis.

Four *Brahmavihāra*

The Four *Brahmavihāra* are a traditional meditation subject that have been transformed and heavily appropriated by Engaged Buddhists. The *Brahmavihāra*, or "Sublime Abodes," are *mettā* (loving kindness), *karuṇā* (compassion), *muditā* (sympathetic joy), and *upekkhā* (equanimity). Traditionally, they are meditation subjects associated with concentration and the production of states of trance. In the hands of contemporary Engaged Buddhists, they have come to represent four desirable emotions that the practitioner should intentionally cultivate, sometimes meditatively, and take as motivation for action.

The four *Brahmavihāra* have played central roles in Sarvodaya for decades. Of the four, *mettā* is the most important. It is the key motivation of service for the community. Joanna Macy relates that the Sarvodaya Movement "promotes it through sermon, song, and slogan, and also through the practice of the *metta* meditation, which is expected of all participants." Of *karuṇā*, a Sarvodaya guideline says, "Feeling sorry for people is not enough. Act to help them." Sympathetic joy is to arise upon seeing the results of one's service work. Equanimity maintains contentment, whether one succeeds or fails, is praised or blamed.[47]

In recent years, Ariyaratne has come to rely heavily upon popularizing *mettā* meditation as part of his initiative to bring peace to Sri Lanka. He holds mass peace meditations, the most recent attracting 650,000 participants, and teaches them the meditation on *mettā*. Participants pledge, "I am a participant in the mass meditational effort to bring about spiritual awakening within the country and across the entire planet. I make my contribution to unite people of all ethnic backgrounds, nationalities, religions, political views, without any difference whatsoever. Through this endeavour of mine, ours, may violence and war cease to exist."[48] With this intention, participants are taught walking, breath, insight, and *mettā* meditation. At the end of the session, participants are directed to spend five minutes radiating their loving kindness out to everyone.

With this program, Ariyaratne intends not only the transformation of the participants, but also ultimately the ending of the violence in Sri Lanka. Those who attend the mass peace meditations are asked to continue to practice the *mettā* meditation at home and to radiate their peaceful and loving-kindness energy out, thereby transforming the "psychosphere"—that is, transforming the overall psychological climate of Sri Lanka.

Another use of the Four *Brahmavihāra* by Engaged Buddhists is found in Tzu Chi. Master Cheng Yen has interpreted the four missions of Tzu Chi as expressions of the four *Brahmavihāra*. Thus, the mission of charity is equated with compassion;

the mission of medical care is equated with loving kindness; the cultural mission is equated with sympathetic joy; and the education mission with equanimity, interpreted as impartiality.[49] This use appropriates a well-known tradition to validate the innovative practices of Tzu Chi.

Cultivating Altruism

The Dalai Lama advocates engaging in meditative practice to develop one's caring for others and one's altruism intentionally. There are many practices for this purpose. One that he often mentions is to contemplate rebirth. When you contemplate that rebirths are infinite, he writes, you come to realize that everyone has at one time been a mother to you. "When you contemplate in this manner, the one-pointed apprehension of some persons as friends and others as enemies . . . will become weaker in strength."[50]

Another, more advanced, practice that His Holiness often mentions is "giving and taking." Quoting from, and then commenting upon, the *Eight Stanzas for Training the Mind*, he writes,

> In short, I will learn to offer to everyone without exception
> All help and happiness directly and indirectly
> And respectfully take upon myself
> All harm and suffering of my mothers.

> This stanza sets forth the practice of giving and taking—out of love giving your happiness and causes of happiness to others and out of compassion taking from others their suffering and the causes that would make them suffer.[51]

Here the "mothers" of the last line refers to all beings, since, as the first practice showed, all beings have been one's mother in past lives. Again, once one realizes this, one will begin to want to offer others one's own happiness and take from others their suffering, as one naturally would do with one's mother. The Dalai Lama admits that this is a difficult practice to do in reality but suggests that even reciting these lines—putting this thought before oneself repeatedly—helps one to make progress in this direction.[52]

GIVING

Giving is another value that is ubiquitous in Engaged Buddhism. The Dalai Lama comments on the value of giving for both the giver and the recipient:

> Giving is recognized as a virtue in every major religion and in every civilized society, and it clearly benefits both the giver and the receiver. The one who receives is relieved from the pangs of want. The one who gives can take comfort from the joy their gift brings to others.[53]

Cheng Yen has made the experiential recognition of the joy of giving one of the foundations of Tzu Chi:

> It is a privilege to extend our helping hands to people regardless of who or what or where they are . . . love and mercy transcends [sic] races, nationalities and geographical distance. And we owe our hearty thanks to our receivers, because it is their unfortunate condition that makes it possible for us to know the joy of giving.[54]

A good example of this joy in giving is provided by the Tzu Chi member Lin-mei Chai, who, after suffering from polio and rheumatic fever, spends her days bedridden, barely able to speak, and living on government assistance. Nevertheless, the funds she receives are more than she feels she needs, so she donates the remainder to Tzu Chi on a monthly basis.

Master Cheng Yen's organization strongly emphasizes the importance of giving, both financial giving and giving of oneself. This is a practice that involves much more than a material exchange; it is a potentially profound self-transformative practice.

> In our charity work, we provide material necessities, medical care, and spiritual consolation for the sick and elderly. We not only help the poor, but also educate the rich by showing them that giving and service are more meaningful than pursuing wealth, power, and prestige. We are grateful to both our long-term care recipients and to disaster victims when we give them food, clothing, care, and companionship, for without their misfortune we would find no opportunity to serve. The poor and wretched receive help, the rich and fortunate activate their love, and thus both can be grateful to each other. . . .

Give whatever you can, whether a little or a lot. Strive persistently
with equanimity and patience. You will soon reach the level at which
"There is no giver, there is no receiver, there is no gift." Giving and receiving will be nothing more than part of the natural order of things. This
may seem like an impossible ideal, but in fact anyone who really wants to
can become a bodhisattva in this world.[55]

Here Cheng Yen interprets fundamental practices of her organization in terms of
the highest Mahayana ideals of the bodhisattva's insight into the emptiness of
"giver," "recipient," and "gift." She speaks of the giver feeling gratitude to the recipient—the one who gives us an opportunity to develop our generosity by enabling us to give. Thus, she highlights the idea that the wealthy need to give as
much as the poor need to receive. Yet as long as such ideas exist, from the Mahayana emptiness perspective, the giving is not yet pure giving; it is giving tainted
by the idea of self. As one gives one should begin to realize how much more one
has received in the "natural order of things" from life than the little that one has
given. In this way, ideas of "giving," "one who gives," and "one to whom one gives"
will lose their power and gradually fade.

Giving is one of the central practices in Sarvodaya Shramadana; "shramadana" in fact means "giving" (dāna) labor or human energy. The shramadana camp
is an opportunity for each person to give his or her labor to a project that will serve
the community as a whole. In addition to one's labor, there are also community
meals to which each person gives food. Macy, a longtime participant-observer with
Sarvodaya, gives this account:

> Villagers are not given sermons so much as opportunities to experience
> their own innate generosity. Whether it is a small child bringing her
> matchbox of rice to the Sarvodaya preschool or a landowner invited to
> give right of way for an access road through his tea estate, the operative
> assumption is that the act of giving empowers the giver and is the soil out
> of which mutual trust and respect can grow.

She quotes a Sarvodaya district coordinator:

> She is a day-laborer—and for rice for the shramadana she gave me more
> than she earns in a whole day. But it was worth it to her—and to us—for
> she feels important to the village now in a way she did not before.[56]

Thus, in the Sarvodaya Shramadana movement, as in Tzu Chi, giving is a key practice for both rich and poor. Giving is a practice for developing oneself, for growing as a human being with the potential of Buddhahood. At the same time, it gives something that is needed, heightens awareness of interdependence, and builds community.

SYMBOL AND CEREMONY, DEVOTION AND INSPIRATION

Engaged Buddhists engage in devotional and ceremonial practices old, new, and old with a new twist. Teaching new Buddhists in the West how to establish their practice, Nhat Hanh recommends that each home have a small meditation room. In that room go cushions, a bell, some flowers, and, perhaps, a Buddha statue— concerning which, Nhat Hanh has some advice: "If you want to have a statue or a painting of a Buddha, please be choosy. Many times I see Buddhas who are not re- laxed and peaceful. . . . A Buddha should be smiling, happy, beautiful, for the sake of our children. If they look at the Buddha and don't feel refreshed and happy, then it is not a good statue. If you don't find a beautiful Buddha, wait, and have a flower instead. A flower is a Buddha. A flower has Buddha nature."[57] The devotional and inspirational intention here is nothing new. For Nhat Hanh, the purpose of regular meditation in such a room is to help people develop their peacefulness and hap- piness, their personal "being peace." Thus prepared, they are better able to help others when they re-enter society.

Another Engaged Buddhist use of symbol is seen in the Nipponzan Myohoji peace movement's placing of peace pagodas and peace pillars in public places all over the world as constant physical reminders of the hope and possibility of peace. The pagodas are clearly Buddhist in origin; the pillars simply have "may peace pre- vail on Earth" written on them in many languages. Standing there as almost mute symbols, they are open to a great variety of interpretations, and no doubt people make of them what they will—like a work of art, perhaps, they have the capacity to move the heart without anyone being able to say exactly what they mean.

In Cambodia, after the fall of the Khmer Rouge, the first Dhammayietra, or walk for peace, accompanied the refugees home. During that peace walk, a spon- taneous blessing ceremony developed. Monks throwing water as a form of blessing is traditional in Cambodia during the Khmer New Year celebration. It is also part of auspicious events like weddings. During the Dhammayietra, water blessings oc- curred spontaneously throughout the month of the walk. People came out, "along the roadside with buckets of water seeking the walkers' blessing by asking the walkers to throw it over them. Walkers would do so with their dippers or leafy branches and murmur . . . 'The war is over!'" Maha Ghosananda explained, "Mine are a simple people. To us water means cleansing. We are washing away the blood."[58]

This is a good example of a traditional ceremonial practice with a new twist. There clearly was a sense among the people along the path of the walk that the Dhammayietra was a sacred and highly auspicious event, and they felt it necessary to celebrate it in some way that would let them proclaim and participate in those qualities. It is important to note that any of the walkers, ordained or not, was able to perform the water ceremony; by participating in the Dhammayietra, it seems that a walker's status was temporarily raised to a level sacred enough to perform the ceremony the same way that a monk ordinarily would.

Sarvodaya Shramadana presents us with an example of a ceremony intended to transform an entire community, rather than an individual: the family gatherings at shramadana camps. These work camps are conducted at the local village level throughout Sri Lanka. They begin, and are interspersed, with "family gatherings." These feature meditations on loving kindness for all beings, as well as songs, dances, and prayers, drawn from the various religions and cultures present in the village, all promoting the idea of "one world, one people." Ariyaratne writes, "The idea behind the term 'family gathering' is that the whole world is one family, and all of them represent humanity in microcosm. All religious, caste, race, linguistic, class, national, or political differences are of no importance in these family gatherings."[59] This practice is clearly intended to transform the community as a whole from one that sees itself as composed of ethnic and religious groups to one that experiences itself as a unified, family-like whole.

In India, there are many former Untouchables who have converted to Buddhism as a social and political act that renounces the caste system and its power over their lives. In TBMSG (Trailokya Bauddha Mahasangha Sahayaka Gana), an organization of these "new Buddhists," (also called dalit, or "oppressed," Buddhists), the conversion ceremony "Going for Refuge" to Buddha, Dhamma, and Sangha is "the central and definitive act of the Buddhist life." This ceremony represents not just a change in religion, but also a rebirth in which one leaves behind the old life within the caste system and is reborn as a Buddhist with status equal to anyone else. Thus, Dr. Ambedkar himself said at his conversion to Buddhism, "Now I have taken a new life."[60]

In sum, as in any other form of Buddhism, symbols and ceremonies, devotion and inspiration play important roles in Engaged Buddhism. Such things contribute to the personal transformation that prepares an individual to engage the problems of society.

WORK

Self-transformation through work is the hallmark of two Engaged Buddhist groups and is important in a third. In Sarvodaya Shramadana, the shramadana work camp is an example of a practice that uses work to transform both the individual and the group. In a shramadana camp, the villagers decide on the work to be done and make all the preparations. At the appointed time, everyone works together on a concrete project, such as building a road or digging a well. But these are not just development projects in the material sense of the word. As the Sarvodaya slogan says, "We build the road and the road builds us." Very substantial changes are made in a village through work camp projects, but roads and wells could deteriorate or be destroyed. Thus, most significant are the psychological and social changes in the group: self-respect and mutual respect; skills in listening, sharing, and working together; the development of initiative, self-reliance, and cooperation. Drawing upon these foundations, many more projects may come to fruition and the community itself may be rejuvenated.

Tzu Chi is another example of a group that puts work at its core. The general remarks introducing Tzu Chi on the group's Web page refer to the importance of service work not only for achieving its immediate ends, but also for the transformation it produces in the one who gives the service.

> Master Cheng Yen understands that misery in this world is not solely due to poverty, but, also, to a lack of meaningful purpose in life. She believes that the most meaningful life is one of service to those in need. . . .
> In the spirit of "There is no one I do not love, trust, or forgive," she seeks to help make this world one of kindness, compassion, joy, and equality by relieving the material and physical suffering of the needy, and guiding the Tzu Chi volunteers toward personal and spiritual growth.[61]

Thus, Master Cheng Yen identifies not only poverty among the lower economic class, but also meaninglessness among the upper class; not only the need for health care, but also the need to give love as core issues for the Taiwanese. One could say, then, that Cheng Yen identified Taiwan as a place with both poor and wealthy people in which the wealthy were doing little to help the poor and then addressed that identified problem not only by providing much needed services, but also by transforming attitudes and behavior.

The personal transformation Cheng Yen seeks for her followers is not only an increase in generosity, but also the kind of transformation brought about by the inevitable frustrations of working together with other people. She says, "When working together, conflicts are unavoidable. We should take such opportunity to train our minds and to undo our habitual negative behavior. Seeing everyone working harmoniously together brings me joy. I am very saddened if people hold a grudge against each other."[62]

Even though Tzu Chi is so thoroughly oriented toward service work, the ultimate goal is still enlightenment or Buddhahood. One works toward that goal precisely by working for others and with others here and now. She writes, "Everyone should use humility to nurture wisdom and to correct all bad habits in order to reclaim their pure nature. . . . [L]et us not forget that our goal is to transcend the state of ordinary human beings."[63]

Work also plays an important role in TBMSG. We saw above that, in TBMSG, the central act in the new Buddhists' lives is the conversion ceremony. Dhammachari Lokamitra, however, reports that the new Buddhists face serious obstacles in consolidating their new identity as Buddhists psychologically free of the caste system. The caste system by its very nature is divisive, and new Buddhists, like others conditioned by this system, tend to think in terms of their divisions into families, regions, and so forth. This "groupism" weakens their ability to work together for a common cause. Thus, for these new Buddhists, the Buddhist identity that unites them is not something achieved at the conversion ceremony once and for all but something that must be brought to mind and built upon again and again. "In the spiritual community our common commitment to Buddha, Dhamma, and Sangha has to exert a stronger pull than the differences and tensions between us. If it does, we can destroy the roots of caste conditioning, individually and collectively."

For TBMSG, friendship within the Buddhist community is central to this process; teamwork has become a way of promoting personal growth as well as solidifying relationships within the Buddhist community. "Teamwork has many challenges, and a strong Dhammic base is necessary to help take them on. When we work together, as opposed to come together to practice meditation or study, our level of consciousness can easily drop, resulting in worse communication, not better. Our psychological weaknesses and negative social conditioning will be ready to exploit any cracks in the harmony of the team. If we have established a strong atmosphere of trust through the practice of Kalyana Mitrata [spiritual friendship], we will be able to reflect upon, take responsibility for, and work on our individual and collective shortcomings."[64] In this way, teamwork has become a central practice. It effectively encourages each individual to think of him- or herself as capable, to do what is best for the group, to overcome self-centeredness by putting the group and its project first, and to think of the group as a unit, over-coming divisiveness and solidifying Buddhist identity.

NONVIOLENCE

Nonviolence is a defining characteristic of Engaged Buddhism. The primary source in the Dharma of teaching on nonviolence to which Engaged Buddhists refer is the first precept: "I undertake the precept to abstain from the taking of life." Similarly, the *Dhammapada* exhorts,

> All are frightened of the rod.
> For all, life is dear.
> Having made oneself the example,
> One should neither slay nor cause to slay.[65]

And the *Mettā Sutta* puts it thus:

> Whatever living beings there be: feeble or strong, tall, stout or medium, short, small or large, without exception; seen or unseen, those dwelling far or near, those who are born or those who are to be born, may all beings be happy!

> Let none deceive another, not despise any person whatsoever in any place. Let him not wish any harm to another out of anger or ill will.

> Just as a mother would protect her only child at the risk of her own life, even so, let him cultivate a boundless heart towards all beings.[66]

In short, there is no shortage of exhortations to nonviolence in the Buddhist canon. Nonviolence is an important theme in traditional Buddhism, and Engaged Buddhist leaders and movements such as the Dalai Lama and the Tibetan Libera-tion Movement, Nhat Hanh and the Vietnamese Struggle Movement, and Suu Kyi and the movement for democracy and human rights in Burma have engaged in heroic nonviolent responses to the most intense forms of violence and brutality.

3   Engaged Buddhist Ethical Theory

There has been considerable discussion among scholars of late regarding what kind of ethical system Buddhism has. Much of this discussion has compared Buddhist ethical thinking to the varieties of Western ethical thought. Like Padmasiri de Silva, though even more inclusively, I see elements of most Western ethical theories in the ethics of Buddhism.[1] Like James Whitehill and Damien Keown, I give pride of place among these theories to virtue ethics.[2]

The Dalai Lama gives a good example of how Buddhist ethics includes elements of many ethical systems considered distinct in Western philosophy:

> [O]ne of the things which determines whether an act is ethical or not is its effect on others' experience or expectation of happiness. An act which harms or does violence to this is potentially an unethical act. I say *potentially* because although the consequences of our actions are important, there are other factors to consider, including both the question of intent and the nature of the act itself. We can all think of things which we have done that have upset others, despite the fact that it was by no means our intention to do so. . . .
>
> Again, it is not difficult to imagine a case where an individual may suppose their actions to be well intended and directed toward the greater good of others, but where they are in reality totally immoral. Here we might think of a soldier who carries out orders summarily to execute civilian prisoners. Believing the cause to be a just one, this soldier may suppose such actions are directed toward the greater good of humanity. Yet, according to the principle of non-violence I have put forward, such killing would by definition be an unethical act. . . . In other words, the content of our actions is also important in determining whether they are ethical or not, since certain acts are negative by definition. . . .
>
> In Tibetan, the term for what is considered to be of the greatest significance in determining the ethical value of a given action is the individual's *kun long.* . . . It . . . denotes the individual's overall state of heart and mind.[3]

This one passage contains elements of teleology ("an act which harms or does violence . . . is potentially an unethical act"), deontology ("certain acts are negative by definition"), and virtue ethics ("the individual's overall state of heart and mind" is the most important factor "in determining the ethical value of a given action"). Although the state of heart and mind is cited as the most important factor, the other factors are still part of the ethical picture.

As the quotation shows, Buddhist ethical thought does not fit neatly into any Western school of ethical thought. Therefore, rather than trying to fit Buddhist ethics into an alien thought system, in this chapter, I intend to characterize the Engaged Buddhist ethical system in terms of the most prominent features that I observe in it. In other words, I will take an inductive approach, examining the important features of Engaged Buddhist ethics one by one. This will allow us to understand the internal conceptual structure of Engaged Buddhist ethics, resulting in a verbal portrait of Engaged Buddhist ethics sui generis.

I do not wish to imply that all of the following features can be found in the thought of all of the Engaged Buddhists. Only some of the leaders of this movement are philosophers, and perhaps only the work of Phra Prayudh Payutto begins to approach the completeness of a systematic philosophy. Therefore, we should not expect to be able to study the speeches and writings of the Engaged Buddhists and examine the status of a particular concept or issue in each of them. Furthermore, not all of the Engaged Buddhists discuss all of the important issues. My intention, therefore, is to identify particular features of ethical thought wherever they are found among the Engaged Buddhists and to investigate their meaning and significance.

NATURAL LAW

Philosophically, natural law plays an explicit foundational role in the ethical thought of two Engaged Buddhists, Payutto, and Buddhadasa Bhikkhu. Natural law is implicit in the thought of some other Engaged Buddhists, and some of them speak in natural law language from time to time. Because only Payutto and Buddhadasa have philosophically developed accounts of natural law in their thinking, however, I will focus on their thought. I speak of natural law as "foundational" in Payutto and Buddhadasa's thought in the sense that they demonstrate Buddhist ethics to be moving from "is" to "ought"—that is, from a description of what is, the nature of reality, to a description of what we ought to do, correct behavior. In other words, their account of ethical behavior is based upon their account of the nature of reality.

The idea of natural law is "the view that there is an unchanging normative order that is a part of the natural world."[4] Put another way, contrary to the view that ethics are merely the invention of human beings, and contrary to the view that ethics derive from a supernatural source, God, natural law theory holds that ethics ultimately derive from the natural world. Thus, in this view, ethics are neither arbitrary or conventional nor culturally relative; they are part and parcel of the structure of the cosmos, hence universal and objective.

One form of the natural law view holds that the natural world contains within itself a normative moral law that is inherent in the structure of the universe. One of the simplest and most straightforward examples of this is classical Confucianism. In Confucianism, the Tao is a moral law that is as much a part of the structure of the universe as the fact that "Heaven is up and Earth is down." Thus, for example, filial piety, as part of the Tao, is a normative moral requirement, unvaryingly incumbent on all people in all times and places. That this normative moral law is as much a part of the structure of the universe as is any physical law, and indeed tied in with it, is demonstrated by the mandate of Heaven: immoral behavior on the part of the emperor results in disturbances manifest, among other ways, in disturbances in the seasonal weather pattern, earthquakes, and the like.

Payutto and Buddhadasa's thought contains a version of natural law ethical theory that differs from this. Rather than declaring that the natural world contains within itself a normative moral law, they instead see the natural world as containing within itself certain features that, with the addition of one simple observation about the nature of sentient beings, mandate for us a set of ethical behaviors. Thus, as we will see, although "good" and "bad" are not part of the structure of the universe, "skillful" and "unskillful" are certainly part of the human response to the way the universe is, and in this skillfulness and lack thereof lies morality.

Now let us lay out the structure of natural law thinking in Payutto and Buddhadasa. In both Payutto and Buddhadasa, the term translated in English as "natural law" is the Thai *kot thammachat*, with *kot* meaning "law" and *thammachat* meaning "nature," "natural," or "naturally arising." The question then becomes, what do Buddhadasa and Payutto have in mind by this "nature" and what is the pattern of its lawfulness?

Buddhadasa explicitly equates the Dhamma with nature and the laws of nature:

> In the original Pali language the word *Dhamma* was used to refer to all
> the intricate and involved things that go to make up what we call *nature*
> (*dhammajāti*). In the main, Dhamma embraces

1. Nature itself
2. The laws of nature
3. A person's duty to act in accordance with the laws of nature
4. The benefits to be derived from acting in accordance with the laws of nature.[5]

Buddhadasa may be innovative in directly equating Dhamma with nature and the laws of nature, but I see nothing in this equation that is discordant with the Pali scriptures, as long as we are clear that by "nature" he means "what is." The Dhamma is ordinarily understood as truth and reality, a true statement of what is and the reality of what is. The latter is nature. Nature, of course includes the laws, or patterns that are manifest in its workings. These are the natural laws that both Buddhadasa and Payutto have in mind.

The Dhamma of the Buddha articulates these natural laws, paying special attention to those that are most significant for the living of human life. The broadest term for the natural law by which the cosmos functions is causality or conditionality; more specifically it is *paticca-samuppāda* (conditioned origination). According to this law, all things come into being conditionally and interdependently (*paticca-samuppāda*), that is, in dependence upon other things. This is a universal, natural law. Payutto quotes the Buddha in this respect, who said, "whether an enlightened Tathāgata were to appear in this world or not, this principle would still prevail as an enduring aspect of the natural order—that is, conditionality (*idappaccayatā*)."[6] In other words, the Buddha simply describes the world as it is; he is, of course, not responsible for making things that way, nor can he change the way the world is. He simply has the wisdom to perceive the natural law and to interpret what it means for sentient beings.

Once one knows the way things are, the Dhamma, one can then begin to understand what one should do. In other words, correct behavior takes the form it does because it must fit the way the world is. The Buddha's teachings encompass both a description of the way the world is and a recommendation of how human beings should behave in light of the nature of the world.

Maha Ghosananda speaks the language of natural law as well: "The Buddha said, 'I teach only two things—suffering and the end of suffering.' What is the cause of suffering? Suffering arises from clinging. . . . As long as the mind clings, it suffers. . . . Clinging always brings suffering. This is a natural law, like the law of fire. It does not matter whether you believe that fire is hot. When you hold fire, it will burn you."[7] It is a law of nature that, just as fire burns, so clinging, or mental/emotional attachment, produces suffering. The teachings of the Buddha, and his directives for practice, are based upon his knowledge of the natural laws that produce human suffering.

Payutto brings this discussion into the ethical realm:

> If we divide the Buddhadhamma [Buddhist teachings] into two parts, *sacca-dhamma* and *cariyadhamma*, . . . defining *saccadhamma* as the part that shows the conditions or true characteristics of Dhamma, and defining *cariyadhamma* as the rules of conduct, it can be seen that *saccadhamma* in Buddhism refers to the teachings related to the conditions of all things, or nature, and the ordinary course of things, or natural law. *Cariyadhamma* refers to taking advantage of knowing and understanding the conditions and course of things, or knowing natural law and then applying it in an advantageous way. In other words, *saccadhamma* is natural law, while *cariyadhamma* is knowledge pertaining to the application of *saccadhamma*.[8]

For Payutto, Buddhism's ethical principles are fundamentally based upon natural law. "According to Buddhadhamma, the moral code constitutes a set of principles of behavior established in accordance with causes and effects that follow natural law."[9]

In what way are the Buddhist principles of ethical behavior based upon the natural law of causality or conditionality? To answer this, we must move from Payutto to Buddhadasa. "The real meaning of morality, the deep meaning as it is in nature (*dhammajāti*) is overlooked. This meaning is indicated by the Pali term for morality, *sīla*. *Sīla* means normalcy, or at equilibrium (*pakati*). If anything conduces to normalcy and not to confusion it is called *sīla*, and the Dhamma (truth, reality) that brings about that state is called *sīladhamma*."[10]

Morality, then, is normalcy and equilibrium. What does he mean by this? For Buddhadasa, human normalcy is "the normalcy of being balanced and harmonious in thought, word and deed. Pakati . . . means not colliding with anyone, even oneself, not disturbing one's state of calm; not clashing with others and disturbing their state of equanimity."[11] To be moral, then, is to be "normal," and to be normal is to behave appropriately, to fit in with the way things are, with the Dhamma, with natural law. Living in harmony with the law of nature results in both personal, internal harmony and societal harmony. In sum, Buddhadasa states, "Morality should aim at enabling individuals to bring their minds to equilibrium (pakati), and to enable societies to be pakati, to live together in peace and harmony. This is morality."[12] Thus, one who is in harmony with natural law is in balance, internally and externally; she or he is personally and socially peaceful and harmonious.

The fundamental natural law, again, is conditionality or interdependence, the law that all things come into being in dependence upon other things. All things and all beings, thus, are utterly dependent upon other things. They cannot exist by themselves. They have no existence without other things. In the case of human beings, we cannot live without both our natural world and our social world. To try to live as if one were or ever could be independent of other beings, things, and processes—human, animal, vegetable, mineral, microscopic and macroscopic realities—is out of balance and—in this sense—wrong. To live in harmony with this law is *pakati*, normalcy and balance. It also makes us happy.

The Dalai Lama thinks of human sociability in terms of natural law. "After all, we are social animals. Without human friendship, without the human smile, our life becomes miserable. The lonely feeling becomes unbearable. It is a natural law—that is to say, according to natural law we depend on others to live."[13] It is a biological fact, a natural law, that we cannot live without others. It seems to be a corollary of this law that living together well produces a condition of *pakati*, a condition of inner and outer harmony, ease, and well-being. By living in harmony with the natural law, one behaves correctly and avoids causing pain for others and for oneself. Self-centered, other-disregarding behavior violates the law of nature and clashes with the way things are, thus producing pain for others and for oneself.

Of course, there is another, very important, component of morality in Buddhism constituted by another aspect of conditionality or causality. For sentient beings, the broad natural law of conditionality includes the natural law of karma (Pali *kamma*), which functions as follows. If one violates the moral law, or, in other words, behaves in an anti-*Dhammic* fashion, it is inevitable that unpleasant consequences will follow, because that is how the universe is constructed. That is, if one behaves immorally, the law of karma sees to it that one suffers a negative consequence sometime in the future, either in this life or a subsequent one. If one behaves morally, one will enjoy appropriate pleasant consequences in the future.

That this is not just Payutto and Buddhadasa's idiosyncratic interpretation of the Buddha's teachings is demonstrated by the findings of Bruce Reichenbach in his study of karma: "[T]he law of karma is a special application of the law of universal causation, an application which uses the metaphysics of causation both to explain a moral phenomenon and to vindicate the moral order by applying universal justice to human moral actions. . . . This vindication accords with the fact that the law of karma presupposes an objective ethic. It affirms that intentions and actions can be objectively determined to be right and wrong, so that the proper or just consequences can result or be apportioned."[14]

The important point in this for us is the objectivity of the law of karma. The idea of karma does indeed presuppose that "intentions and actions can be objectively determined to be right and wrong, so that the proper or just consequences can result." A. T. Ariyaratne comments on the objectivity of karma in more homely fashion: "[T]he biggest blunder Western culture has made is that there is no standard to measure good and bad. It is lost in liberal thinking. In other words, there is nothing called sin and merit. You are not accountable because you do not know whether you will be reborn or not. In Sri Lanka, we believe in rebirth. We believe in sin and merit."[15]

Ariyaratne deplores the relativism that he perceives in "Western" culture and ethics. He believes people need objective standards of right and wrong—like the system of accountability in the karma system: a "bad" or "sinful" action causes unpleasant consequences in a subsequent birth (thereby demonstrating the unskillfulness of the act), while a "good" or meritorious action causes pleasant consequences (thereby demonstrating its skillfulness).

Payutto also sees karma as a natural process of justice: "For Buddhism, the results of following or not following the moral code are part of a natural process . . . that is, the results of actions have their own natural justice called the law of kamma. These fruits of action have their genesis in the mind and then extend out to a person's character and lifestyle—be it in this life or the next."[16]

This naturalistic understanding of karma as part of natural law makes clear what kind of thing karma is. It is, of course, neither the act of a superhuman agent nor a system of rewards and punishments in which the universe, as a stand-in for God, has a list of good and bad behaviors and wishes to mold us in the right direction by using rewards and punishments. Naturalistically, karma is simply a matter of conditionality: behavior that is out of harmony with the interdependent, cooperative and interconstructive nature of the cosmos (or, to say the same thing in another way, behavior that is motivated by one or more of the three poisons, greed, hatred, and delusion) naturally causes pain for oneself and those around one. Harmonious, cooperative behavior simply participates in the natural flourishing of life.

Note that, in this view, being out of balance, or out of step with the nature of the world, is what constitutes wrongness. This is wrongness in the is/ought sense of not being the way things are and, consequently, being improper. Thus, Buddhadasa states, "nature (dhammajāti) follows its own particular way. If we transgress its fundamental laws we are, in effect, transgressing natural morality; that is, we lack morality according to the dictates of nature."[17]

We have seen what kinds of human behavior are "in balance" and "fit in" with the nature of reality. All things come into being in dependence upon conditions outside of themselves. Nothing exists even for a moment by depending only upon itself. If one fits in with the interdependent nature of all things, one behaves skillfully and correctly. Thus, nonegocentric, cooperative, and mutually beneficial behavior is in accord with the Dhamma, or law of nature. Contrarily, self-centered, other-disregarding behavior violates the law of nature and clashes with the way things are. The properness and improperness of these behaviors are universal for all sentient beings. They are constant through the multiplicity of cultures—indeed, throughout the natural world. Buddhadasa writes, "If we are observant, we will notice what nature's secret plan has been from the very beginning: the entire natural world should exist in harmonious balance for it to survive, develop and thrive. We may call this interdependence and equilibrium the plan or direction of nature."[18] This is the meaning of "good" and "bad" and its foundation in natural law, as understood in this system of thought: "good" means skillful and correct in the light of natural law, and "bad" means unskillful and incorrect in the light of natural law.

Payutto links is and ought in a similar fashion. Incorrect behavior works as follows: ignorance and delusion as to the way things are cause selfish desire or greed. If one's desires are frustrated, ill will, frustration, and destructive tendencies arise. From these, in turn, a host of tendencies and habits develop, such as "a miserly disposition, envy, paranoia, irrationality, anxiety, fear, feelings of vengeance, laziness, and so on." The alternative approach, of course, is correct behavior: "The opposite course of action involves . . . knowing the way of all things and how to relate to them with wisdom. . . . You should know how to live in harmony with nature by acting virtuously: with mettā—love and good intentions for others; karuṇā—helpful intentions; muditā—joy in the success of others; upekkhā—equanimity and even-mindedness . . . , sāmaggī—unity and cooperation."[19] Like Buddhadasa, Payutto sees the "ought" developing out of the "is." One needs first to know the truth, the Dhamma. Once one knows "the way of all things," one is in a position "to relate to them with wisdom."

In this passage, moreover, Payutto sees in the natural law the foundation for the positive virtues, such as benevolence, generosity, and sympathetic joy. Elsewhere, Buddhadasa expresses a similar view, stating, "the conflict in the world today is a form of insanity. . . . The only real solution is to live in terms of the true nature of things . . . , that alone which possesses absolute power, sustains morality, and which can produce the cooperative social conditions of love and compassion (*mettā* and *karuṇā*)."[20] In what way does the true nature of things produce the cooperative social conditions of love and compassion? Buddhadasa gives us an example: "What is needed is an approach that emphasizes not taking more than is needed and at the same time is in accordance with the laws of nature, for then people would share whatever extra they had out of *mettā-karuṇā*—compassion and loving kindness. People would set aside for themselves only what they needed; anything in excess of that would be left for society."[21]

This, Buddhadasa demonstrates, is in accord with the law of nature; all forms of life—stomachs, birds, insects, trees—"all consume only as much as nature has given them the means to take in, a level of consumption perfectly adequate for their needs."[22] Only humans hoard, amass things, and develop greed. If we were to be "normal," like the rest of nature, we would cease this behavior and *mettā-karuṇā* would result.

Now let us consider exactly how we get from the natural law to the rules of conduct, from is to ought. There is one further step that is implicit in Theravada thought, but neither Payutto nor Buddhadasa mentions it. To get to ethics from the natural law of the Dhamma, we must begin with a simple observation about the nature of sentient beings: sentient beings attempt to avoid pain and maximize pleasure or happiness. This observation *and a reaction to it* are implicit in the Four Noble Truths and in the very conception of Buddha and the Middle Path.

The first Noble Truth, while neutrally observing that suffering, or *duḥkha* (Pali *dukkha*), is an inevitable part of life as we know it (samsara) also assumes that this is a problem. *Duḥkha*, as experienced primarily by human beings (because humans have the fortunate birth that allows us to do something about this problem), is the problem, the illness, for which the Buddha is the physician and Buddhism is the cure.

Although the observation that samsaric life is laced with *duḥkha* is a neutral statement, the assumption that this is a problem is not neutral. This is a morally engaged assumption; it engages the Buddha and Buddhists to respond to this problem and do something about it. As an assumption, this is the starting point of Buddhism as a religion: the understanding and experience that life as we know it has a structural problem. As a moral assumption, it engages a human response: Buddhism responds to this problem and invites us to do something about it. Why is it a problem that humans, and other sentient beings, suffer? Buddhism does not explain this. It simply points out that, upon observing that humans and other sentient beings suffer, the Buddha (and all Buddhas) responds with a feeling of compassion. There is no explanation as to why Buddhas have compassion, it is just a given that they do. Buddhas, the perfected human beings, respond to the human condition (and the condition of all sentient beings) with compassion, caring, and empathy. Thus, *duḥkha* is a negative thing; it is to be minimized, prevented, uprooted, eliminated. It is good to remove suffering. The other three Noble Truths build upon this assumption. Because it is good to remove suffering, we need to understand suffering as thoroughly as possible (Noble Truth 2); believe that it is possible to radically uproot suffering (Noble Truth 3); and learn how to eliminate suffering (Noble Truth 4).

Thus, there seem to be two irreducible foundations of morality: (1) natural law, the Dhamma (conditionality); and (2) an empathetic, caring, compassionate response to the suffering of sentient beings. Empathy, caring, and compassion, fully manifest in Buddhas, are implicit in the whole enterprise of Buddhism. The first foundation, the claim that conditionality and interdependence universally characterize samsara, Buddhist thought extensively strives to demonstrate (though, of course, whether it succeeds is a separate issue). The second, the perception that suffering is bad, Buddhism assumes, but few would probably want to challenge this assumption. It is actually the second foundation—the assumption that suffering is a problem and that caring is a response to that problem—that takes us from *is* to *ought*, from metaphysics to ethics.

DEVELOPMENTAL PERSPECTIVE: PROGRESSIVE ALTRUISM

Mark Johnson writes,

> [T]he idea that what is moral is somehow utterly separate from and unrelated to our quest for well-being makes morality into an inexplicable fact that has no explanatory connection to what we know about ourselves. To divorce morality from prudence makes it virtually impossible to understand why we have the moral values we do and why we regard them as so significant. It makes morality seem as though it comes out of nowhere from on high, with only the most external relations to the kinds of beings we are, the motivations we entertain, and the purposes that give direction to our lives. . . . In short, the idea that morality has nothing to do with our purposive search for well-being and happiness would make morality utterly inexplicable, at best, and a cruel joke, at worst.[23]

This insight, from the perspective of a critic of traditional Western ethical theory, points to the reason why Buddhist ethics do not neatly fit into the categories of

Western ethical theory. From a Buddhist perspective, there is a moral continuum between the ethical egoist who behaves morally because it is good for him and the altruist who does the same purely out of compassion for others. The reason lies in the developmental nature of Buddhist ethics.

The developmental aspect of Engaged Buddhist ethics is one of the keys to its structure. How this is so can be seen in the Buddhist precepts. The most popular and well-known Theravada principles of conduct are the *pañca-síla*, the Five Precepts for Buddhist Laypeople, frequently discussed by all the Theravada Engaged Buddhists, as well as by Thich Nhat Hanh. These state that one undertakes to observe the precepts (1) to abstain from the taking of life; (2) not to take that which is not given; (3) to abstain from misconduct in sensual actions; (4) to abstain from false speech; (5) to abstain from liquor that causes intoxication and indolence.[24]

These are training precepts. One undertakes these precepts as a part of one's Buddhist practice, one's effort to gradually transform oneself into a person capable of attaining freedom from samsara and realizing nirvana. One may approach this practice, however, with many different motivations. It is possible, and not at all unusual, to look at the precepts from an enlightened self-interest perspective (the ethical egoist). From this perspective, to observe the precepts is to act for one's own welfare. If I were to kill or harm another, I would earn a painful karmic consequence in this, or a future, lifetime. To protect myself from negative consequences in the present life and in future lives, I need to observe the precepts. In this light, these precepts seem to be concerned with responsibility *to* and *for* oneself. Because of the interdependent nature of the world, however, this responsibility to and for oneself can only be exercised through a practice of responsibility to others. That is, I can look after my own welfare by observing the first precept and not harming you. If I fail to observe the first precept and harm you, I harm myself. Not harming you physically is only the beginning; I need to progress to not harming you emotionally, to not harming you verbally, to not having any impulse to harm you. The same applies to the other precepts. It is good for me, as a karmic being and as a being on a path of self-transformation, to become less and less self-concerned and more and more other-concerned. It is because of my own enlightened self-interest, my responsibility *to myself* that I should strive every day to become a person more and more mindful of and responsible *to others*. Ultimately, this can only be achieved by learning, progressively, to forget about myself. That is, my responsibility to myself is fulfilled in forgetting about myself and concerning myself with the welfare of others. Thus, in the end, responsibility to oneself and responsibility to others, my good and the good of others come to coincide. The former is fulfilled in the latter; that is, the two become, in a practical sense, coinherent. It is still good for others that the ethical egoist pursues moral behavior, even if his motivation is self-centered, and it is still good for the altruist's own spiritual development and progress toward enlightenment that he acts out of concern for others—the self-concern may be forgotten, but it is still true that he helps himself by helping others.

Let us look further at these precepts. They are usually stated in the negative: do not kill, do not steal, and so forth. This negative formulation mandating self-restraint from unskillful behavior is regarded in the tradition as the ethical minimum enjoined upon Buddhists. But this is no more than the starting place of Buddhist ethics. Because Buddhism is fundamentally about self-transformation (in the context of the understanding that there is no self or soul, no unchanging essence that one "is"), Buddhist ethics are fundamentally developmental in another sense: the ethical possibilities grow with the moral-spiritual development of the person. That is, although the Five Precepts may appear to be rules, they are rules only for the least developed, for those who need to think in terms of rules in order to avoid harmful behaviors. For those who understand nothing but self-interest, the precepts may be taught as rules of self-restraint that one follows for one's own sake.

The precepts, however, are not merely negative, and in their constructive dimension we can see that they are also not rules. Each precept has an open-ended, positive correlate. One who follows—or, better, lives in harmony with—the first precept not only avoids taking life, not only avoids harming life, but also positively develops *mettā*, loving kindness.[25] Loving kindness, of course, comes in many kinds and degrees, the lowest of which is avoiding killing, the highest of which is exemplified in the life of the Buddha, who is understood to have manifested compassion in all of his actions following his enlightenment. The core virtue of *mettā* is described thus in the *Mettā Sutta:* "May all beings be happy and secure, may their hearts be wholesome. . . . / Just as a mother would protect her only child at the risk of her own life, even so, let him cultivate a boundless heart towards all beings. / Let his thoughts of boundless love pervade the whole world: above, below and across without any obstruction, without any hatred, without any enmity."[26] Living in harmony with the first precept comes in degrees. It is a long way from the minimal avoidance of killing entailed in observing the first precept to the *Mettā Sutta*! The idealism of the latter demonstrates the open-endedness of this virtue. How well, how fully, how tirelessly, how consistently, in which capacities and dimensions is one able to manifest loving kindness? The answer depends upon how far one has come in one's multi-lifetime project of self-transformation. Thus, moral responsibility in Buddhism is very much a matter of response-*ability*. According to

Nhat Hanh, "To practice ahimsa, first of all we have to practice it within ourselves. . . . Depending on our state of being, our response to things will be more or less nonviolent. Even if we take pride in being vegetarian, for example, we have to acknowledge that the water in which we boil our vegetables contains many tiny microorganisms. We cannot be completely nonviolent, but by being vegetarian, we are going in the direction of non-violence."[27] This quotation expresses very clearly the open-ended quality of the positive counterparts of the precepts and the Buddhist virtues generally: we will never reach the ideal or perfect level of development, but we orient ourselves by reaching toward it and we never stop trying to get closer.

Buddhadasa also affirms that goodness and badness are not fixed, but progressive. "If a certain person, when making contact with the world, increasingly develops along the lines of mindfulness and wisdom, we call that 'goodness' or 'virtue' (puñña). If another person, when making contact with the world, increasingly develops along the lines of stupidity and delusion, we call that 'evil' (pāpa)."[28] Correct and skillful living includes living a life of loving kindness to the limits of one's ability. This is not a matter of following a rule or obeying a commandment, a duty or an obligation, but of living as fully as one is able one's potential as a human being on the way to Buddhahood. Phra Payutto writes that "the 'negative' aspects of the moral code are a way of expressing the most general aspects of the practice—they keep an eye on evil until all seeds of evil intention are rooted out. But as for the positive aspects of the moral code, they continue on without end."[29]

What has been said with respect to the first precept is true as well of the other precepts. The second precept negatively declares one's intention to avoid stealing; this is a moral minimum, taken as a rule only by the least morally developed. Positively, however, the second precept is embodied in giving and generosity of all kinds, including giving of oneself, a very open-ended virtue when one considers the endless needs to which one might give oneself. The third precept, avoiding sexual misconduct, is expressed positively in sexual restraint and more broadly in contentment and self-mastery; the fourth, to avoid lying, is expressed of course in truthfulness; and the fifth, avoiding intoxicants, is positively expressed in mindfulness.[30] Loving kindness, giving, self-mastery, truthfulness, and mindfulness are all important, open-ended Buddhist virtues, understood to be modeled to perfection in the Buddha.

Maha Ghosananda writes, "The Buddha said, 'You must work out your own salvation with diligence.' What does this mean? Each of us is responsible for our own salvation. . . . [But] personal salvation does not mean salvation exclusive of the rest of humanity. If we follow the eightfold path, the path toward an end to suffering, our growing union with the universal spirit unfolds naturally, and our love comes to embrace all living beings. Personal salvation is but a microcosm of human salvation."[31]

Here we see very clearly the progressive altruism of this developmental ethic. For this Theravada Engaged Buddhist, as we work out our personal salvation, our loving kindness and hence our devotion to others grows and unfolds naturally until it embraces all living beings. The developmental perspective is also something a good teacher bears in mind. The Dalai Lama says, "If you want to be selfish, you should be selfish-with-wisdom, rather than with foolishness. If you help others with sincere motivation and sincere concern, that will bring you more fortune, more friends, more smiles, and more success. If you forget about other's rights and neglect others' welfare, ultimately you will be very lonely."[32]

Buddhist ethics being fundamentally developmental does not in any way imply that "the Good" is one thing for one person and another for another person. On the contrary, it is always good to be as selfless and loving as one is able. This is constant. A given person, however, is truly capable of only so much at any particular point in his or her development. In this quotation, the Dalai Lama shows he has no reluctance to address people where they are developmentally. If they have developed to the point of having sufficient detachment and objectivity to see that it is best to put the needs of the greater number ahead of one's own individual interests, then he will meet them there. If all they can appreciate is their own self-interest, he will meet them there.

Payutto agrees: "If craving receives the proper inducement, it can be a tool for getting rid of ignorance and craving in the future. . . . If you are unable to do anything else, choose craving that aims at the good, which, in turn, will have an effect on your actions. But if possible, refrain from both good and bad craving and choose the way of wisdom, which is pure, liberating, and does away with dukkha."[33] We are all someplace on the developmental continuum. What counts in Engaged Buddhist ethics is to do one's best and to strive consistently to become more and more capable of doing better and better.

PRINCIPLES, PROTOTYPES, AND VIRTUE

We have seen that the precepts should not be conceived as rules, except for the morally undeveloped, who need rules to get started on a path of moral development. How, then, should we conceive them? I believe that the Buddhist precepts, *with* their positive analogues, are best understood as *principles* embodying core virtues. Shakyamuni Buddha's behavior during his lifetime presents the prototype examples of these principles. Let me elaborate this concept.

My understanding of moral principles, as distinct from rules, has been shaped by Mark Johnson, who writes as follows, citing John Dewey.

> It is critical to distinguish *rules* . . .—which are supposed to tell you how to act—from general *principles*—which are summaries of our collective moral insight. The crucial distinction I have in mind was made by Dewey, who understood rules as ready-made, fixed precepts that become divorced from their origins in concrete situations and are then "applied" to new situations according to an objectivist model of cases being "brought under" laws.
>
> Principles, on the other hand, are crystallizations of the insights that emerge out of a people's ongoing experience. As such, they provide ideals that establish standpoints from which to view and evaluate our experience and our proposed actions. For Dewey . . . "the object of moral principles is to supply standpoints and methods which will enable the individual to make for himself an analysis of the elements of good and evil in the particular situation in which he finds himself."
>
> . . . Dewey continues, "A moral principle, such as that of chastity, of justice, of the Golden Rule, gives the agent a basis for looking at and examining a particular question that comes up. It holds before him certain possible aspects of the act; it warns him against taking a short or partial view of the act. It economizes his thinking by supplying him with the main heads by reference to which to consider the bearings of his desires and purposes; it guides him in his thinking by suggesting to him the important considerations for which he should be on the lookout."[34]

A moral principle, then, is not a rule, inasmuch as it does not attempt to tell one what to do in all situations. It nonetheless gives guidance and maintains a measure of objectivity by embodying an ideal. In Buddhism, this ideal carries the primary authority of the Buddha and the secondary authority of the Buddhist tradition. Although the Buddhist moral ideal is very generally, and in that sense vaguely, embodied in the moral precepts and their positive counterparts, the vagueness of the principles is not a shortcoming but rather is what permits the open-endedness of the Buddhist precepts, which grow in their challenge with the growth in each individual's development in response-ability. Thus, a rule is completely constraining—action must in all cases be "brought under" the rule. A principle, on the other hand, is partially constraining—behaviors utterly in violation of the principle will be out of the question—but also very open-ended. The open-endedness of a principle invites a creative response to the interface—unique in each case—between the particularity of the situation in which one finds oneself and the particularity of one's developmental response-ability. As Payutto writes, "Good deeds can be far reaching, endless, and changeable, depending on particular circumstances and contexts."[35]

It is important to bear in mind that the precepts retain their insistence upon a minimum level beneath which one should never fall. That is, they clearly indicate that it is wrong to intentionally kill, steal, commit adultery, lie, or intoxicate oneself. That being so, it is clear that the higher-level expression of the precepts as open-ended moral principles is by no means an open door to complete subjectivity or relativity. There are clear standards with minimum thresholds that one should not cross, and at the same time there are ideals that it may be impossible to perfect. Many Engaged Buddhists have remarked that nonviolence is such an ideal, always calling us to a higher and higher standard. There is, thus, a rule at the lowest level: do not kill! But at the higher level of ever-subtler nonviolence it is impossible that there could ever be a rule. Instead, there is a virtue, nonviolence, embodied in the prototype of the Buddha.

The Dalai Lama clearly distinguishes between rules and principles. He rejects moral rules, declaring that "no one should suppose it could ever be possible to devise a set of rules or laws to provide us with the answer to every ethical dilemma, even if we were to accept religion as the basis of morality. Such a formulaic approach could never hope to capture the richness and diversity of human experience." This, however, does not mean that we must accede to moral relativism. Indeed, he says, it is "essential . . . to construe principles which can be understood as morally binding." In particular, "we must be able to show that violence toward others is wrong." Our goal should be to find a way of doing this that "avoids the extremes of crude absolutism on the one hand, and of trivial relativism on the other." How does he manage this? "My own view . . . is that establishing binding ethical principles is possible when we take as our starting point the observation that we all desire happiness and wish to avoid suffering. We have no means of discriminating between right and wrong if we do not take into account others' feelings, others' suffering."[36] For the Dalai Lama, then, although the idea of adequate ethical rules is an illusion, objective ethical principles are a necessity. The search for an objective starting point for such principles does not detain him long, and here we are on familiar ground: the Dalai Lama, like Payutto and Buddhadasa, grounds his ethical principles in the first Noble Truth of Shakyamuni Buddha, in which suffering is defined as a problem. On this basis, he concludes that nonviolence is a correct ethical principle.

His Holiness comments that the morally best thing is to develop oneself spiritually such that one is a loving and compassionate person capable of putting one's personal wishes aside and responding spontaneously for the good of all. If one has done this, our spontaneous actions will tend to be correct. Most people, however, have not reached such an ideal state, and therefore our spontaneous actions may be unreliable or destructive, especially in cases when we do not have time to think things over and our bad habits take control. In these situations, that is, for most of us, he says, "it is very useful to have a set of basic ethical precepts to guide us in our daily lives. These can help us to form good habits." He adds that we should think of such precepts "less in terms of moral legislation than as reminders always to keep others' interests at heart and in the forefront of our minds."[37] Ethical precepts, then, are training devices. When we have trained to the point of spontaneous moral behavior, we will no longer need them, but at that point our behavior will embody them.

The Dalai Lama, in his work for a broad, non-Buddhist audience, claims an area of consensus on the content of ethical precepts. He states that all the world's major religions, as well as the humanist philosophical tradition, agree in ethics, despite their disagreement in metaphysics. "The consensus among them," he states, is "compelling. All agree on the negativity of killing, stealing, telling lies, and sexual misconduct."[38] One glance will tell the reader that this consensus area of agreement on ethical precepts is the same as four of the Five Lay Precepts of Buddhism (avoiding intoxicants is missing). There is no need to respond to such a disclosure with cynicism, however, if one briefly reflects upon the unlikelihood of any society surviving that did not attempt to minimize such behavior.

The Dalai Lama explicitly points out that such precepts are not "legislation," but reminders. He is quite right to point this out, because in Buddhism there is, after all, no one (no God) to legislate such a rule. One chooses whether to practice the precepts on the basis of one's understanding of their value. The "reminder" that the precepts give is based upon natural law. The precepts remind us that, because the world is as it is (interdependent and with the law of karma operating), so certain consequences will inevitably follow from certain behaviors. Out of his compassion, the Buddha has advised us to behave wisely, or skillfully, with respect to these facts of life. The precepts remind us of the natural law, *saccadhamma* and *cariyadhamma*.

This idea of ethical precepts as reminders suggests Johnson's idea of the role of prototypes in the moral life. As mentioned above, the Buddhist moral ideal is only generally, and in that sense vaguely, embodied in the moral precepts and their positive counterparts, but it is fleshed out in the prototypical examples of the Buddha's actions during his lifetime. Building upon the discoveries of cognitive science, Johnson explains how prototypes function in the ethical domain. "Psychologists, linguists, and anthropologists have discovered that most categories used by people are not actually definable by a list of features. Instead, people tend to define categories (e.g., bird) by identifying certain prototypical members of the category (e.g., robin), and they recognize other nonprototypical members (e.g., chicken, ostrich, penguin) that differ in various ways from the prototypical ones. There is seldom any set of necessary and sufficient features possessed by all members of the category."[39] Johnson adds that, "moral precepts turn out to be formulated only with reference to prototypical ('clear') cases. Those precepts seem to work unproblematically only for prototypical cases."[40] Compassion, for example, is a basic Buddhist moral value or principle. As such, it is not a moral "rule." It does not tell us exactly what to do and what not to do in all situations. The prototype of Buddhist compassion is, perhaps, based on the image of the Buddha as the Great Physician, the one who relieves the suffering of humankind and also heals a sick monk. Thus, a Buddhist knows very well the morally right thing to do when confronted by a sick person. A Buddhist understands well enough to strive to relieve the suffering of a person in pain, giving physical and psychological care, motivated by compassion. This provides sincere Buddhists with an image and with an ideal, but it is a rather fuzzy ideal. Many situations are close enough to prototypical that one knows what to do: feed a hungry man, listen to a troubled friend, comfort a crying child. But there is, again, no rule that tells one exactly what to do when confronted by a dilemma that is less prototypical, for example, a student begging a teacher for a passing grade, despite having earned failure, or by situations involving choices between two mutually exclusive options, both of which seem compassionate, for example, participating in an antiwar march or visiting with an elderly person who cannot march. Such cases require moral judgment, a judgment made with as much compassion and practical wisdom as one has developed, and with the prototype as a guide, but with no rule to follow.

Even though he believes that it is important to accept ethical precepts, the Dalai Lama is clear that this does not mean that Buddhist ethics amount to an ethic of following rules. For example, although there is a precept against harming, "ethically sound conduct depends on us applying the principle of non-harming." Moreover, "there are bound to be situations when any course of action would appear to involve breaking a precept. Under such circumstances, we must use our intelligence to judge which course of action will be least harmful in the long run."

Here he gives the example of telling a lie in order to save a life. He concludes that "the moral value of a given act is to be judged in relation both to time, place, and circumstance and to the interests of the totality of all others in the future as well as now."[41] One uses moral judgment to adapt one's action to the demands of one's particular situation, but the moral principles behind one's actions remain constant.

Payutto goes even further, with scathing words for rule following, even identifying Buddhism itself with the elimination of rule following: "[S]trict adherence to mere rule and ritual . . . was present in ancient India and is still an aspect of life there today. The elimination of these kinds of beliefs and practices was clearly the aim of Lord Buddha and continued to be a major aspect of Buddhist practices and teachings. . . . Adherence to mere rule and ritual increased with the decline of Buddhism in India, but such adherence . . . also contributed to this decline. . . . [I]t can be said that wherever this adherence prospers, Buddhism degenerates."[42] In sum, along with natural law and the developmental perspective, another helpful concept for understanding Engaged Buddhist morality is the concept of moral principles. In Buddhism, these moral principles have both a negative and a positive pole. The precepts are the negative pole. They serve as reminders, establishing a moral floor below which one should not fall. They may serve as rules for the least morally developed: "for your own sake, don't do these things." In the context of the developmental nature of ethics, though, the precepts flow seamlessly into their positive counterparts. They are thus inherently open-ended. The positive counterparts, indeed, represent virtues that are infinitely perfectible. The moral principles to which Engaged Buddhism adheres are embodied in the positive counterparts of the precepts and in the Buddhist virtues in general.

This brings us to virtue ethics, another useful category for understanding Buddhist ethics. Whitehill, in his classic paper on virtue ethics and Buddhism, gave a brief and clear account of the meaning of virtue ethics. He defines "ethics of virtue" as "an ethics that is character-based . . . , praxis-oriented, teleological, and community-specific." He goes on, "The goal of ethics is to become a person who does good or virtuous things freely from the ground of a well-tempered character, supported by a matured, resolute, and reasonable knowledge of what one is doing. The path of Buddhism does not dissolve character (which is different from ego and personality). It awakens and illuminates moral character and establishes a 'noble' selfhood in the wide, deep, expressive freedom of creative forms of life and its perfections."[43]

This characterization of virtue ethics exactly fits the account of Engaged Buddhist ethics that I have given in this section. Probably the most important consideration in this light is the developmental nature of Engaged Buddhist ethics.

For Engaged Buddhists, ethics are an intrinsic part of one's spiritual development. Actually, spirituality and ethics are two aspects of the same thing, or even two ways of talking about the same thing. By practicing Buddhism, one is endeavoring to become more and more selfless, more and more capable of higher and higher levels of nonviolence, loving kindness, and altruism. The Buddhist path is all about transforming and developing one's character in a specific way defined by the Buddhist community. Moreover, the Buddha as prototype embodies that perfection of character. Thus, to work from Whitehill's definition, Engaged Buddhist ethics are character-based (one wants a character like that of the prototype, the Buddha, that is, maximally wise and compassionate); praxis-oriented (this applies on two levels: one both engages in practice in order to develop one's character, and, as one develops one's character, one is expected to express that character in praxis, that is, in concrete, practical acts on behalf of others); teleological (one is reaching toward ever-greater levels of perfection); and community-specific (all of this is based upon the Buddhist picture of the path).

Buddhadasa summarizes the virtue ethics perspective of Engaged Buddhism in the quotation we have already seen: "If a certain person, when making contact with the world, increasingly develops along the lines of mindfulness and wisdom, we call that 'goodness' or 'virtue.'" Virtue is the continual and progressive development of one's character in the direction of ever-greater mindfulness and wisdom (one could add other important Buddhist virtues).

The Dalai Lama also expresses a virtue ethics perspective when he writes, "In Tibetan, the term for what is considered to be of the greatest significance in determining the ethical value of a given action is the individual's *kun long*. . . . It . . . denotes the individual's overall state of heart and mind. When this is wholesome, it follows that our actions themselves will be (ethically) wholesome. . . . The aim of spiritual and, therefore, ethical practice is . . . to transform and perfect the individual's *kun long*."[44]

For the Dalai Lama, the overall state of heart and mind is most important not, as in more classical theories, because it determines the karmic value of an action, but because it is "that which drives or inspires our actions—both those we intend directly and those which are in a sense involuntary" and thus determines the nature of the action itself.[45] What is important is to develop one's character such that all our actions, including the spontaneous, are ethically wholesome.

Spontaneous actions get special attention because, as His Holiness points out, "the more spontaneous our actions, the more they will tend to reflect our habits and dispositions in that moment. If these are unwholesome, our acts are bound to be destructive."[46] Conversely, a wholesome inner state produces a wholesome act. In other words, our character is composed of our habits and dispositions. A wholesome character, with wholesome habits and dispositions, will naturally manifest in wholesome actions—loving and compassionate actions—while the reverse also is true. It is these habits and dispositions upon which Engaged Buddhism, like many other forms of Buddhism, works.

Moreover, just as the Dalai Lama sees an area of consensus among the religions and humanist philosophies on the content of moral precepts, as we saw earlier, so he also sees an area of consensus on motivational factors, stating, "all agree on the negativity of killing, stealing, telling lies, and sexual misconduct. In addition, from the point of view of motivational factors, all agree on the need to avoid hatred, pride, malicious intent, covetousness, envy, greed, lust, harmful ideologies (such as racism), and so on."[47]

The preceding is a list of unwholesome motivational factors. There are many lists of wholesome motivational factors, or character states, or virtues. Here is a representative comment from the Dalai Lama: "It is . . . important to realize that transforming the mind and heart so that our actions become spontaneously ethical requires that we put the pursuit of virtue at the heart of our daily lives. This is because love and compassion, patience, generosity, humility, and so on are all complementary."[48] This quotation exemplifies three of the themes of this section. First, virtue is found in the pursuit of virtue; it is not an unchanging state of being. Second, persons of virtue are pursuing virtuous character traits in a developmental, teleological fashion so that the spontaneous actions that inevitably manifest character will become more and more ethical. Third, the virtues are complementary because they represent different but interdependent aspects of the character or *kun long*, the overall state of heart and mind. A loving person will be generous; a patient person will be humble, and so forth.

The particular lists of virtues one sees among the Engaged Buddhists vary, but they always place a heavy emphasis upon the virtues of beneficence, especially compassion, loving kindness, and generosity or giving. The other most frequently found components of such lists are the virtues of wisdom or understanding. A comment from Ariyaratne, including another list of virtues, is illustrative: "Sarvodaya is not a movement of Buddhists exclusively. It is a movement for all religious groups and also for those who have no particular religion. We in Sarvodaya believe that religions should assist human beings and human groups to overcome internal defilements such as greed, ill will, and egotism, and promote internal spirituality so that beneficence, sharing, morality, and enlightenment will evolve within them. The ultimate objective of Buddhists and other religious individuals should be building a critical mass of spiritual consciousness on this planet—which is the

surest way to live in a culture of peace."⁴⁹ Like the Dalai Lama, Ariyaratne is confident that the Buddhist list of virtues and vices—or wholesome and unwholesome
states of heart and mind—applies universally. As with the Dalai Lama, and the
other Engaged Buddhists, overcoming vices must be supplemented by practices
that intentionally cultivate virtues. Ariyaratne's list of virtues here includes both
the virtue of beneficence and the wisdom virtue of enlightenment. Again, it is
understood that these are qualities that one develops.

Ariyaratne also makes the important claim here that, if enough people were
to develop such moral/spiritual character traits, a culture of peace would develop.
Ariyaratne is not alone in this view; there is a widespread, though not universal,
belief among the Engaged Buddhists that the way to eliminate our worst social
problems—such as war—is for a large number of individuals to develop their moral
character properly. In other words, the Engaged Buddhists believe that it is essential for individuals to develop their character, their overall state of heart and mind,
by practicing spiritual discipline. They believe that this is not only for the good
of the individual and his or her progress in spiritual development, but also for the
good of society. After all, the reasoning goes, society is made up of individuals;
therefore, if enough individuals become noticeably more benevolent, the overall
society must become more benevolent as well. Nhat Hanh writes, "Meditation is
to see deeply into things, to see how we can change, how we can transform our
situation. To transform our situation is also to transform our minds. To transform
our minds is also to transform our situation, because the situation is mind, and
mind is situation. Awakening is important. The nature of the bombs, the nature
of injustice, the nature of the weapons, and the nature of our own beings are the
same. This is the real meaning of engaged Buddhism."⁵⁰

"The situation is mind, and mind is situation." Change the mind, and you
change the situation; change many minds, and you noticeably change the social
situation. If there is a bomb in the mind of many people in a society, that society
will have a bomb (and vice versa). Therefore, if you want to change a society's character, to make it less violent for instance, you must change the character of many
individuals within that society. For Engaged Buddhists, that requires a sustained
effort at Buddhist practice.

HOLISM

Holism in Engaged Buddhist ethics is simply a manifestation of interdependence:
because the various aspects of human life and spiritual development are interdependent, moral thought will inevitably take this into account. Buddhist thought

has always embraced psychophysical unity in the human being. The Eightfold Path has always included moral discipline, mental discipline, and the cultivation of wisdom. Wisdom and compassion have always been the two wings of Mahayana Buddhism. Engaged Buddhism simply builds on these roots.

Reason, emotion, meditation, mindfulness, ethics, and action are interrelated in Engaged Buddhist thought in virtually every possible way. To clarify some of these interrelationships, we will begin by looking at the domain of the intellect in relation to ethics—which is quite complex in itself—and later add emotion into the mix.

The Domain of the Intellect: Understanding, Reason, Mindfulness, Wisdom, and Ethics

Unlike the dominant Western ethics, in Engaged Buddhist ethics the intellectual realm is divorced from neither emotion nor action; nor is it uniquely privileged, though it is quite important. Payutto explains intellectual development as a central element in a person's overall development toward enlightenment. His discussion of "proper understanding" (the first component in the Eightfold Path) illustrates this intellectual development. "Proper understanding" refers to knowledge of the basic teachings of the Buddha: the Four Noble Truths, dependent origination, and so forth. For Payutto, understanding is a part of every stage of the Buddhist path. Understanding begins with saddhā, or confidence in a teaching that comes at first from another. It progresses through reason proper, in which one intellectually tests and ultimately assents to the teachings that one has heard. Next, one focuses one's formal practice upon what one intellectually understands and tests it in one's lived experience. When this kind of understanding has been thoroughly accomplished—that is, when understanding has become experiential—one has reached "proper knowledge or insight (sammāñāṇa)" and liberation.[51]

Thus, understanding is both the beginning and the end of the path. It is a core component of the path, interdependent with other factors and highly developmental, transforming not only in degree, but also in kind from the faith or confidence that dimly grasps and hopes, to mature, experiential, liberating insight. That is, it is because of its developmental nature that understanding is able holistically to embrace everything from faith, through reason, to experiential knowledge and liberation—things that in Western philosophy and ethics are held to be quite distinct, antagonistic to each other, and even mutually exclusive.

Payutto quotes the Buddha on the two most important factors in developing proper understanding:

1. For bhikkhus, those in the process of learning . . . I see no other external factor more beneficial than having a spiritual friend (kalyāṇamitta).
2. For bhikkhus, those in the process of learning . . . I see no other internal factor more beneficial than critical reflection (yonisomanasikāra).[52]

Having a spiritual friend refers to having a qualified and caring spiritual teacher. With respect to reason, our interest is with yonisomanasikāra, or critical reflection, which Payutto defines as "engaging the mind, considering matters thoroughly in an orderly and logical manner through the application of critical or systematic reflection" and further interprets as "a principle based on wisdom that contemplates how teachings should be correctly applied."[53] The point for our purposes is that this kind of purely intellectual understanding is a necessary but not sufficient element in personal development, both for ethical and for spiritual purposes—purposes that are certainly inseparable for the Engaged Buddhists.

Because reason is necessary but not sufficient for intellectual development, it is supplemented by other factors. One important such factor is mindfulness, sati. Payutto defines sati negatively as "non-forgetting," "non-carelessness," "non-distraction," and "non-fuzziness," and positively as "carefulness, circumspection, and clarity . . . and the condition of being constantly prepared to deal with situations and respond appropriately." Payutto goes on, "Buddhadhamma emphasizes the importance of sati at every level of ethical conduct. Mindfully conducting your life and your practice of the Dhamma is called appamāda, or conscientiousness [and it] is of central importance to progress in the Buddhist system of ethics."[54] Thus, mindfulness is a quality of mind—clarity, attentiveness—that one brings to the performance of one's everyday life tasks as well as formal Buddhist practice. While it is not rational as such, it is involved in rationality, the use of reason.

Payutto goes on to say, "yonisomanasikāra is a member of the paññā [wisdom] section of the Path; it is a tool to be used. Appamāda, on the other hand, is a member of the samādhi [concentration] section; it governs the use of the tool of yonisomanasikāra and serves as a motivating force to further progress."[55] It is well known that the factors of the Eightfold Path fall into three categories: ethics, mental discipline, and wisdom. Here we see that the factors can assist each other across these divisions. In the above quotation, we see mindfulness, a factor associated with the meditation group, assisting critical reason, a factor in the wisdom group. In this sense, mindfulness has an instrumental value for reason.

Similarly, ethics have an instrumental value. For example, Payutto writes, "Buddhism teaches that proper ethics have value because they nurture and improve the quality of the mind; ethics make the mind clean, clear, and pure; . . .

they allow the mind and life itself to flourish and blossom; and finally they lead to liberation and freedom of the mind, which allows a person to go forth and act with wisdom in skillful and wholesome . . . ways."[56] This statement reflects the traditional idea that the three categories of development in the Eightfold Path are progressive, that is, that ethical development comes first and prepares the person for mental disciplines which in turn lead to the development of wisdom. Here we see that ethics—or, more accurately, progress in ethical development—actually contributes to the transformation of the nature of the mind, making it clean, clear, and pure. In this way, ethical development contributes to liberation itself, which, interestingly, is not portrayed as the end of the story, but "allows a person to go forth and act with wisdom in skillful and wholesome ways." Here, then, we come full circle: ethical behavior ultimately leads to the transformation of liberation, which, in turn, allows a person to act skillfully, wholesomely and with wisdom, that is, in a consummately *ethical* manner. Once again we see how developmental the Buddhist path is: one begins with ethics and ends with ethics, yet from the beginning point to the end point, the *ability* to behave ethically has developed so much that it goes by another name: wisdom.

In the end, in this holistic system, wisdom and ethics are inseparable. Payutto puts this very plainly: "If the principles or teachings related to a quest for truth and wisdom do not reveal ethics and a method of practice that can be applied in daily life, then such principles cannot be considered Buddhism—this is especially true for that which is held to be the original body of teachings of Lord Buddha."[57] Hence, for a thinker like Payutto, an Engaged Buddhism—a Buddhism that takes the practice of the ethical dimension of Buddhism seriously—is a necessity.

The implications of these ideas are familiar to an activist such as Sulak Sivaraksa, who sounds much like Payutto as he writes, "Calm and the development of yonisomanasikara in turn lead to the development of *panna*, genuine understanding. *Panna*, which comes from both the head and the heart, is very different from purely intellectual knowledge. It helps one to become aware, humble, and to know one's limits, even as it promotes *metta* and compassion in sharing the sufferings of others and attempting to eliminate the causes of suffering."[58] For Sulak, all of these factors of enlightenment are interrelated and mutually supportive, and, inasmuch as they reflect one's progressive transformation, they all manifest themselves in one's way of being-in-the-world. Inasmuch as understanding, *mettā*, and compassion are progressively developed, action in the world to reduce the suffering of others becomes inevitable.

ADDING EMOTION TO THE MIX: REASON-EMOTION-ETHICS-ACTION

Of particular interest for Western ethicists may be the fact that Engaged Buddhist ethics do not separate the domains of the intellect and the emotion. Because they do not separate these domains, Engaged Buddhist ethics also do not privilege the intellect over emotions in the ethical domain. On the contrary, it is central to Engaged Buddhist ethics that we develop emotionally as much as intellectually.

Upon reading these words, the reader may wonder what has happened to the detachment that many have taken to be a hallmark of traditional Buddhism. Detachment, of course, is subject to many interpretations, but it is often understood to indicate coolness and uninvolvement to the point of not being concerned, especially in popular understandings of Theravada. Engaged Buddhists see this as a misunderstanding.

Regarding the misunderstanding of detachment as coolness, uninvolvement, and not being concerned, Buddhadasa has helpful insights. Let us look again at a passage seen already in chapter 2.

> Having not fully appreciated or examined the Buddha's teaching regarding *dukkha*, many people have misunderstood it. They have taken it to mean that birth, old age, sickness, death, and so on are themselves *dukkha*. In fact, those are just its characteristic vehicles. The Buddha summarized his explanation of *dukkha* by saying, . . . anything that clings or is clung to as "I" or "mine" is *dukkha*. . . . Therefore birth, old age, sickness, death, and so on, if they are not clung to as "I" or "mine," cannot be *dukkha*. . . . The body and mind are the same. Don't think that *dukkha* is inherent in the body and mind.[59]

Rather than speaking of detachment, Buddhadasa emphasizes not clinging, a subtle but important distinction. This change makes it clear that the problem is not life itself, but our mental attitude. Thinking that the problem is inherent in life, in the world is a misunderstanding. Therefore there is no need to detach oneself from the world itself; the need is simply to transform our minds such that "I" and "mine" cannot be found in them.

Engaged Buddhists, in fact, do not emphasize detachment. Sulak speaks directly to the issue of detachment and what Engaged Buddhists prefer in its stead.

> Once one understands the Dhamma, one can change one's inner condition with a detached view of the world, feeling less greed, hatred, and delusion.

One is fairly content. Yet the external world remains unjust and dangerous. . . . The majority of people are deprived of basic human rights. Starvation, malnutrition, unemployment, prostitution, robbery and drug addiction are still prevalent. According to the Buddha, to ignore such a situation is to fall into a state of heedlessness, to be trapped by a false happiness. . . .

In other words, we should adjust our inner condition, which should be calm and mindful, to be aware of the unjust external world. It is wrong to try to adjust the external world without training one's mind to be neutral and selfless. It is also wrong to be calm and detached without a proper concern to bring about better social conditions for all who share our planet. . . . In life it is our duty to restructure our consciousness to deal with human society selflessly and harmoniously with loving kindness, compassion, wisdom, and sympathetic joy.[60]

If one must speak of detachment, for Sulak, one should see it as detachment from the *objects* of greed, hatred, and delusion. It is from these that we should turn away. When we do so we will find ourselves in a state of calm, but not an uncaring calm and not a calm supported by turning away from the problems of the world. We are interdependent with the world; we cannot turn away from it. To turn away from the world is heedlessness, and we should be mindful of our surroundings. The state that Sulak, and most of the other Engaged Buddhists, seeks is a state of calm suffused with the virtuous caring emotions of loving kindness, compassion, and sympathetic joy.

Let us turn now to the Engaged Buddhists' holistic view of reason and emotion. We have seen that, for the Dalai Lama, the very foundation of ethics is "the individual's overall state of heart and mind [*kun long*]." "Heart and mind" are cited together in this way, because in Tibetan "the word for 'mind,' *lo*, includes the ideas of consciousness, or awareness, alongside those of feeling and emotion. This reflects an understanding that emotions and thoughts cannot ultimately be separated." The impossibility of separating emotions and thoughts is demonstrated, he points out, by the turmoil both heart and mind are in when they are gripped by powerful negative emotions such as hatred and anger.[61] Thus, "heart and mind," reason and emotion, are a single thing for the Dalai Lama and together serve as the root of ethical concern. When the heart/mind is in the power of negative thoughts and afflictive emotions, our actions will be unethical and we will harm others. Conversely, when the heart/mind is in the power of positive thoughts and emotions such as understanding and compassion, our actions will be ethical and tend to help others.

For the Dalai Lama, the interplay of feeling and reason clearly pertains to the ethically crucial state of heart and mind, compassion.

> Although it is clear . . . that nying je, or love and compassion, is understood as an emotion, it belongs to that category of emotions which have a more developed cognitive component. Some emotions, such as the revulsion we tend to feel at the sight of blood, are basically instinctual. Others, such as fear of poverty, have this more developed cognitive component. We can thus understand nying je in terms of a combination of empathy and reason. . . .
>
> To me, this suggests that by means of sustained reflection on, and familiarization with, compassion, through rehearsal and practice we can develop our innate ability to connect with others, a fact which is of supreme importance given the approach to ethics I have described. The more we develop compassion, the more genuinely ethical our conduct will be.[62]

Emotions, then, can have greater or lesser cognitive components; however, the emotions that are particularly important for ethical development have larger cognitive components. Thus, we can apply the intellect to our emotional development. This, in fact, is the approach Buddhism has traditionally taken in many meditation practices.

As we have seen, the Dalai Lama sees ethics as rooted in the feelings of empathy or caring. It has always been intrinsic to Buddhism to intentionally nurture desirable emotions. Such intentional training plays a crucial role for Engaged Buddhists as well. The Dalai Lama states,

> [T]he capacity for empathy . . . is of crucial importance when it comes to ethics. . . . We find that in practice, if we are not able to connect with others to some extent, if we cannot at least imagine the potential impact of our actions on others, then we have no means to discriminate between right and wrong. . . . It follows, therefore, that if we could enhance this capacity—that is to say, our sensitivity toward others' suffering—the more we did so, the less we could tolerate seeing others' pain and the more we would be concerned to ensure that no action of ours caused harm to others.[63]

To develop compassion, loving kindness, and the other positive emotions is only part of what needs to be done. The Dalai Lama contends that we not only need to continually develop our compassion, or caring about the other, but also need reason, imagination, critical thinking, and judgment, to help us determine what to do in the unique circumstances of any ethical dilemma. We need, in fact, *yonisomana-sikāra*, which Payutto explained as "a principle based on wisdom that contemplates how teachings should be correctly applied." Feeling for and with others clearly does not mean losing rationality. We need what the Dalai Lama calls "the union of skillful means and insight," ensuring that our deeds are motivated by compassion and guided by "the faculty of wise discernment."[64]

Classical Mahayana frequently refers to wisdom and compassion as insepa-rable, interdependent or even the same, as "two wings of the bird" or "two sides of a single coin." The Tibetan tradition frequently refers to this pair as skillful means and insight or wisdom. The idea is that realization of one member of the pair auto-matically entails realization of the other. That is, if one lets go of the illusion of a separate, independent self (wisdom or insight), the care that one formerly reserved for oneself will be automatically extended to all beings. Similarly, if one succeeds in cultivating one's care for others to the extent that one forgets oneself or loses one-self in one's concern for "others," that self-forgetfulness itself constitutes nascent wisdom.

Nhat Hanh refers frequently to the interrelationship between compassion and wisdom—or love and understanding, as he calls it—following this classical Mahayana tradition. This is how he puts it:

> Understanding and love are not two things, but just one. Suppose your son wakes up one morning and . . . decides to wake up his younger sister, to give her enough time to eat breakfast before going to school. It happens that she is grouchy and instead of saying, 'Thank you for waking me up,' she says, 'Shut up! Leave me alone!' and kicks him. He will probably get angry. . . . But then he remembers that during the night his sister coughed a lot, and he realizes that she must be sick. . . . He is not angry any more. At that moment there is *buddh* in him. He understands, he is awake. When you understand, you cannot help but love.[65]

Nhat Hanh often focuses in his teaching on developing understanding in his students; between love and understanding, understanding would seem to be the element more readily available to a teacher to work with, especially in the con-text of lecturing to groups and writing books. In addition, however, Nhat Hanh believes that "when you understand, you cannot help but love." This idea seems to be based on a belief in Buddha nature, according to which human beings are innately loving beings. When we fail to love, it is because an element of ignorance has intruded into our experience, submerging our natural impulse to love. If we can remove the ignorance, by coming to understand, our natural caring will cease to be blocked and be able to come forth.

Sometimes, though, Nhat Hanh works directly on the caring. In his Tiep Hien Precepts (now called Fourteen Mindfulness Trainings of the Order of Interbeing) and his commentary on them, Nhat Hanh writes, "Do not avoid contact with suffering or close your eyes before suffering. Do not lose awareness of the existence of suffering in the life of the world. Find ways to be with those who are suffering by all means, including personal contact and visits, images, sounds. By such means, awaken yourself and others to the reality of suffering in the world. [Comment:] If we get in touch with the suffering of the world, and are moved by that suffering, we may come forward to help the people who are suffering."[66] Being with suffering can arouse strong emotions. We often keep suffering at a distance and hide our eyes from it precisely so that we will not have to feel. For Nhat Hanh, this is allowing ignorance to intrude. If we allow ourselves to "be with" suffering, both understanding (we awaken to the situation) and caring will usually develop immediately. Again, there is no reason/emotion dichotomy here. In the passage from Nhat Hanh, we can see the extent to which right action is a response not just to emotion, but also to a state composed of both knowledge and emotion, being "in touch with suffering." Though compassion is primarily an emotion, it is not for that reason regarded as being irrational in the sense of unwise or exhibiting poor judgment. The prototype portrays it in exactly the opposite manner: ideally, compassion is to be accompanied by practical wisdom and wisdom by compassion.

Maha Ghosananda illustrates this point with the following story:

There was a farmer who went into the forest with his friend to gather wood. When the farmer struck a tree with his axe, he disturbed a beehive, and a swarm of angry bees flew out and began stinging him.

The farmer's friend was filled with compassion. He grabbed his axe and killed the bees with swift, mighty blows. Unfortunately, he also killed the farmer.

Compassion without wisdom can cause great suffering. We might even say, "It is better to have a wise enemy then a foolish friend."

Wisdom and compassion must walk together. Having one without the other is like walking with one foot. You may hop a few times, but eventually you will fall. Balancing wisdom with compassion, you will walk very well—slowly and elegantly, step by step.[67]

For Engaged Buddhists, reason and emotion are not antagonists; they are not dichotomous. Wisdom and compassion need each other. Unlike Western ethical thought, there is no notion in Engaged Buddhist ethical thought of actions motivated by reason as being generally more trustworthy than actions motivated by emotion. Engaged Buddhists do dichotomize, but their dichotomies fall along lines other than the reason/emotion line. They, like other Buddhists, dichotomize between "unskillful" actions motivated by one or more of the "three poisons," greed, hatred, and delusion (notice the mixture of emotion and ignorance in these motivations), and "skillful" actions with motivations free of the poisons, motivations characterized by nongreed, nonhatred, and nondelusion or by selflessness, compassion, and loving kindness (again, motivations displaying a mixture of emotion and understanding).

NONADVERSARIAL STANCE

Perhaps the most fundamental philosophical basis of the nonadversarial element in Engaged Buddhist ethics is the perception that "self" and "other" are interdependent and therefore have common interests. The Dalai Lama writes,

> If the self had intrinsic identity, it would be possible to speak in terms of self-interest in isolation from that of others. But because this is not so, because self and others can only really be understood in terms of relationship, we see that self-interest and others' interest are closely interrelated. Indeed, within this picture of dependently originated reality, we see that there is no self-interest completely unrelated to others' interests. Due to the fundamental interconnectedness which lies at the heart of reality, your interest is also my interest. From this, it becomes clear that "my" interest and "your" interest are intimately connected. In a deep sense, they converge.[68]

This is the root *logical* foundation of the nonadversarial element in Engaged Buddhist ethics. If self and other are not in reality separate from each other, it is logically impossible for their interests to be separate from each other. As we have seen in Buddhist natural law thinking, what *is* has implications for what one *ought* to do. Knowing that we are interconnected and that our interests are interconnected, when we are in a conflict situation, we *ought*, if we are skillful in our behavior, to look for a win-win outcome that will fulfill the true interests of everyone involved.

Of course, logic only goes so far in motivating behavior. Experiential knowledge with elements of both understanding and emotion is much more powerful. It is natural, therefore, that many Engaged Buddhists cite a *feeling* of nonseparation from others as the foundation of their desire to engage in altruistic behavior. Nhat Hanh reports that, during the war in Vietnam, the monks and nuns, though safe in their monasteries, said that the bombing and oppression of the Vietnamese people "hurts us too much. We have to react." That is, though the bombing was miles away, they felt the pain of the bombing of others—from whom they did not feel separate—as if it were in some sense their own pain. They had to react—take action to stop the bombing—because they were in so much pain.[69] In a similar vein, Master Cheng Yen, founder of the Tzu Chi movement with its many free hospitals, says, "If there were no suffering, society would be perfect. When everyone is happy, only then am I happy. When everyone is healthy, only then am I healthy. When human suffering ends, my suffering ends."[70]

For some Engaged Buddhists, as we develop altruistic behavior and attitudes toward others we increase our own personal peace and happiness. The Dalai Lama claims, "The principal characteristic of genuine happiness is . . . inner peace," and this peace "is rooted in concern for others." He asks, "Does this proposition stand up to analysis? . . . Consider the following. We humans are social beings. We come into the world as the result of others' actions. We survive here in dependence on others. Whether we like it or not, there is hardly a moment of our lives when we do not benefit from others' activities. For this reason, it is hardly surprising that most of our happiness arises in the context of our relationships with others. Nor is it so remarkable that our greatest joy should come when we are motivated by concern for others."[71]

We have seen that, for the Dalai Lama, "due to the fundamental interconnectedness which lies at the heart of reality, . . . 'my' interest and 'your' interest" ultimately converge. Therefore, it should not surprise us that sympathetic joy— your happiness producing my happiness—is a part of human emotional life. Because there is in reality no individual human self, it should also not surprise us that "our greatest joy" comes when we forget ourselves and think of others—this also is a manifestation of the nature of reality. Therefore, for the Dalai Lama, one's own inner peace and happiness are best served by forgetting about oneself and helping others to achieve happiness.

Maha Ghosananda also writes of benefits to oneself resulting from other-regarding behavior:

> Buddhist scriptures . . . tell us that those who practice loving kindness sleep well. They have no bad dreams. They wake up happy. . . .

When we love all beings, we gain the blessing of fearlessness. Our speech and all of our physical and mental actions become clear, and we become free.

With loving kindness, we are like a fish in clear water, never submerged by the burdens of the world. . . . We have clear comprehension about the purpose of our life and about how to live happily.[72]

Thus, a whole host of personal rewards come to us when we forget about ourselves and concentrate on loving others.

We have seen that the nonadversarial ethical position is rooted intellectually in understanding of the interdependence of self and other and rooted emotionally in experientially feeling a connectedness with others. We have noted that beneficent, other-regarding behavior benefits not only others, but also oneself. These seeds and roots of interpersonal connectedness culminate for the Engaged Buddhists in their ethical stance of a nonadversarial position in situations of conflict.

Maha Ghosananda frequently expresses the nonadversarial stance in conflict situations. "How do we resolve a conflict, a battle, a power struggle? What does reconciliation really mean? Gandhi said that the essence of nonviolent action is that it seeks to put an end to antagonism, not the antagonists. This is important. The opponent has our respect. We implicitly trust his or her human nature and understand that ill will is caused by ignorance."[73] Maha Ghosananda, like many other Engaged Buddhists, is greatly indebted to Gandhi and agrees with him on many points. Without Gandhi's belief in Atman, the divine soul within recognized in Hinduism, Maha Ghosananda can still speak of trusting the human nature of others. How does this work in Buddhism? Aung San Suu Kyi gives an example:

Alan Clements: Obviously, in your call for dialogue and reconciliation with SLORC [the Burmese military regime] some level of forgiveness is essential, balanced with some degree of justice. But what do you think is the core quality of forgiveness that allows one to genuinely forgive one's oppressors?

Aung San Suu Kyi: To forgive, I think, basically means the ability to see the person apart from the deed and to recognize that although he has done that deed, it does not mean that he is irredeemable. There are aspects of him that are acceptable. To wholly identify a person with his deed is the sign of a real inability to forgive. For example, if you always think of a murderer in terms of the murder, you will never be able to forgive him. But if you think of the murderer objectively, as a person who has committed a murder, and there are other aspects to him besides that deed he has committed, then you're in a position to forgive him.[74]

As in Gandhi, we have here the principle "hate the deed, not the doer." For Suu Kyi, this kind of thinking comes to mind when she is asked about how she will relate to the current military rulers of Burma (who have kept her under arrest for many years and brutalized the country) in the future, when she has more freedom. Her call for dialogue and reconciliation with them instead of victory for herself and her party and loss for them depends upon her avoidance of feelings of ill will toward those who have oppressed her and her country. To have such an attitude while still rejecting their oppressive actions, it is necessary for her to be able to separate the deed from the doer.

In the two passages above, we see how the Engaged Buddhist nonadversarial stance is rooted in the interaction of two fundamental ideas discussed in chapter 2: *anātman* and human enlightenability. Because humans lack a soul, whatever is wrong in our behavior can be addressed by identifying and changing the causes of that behavior. When there is no need to blame the person doing "wrong," conflict is depersonalized; we can address the causes of—for example, ignorant behavior—and not just criticize the person or his or her behavior. Second, because humans are educable and even enlightenable, we have reason for optimism, reason to hope that if we change causes and conditions of behavior, eliminating seeds that cause ignorant behavior and planting seeds that cause wiser behavior, the behavior that concerns us will change for the better.

We saw another example of the nonadversarial nature of Engaged Buddhist ethics in our discussion of the Five Lay Precepts above. There we saw that my observance of the precept of not harming while being directly good for you is also very much good for me. This way of thinking is in the background when Maha Ghosananda writes, "Taking care of others is the same as taking care of myself. . . . When we protect ourselves through mindfulness, we are protecting others as well. When we protect other living beings through compassionate action, we are also protecting ourselves."[75] Why is it that "taking care of others is the same as taking care of myself"? There are basically two ideas here. First, if I take proper care of myself, I will not hurt others. Also, if I take proper care of myself, I become the kind of person who is able to help others, the kind of person who has nurtured a loving disposition that he or she can therefore extend to the world.

Many of the Engaged Buddhists are well known to have expressed their non-adversarial ethic by refusing to regard anyone as an enemy. Again, Maha Ghosananda discusses his willingness to work with the Khmer Rouge to build a temple at the border:

> "Oh," thought many people, "he is talking to the enemy. He is helping the enemy! How can he do that?" I reminded them that love embraces all beings, whether they are noble-minded or low-minded, good or evil.
>
> Both the noble and the good are embraced because loving kindness flows to them spontaneously. The unwholesome-minded must be included because they are the ones who need loving kindness the most. In many of them, the seed of goodness may have died because warmth was lacking for its growth. It perished from coldness in a world without compassion.
>
> . . . Reconciliation does not mean that we surrender rights and conditions, but rather that we use love in all of our negotiations. It means that we see ourselves in the opponent—for what is the opponent but a being in ignorance, and we ourselves are also ignorant of many things. Therefore, only loving kindness and right mindfulness can free us.[76]

For Engaged Buddhists like Maha Ghosananda, because of the lack of a self or soul, no one should be branded "bad" as a fixed and final state of being. There were reasons that made this person turn out this way—a lack of love, ignorance. The proper response to such a person is loving kindness and compassion.

During the war in Vietnam, Buddhists in the "Struggle Movement" trying to stop the war took a principled nonadversarial stance. In their case, that meant refusing to side with North Vietnamese Communists or South Vietnamese anti-Communists.

> We were able to understand the suffering of both sides, the Communists and the anti-Communists. We tried to be open to both, to understand this side and to understand that side, to be one with them. That is why we did not take a side, even though the whole world took sides. We tried to tell people our perception of the situation: that we wanted to stop the fighting, but the bombs were so loud. . . . We wanted reconciliation, we did not want a victory.[77]

Nhat Hanh extended this thinking to the Cold War situation as well. In 1987, he wrote,

People completely identify with one side, one ideology. To understand the suffering and the fear of a citizen of the Soviet Union, we have to become one with him or her. To do so is dangerous—we will be suspected by both sides. But if we don't do it, if we align ourselves with one side or the other, we will lose our chance to work for peace. Reconciliation is to understand both sides, to go to one side and describe the suffering being endured by the other side, and then to go to the other side and describe the suffering being endured by the first side. Doing only that will be a great help for peace.[78]

Later, the same reasoning was expressed in response to the beating of Rodney King:

We all saw the video of the Los Angeles policemen beating Rodney King. When I saw those images, I identified with Rodney King, and I suffered a lot. You must have felt the same. We were all beaten at the same time. But when I looked more deeply, I saw that I am also the five policemen. I could not separate myself from the men who did the beating. They were manifesting the hatred and violence that pervades our society. . . . We have helped create them through our forgetfulness, through the way we live our daily lives. In my heart I feel no blame for anyone. Arresting and imprisoning the policemen will not help them or solve the problem. The problem is much deeper than that. Violence has become the substance of our lives.[79]

The Tibetan case is probably the best-known example of nonadversarial attitudes in the face of the greatest provocation. Here is a typical statement from the Dalai Lama:

In my particular case, we Tibetans are carrying on a struggle for our rights. . . . We Tibetans have a unique and distinct cultural heritage just as the Chinese have. We do not hate the Chinese; we deeply respect the riches of Chinese culture which spans so many centuries. Though we have deep respect and are not anti-Chinese, we six million Tibetans have an equal right to maintain our own distinctive culture as long as we do not harm others. . . .

I am serving our cause with the motivation of service to humankind, not for reasons of power, not out of hatred. Not just as a Tibetan but as a human being, I think it is worthwhile to preserve that culture, that nation, to contribute to world society.[80]

The nonadversarial attitude is more widespread among Tibetans than one might expect. The Dalai Lama tells the story of a monk named Lopon-la who had been imprisoned and tortured by the Chinese. His Holiness relates,

> When I asked him whether he had ever been afraid, he admitted that there was one thing that had scared him: the possibility that he might lose compassion and concern for his jailers.
>   I was very moved by this, and also very inspired.[81]

The Dalai Lama has gone so far into the nonadversarial attitude that he even regards his enemies as his benefactors.

> Only when someone criticizes and exposes our faults are we able to discover our problems and confront them. Thus is our enemy our greatest friend. He provides us with the needed test of inner strength, tolerance and respect for others. Instead of feeling anger toward this person, one should respect him and be grateful.[82]

In Burma, a colleague of Suu Kyi expresses the nonadversarial attitude when interrogated by the widely feared military intelligence. She tells the story. "When Uncle U Kyi Maung was under detention, one of the Military Intelligence officers interrogating him asked, 'Why did you decide to become a member of the National League for Democracy?' And he answered, 'For your sake.'"[83]

Nonadversarial attitudes like these will inevitably have a major effect on these Engaged Buddhists' approaches to real-world conflict situations. Those with nonadversarial perspectives cannot and do not approach a conflict situation determined to defeat their opponents. They must and do seek common ground, a win-win situation, reconciliation.

The nonadversarial perspective seems to be the dominant view among Engaged Buddhist leaders, but there are some among them whose view with respect to adversariality is less clear. We can briefly consider this issue in the ex-Untouchable *dalit* Buddhist groups and in the Soka Gakkai.

Both the *dalit* Buddhist groups and the Soka Gakkai initially maintained strongly adversarial postures. The initiator of the *dalit* Buddhist movement, B. R. Ambedkar, was himself born an Untouchable, and though he amazingly rose to be one of the most important leaders of the newly independent India, his outcaste status followed him. He dedicated his life to the cause of the former Untouchables, trying to reform Hinduism from within, but failed. He ultimately converted to Buddhism as a rejection of Hinduism and the caste system. Thus, conversion for him was itself an adversarial act. He wanted to see the elimination of the entire caste system and urged his followers to join the "battle": "My final word of advice to you is educate, agitate, and organize, have faith in yourself. With justice on our side, I do not see how we can lose our battle. The battle to me is a matter of joy. The battle is in the fullest sense spiritual. There is nothing material or social in it. For ours is a battle not for wealth or for power. It is a battle for freedom. It is a battle for the reclamation of human personality."[84]

Many *dalit* Buddhist groups to this day focus on the political and social issues in their struggle with the larger Indian society and maintain a clearly adversarial position. The *dalit* Buddhist group TBMSG, however, has a different posture. It has turned its focus away from the conflict with the larger society and onto the development of its own *dalit* membership. While the *dalits* continue to experience terrible discrimination and even attacks, TBMSG has determined that the best way for them to be helped is for them to be transformed from within by Buddhist practice and the Buddhist way of life. They have picked up the part of Ambedkar's thought that emphasized this kind of change. Thus, the TBMSG leader, Dhammachari Lokamitra, quotes Ambedkar: "The greatest thing that the Buddha has done is to tell the world that the world cannot be reformed except by the reformation of the mind of man and the mind of the world."[85] Consequently, TBMSG has taken as its work the huge task of bringing Buddhist learning, practice, and way of life to the former Untouchable Buddhist community. They have simply put aside the struggle with the larger community. Consequently, there is no occasion for them to take up an adversarial posture for the time being. Whether they would take up an adversarial or nonadversarial posture if and when they once again take up the struggle with Indian caste society is an open question.

The Soka Gakkai for most of its existence also maintained a strong, indeed strident, adversarial position. They became notorious for their harshly combative posture with respect to other religions and other Buddhist groups. It should be noted that their adversarial habits served them well in their ability to maintain a position of opposition to the totalitarian government in Japan during World War II, while other Buddhist groups weakly submitted.

In the last decade, the Soka Gakkai broke from its parent group, Nichiren Shōshū, and quickly began to adopt a much less adversarial posture. Remarkably, its rhetoric has turned from the *shakubuku* ("break and flatten") rhetoric used in the past in its aggressive proselytization efforts to rhetoric—and action—of dialogue. Daisaku Ikeda, president of the Soka Gakkai International, writes, "My stance as a Buddhist is always to see things from the standpoint of respecting and trusting in other human beings. I believe that mutual understanding is always possible when we conduct dialogue from the common ground of our shared humanity."[86] Acting on these commitments, Ikeda has founded the Boston Research Center for the 21st Century as an institution devoted to promoting genuine dialogue between religions and civilizations in the interest of global peacebuilding. The center organizes many conferences every year, gathering representatives from a great variety of perspectives to dialogue on equal terms. It annually gives out awards to persons of all backgrounds who are doing outstanding work for peace and on behalf of humanity—Ikeda's bodhisattvas-*cum*-global citizens. The SGI also cooperates in a harmonious spirit with other religious and secular institutions in a variety of programs based upon mutual interest in making the world a better place. Taking these things into account, the present posture of this international wing of the SGI cannot be said to be adversarial. Its transformation from an adversarial to a nonadversarial, dialogical, cooperative posture has been a remarkable and rapid turnaround.

PRAGMATISM

The pragmatism of Engaged Buddhism is rooted in the strong streak of pragmatism in traditional Buddhism, especially the teachings of the Buddha. Payutto, Buddhadasa, and Maha Ghosananda are all fond of quoting the Buddha's statement, "I teach only two things—suffering and the end of suffering." If this teaching is taken at face value then the entire purpose of Buddhism is pragmatic: to end suffering.

Buddhadasa's disciple, Santikaro Bhikkhu, links Buddhadasa's following of this saying of the Buddha to his interest in social issues:

> The Buddha himself declares the purpose and scope of his teaching: "In the past, Bhikkhus, as well as now, I teach only *dukkha* and the utter quenching of *dukkha*."
>
> Buddhadasa Bhikkhu referred to these words repeatedly, and they provide the proper context of his own life and work. . . . None of Ajarn Buddhadasa's words can be understood properly, except in this context. In particular, his social commentaries require this context in that the reason why we must discuss politics and economics is that they are the sources of so much *dukkha* in individuals and conflicts in society.
>
> . . . For Buddhadasa Bhikkhu, something is Buddhist solely because it quenches *dukkha*. When asked if something is "good" or "correct," Ajarn Buddhadasa asked in return, "Does it quench *dukkha*?"[87]

In other words, the test of value is pragmatic: if something quenches *dukkha*, it is "good," it has value. Nothing else is really worth worrying about.

Ambedkar, initiator of the *dalit* Buddhist movement, felt that pragmatic value was so invariably present in the Buddha's teachings that any teaching without such value could not be the teaching of the Buddha. He writes, "The Buddha never cared to enter into a discussion which was not profitable for man's welfare. Therefore anything attributed to the Buddha which did not relate to man's welfare cannot be accepted to be the word of the Buddha."[88]

Payutto repeatedly emphasizes the pragmatic nature of the Buddha's teachings. He writes, "There is one thing that is recognized as part of the nature of the Buddhist teachings: In teaching the truth, only the things that can be put to use in this life are of value; the things that do not lead to beneficial results in this life, even if they may be true, are not taught."[89] Thus, for Payutto, Buddhist teachings should always be able to give something of value to human life. Ideas without such a pragmatic purpose have no place in Buddhism. Although such may have been the intention of Shakyamuni, Buddhism has by no means adhered to this rule over the millennia. With their commitment to the elimination of suffering, however, Engaged Buddhists are naturally drawn to this element of the Buddhist tradition.

Looking through his Buddhist eyes, the Dalai Lama sees religion in general in the same pragmatic way. For His Holiness, all the religions have a pragmatic element that can be drawn upon to help the world solve its problems. This element is the religions' ability, as he sees it, to transform the individual to become more caring about others. "Despite different conceptions of the universe such as life after death, etc., all religions essentially teach one to become a better human being and to develop a kind heart."[90] For decades His Holiness has taught this principle around the world as the key to the survival of life on planet Earth.

Nhat Hanh made Buddhist pragmatism the key to the First Precept of the Order of Interbeing, which he developed during the war years. This precept states, "Do not be idolatrous about or bound to any doctrine, theory, or ideology, even Buddhist ones. All systems of thought are guiding means; they are not absolute truth."[91] The idea that a body of teachings is something to be used, rather than something that has captured "truth," is an explicitly pragmatic idea. For Nhat Hanh this pragmatic approach to religion and ideology was a crucial point, because the Vietnam War made it all too clear, as he said, that "in the name of ideologies and doctrines, people kill and are killed." He contrasted such an approach with Buddhism, in which, "peace can only be achieved when we are not attached to a view."[92] Thus, pragmatism becomes not just a characteristic that Buddhism happens to have, but also something important for the possibility of peace in the world.

THE IMPERATIVE TO ACT

The feature of Engaged Buddhist ethics that most differentiates it from more traditional Buddhist ethics is the imperative to act. The "Chief of all Sayings" (*Dhammapada* 183) urges disciples of the Buddha in this way:

> Refraining from doing evil
> Doing only good
> Purifying the mind
> This is the Heart of Buddhism.[93]

There is also a Mahayana variant: "avoid evil, cultivate good, save all beings." These are taken as summaries of the Buddhist path.

It is characteristic of Engaged Buddhist ethics to believe that it is as imperative to "do good," as it is to "refrain from evil." Engaged Buddhist leaders see traditional Buddhist moral practice as often contenting itself with refraining from evil, as if it were enough to keep one's own hands clean. That is, a popular traditional view is this: the goal of Buddhism is to attain liberation from samsara. If one commits a moral misdeed, one will cause oneself karmic harm, placing oneself further from the goal of liberation. From an Engaged Buddhist point of view, if this is one's motivation and the context within which one thinks, one's moral development is at a very early stage. The motivation in this traditional view is selfish; missing is any true compassion or altruism, a concern that *other* people not suffer. Therefore, the Engaged Buddhists make it a point to emphasize the importance of actively doing good for others.

Tzu Chi is one of the organizations that strongly emphasize the importance of all their members engaging in service work. One of their slogans is "Just do it." As the Tzu Chi web site puts it, "Tzu Chi people have walked the path of love for more than thirty years. We have experienced success and disappointment, but we have always fearlessly upheld the attitude of 'Just do it!'"[94] In fact, Cheng Yen explicitly emphasizes the importance of moving from the first level of the "Chief of All Sayings" to the second. "The world not only needs people to not do bad deeds, but it needs more people to do good deeds. Once everyone is on the right path, peace and happiness will be brought into the world. Shunning evil deeds is good, but performing good deeds is more important."[95]

Ikeda highlights three virtues as the center of SGI's practice: a sense of responsibility, compassion, and wisdom. We have already heard much about compassion and wisdom as core Buddhist virtues. SGI's practice of naming a sense of responsibility as an equally important virtue captures the constancy with which SGI focuses on activism. For Ikeda, "a sense of responsibility refers to the responsibility to protect the right to life shared by humankind and all living things. It is a tenacious determination to work for the creation of peace."[96]

Nhat Hanh and Sulak are both very clear in their commitment to move the practice of Buddhist morality from the level of avoiding evil to the level of doing good. This can be seen in the rethinking of the Five Lay Precepts (pañca-śīla) that each has done. As we saw in chapter 2, each of them rethought the Lay Precepts, adding the proactive dimension. So, for example, the first precept, to avoid doing harm, was expanded by Sulak to include an invitation to "shape a politically just and merciful world" and by Nhat Hanh to the rewritten precept, "I am determined not to kill, not to let others kill, and not to condone any act of killing in the world, in my thinking, and in my way of life." Thus, the ethical standard moves from a passive to an active ethic.

Similarly, Ariyaratne's Sarvodaya Shramadana has transformed the four Brahmavihāra from subjects for transic meditation practiced in withdrawal from society to values that need to be put into practice. Two typical quotations express this transformation:

Feeling sorry for people is not enough. Act to help them.
(Shramadana guideline)

Nonviolence is more than not walking on insects in the road. It is to be of service to our fellow-beings.
(Sarvodaya organizer)[97]

Suu Kyi also makes an explicit point of interpreting traditional values in an activist direction:

Engaged Buddhism is active compassion or active metta. It's not just sitting there saying, "I feel sorry for them." It means doing something about the situation by bringing whatever relief you can to those who need it the most, by caring for them, by doing what you can to help others.

Of course, the "sending of loving-kindness" is very much a part of our Burmese Buddhist training. But in addition to that we have got to do

more to express our *metta* and to show our compassion. And there are so
many ways of doing it. For example, when the Buddha tried to stop two
sides from fighting each other, he went out and stood between them. They
would have had to injure him first before they could hurt each other. So he
was defending both sides. As well as protecting others at the sacrifice of his
own safety.[98]

She interprets nonviolence in the same way:

Non-violence means positive action. You have to work for whatever you
want. You don't just sit there doing nothing and hope to get what you
want. It just means that the methods you use are not violent ones. Some
people think that non-violence is passiveness. It's not so.[99]

It seems that a good deal of Suu Kyi's task is in fact to convince the Burmese people
that they need to be more activist, and this task in turn involves convincing them
that their traditional understanding of Buddhist teaching is wrong. "Some people
think of *karma* as destiny or fate and that there's nothing they can do about it.
It's simply what is going to happen because of their past deeds. This is the way in
which *karma* is often interpreted in Burma. But *karma* is not that at all. It's doing,
it's action. So you are creating your own *karma* all the time. Buddhism is a very
dynamic philosophy and it's a great pity that some people forget that aspect of our
religion."[100]

Suu Kyi is quite right in saying that the Buddha did not teach a doctrine of
passivity. The Buddha emphasized making wise choices and taking skillful action
now in response to whatever comes one's way, part of which is determined by
karma. This is a good example of an Engaged Buddhist having to argue against a
popular misunderstanding of the Buddha's teachings and urging in its place a view
closer to what the Buddha taught than the current popular view.

Taking action applies to monks as well as to laypeople. Buddhadasa justifies
this understanding with a homely image:

Buddhist monks are wanderers, not hermits. That is to say, they wander
about in order to be involved with people who live in the world, rather
than living in the forest cut off from social contact. Their duty is to help
the people of the world in whatever way is suitable so that they do not
have to suffer or, in the words of a Thai proverb, so that they can know
"how to eat fish without getting stuck on the bones."

> Buddhist monks . . . are always involved in society in order to teach
> people about the true nature of the world, to overcome suffering and avoid
> choking to death on the bones of life.[101]

Although teaching laypeople is certainly a form of engagement with the world
and its problems, monks involved with Engaged Buddhist movements often are
involved with society in highly untraditional ways. Monks involved in the Sarvodaya Shramadana movement are involved with all aspects of the work, from
organizing to visiting government officials to digging in the Earth, legitimizing
and sacralizing with their presence whatever activities they are involved with. A
Sarvodaya monk may exhort other monks thus: "Don't sit in your temple like a
rich monk waiting for dana [gifts]. Go to the people, go to the poorest, work with
them."[102] While large numbers of Sri Lankan monks have responded positively to
this invitation, it has taken some time for laypeople to accept the monks in these
new roles. Many laypeople prefer to see the monks more aloof from society, often
because that makes them seem more fitting recipients of their *dāna*. Maha Ghosananda has had to contend with the same problem. He responds lyrically to such
concerns:

> We Buddhists must find the courage to leave our temples and enter the
> temples of human experience, temples that are filled with suffering. If we
> listen to the Buddha, Christ, or Gandhi, we can do nothing else. The refu-
> gee camps, the prisons, the ghettos, and the battlefields will then become
> our temples. We have so much work to do.
> This will be a slow transformation, for many people throughout Asia
> have been trained to rely on the traditional monkhood. Many Cambodians
> tell me, "Venerable, monks belong in the temple." It is difficult for them
> to adjust to this new role, but we monks must answer the increasingly loud
> cries of suffering. We only need to remember that our temple is with us
> always. We *are* our temple.[103]

Of course, the most important evidence of the imperative to act as a component
of Engaged Buddhist ethics is the many activities in which they are involved, their
work to stop war, develop an impoverished country, unseat a brutal government,
develop a culture of peace, provide medical care to the poor, empower the oppressed, and much more.

ENGAGED BUDDHISM AND TRADITION

Engaged Buddhism represents a continuous development of Buddhism, not a radical break from it. It is therefore not surprising that there is no single feature of Engaged Buddhist ethics that cannot be found in more traditional Buddhist ethics. The most prominent features of Engaged Buddhist ethical theory are natural law ideas; a developmental perspective; use of principles, prototypes, and virtue ethics; holism; a nonadversarial stance; pragmatism; and the imperative to act. Every one of these features can be and is justified by the Engaged Buddhist leaders by an appeal to tradition. What, then, makes Engaged Buddhism different from traditional forms of Buddhism? In some cases, the Engaged Buddhist leaders are arguing against what they see as misinterpretations that have taken root in popular forms of Buddhism, such as the idea that karma means fate, or the idea of passivity. Some such arguments are implicit, such as the Engaged Buddhist emphasis on the practical usefulness of Buddhism, whereas traditional Buddhism occasionally tends toward scholasticism or ritualism (not that Engaged Buddhism is devoid of scholars or of rituals!). Engaged Buddhism notably turns away from popular interpretations of detachment as uninvolvement with the world in favor of calm and loving involvement. In many cases, what differentiates Engaged Buddhism is only its insistence upon the necessity of taking practical action in the world. After taking this one step, Engaged Buddhism has shown tremendous creativity in applying such traditional values as holism or the nonadversarial stance to the problems that arise when one does take practical action in the world.

4   Individual and Society

An early question that a social ethics metatheory must address is the nature of the individual and society and the relationship between the two. We shall see that what is clear on the level of ethical theory will produce clarity when the social ethics are applied to particular issues in society; what is ambiguous in theory will produce ambiguities in application.

INDIVIDUAL

Engaged Buddhists take traditional views in their understanding of the human individual. We will review them briefly.

HUMAN NATURE

When asked, "What does being human mean to you?" Aung San Suu Kyi replies, "As a Buddhist, if you really want to consider what we, as human beings, are here for it's quite simple: we are trying to achieve enlightenment and to use the wisdom that is gained to serve others, so that they too might be free from suffering. While we can't all be Buddhas, I feel a responsibility to do as much as I can to realize enlightenment to the degree that I can, and to use it to relieve the suffering of others."[1]

For Suu Kyi and the others, what defines us as human is our potential to achieve enlightenment. At the same time, it is characteristic of Engaged Buddhism that this potential does not mean that we should wait until we achieve enlightenment to start helping others. On the contrary, we should serve others immediately, to the best of our ability, while we continue to strive to develop our Buddhahood.

Of course, it is recognized very well that there are hindrances standing in our way. Again, the list of such hindrances is not unique to Engaged Buddhism, the chief culprits being greed, hatred, and delusion; ignorance; clinging; selfishness; and heedlessness.

When considering our dual nature as human beings who are both enlightenable and yet weighed down with hindrances, the Engaged Buddhists have a tendency to accentuate the positive. Some do this by recognizing that either a nega-tive or a positive future are equal possibilities for us and encouraging us to choose the positive. Maha Ghosananda writes,

> When anger controls us, we harm ourselves and the people around us. Anger burns the mind and the body. The face becomes flushed, the heart weakens, and the hands tremble. . . . When we are angry, our face becomes ugly. Anger is fire, and it burns hundreds of cells in our brain and in our blood.
>
> If we have loving kindness, our faces become brilliant, radiant, and beautiful.[2]

Other Engaged Buddhists, particularly Mahayanists under the influence of the Buddha nature idea, tend to see our nature as more innately good than bad. Certainly the Dalai Lama does this. His Holiness believes that caring is innate— that is, it is our nature to be empathetic and caring. He points to an everyday example to make his case.

> If it is correct that, on some level, we all have the capacity for empathy, it follows that for one individual to harm another, this potential must be overwhelmed, or submerged in some way. . . .
> . . . [C]onsider a child going out to play who gets into a fight with another child. Immediately after, the victorious child may experience a sense of satisfaction. But on returning home, that emotion will subside and a more subtle state of mind will manifest. At that point, a sense of unease sets in. We could almost describe this sort of feeling as a sense of alienation from self: the individual doesn't feel quite "right." In the contrary case of a child who goes out to play and shares an enjoyable afternoon with a friend, afterwards not only will there be an immediate sense of satisfaction, but when the mind has settled down and the excitement worn off, there will be a sense of calm and comfort.[3]

For His Holiness, empathy is more natural to us than antipathy. Consequently, on those occasions when the latter overwhelms the former, we ourselves do not feel right and suffer to one degree or another.

EGALITARIANISM

Though recognizing that the actualization of one's human potential varies greatly from person to person, Engaged Buddhists still emphasize the equality of human-kind.

Phra Payutto emphasizes the equality of humanity based upon at least four major points in the teachings and institutions of the Buddha. His case is this: (1) People could be ordained as monks or nuns in the Sangha regardless of their caste.[4] The Buddha set up the Sangha as an ideal community, equally open to all.[5] (2) Though abilities differ, everyone has an "equal right" to an equal opportunity to achieve whatever they can.[6] (3) The Buddha "gave rights to women" to "bene-fit from Buddhadhamma and reach the final goal of the teachings just the same as men."[7] And (4) the Buddha "taught Buddhadhamma with a common tongue so that people of any educational background could benefit from this Dhamma."[8]

Sri Lankan scholar L. P. N. Perera wrote a commentary on the United Na-tions Universal Declaration of Human Rights in which he draws support for each article in the declaration from the Pali texts and Theravada tradition. Article 1 of the declaration begins, "All human beings are born free and equal in dignity and rights." This statement is the foundational premise of the entire document and of international human rights thought in general. Perera's commentary on it, supporting it from a Theravada Buddhist perspective, draws upon the points mentioned above:

> Buddhism is one of the earliest religions to recognize the fundamental equality of all human beings belonging, as they are, to one community in the sense that peoples' essential natures are the same whatever their indi-vidual differences, due to heredity, environment, and other factors, may be. This sense of equality is further reinforced by the Buddhist view that (a) all human beings, in the final analysis, face the same basic phenomena of birth, decay and dissolution, spelt out as the First Noble Truth, and (b) that at the same time human beings are capable of overcoming these problems by attaining the very highest moral and spiritual level by a development of the human potential through an extension of human capacity. Human life is so placed in the cosmic scheme of things, that human beings alone enjoy the best opportunity of transcending the unsatisfactoriness of existence into the state of *Nirvana*—the state of Highest Happiness . . . in this very life.[9]

Venerable Cheng Yen interprets the story of Siddhartha leaving home in terms of human equality:

> From eliminating inequality in ancient India to purifying all human minds, the Buddha, or Prince Siddhartha, was concerned about human nature not just in one country but in the whole world. This is where Prince Siddhartha's greatness lies. In spite of being born in a palace and living a prosperous life, the prince was able to feel the suffering of the poor and the arrogance of the Brahman religious leaders. This inequality led him to search for a way to end the suffering of all beings. In order to free people from suffering, he had to start with himself. Thus, he left his home to experience the feelings of other living beings and to look for the truth in life.[10]

Cheng Yen sees herself following in Siddhartha's footsteps. In her case, the shock she received upon seeing on a hospital floor the blood of a poor woman who died because of the inability to pay for medical care brought home the significance of human equality: the need of all for medical care and the irrelevance, to her mind, of ability to pay to meet that need.

Struggling to heal a community divided along lines of ethnicity and religion, the Buddhist heritage of egalitarianism has been an important asset for Sarvodaya Shramadana. In a passage we have seen before, A. T. Ariyaratne explains the importance of the "family gatherings" that occur periodically throughout Sarvodaya work camps:

> The idea behind the term "family gathering" is that the whole world is one family, and all of them represent humanity in microcosm. All religious, caste, race, linguistic, class, national, or political differences are of no importance in the family gatherings.[11]

The Dalai Lama interprets human equality as fundamental sameness, and stresses it as one of the foundations of his ethical views:

> For my part, meeting innumerable others from all over the world and from every walk of life reminds me of our basic sameness as human beings. Indeed, the more I see of the world, the clearer it becomes that no matter what our situation, whether we are rich or poor, educated or not, of one race, gender, religion or another, we all desire to be happy and to avoid suffering.[12]

Thus, in a variety of iterations, egalitarianism is an important component of Engaged Buddhist understanding of human nature.

ANĀTMAN

Buddhadasa Bhikkhu succinctly explains the importance of the teaching of *anāt-man* (no self). "Spiritual disease is the disease whose germ lies in the feeling of . . . 'I' and 'mine' that is regularly present in the mind. The germ that is already in the mind develops first into the feeling of 'I' and 'mine' and then, acting through the influence of self-centeredness, becomes greed, hatred, and delusion, causing trouble for both oneself and others. These are the symptoms of the spiritual disease that lies within us."[13]

The problem with believing that the word "I" refers to a real thing that is "me" is not just psychological. Unless we challenge it in a sustained way, this false "I" becomes the center of one's existence and thus leads to a self-centeredness that deeply influences our everyday actions. A world full of self-centered beings constantly confronting each other will cause trouble! Thus, seeing the truth of *anātman* and letting go of the delusion of self will have tremendous ethical consequences.

Thich Nhat Hanh draws out some of the ethical and political implications of ideas of self and *anātman*: "In the West, people have the impression that their body belongs to them, that they can do anything they want to their body. They feel they have the right to live their lives however they please. And the law supports them. This is individualism. But according to the teaching of interbeing, your body is not yours alone. Your body belongs to your ancestors, your parents, and future generations, and it also belongs to society and all other living beings. All of them have come together to bring about the presence of this body."[14] From an individualistic perspective, one that embraces a strong idea of a separate and independent self, one's body is closely identified with one's sense of selfhood. In many societies, the legal system will support such an idea with many laws protecting privacy and allowing oneself to do whatever one wants if no one else is hurt. Societies with less sense of individualism, with less sense of a separate and independent self, will be organized differently. They will think in terms of ancestors and descendents, and not just the present generation. Privacy will be less of an issue, and there will be a greater sense of obligation to kin and community.

As we saw in chapter 3, for the Dalai Lama, the lack of self points directly to our shared interests with others. "Due to the fundamental interconnectedness which lies at the heart of reality, . . . 'my' interest and 'your' interest are intimately connected. In a deep sense, they converge."[15] Without a self, there is nothing to really separate us, and our interest, from others, and their interest. Our interests coinhere. If this is the case, our relations should always be nonadversarial.

INDIVIDUAL AND SOCIETY

In Engaged Buddhism, individual and society are interdependent. Of course, this was true in traditional Buddhism as well, but Engaged Buddhists make a point of saying it and of contemplating its implications.

Payutto declares, "The Buddhadhamma sees the internal life of the individual as intimately related to the external life of society and holds that values in the two realms are inseparably connected, compatible, and are, in fact, one and the same thing."[16] What would be the implications of the internal life of the individual and the external life of society being "intimately related"? Payutto goes on to quote the Buddha (S.V. 168–169),

> Bhikkhus, protecting yourself, you protect others; protecting others, you protect yourself.
>
> And how is it that while protecting yourself you protect others? By earnest practice, development, training, and making the most of it. In this way, when you protect yourself, you protect others.
>
> And how do you protect others by protecting yourself? By proper resolve (chanda), by non-violence, by possessing a heart of loving-kindness and compassion.[17]

Here again is the nonadversarial element of Buddhist ethics that we saw in the discussion of the precepts. By engaging in Buddhist practice, one transforms oneself into a person with less violence and more loving kindness and compassion; this is good for the individual and good for society. One is, after all, a part of society, not separate from it; society is the sum total of many such individuals. Thus, the internal life of the individual and the external life of society are "intimately related."

Nhat Hanh has written the classic Engaged Buddhist statement of the relationship between individual and society. Drawing upon the idea of emptiness, which he explains with characteristic simplicity, Nhat Hanh demonstrates his understanding of the interdependence of individual and society.

> When we go to a meditation center, we may have the impression that we leave everything behind—family, society, and all the complications in-

volved in them—and come as an individual in order to practice and to search for peace. This is already an illusion, because in Buddhism there is no such thing as an individual. . . .

[T]he individual is made of non-individual elements. How do you expect to leave everything behind when you enter a meditation center? The kind of suffering that you carry in your heart, that is society itself. You bring that with you, you bring society with you. You bring all of us with you. . . .

Leaves are usually looked upon as the children of the tree. Yes, they are the children of the tree, born from the tree, but they are also mothers of the tree. The leaves combine raw sap, water, and minerals, with sunshine and gas, and convert it into a variegated sap that can nourish the tree. We are all children of society, but we are also mothers. We have to nourish society. If we are uprooted from society, we cannot transform it into a more livable place for us and for our children.[18]

The relationship between individual and society is one of interpenetration; the individual contains society within himself and society is constructed of individuals. We are children and mothers of society and society is our mother and our child. We produce each other.

For Sulak Sivaraksa, the interdependence of the individual and society has practical implications. What is good for society is good for the individual and vice versa, whether viewed from a material or a spiritual perspective. A stable and harmonious society is the best support for Buddhist practice. Buddhist practice, in turn, should make one a better person, with more helpful contributions to bring to society. Sulak writes, "Hence we should all take responsibility both for our own development and for the development of our common society, both of which are inseparably intertwined."[19] This is the kind of thinking that is also at the foundation of the Sarvodaya Shramadana movement, which has as its goal the "dual awakening" of both individual and society.

RESPONSIBILITY

For the Dalai Lama, the interdependence of individual and society has important ethical implications. "We are social animals. . . . Because of our nature, we have to live in a cooperative setting. People who have no sense of responsibility for the society or the common good are acting against human nature."[20] Because our nature is social and we *cannot* live in solitude, for His Holiness it follows that acting responsibly for the common good is to act in harmony with human nature. We see here again an element of natural law thinking on His Holiness's part, moving as in the thought of Payutto and Buddhadasa from *is* to *ought*, in this case, from what our human nature is (we are social) to what our behavior ought to be—cooperative and responsible for the common good.

Although many Engaged Buddhists are interested in promoting the idea of social responsibility—indeed, social responsibility is a basic premise of Engaged Buddhism—the Dalai Lama has done more to develop this idea than anyone else. In addition to the case for responsibility that he makes from human nature, His Holiness also makes a logical case for responsibility: each of us is only one individual, while others are "infinite." No individual's value, no matter how important, can outweigh the combined value of all others: "Because of numbers, the infinite numbers of others' rights and welfare naturally become most important. The welfare of others is important not only because of the sheer number, but also if you were to sacrifice the infinite others for your own happiness eventually you will lose. If you think more of others, taking care of others' rights and serving others, ultimately you will gain."[21]

Here His Holiness's belief in human equality, or sameness, combines with a utilitarian argument that the good of the greater number is, objectively, more important than the good of any individual. Therefore, the good of the group is more important than my narrowly conceived individual good, and I should act for the good of the group. There is an additional argument based upon interdependence: because my good is interdependent with the good of others, if others suffer I will suffer, too. Therefore, I should look after the good of the many, putting aside my narrowly conceived individual good if necessary, even for my own sake, as seen from the perspective of enlightened self-interest. We can also see the combination of these arguments as an implicit natural law argument: we cannot survive without society; society can survive without any one of us; therefore, it is "normal," as Buddhadasa would say, for us to put our individual interests aside for the sake of society. We shall see below, in fact, that Buddhadasa does see things in this way.

These kinds of reasons and sentiments result in His Holiness's well-known promotion of "universal responsibility":

> I am convinced that it is essential that we cultivate a sense of what I call universal responsibility. . . . What is entailed . . . is . . . a reorientation of our heart and mind away from self and toward others. To develop a sense of universal responsibility—of the universal dimension of our every act

and of the equal right of all others to happiness and not to suffer—is to develop an attitude of mind whereby, when we see an opportunity to benefit others, we will take it in preference to merely looking after our own narrow interests.[22]

Universal responsibility, then, is based upon human sameness ("the equal right of all others to happiness and not to suffer") and expressed in altruistic behavior, putting oneself second and others first. In the end, responsibility translates into a positive moral duty to care for others.

> A sense of responsibility toward all others also means that, both as individuals and as a society of individuals, we have a duty to care for each member of our society. . . . We need, therefore, to ensure that the sick and afflicted person never feels helpless, rejected, or unprotected. Indeed, the affection we show to such people is, in my opinion, the measure of our spiritual health, both at the level of the individual and at that of society.[23]

As individuals need to be responsible to society, so also society needs to be responsible to individuals. The rationales for these two forms of responsibility differ, however. The individual needs to be responsible to society because the good of the entire society outweighs the good of the individual. Society, however, needs to be particularly responsible to those individuals who need help. Those individuals who can take care of themselves have no special call on society's attention; it is the needy who require our care. The rationale for society's responsibility toward individuals, then, is compassion. We can see here one of several reasons why the Dalai Lama is sympathetic to human rights. Human rights are designed to protect people, whether individuals or in groups, who need protection from more powerful individuals or groups. They also can be seen as an expression of compassion.

BALANCING THE INDIVIDUAL AND SOCIETY: KARMA AND CONDITIONING, SELF-RELIANCE AND RESPONSIBILITY

There is no such thing as a "free will" in Buddhism. That such a "will," alone in the universe, could exist as some kind of entity free of all causal and conditioning influences from outside itself is an impossibility from a Buddhist perspective. This does not mean, however, that Buddhism sees humankind as fully determined. The entire enterprise of Buddhism is based upon the Buddha, and subsequent teachers, encouraging people to make wise choices. This enterprise would make no sense if people could not choose! From a Buddhist point of view, free will and determinism are the poles of a false dichotomy. The Western preoccupation with this issue may be traced to European Enlightenment thinking, epitomized by Descartes and carried forward by Kant, in which a person is regarded as an autonomous individual in which a transcendent reason and a free will are essential to the individual's identity. None of the terms in this constellation of concepts exist in Buddhist notions of the human person.

As we know, the starting point in Buddhist thought is very different. Buddhism sees the human being as a composite being, lacking in selfhood and highly interdependent with his or her surroundings. As Nhat Hanh says, "The individual is made of non-individual parts," and, as Maha Ghosananda says, "There is no self. There are only causes and conditions." These views open up an entirely different approach to certain ethical issues, an approach not without its own difficulties.

To see more clearly the ethical implications of *anātman* and the interpenetration of individual and society, I would like to focus on the issue of causation with respect to an individual's choices and actions. We have seen that Buddhists do not accept free will. What, then, is behind an individual's choices and action?

First of all, it is not the case that everything we do, including our present choices, is determined by past karma. This is a point heavily emphasized by the Buddha.

Payutto quotes the Buddha twice:

> Bhikkhus, when people take the kamma that they have done as the essential cause, then proper resolve (*chanda*), effort, and "this should be done — this should not be done" do not exist. When what should and should not be done are not established with seriousness and certainty, then it is as if these recluses and brahmins have lost their mindfulness, their control. The words of these recluses are not in accord with the Dhamma.[24]

> Bhikkhus, anyone who says that, "This person has performed this kamma and so now he is subject to this and that kamma," leaves no room for leading the Holy Life (*brahmacariya*), because he is blind to the way that leads to the complete elimination of dukkha.[25]

In other words, if people feel that their lives are predetermined, they will not make any effort either to live a moral life or to engage in religious practice. They will become passive, letting things happen to them, rather than trying to guide their own lives in a direction of their own choosing. The Buddha goes on to say that he came into this world precisely to exhort humankind not to commit moral misdeeds. The point of the Buddha's teaching about karmic causation is to persuade people to give up moral misdeeds now in order to eliminate karmic suffering in the future, not to feel trapped by any misdeeds committed in the past. In other words, it is essential that they exert themselves to make wise choices. They will not do that unless they believe that those choices are not simply fated, but real.

Having established that our present choices and actions are not determined, or fully caused, by our past karma, Payutto considers the role of external factors in influencing our choices. Payutto points to two factors, one internal and one external, that are especially stressed by the Buddha as important to Buddhist practice. "[O]ne, critical reflection (yonisomanasikāra), is the principle used in the Buddhist method of reflection and is considered very important to the internal, psychological process; two, association with good people (= having spiritual friends, kalyāṇa-mitta [Sanskrit] kalyāṇamitra), shows the importance of having the support of social factors, and it is held to be an important external factor."[26] Here we see that in a person's spiritual development both internal and external factors are regarded as important. We will discuss critical reflection later in this chapter; for now, let us learn more about the role of the kalyāṇamitta.

Again, Payutto quotes the Buddha: "Ananda, having a good spiritual friend (kalyāṇamitta) amounts to the whole of the Holy Life, because those who have found a good friend . . . have the desire to progress along the Noble Eightfold Path, and they will make great strides down this path."[27] Citing Pali texts, Payutto specifies that persons having a kalyāṇamitta gain several benefits. Monks would be aware of the rules of the order, which will help them to be virtuous. (By extension, a layperson would be aware of the Lay Precepts, which would also help them to be virtuous.) They would have the opportunity to hear and discuss the Buddhist ideals, which will hone and polish their character and cleanse their minds. They will have the support of a community that will help them to make their efforts well established — that is, to form good habits and practices.[28] Elsewhere the Buddha also makes it clear that practitioners benefit from living in a peaceful and harmonious society.

In other words, the Buddha recognized the role of external conditioning as a crucial support to personal development. Given that, as Maha Ghosananda says, 'there is no self; there are only causes and conditions,' it is clear that the causes and conditions to which one is exposed will play a very great role in shaping the beliefs, values, attitudes, inclinations, habits, and behaviors that constitute "the individual." Thus, it was natural, indeed inevitable, that the Buddha would emphasize the importance of external factors in influencing the future development of an individual engaged in Buddhist practice. If such a person has a *kalyāṇamitta*, which is to say a teacher, he or she would have access to the entire world of Buddhist teaching and Buddhist community. This would constitute wholesome causes and conditions shaping the individual and obviously make it far more likely that such a person would make progress on the Buddhist path.

In sum, though, as we saw above, each individual's moral choice is heavily emphasized, the importance of external conditioning agents is, at the same time, emphasized as playing a crucial role in influencing the individual's moral and spiritual development. If one were to ask which ultimately plays the greater role, self-determination through choice or the conditioning influence of external factors, one would have to say that one determines or constructs oneself, one's character, through one's choices. One uses critical reflection (*yonisomanasikāra*) in making these choices, and, at the same time, these choices are heavily influenced by the external factors to which one has been exposed and to which one has chosen to expose oneself. Thus, personal choice is the decisive factor for the Buddha, but that choice is neither "free" (totally isolated from external influence) nor "determined" (totally caused by external factors), but *influenced*. Buddhism stresses both the vital importance of human choice—half the point of Buddhism as a teaching is to urge people to make the right choices—and the vital importance to those choices of wholesome external influences—the other half of the point of Buddhism is to convey to people what the right choices are and to provide community to support those choices.

We now need to move on from the words of the Buddha and bring this issue into the contemporary thinking of the Engaged Buddhists. We have seen that the causal role played by society in conditioning the actions of the individual was recognized in a limited way in the teachings of the Buddha—the importance of a *kalyāṇamitta*, of living in a peaceful society, of knowing Buddhist teachings are all recognized. One of the achievements of Engaged Buddhism has been to enlarge that understanding with knowledge, often gained from Western social sciences, of the influence of such things as poverty and oppression on an individual's choices. Sarvodaya Shramadana premises its large and complex development program upon the interdependence of all factors—psychological, social, economic, cultural, religious, environmental—in influencing the health or dysfunction of a community and the individuals within it. Such an assumption is a given in Engaged Buddhism. We now need to examine how this enlarged understanding challenges the established understanding of the balance between internal and external, or individual and social, factors in influencing the choices an individual makes. We begin with the Dalai Lama:

[T]hose who would harm us give us unparalleled opportunities to practice disciplined behavior.

    This is not to say that people are not responsible for their actions. But let us remember that they may be acting largely out of ignorance. A child brought up in a violent environment may not know any other way to behave. As a result, the question of blame is rendered largely redundant.[29]

This sounds convincing. We know that His Holiness is right in his comment upon the child not knowing any other way, and it does follow that in such a case issues of blame seem inappropriate, but how far are we willing to take this idea? Will the same child, when he reaches adulthood, still be exempt from our blame?

    Nhat Hanh's most famous poem, "Please Call Me by My True Names," is a powerful statement of a nonjudgmental, yet highly moral, ethos. For many people, it raises questions regarding personal and social responsibility. I quote an excerpt:

> I am the mayfly metamorphosing on the surface of the river,
> and I am the bird which, when spring comes, arrives in time to eat the mayfly.
>
> I am the frog swimming happily in the clear water of a pond,
> and I am also the grass-snake who approaching in silence, feeds itself on the frog.
>
> I am the child in Uganda, all skin and bones, my legs as thin as bamboo sticks,
> and I am the arms merchant, selling deadly weapons to Uganda.
>
> I am the 12-year old girl, refugee on a small boat, who throws herself into the ocean after being raped by a sea pirate,
> and I am the pirate, my heart not yet capable of seeing and loving.[30]

In his comment on this poem, Nhat Hanh wrote,

> In my meditation I saw that if I had been born in the village of the pirate and raised in the same conditions as he was, I am now the pirate. There is a great likelihood that I would become a pirate. I cannot condemn myself so easily. In my meditation, I saw that many babies are born along the Gulf of Siam, hundreds every day, and if we educators, social workers, politicians,

and others do not do something about the situation, in 25 years a number of them will become sea pirates. That is certain. . . . If you take a gun and shoot the pirate, you shoot all of us, because all of us are to some extent responsible for this state of affairs.[31]

Nhat Hanh is drawing on the idea of *anātman* to reach the ethical position he occupies in this comment. With *anātman*, there is no self or soul to "be" good or bad. There are causes and conditions that lead to particular results. Sociological studies indicate that, statistically speaking, he is quite right in saying that "a number of them" will become pirates if social and economic factors remain the same. As members of society, we allow society to be as it is. On this basis, Nhat Hanh introduces the term "co-responsible" to refer to the shared responsibility of the pirate and his society—even the entire human community—for the rape of the twelve-year-old girl.

Some people balk at the idea of sharing responsibility for that rape. Even the Dalai Lama, despite the fact that he promotes "universal responsibility," does not see this matter as Nhat Hanh does:

> When I say that on the basis of concern for others' well-being we can, and should, develop a sense of universal responsibility, I do not . . . mean to suggest that each individual has a direct responsibility for the existence of, for example, wars and famines in different parts of the world. It is true that in Buddhist practice we constantly remind ourselves of our duty to serve all sentient beings in every universe. . . . But clearly certain things, such as the poverty of a single village ten thousand miles away, are completely beyond the scope of the individual. What is entailed, therefore, is not an admission of guilt but, again, a reorientation of our heart and mind away from self and toward others. . . . [T]hough, of course, we care about what is beyond our scope, we accept it as part of nature and concern ourselves with doing what we can.[32]

For His Holiness, then, even though interdependence does bind us all together, interdependence does not reach so far as to cause us to share responsibility for the pirate's act of rape. Considering both Nhat Hanh's and the Dalai Lama's perspective, it seems that our understanding of the relationship between interdependence and responsibility requires some fine-tuning. Although interdependence is a fact universally accepted by Buddhists, Indian Buddhist philosophy tends to see causality in degrees, with direct and indirect causes, supporting conditions, and so forth, sorted out and differentially weighted; in contrast, East Asian thought often sees causality in a more totalistic, sweeping, all-inclusive way. Is this why the Dalai Lama (Indo-Tibetan tradition) and Nhat Hanh (East Asian tradition) see this matter in different ways? Should we be taught by the Dalai Lama here and consider responsibility along the lines of Indian thought, with primary and secondary responsibility, or with degrees of responsibility? Would, for example, 90 percent responsibility for the pirate, 9 percent for Thai society, and 1 percent for the rest of us be fair? How about 50 percent for the pirate and 50 percent for society? Even U.S. law courts admit mitigating factors during the sentencing portion of a trial (after guilt is determined), but, on the other hand, our jails are full of people from impoverished backgrounds, racial minorities, people abused as children, and the like—and, even worse, we execute disproportionately large numbers of these populations. Are Engaged Buddhists able to shed light on this morass?

Returning to the poem, a related and even more controversial element is its treatment of the pirate and the arms merchant. The poem places them in a parallel position with the snake and the bird, thus suggesting that we should no more blame the human killers than the animal killers. In their situation, with their background, we would do the same. The poem suggests there is no place here for judgment or blame.

For many Westerners, this aspect of the poem has been a revelation and a liberation from the prison of judgmental thinking. This poem very successfully counters the tendency to complacent self-righteousness, distancing oneself from the "evil-doers," while judging them like God from above. It invites us to enlarge the compass of our compassion to embrace the pirate as well as the twelve-year-old girl and preserves morality without the need of judgment. But this very nonjudgmental thinking also makes many people uneasy. We can see Nhat Hanh's point: yes, in their situation, with their background, we probably would do the same (given *anātman*, in their situation, with their background, we would *be* them); yes, statistically speaking, it is inevitable that a certain number of those born into the same conditions will become pirates. But here is the rub: statistically speaking there is an inevitability that a certain number will become pirates. But what can we say of any given individual? Statistics cannot predict the actions of individuals. And why? Because humans have choices. That choice is conditioned; it does not occur in a vacuum, but choice is there. There is no inevitability when it comes to an individual's actions. We should recall that Buddhism traditionally does stress one's own responsibility for one's actions. That particular pirate was by no means fated by his background to rape that child. Both the Buddha and contemporary Engaged Buddhists passionately reject fatalism as utterly destructive of morality and the spiritual path. The pirate chose to rape the child, though that choice was heavily influenced by many causes and conditions outside himself.

Let us look at this issue from a very different perspective within the Engaged Buddhist world. We have seen that Thich Nhat Hanh removed responsibility for his deeds from the pirate by sharing that responsibility with society at large. In the *dalit* (ex-Untouchable) new Buddhist community founded by Ambedkar, we can see the exactly opposite principle at work. Dhammachari Lokamitra, a leader of the TBMSG in India, emphasizes the importance for the *dalit* new Buddhists of their consciously taking responsibility for their own actions and inactions. Decrying the "appalling living conditions and limited employment prospects" that plague the *dalit* Buddhists, Lokamitra points out that such conditions lead to resentment, insecurity, "and, perhaps worst of all, a victim mentality which only serves to perpetuate the helplessness and dependency that are part of the heritage of Untouchability." Referring to the writings of Ambedkar, Lokamitra writes,

> "Going for Refuge" means taking responsibility: not putting responsibility for unskillful thoughts, speech, and actions on to others or on external conditions; accepting responsibility for cultivating skillfulness of body, speech, and mind. . . .
>
> In India, Untouchability has led to attitudes of social, psychological, and material dependence for many. It is common to think that one can do nothing for oneself—any change must come from those in power. Feelings of worthlessness, helplessness, inertia, and passivity inevitably follow this attitude. . . . Dependence fosters a victim mentality, a state of paranoia in which everything unpleasant that befalls one is part of a conspiracy against one and the social community to which one belongs (from my experience in India there are objective validations for such paranoia, despite it being a subjective state). . . .
>
> Taking active and practical responsibility challenges such attitudes and demands change. We begin to develop self-reliance, confidence, initiative, and creativity. We learn that we can change our mental states, even in the most difficult circumstances. Instead of being a victim of circumstances, we see that we can positively affect others and the environment in which we live.[33]

Here Lokamitra makes clear the negative consequences of removing responsibility from someone—ultimately it means removing self-respect, individual initiative, and efforts at self-improvement. Responsibility is highly interrelated with power.

Those who do not have the power to do something cannot have the responsibility for doing it. Convince someone that she or he has responsibility to do something and she or he may become empowered, that is, begin to take action. For Lokamitra, therefore, it is an urgent priority in his work to support the *dalit* population in owning *more* responsibility for their condition, not less, despite the fact that they are, objectively, the victims of an immense injustice.

A similar way of thinking seems to be at work in the Sarvodaya Shramadana movement, which also consciously places self-reliance and empowerment at the center of its program. The reader may recall that everyone — even the poorest family — is expected to bring a contribution of food to a Sarvodaya community meal. A Shramadana organizer says of this, "Of course, her family is poor and of course we do not really need her little bit of rice or her betel leaf. But in giving it, she gets a new idea about herself."[34] What is the new idea that she gets about herself? That she is a person who is a giver, not always a receiver, that she contributes to her community, that she is a full member of it equal to the rest, that she helped to make this happy event possible. The thought is planted in her mind: if she can do this, what else might she be able to do?

Ariyaratne writes, "We believe that by raising the level of spiritual consciousness of people in a physical and social environment where needs are satisfied *as a result of self-reliance*, we are laying a strong psychological foundation for lasting peace within human minds and among human communities."[35] For Ariyaratne, "a Buddhist approach to development . . . is based on self-reliance and community participation at all stages."[36] As for Lokamitra, Ariyaratne also finds self-reliance — which presupposes taking responsibility for oneself — inherently empowering.

Having read the views of Nhat Hanh, the Dalai Lama, and Dhammachari Lokamitra and seen the practice of Sarvodaya Shramadana, what can we make of Engaged Buddhist thinking about who bears responsibility for an individual's action?

We have seen that the Engaged Buddhists all recognize the interdependence of individual and society. As Nhat Hanh puts it, the individual is made of non-individual parts (from society and nature) and society is made up of nonsociety parts (individuals). There is and can be no clear line between the two, because one shades into the other. This perspective points in the direction of a need for Engaged Buddhist ethical theory to identify the correct balance between the roles of individual and society as they interact in various ways; however, precisely because one shades into the other, the details of their interaction are unclear.

Buddhistically, we know that it is the case both that the pirate is creating terrible karma for himself when he harms another and that society also is creating terrible karma for itself when it allows conditions to exist that inevitably result in violence, disorder, and suffering. Both the individual pirate and society are harmed by allowing current conditions to exist. In this sense, their interests are nonadversarial, and, from both a Buddhist and a societal perspective, it is clearly best for society to intervene before more pirates are produced, by changing socioeconomic conditions for the better. In this sense, understanding the interdependence of individual and society clarifies matters. Leaders within society should be able to see their responsibility and act in good time, before problems develop.

With respect to criminal justice, however, understanding the interdependence of individual and society seems to have muddied the waters. Having added an expanded awareness of social causation to individual choice, Engaged Buddhism leaves us wondering to what degree social responsibility should be factored in alongside individual, personal responsibility when considering who bears responsibility for an action. We have seen that the Engaged Buddhists vary in their views of the relative weight for moral responsibility that should be given to individual choice and to societal influence. In practice, a society needs to come to a decision on this issue for criminal justice purposes. The ideal society based upon Engaged Buddhist principles would find some kind of balance between the two. But what is the correct balance? Is the pirate blameless, like the child the Dalai Lama mentioned, because of what his society did to him from the time he was a child? What would such an idea imply for a system of criminal justice? On the other hand, would it actually be in the interest of the pirate to be blamed for his act and held legally responsible for it, as Lokamitra and Ariyaratne could be interpreted as implying? If Engaged Buddhists ever governed a country, what would their legal system look like? Could they even have a criminal justice system? How can Engaged Buddhists properly balance individual and social responsibility? We will return to this subject in chapter 7, under the heading of "Criminal Justice."

These questions represent only one example of the inherent difficulty of identifying a correct balance between two things, individual and society, which are considered neither identical nor different. Let us examine another.

BALANCING THE INDIVIDUAL AND SOCIETY: POLITICAL THEORY

That it is not clear how the balance between individual and society is to be struck can be seen again in the contrasting views of Payutto and Buddhadasa as they explore the broad outlines of political philosophy for an ideal society built upon the values of Engaged Theravada Buddhism. I shall also bring Suu Kyi into the discussion from time to time.

As we saw in chapter 2, in the section on natural law, Payutto and Buddhadasa speak of the ethically good life as one in which one lives harmoniously in the midst of the web of interconnectivity. This view inevitably raises certain questions. We may formulate two of them as follows: (1) To what degree does this ethic recognize something of value in the individual *per se* and in individual freedom? And (2) in an interdependent world, how can one challenge injustice or a brutal government? Let us begin with the second question.

What Buddhadasa and Payutto describe as the moral necessity of living in harmony in the web of interdependence might be taken as supporting a laissez-faire response to the actions of oppressive governments. Do Buddhadasa's and Payutto's natural law ethics, with their emphasis on harmony and fitting in with the larger whole, in fact tacitly support government and cultural insistence upon mute obedience and resignation to the whims of powerful authority? Within this worldview, is one authorized to step out of the web of interdependence to say "no," or is such behavior "incorrect" by virtue of its disharmony?

To answer immediately, I do not believe that oppressive social and political consequences follow from the natural law ethic that I have outlined. Nor does it take a subtle argument to see that this is so. In the case of a government that brutalizes or oppresses its people, it is the government that is out of step with "the way things are" inasmuch as the Dhamma indicates that rulers and ruled live in mutual dependence and that "correctness" in their relationship is found in mutually beneficial support and harmony. A government that requires of its people in the name of harmony or fitting in with the greater whole that they accept brutal or oppressive government institutions and behavior is simply distorting the Dhamma. The Dhamma portrays a vast and complex web of interdependence with no particular center or pinnacle. It does not support one-sided insistence that "you harmonize with me" with no balancing in the opposite direction! "Fitting in with the way things are" simply means nonegocentrism and consideration of others; it applies to rulers as much as to the ruled. "The way things are," with which one *must* harmonize, refers to the natural law of conditionality; it does not refer to a particular social system that just happens to be in place. Indeed, from a Buddhist perspective, every social system is brought into existence by causes and conditions and will go out of existence when those causes and conditions change; there is clearly nothing ultimate or unchanging about a social system.

Moreover, an unjust or brutal government can be challenged on two grounds: (1) A social system that does not fit in with the natural law of conditionality could be indicted by virtue of that fact. That is, a government that pretends that it is ultimate and unchallengeable, that brutalizes or oppresses the people upon whom it depends would be so far out of harmony with the natural law of conditionality and mutual dependence that its existence would be utterly unjustified in Buddhadasa's and Payutto's terms. (2) A government that caused its people to suffer could easily be challenged on that ground, simply for the sake of putting an end to suffering. Eliminating suffering has always been the raison d'etre of Buddhism; compassion has always been one of its major virtues.

Buddhadasa actually writes that there are occasions when revolution may be justified, basing his view upon the ancient concept of the *dasarajadhamma*, the ten virtues that a king or ruler should embody: generosity, morality, liberality, uprightness, gentleness, self-restraint, nonanger, nonhurtfulness, forbearance, and nonopposition. He writes, "Do not blindly follow the political theories of someone who does not embody the dasarajadhamma system. . . . Indeed, revolution has a place in deposing a ruler who does not embody the dasarajadhamma, but not a place within a revolutionary political philosophy which espouses violence and bloodshed."[37]

What Buddhadasa seems to mean is that a government that embodies the ten virtues of a ruler should be respected and supported. One that lacks these qualities may, however, appropriately be replaced (though he qualifies this by saying that this is not appropriate if those who seek to overthrow the government are themselves violent, that is, lacking in the *dasarajadhamma*). Indeed, the idea of the *dasarajadhamma* itself confirms what was stated above, that this ethic of living in harmony with the larger whole certainly applies to rulers as much as to the ruled and requires of both nonegocentric and considerate behavior. In fact, Payutto asserts that, although everyone should cultivate the four Sublime States of Mind (*Brahmavihāra*, loving kindness, compassion, sympathetic joy, and equanimity), "great people, in their positions of status and leadership, should practice these values first and set a good example for others to follow."[38]

Granted that this ethic of fitting in harmoniously with the larger whole does not justify governmental oppression, let us widen the focus of this issue now by considering whether this ethic permits an individual to stand outside the group and say "no" to actually challenge an oppressive government. And let us consider this in the context of the first issue mentioned above, the question to what degree this ethic recognizes something of value in the individual per se and in individual freedom. These issues require clarification of the place of the individual and individualism within this system that emphasizes interconnectivity, harmony, and fitting in with the whole.

When we examine Buddhadasa's and Payutto's writing for their views on individualism, we see areas of agreement and of difference. The two agree on a crucial point, well rooted in tradition: the necessity of personally and independently engaging in critical thinking to develop insight, understanding, and wisdom. Buddhadasa states that, after one learns meditation and has gained "a workable mastery over the mind," one needs to develop insight. To do this, "one has to maintain the freedom of mind by not harboring attachment or clinging to any sectarian view or philosophy." Likewise one must remain unattached to "sectarian views" and to the *arhats*. "We should not even think that the Buddha can help us or can lead the way, because he says that we must search for the Truth by ourselves."[39] Thus, Buddhadasa, in line with tradition, emphasizes the importance of thinking for oneself, of maintaining intellectual freedom. With respect to our issue, we may conclude that a person who was trained in this way should have sufficient intellectual freedom to be able to say "no" when necessary, whether this required disagreeing with a personal acquaintance, with conventional wisdom, or (given sufficient courage) with an oppressive government.

Payutto also stresses the importance of critical reflection (*yonisomanasikāra*). He defines the latter as "engaging the mind, considering matters thoroughly in an orderly and logical manner through the application of critical or systematic reflection." He goes on:

Most people with undeveloped wisdom must still depend on the suggestions and encouragement of others and gradually follow these people until they achieve their own intelligence. But eventually these undeveloped people must practice until they are able to think correctly for themselves and can then proceed to the final goal on their own.

He then quotes the Buddha:

1. For bhikkhus, those in the process of learning, . . . I see no other external factor more beneficial than having a spiritual friend (*kalyāṇamitta* [in this context, a teacher]).
2. For bhikkhus, those in the process of learning. . . . I see no other internal factor more beneficial than critical reflection (*yonisomanasikāra*).[40]

Payutto emphasizes that "critical reflection works beyond the level of confidence (*saddhā* [often translated as "faith"]) because this is the stage at which people begin to think freely for themselves."[41]

We may take it, then, that Buddhadasa and Payutto agree on the importance of developing the ability to be independent, critical thinkers as an essential part of the Buddhist path. They both recognize intellectual freedom as a necessary good. Thus, a well-trained Buddhist should have the ability to say "no" when necessary.

It is interesting to note the comments on critical thinking of Suu Kyi, for whom these are real and urgent issues.

> I've always said that [the Burmese people] really must learn to question people who order them to do things which are against justice and existing laws. Ask, according to which law are you forcing me to do this? What right do you have to make me do this? They've also got to ask themselves, should we do this? People must ask questions and not just accept everything.
>
> . . . Intellectuals are very important in any society. Because they are the ones who . . . are provoking people, opening them to new ideas, pushing them along to new heights. . . . The intellectual with his questioning mind threatens the totalitarian mind which expects orders to be carried out and decrees to be accepted without question. There will always be clashes between the authoritarian mind and the questioning mind. They just cannot go together.[42]

For Suu Kyi, then, a habit of critical thinking is crucial to society. Because the questioning (or questing) mind and the totalitarian mind are antithetical, it would seem that the promotion of critical thinking would be in the interest of a society that wanted to avoid totalitarianism.

Despite the fundamental agreement between Payutto and Buddhadasa on the subject of intellectual freedom, when we turn to their views on political freedom, we find a striking disagreement between the two, one that has strong implications for their understandings of individuality and its value.

Buddhadasa writes,

> Liberal democracy . . . upholds the ideal of freedom. . . . But the freedom it upholds is so ambiguous that it seems always to be controlled by the power of human defilements (kilesa). . . . The liberal philosophy or ideology of freedom does not have the power to resist the strength of human defilements. The ambiguity of the meaning of liberal democracy promotes the idea that anything one wants to do is all right. The thug as well as the wise man claims freedom for himself. . . . We must accept the fact that we all have defilements. . . . Liberal democracy cannot deal effectively with this fact. . . .

The word *freedom* as it is widely interpreted is actually inconsistent with the fundamental meaning of politics. If we think of politics as something that concerns groups of people living together, then the emphasis of a political system would be the well-being of the entire group. *Freedom*, on the other hand, is an individual matter. An emphasis on personal freedom shifts the focus from the group to the individual. Such a focus is at odds with the meaning of politics.[43]

In light of his strong commitment to independent, critical thinking and his own magnificent practice of it, it is puzzling that Buddhadasa was so suspicious of individual political freedom. The last paragraph of the above quotation demonstrates that the tension between individualism and the web of interconnectivity is at the bottom of this issue for Buddhadasa. For him, politics is about the group, not the individual. The individual and his or her claims of freedom take a backseat to the good of the entire group.

Payutto agrees with Buddhadasa up to a point. He agrees that liberty will be misused by those whose minds are in the power of the defilements.

Liberty can only be successful and lead to true democracy when people use it with a wisdom that is impartial and sincere. If the mind is in the grip of the defilements, how can impartiality and sincere wisdom arise? As long as we are guided by greed, aversion and delusion, our "wisdom" is also guided by these things. Our thinking will be attuned to personal gain and destruction of our enemies, and immersed in delusion. It is impossible for any benefit to arise in society in such a situation.[44]

Payutto, however, also discusses freedom in a much more optimistic manner. Payutto immediately dismisses any idea of freedom meaning that one can do anything that one wants, acknowledging that, because human beings must live together, social and political freedom, or liberty, can never be absolute. He recognizes that there are various kinds of political liberty, the best of which is "a balance or harmony" that is "a product of wisdom and understanding" in which one's own liberty is "related to the liberty of other beings."[45] He then, unlike Buddhadasa, goes on to discuss the potential positive consequences, for society, of individual freedom.

The democratic system is the system of government which seeks to provide maximum opportunity for people to express their social potential. Liberty here, then, is the ability to contribute personal potential to overall social growth. Everybody has their potential and abilities, but they cannot be expressed without freedom. Without liberty, people cannot voice their views or make use of their intelligence. Society in turn derives no benefit from their potential.[46]

Here it is clear that individual freedom can be a positive good that has the potential to add something constructive to human society and without which society is definitely the poorer.

From the perspective of her firsthand experience, Suu Kyi entirely agrees with Payutto on this point: "Under authoritarian regimes, where you are only allowed to express certain things, the growth of talent becomes distorted. It can't flower. Like a tree that becomes distorted because it's trained to go just one way—the way that's acceptable to the authorities. So there can never be a genuine flowering or burst of talent and creativity."[47] Despite their shared natural law view of Buddhist ethics, Payutto and Buddhadasa come to significantly different conclusions on the issues of political freedom and the relationship between the individual and society. In turn, this produces different views on the more desirable political system. Payutto favors a "dhammic democracy" that balances the interests of individual and society, in which all social institutions—government, education, religion, media, family, and so forth—strive to shape individuals in the direction of dhammic values—freedom from the three poisons (greed, hatred, and delusion) and nurturance of the four Sublime States (loving kindness, compassion, sympathetic joy, equanimity) and of mindfulness and wisdom. "The aim is to create a society that is of optimum benefit to both the individuals within it and the collective whole, and this aim is realized by carefully looking into things and perceiving that which is based on truth, benefit and goodness."[48]

For Payutto, then, "to demand democracy is to demand development," because liberty is only a good when in the hands of those with developed minds. Note, however, that all people have this potential:

All people have a potential that is capable of development and utilization to realize a fulfilling life and constructive and harmonious community.

The recognition of human potential also implies that human beings require development. Their wisdom and mindfulness need honing so that they can look at things with discernment and use their liberties intelligently.[49]

Payutto is concerned that democracy often is in the hands of the undeveloped, and in those cases it functions poorly. If it is in the hands of those who adhere to Dhamma, though, democracy can function well.

> By adhering to Dhamma even in a negative sense, by giving up pride, craving and views in favor of the Dhamma, people are capable of governing themselves. When they have this capability, democracy becomes a viable reality. The kind of people who can govern themselves are those who uphold the Dhamma.
>
> Therefore, in a [Dhammic] democratic society, people will yield to each other for the sake of truth, goodness, reason and benefit, for that condition which is really attuned to solving problems.[50]

Suu Kyi has the same kind of reservations about democracy that Payutto and Buddhadasa express: concern that human selfishness will take advantage of the freedom available in democracy. But, like Payutto, she endorses democracy as the best form of government. Indeed, she has staked her life and liberty upon the struggle for democracy in Burma:

> I have always said that once we get democracy, there will be people who misuse their democratic rights and use them just for their own pleasure or personal gain. . . . Democracy is far from perfect. . . . I don't agree with everything that's happening in the West, which is why I say that I would like our democracy to be a better, more compassionate and more caring one. That is not to say we have fewer freedoms. But that we will use these freedoms more responsibly and with the well-being of others in mind.[51]

Thus, although Suu Kyi is concerned about the misuse of the liberty available in democracy, she sees the answer to this problem in greater measures of responsibility and compassion, that is, in more concern for others and the good of the whole. Payutto also speaks of the importance of responsibility. "The more freedom there is, the more is a sense of responsibility necessitated. If liberty is coupled with a sense of responsibility, a balance—a Middle Way—will result, ensuring the creation of a true democracy."[52]

Buddhadasa, on the other hand, favors a dhammic socialism, one in which the interests of the individual take a definite backseat to the interests of the group.[53] "A more controlled form of democracy which is better able to cope with human defilement is socialism . . . which is opposed to the ideal of the individual freedom of liberalism. Socialism focuses on social utility, and the examination and correction of social problems. Liberalism cannot provide a basis for social utility because it promotes selfishness, individual benefits rather than social benefits. . . . Dhammic socialism can save the world from what appears to be its self-destructive course."[54]

It seems that Buddhadasa may have been more pessimistic than Payutto regarding the degree of realistic expectation he was willing to grant human potential. In political liberty, Buddhadasa sees only license for the *kilesa* to run amok. Payutto, though acknowledging that the *kilesa* are in fact running amok in the world today, still hopes that with proper education and social engineering we may control our *kilesa* sufficiently for our human potential to flourish constructively, and, moreover, he sees no other way forward.

In addition to this judgmental difference, there is a deeper and more substantive difference between the two regarding their philosophical understandings of the relationship between the individual and society. Both thinkers assume the interdependence of individual and society. Let us, however, imagine them faced with the following question: when a choice must be made between one or the other side of this interdependent pair—individual and society—which one should be favored?

Buddhadasa clearly favors society over the individual, apparently for two reasons. First, as we have seen, Buddhadasa strongly emphasizes the extent to which the individual is severely afflicted with the *kilesa*, causing him to greatly fear that those *kilesa* will cause the individual to harm himself and society. Second, Buddhadasa stresses more than Payutto the idea that morality involves harmony, balance, and "fitting in." He believes that, although all parts of life are interdependent, the smaller units must give way to the larger units. To seek one's individual good at the expense of the good of the group would be purely selfish and for that reason unjustifiable. The good of the group, of society, is the appropriate concern of politics. Social benefits, he says, are the proper focus of our concern, not individual benefits. In short, the focus of his thinking about interdependence is the interdependence among individuals that constitutes the group; this, to Buddhadasa, implies the transcendence of the group over the individual.

Payutto differs from Buddhadasa inasmuch as, though he acknowledges it, he does not emphasize the defilement-bound present condition of humankind, but rather emphasizes our *potential* to be *either* defilement-bound *or* relatively defilement-free. Nonetheless, it is certainly not the case that he favors the individual over society in the sense that, if forced to favor one over the other, he would favor the individual and let society suffer. I believe that, for Payutto, the individual and society are so interdependent that he would regard the question of choosing between them as improper. In his view, interdependence means not only the interdependence of individuals within the group, but also of the individual and society. Thus, even though individual freedom has indeed led to a great deal of misery for human society, it is still necessary to society that sufficient freedom be granted to the individual, or society itself will suffer anyway: society cannot improve from its present level of degradation without constructive contributions from individuals. Because the individual and society are interdependent, the only hope is for wise people to use their interdependence with others to shape others, both through individual influence and institutional structures (for example, schools) that cultivate our potential for good. If society were to use its power to radically limit individual freedom, both the individual and society would lose. If society allows individuals a great deal of freedom and establishes institutions that promote wholesome human development, both individual and society gain.[55]

Buddhadasa and Payutto are arguably the two greatest Buddhist thinkers of modern Thailand. As such, their ideas represent some of Thailand's most important and best-known modern interpretations of Theravada Buddhism. Though the core of their natural law ethical views is similar, their nuances are sufficiently different that they ultimately recommend substantially different paths for the development of political institutions in Thailand (and, potentially, other modernizing Theravada Buddhist countries). Their views may be a good indication of both the range of political options that is defensible on the basis of a modern reading of Theravada thought and values—from dhammic democracy to dhammic socialism—and the limits of such options—a government that does not embody the self-restraint, morality, and good will of the *dasarajadhamma* is simply illegitimate from a Buddhist perspective.[56]

Before leaving this subject, we should consider the views of two Engaged Buddhists who are not so much philosophers, as are Buddhadasa and Payutto, but more activist leaders: Ariyaratne and Sulak. Both advocate a small-scale, participatory democracy as the desirable political form.

Sulak discusses the effects of the globalization of trade on the traditional way of life in a country like Thailand—effects that may include losing the land on which families live and farm, forcing them to move to the cities to earn a livelihood. When that happens, says Sulak, the institutions that govern our lives become centralized and remote, precluding meaningful participation in the decision-making process. As a consequence, "the ethical values which are dependent upon an appreciation of oneself as a member of a community with a responsibility for the welfare of others in the community cannot be sustained." That is, with dislocation and urbanization, one is no longer part of a small community in which the members of the community together make the decisions that affect them. Even though these decisions are community decisions, the individual participates in those decisions and is part of them. Dislocation from this kind of community therefore takes out of the hands of the individual a considerable part of his control over fundamental aspects of his life. In this way, the individual loses an important part of his freedom. Hand in hand with this loss of control, or individual freedom, goes the disintegration of a community life based upon mutual concern and responsibility. Sulak claims that "it is only through the establishment of a public sphere where one becomes engaged in the process of making decisions which will affect himself and other members of the community that one comes to recognize social responsibilities and the nature of human interdependence."[57]

What Sulak has in mind here is a kind of small-scale village or town community in which each individual (ideally) might participate in making decisions in a context in which everyone recognizes the importance of looking after the good of the entire group. Thus, very little conflict of interest is presumed between the individual and the group because each individual can very clearly see that his or her good is inseparable from the good of the entire group. For Sulak, such a system presupposes a small enough scale that each individual can participate in the decision-making process. It would also presuppose that each individual intends to remain in the community and presumes that his or her children and grandchildren likewise will remain in the community. In such a context, one can indeed see that the good of the group does *generally* tend to be the good of the individual and vice versa.

Thus, Sulak sees the encroachment of globalizing power upon such village life resulting in a situation in which both individual freedom *and* the community of mutual responsibility lose ground. In this scenario, individual freedom and social responsibility are not opposed, but rather are two aspects of a community constituted by individuals engaged in a joint process of decision making that affects each individual and the community as a whole.

The kind of community life to which Sulak alludes, Ariyaratne has been working to construct in Sri Lanka for four decades. The Sarvodaya Shramadana is very much a movement that aims to empower poor people and strengthen community ties. In this way, the strengthening of individuals and the strengthening of the community are approached as interdependent.

How is this done? The classic Sarvodaya institution is the *shramadana* (donating work) camp, the first major event when Sarvodaya enters a village, at the village's invitation, to help organize a project to improve the community. In an underdeveloped country such as Sri Lanka, the projects that are typically undertaken include road building or the construction of clean water systems or latrines. Throughout the planning and execution of the project, the community uses "family gatherings" to organize itself and make decisions. These are highly participatory events in which emphasis is put upon gaining contributions from as many different individuals and different kinds of individuals as possible. Children as well as adults, women as well as men, the powerful and the relatively powerless, are all encouraged to contribute their perspectives and ideas. Decision making is by consensus. Thus, in this single institution, the individual is strengthened, or empowered, by sitting side by side with his or her peers and participating equally in examining the merits of proposed actions and deciding with equal voice what the group shall do. The community is strengthened by having its needs put first, by having the collective insight and energy of the group devoted to it, by having so many of its constituent parts (individuals) feeling empowered, by having the sense of community strengthened among the individuals, and, at the end, by having a new road or well or latrine. All of this draws upon the Buddhist idea of self-reliance, particularly strongly emphasized in Theravada. The community does not wait for the government to come and put in a road; if they want a road, they take care of it themselves. The individual does not let someone else take care of what needs to be done; men, women, and children pitch in side by side with their ideas and physical labor.

Here we see the strengthening of individuals and the strengthening of the community as two interdependent elements of a single process. Reflecting upon decades of this kind of experience, Ariyaratne notes a number of elements in this approach to development that empower both the individual and the community. Because the community's decisions are based upon full participation in the decision-making process and decisions are made by means of consensus, the shramadana camp is an exercise in participatory democracy that enables both individuals and communities to manage their own affairs simultaneously. Because there is a specific project to focus on, individual ideas and initiatives are welcome and may be adopted by the group; at the same time, individuals work in groups. The aim is for power to be held on the local level; when power is held at the local level, as Sulak also says, the individual participates in that power together with others in the community. In this way, self-reliance and community participation merge in a shramadana project.[58] As Ariyaratne says, "Sarvodaya has committed itself to a dynamic non-violent revolution which is not a transfer of political, economic, or social power from one party or class to another, but the transfer of all such power to the people."[59]

Of course, even in an ideal scenario there will always be individual differences in power based upon individual variation in characteristics like timidity, skill, and so forth. The idea here, though, is to maximize the power given to the individual and to the local community. For Ariyaratne, this is done so that the community can lift itself out of poverty and all that goes along with poverty, in order to create optimal conditions supporting the process of the individual's self-development, or progress to awakening. Every step of the way, in Ariyaratne's vision, the good of the community enhances the good of the individual and vice versa.

For Ariyaratne, the Sarvodaya process of community development is a process of village self-empowerment, a process he envisions as developing into what he calls *gram swaraj*, or village self-rule.[60] Many Sarvodaya programs that do, in fact, empower the village and its members economically, socially, and politically are already in place. Preschools established by Sarvodaya in thousands of villages function independently of the government under complete village control. Small business loans are made, clean water is provided, roads are built, self-policing systems are established, and people are trained in practical and social skills, all under village control and without any intervention by government. Because these are services that government often provides, to the extent that Sarvodaya villages provide these services for themselves, they are already embarking upon *gram swaraj*.

Sarvodaya, however, sees the possibility of greater village self-rule. Two programs with far-reaching implications for village self-rule and participatory democracy are Sarvodaya's banking and information technology programs. Sarvodaya is presently in the process of establishing the Sarvodaya Development Bank, which would link the banks it has already established on the village level. Once established, this bank would have resources of 1 billion rupees and serve a half a million people, making it one of the largest banks in Sri Lanka.[61] Sarvodaya's village-level banks support development according to Sarvodaya's values and keep the village's money in the local community and under village control. Linking them will produce a stronger banking system, giving Sarvodaya villages even more autonomy from national financial power. Similarly, Sarvodaya has recently made it a priority to develop information technology (telephone, e-mail, and computers) in the villages, promoting access to the tools of communication in its village and regional "telecenters."[62] Ariyaratne intends to use technology to link the villages electronically, fostering their ability to network and develop themselves economically and politically in an entirely decentralized, grassroots manner, without ever plugging in to national economic and political systems, creating, as he puts it, "highly decentralized communities . . . getting networked together and bypassing the centers of power."[63]

Ariyaratne recognizes that, though Sarvodaya villages have made tremendous strides in development and self-empowerment, they are not immune from the power of the national government and its pursuit of political and economic policies that lead to continued civil war and erode the viability of village life. Ultimately, Ariyaratne believes that the Sri Lankan political system and the present form of national government in Sri Lanka must be replaced by an entirely different form of governance that decentralizes power as fully as possible, building upon self-governing villages (and urban neighborhoods) linked together in a loose federation, putting an end to a system of power held by elites and replacing it with a system of power held by ordinary people. Ariyaratne envisions that such a change could come about in one of two ways: either the present system will crash under the weight of its own corruption and inherent lack of viability or, when a critical mass of Sri Lankan villages have attained self-rule and practical autonomy from the state, they will be able to declare their independence from the state.[64]

In sum, Ariyaratne and Sulak see the best hope for an ideal way of life residing in a small community that uses participatory democracy and is free of outside domination. In such a community, the good of the individual and of the community are interdependent; that interdependence is clear to those who live in the community. Both individual and community are empowered as decision making is collective yet everyone participates in it. We may observe that the balance between individual and society that they portray in such a community seems to embody an Engaged Buddhist ideal: the good of both individual and society is realized, both individual and society are empowered, and the individual's freedom as well as responsibility to the community are both enhanced.

To what extent could such an ideal become a reality? This could be tested in a concrete way by a careful study of Sarvodaya villages. To what extent might such a scenario continue to be viable in our increasingly urbanized and globalized world? That is more difficult to say.

5 Human Rights

Many Engaged Buddhist leaders speak of human rights regularly and even insistently. Here are three examples.

A. T. Ariyaratne, founder and director of the Sarvodaya Shramadana organization of Sri Lanka, is a consistent advocate of human rights in Sri Lanka. The objectives of the organization's peace center, Vishva Niketan ("Universal Abode") are to

> Acknowledge in all activities, inviolable and inalienable human rights as the basis of peace and justice of every community in the world, where all citizens shall be assured of their human worth and dignity while they on their part discharge their responsibilities to others.[1]

Maha Ghosananda, head of Cambodian Buddhism and called the "Gandhi of Cambodia," states,

> Cambodian people must obtain all basic human rights, including rights of self-determination and rights to freely pursue economic, social, and cultural development.[2]

Sulak Sivaraksa, Thai Buddhist layperson and tireless social reformer, writes,

> The defense of human rights takes ethical precedence over national sovereignty. Most people are able to accept this tenet when addressing an obvious abuse such as apartheid. In that case, the claim by the minority whites that the world should not interfere in South Africa's internal affairs is not seen as a legitimate application of national sovereignty. By the same token, other regimes that deny their citizens full, free, and equal participation in the decision-making that affects their lives should thereby lose international recognition of their legitimacy.[3]

In addition, human rights are the cornerstone of the national campaigns of three Buddhist countries embroiled in particularly acute struggles: Tibet, Cambodia, and

Burma. For example, if one looks at the web site of the Tibetan government in exile,[4] one will see that "human rights" is one of the main categories under which they organize information relevant to the Tibetan situation. If one clicks on the "Human Rights" link, another page will come up that lists dozens of individual and collective cases of violations of human rights in Tibet, along with periodic "Human Rights Updates" summarizing the human rights situation there.[5] In the case of Cambodia, if one types "Cambodia" and "human rights" into an Internet search engine, a list of dozens of Cambodian and international nongovernmental organizations will be generated, all of which focus on efforts to ameliorate the human rights situation in Cambodia. Many of these make explicit connections between human rights values and Buddhist values. For example, the web site of the Cambodian Institute of Human Rights discusses the institute's many activities on behalf of human rights in Cambodia. This includes the Human Rights Teaching Methodology project, which has trained 25,000 teachers on "how best to convey messages about human rights, peace, democracy, and nonviolence. These teachers teach almost 3 million Cambodian school children every school year." They then go on to point out,

> Buddhism never vanished from the hearts of the Cambodian people during the dark years. There are parallels between modern ideas like democracy, human rights, and good governance and the ancient teachings of the Buddha—on treating other people with respect and kindness. The principle of non-violence (avihimsa), means less harm is done to others. Besides the initial five Buddhist precepts . . . , four other Buddhist principles of interpersonal behavior are relevant: [namely, the four] Brahmavihara. . . . These ideas, or Buddhism at least, is familiar and acceptable to all Cambodians, including leaders, so they are much more likely to be received favorably than if we simply talked about the International Covenant on Civil and Political Rights or other complicated documents considered Western and even alien.[6]

In Burma, the popular struggle against the military dictatorship understands itself as a movement for democracy and human rights. Aung San Suu Kyi writes,

> The people of Burma view democracy not merely as a form of government but as an integrated social and ideological system based on respect for the individual. When asked why they feel so strong a need for democracy, the least political will answer: "We just want to be able to go about our own

business freely and peacefully, not doing anybody any harm, just earning a decent living without anxiety and fear." In other words they want the basic human rights which would guarantee a tranquil, dignified existence free from want and fear.[7]

Of all subjects connected with Engaged Buddhism, the subject of human rights has generated more discussion than any other. This discussion of Buddhism and human rights, moreover, occurs within the context of a larger discussion regarding the status of human rights in the international context. That discussion centers upon whether human rights are "Western" or truly universal. On this larger question, the leaders of many countries, human rights nongovernmental organizations, religious leaders, and scholars have all had much to say. Spokespersons for a number of Asian countries have been particularly active in these discussions.

This larger discussion, as well as the Buddhist discussion, is shaped by several human rights documents generated and approved by the international community under the auspices of the United Nations. The most important of these documents, and the one to which all interested parties frequently refer, is the Universal Declaration of Human Rights (UDHR), adopted by the General Assembly of the United Nations in 1948. Two subsequent international human rights covenants also stand out: the International Covenant on Economic, Social, and Cultural Rights and the International Covenant on Civil and Political Rights. They were approved by the United Nations in 1966 and entered into force in 1976. Together, these three documents are called the International Bill of Human Rights. Other treaties elaborate aspects of human rights requiring special attention, such as genocide and racism, and pertaining to populations requiring special protection, such as women, children, refugees, and indigenous peoples.

As understood internationally, the term "human rights" refers specifically to the rights protected by the International Bill of Rights. Human rights scholars often point out that the list of rights claimed in these documents developed historically as the international community acted to further elaborate the rights recognized internationally. Such scholars refer to "three generations" of rights that have developed thus far.[8] The first, embodied especially in the UDHR, focuses on the recognition of civil and political rights and liberties. Specified rights in this category named in the UDHR include the right to life, liberty, and personal security; protection from slavery, torture, and cruel, inhuman, or degrading treatment or punishment; equality before the law, protection from arbitrary arrest or detention, and hearings before an independent and impartial tribunal; freedom of movement and residence; the right to a nationality; freedom of thought, conscience, and religion; freedom of opinion, expression, and the press; freedom of assembly and association; the right to political participation; and a government based upon the will of the people. Even in this first human rights document, certain social and economic rights are mandated, specifically a right to work with just remuneration; the right to rest and leisure; the right to an adequate standard of living; the right to an education; and the right to participate in cultural life. Significantly, for our purposes, the UDHR also states, "Everyone has duties to the community in which alone the free and full development of his personality is possible" (Article 29).

The "second generation" of human rights is embodied particularly in the two international covenants mentioned above that came into force in 1976. These do not actually add very much that is new to the basic rights of the UDHR, but they do give special emphasis and further elaboration to the social and economic rights mentioned in the UDHR. The "third generation," which presently is under development, focuses particularly on the collective rights of peoples to self-determination and to the maintenance of their own culture. Quite significant in this category is the Draft Declaration on the Rights of Indigenous Peoples, not yet approved by the United Nations at this writing. This document intentionally refers to the rights of a people as a whole, as opposed to the rights of individuals stressed in earlier generations of United Nations human rights documents. So, for example, the draft document states,

Article 6.
Indigenous peoples have the collective right to live in freedom, peace and security as distinct peoples and to full guarantees against genocide or any other act of violence. . . .

Article 7.
Indigenous peoples have the collective and individual right not to be subject to ethnocide and cultural genocide, including the prevention of and redress for:

(a) Any action which has the aim or effect of depriving them of their integrity as distinct peoples, or of their cultural values or identities; . . .
(c) Any form of population transfer which has the aim or effect of violating or undermining any of their rights.

The Draft Declaration on the Rights of Indigenous Peoples thus reflects a marked evolution in thinking on the subject of human rights—from individual rights to individual and *collective* rights. Although it is not yet in force, because of the opposition of a number of nations, it is very strongly supported by indigenous peoples and many nongovernmental organizations and has made a significant impact on global thinking about human rights.

When the term "human rights" is used, the rights specified in the International Bill of Human Rights are what are generally understood in the international community. Because of the familiarity and prestige of the UDHR, however, many people take a narrower focus and understand "human rights" to be the rights specified in the UDHR alone. The reader will see this reflected in the discussion in this chapter. Although this narrower understanding of the scope of human rights is not correct, human rights scholars correctly stress that the rights specified in the two subsequent "generations" of human rights are all present in embryonic form in the UDHR.

Such is the content of the current human rights agenda. But what are the issues? Again it is useful to place the issues specific to Buddhism and human rights in a larger context. Here the relevant context is the so-called Asian values debate that began in the early 1990s. "Asian values" is the phrase put forward by several Asian officials in order to challenge what they claimed to be "Western" ideas of human rights and civil liberties. They held that such ideas were a part of the Western individualism that has produced the crime, corruption, and general immorality they saw as common in the West, whereas Asian culture, they said, values the family and society over the individual and therefore has produced a more communitarian society, with less disorder. As such, they had no desire for Western values to intrude into Asian society. As Lee Kuan Yew [of Singapore] put it, Asians have "little doubt that a society with communitarian values where the interests of society take precedence over that of the individual suits them better than the individualism of America."[9]

Joanne Bauer and Daniel Bell point out that, although they are politically inspired, these comments by Lee Kuan Yew and similar statements by Prime Minister Mahathir Mohamad of Malaysia struck a sympathetic chord in many parts of Asia and ignited an extended philosophical debate on the nature of human rights and the extent to which they belong to Western culture or are sufficiently universal to apply to all societies and cultures.[10] Specifically, the "Asian values" debate considers whether the civil and political liberties of the international human rights documents presuppose Western individualism and promote adversarial relationships within society, values that, the argument claims, are antithetical to "Asian" society, which is communitarian in nature and places greater emphasis on social harmony than does the West. As a consequence, it is claimed, human rights are not only Western, as opposed to universal, but if imposed upon Asia would funda-mentally alter the nature of Asian society for the worse. Another claim made by the "Asian values" side is that the civil and political liberties proclaimed in human rights documents are a luxury that only rich, developed states can afford to make available to its citizens, while less wealthy developing states must concentrate on economic development.

The earlier chapters of this work will have demonstrated the relevance of the first of these two concerns for Buddhism. Buddhism, as we have seen, though not devoid of individualistic elements, does have strong communitarian instincts. The debate between Buddhadasa Bhikkhu and Phra Payutto regarding the rela-tive importance of individual freedom and "fitting in" harmoniously with the web of interdependent social relations is an indication of how difficult this matter is to resolve within the framework of Buddhist philosophy. We will return to this issue below.

For now, let us begin with an easier issue: the complaint that human rights are not appropriate for Asian societies simply because it is a Western concept. Such complaints play on the fears of developing states and resentment of Western hege-mony. I have not seen a Buddhist activist or scholar make this particular objection. Activists claim that those who make this objection tend to be Asian dictators, whose claims, after some examination, are dismissed as mere rhetoric intended to ward off challenges to their autocratic use of power. Engaged Buddhist leaders are among those who roundly denounce such pronouncements.

Suu Kyi does not mince her words in responding to such claims, claims that the Burmese military rulers also have made. Burma is one of the countries in which Engaged Buddhists have made human rights a cornerstone of their national struggle. Suu Kyi writes,

Opponents of the movement for democracy in Burma have sought to undermine it by . . . condemning the basic tenets of democracy as un-Burmese. There is nothing new in Third World governments seeking to justify and perpetuate authoritarian rule by denouncing liberal democratic principles as alien. . . .

It was predictable that as soon as the issue of human rights became an integral part of the movement for democracy the official media should start ridiculing and condemning the whole concept of human rights, dubbing it a western artefact alien to traditional values. It was also ironic—Buddhism, the foundation of traditional Burmese culture, places the greatest value on man, who alone of all beings can achieve the supreme state of Buddhahood. Each man has in him the potential to realize the truth through his own will and endeavour and to help others to realize it. Human life therefore is infinitely precious. "Easier it is for a needle dropped from the abode of Brahma to meet a needle stuck in the earth than to be born as a human being." . . .

It is a puzzlement to the Burmese how concepts which recognize the inherent dignity and the equal and inalienable rights of human beings, which accept that all men are endowed with reason and conscience and which recommend a universal spirit of brotherhood, can be inimical to indigenous values. It is also difficult for them to understand how any of the rights contained in the thirty articles of the Universal Declaration of Human Rights can be seen as anything but wholesome and good. That the declaration was not drawn up in Burma by the Burmese seems an inadequate reason, to say the least, for rejecting it, especially as Burma was one of the nations which voted for its adoption in 1948. If ideas and beliefs are to be denied validity outside the geographical and cultural bounds of their origin, Buddhism would be confined to north India, Christianity to a narrow tract in the Middle East and Islam to Arabia.[11]

In compelling defense of these words, it is worth noting that human rights ideas became so popular during the struggle for democracy in Burma, that a popular song expressing the longing for democracy incorporated human rights language into the lyrics cited above: "I am not among the rice-eating robots. . . . Everyone but everyone should be entitled to human rights."[12]

A brief look at the history of the framing of human rights declarations will shed light on the issue of the putative "Western" nature of international human rights. As Sumner Twiss sees it, the UDHR came into being in 1948 as a response of the international community to the brutality and genocide of the World War II. In response to this watershed event of inhumanity, representatives of the many nations and cultures in the United Nations agreed that such acts were "antithetical to each and all of their traditions." This judgment was expressed in rights language in the UDHR. "The fact that rights-language was employed was doubtless due to the dominance of the Western legal tradition in the international arena, but the mutually agreed upon judgment about the proscription of certain acts was not exclusively a 'Western' moral judgment."[13]

The subsequent human rights documents of the 1960s and 1970s were an affirmation that the oppression and poverty of developing countries was unacceptable to the global community. It is important to note that non-Western representatives played a much more prominent role in the negotiations leading to these documents. The same was true of the negotiations that produced the 1979 convention on the protection of women's human rights and the 1993 UN Draft Declaration on the Rights of Indigenous Peoples. Twiss's conclusion is that these international documents represent a true global consensus.

> [F]ar from preempting or replacing the rich moral teachings of various cultural traditions, specific expressions of human rights concerns have arisen from the mutual recognition by adherents of these traditions that they have a shared interest in the protection of certain values. Brutality, tyranny, starvation, discrimination, displacement, and the like are recognized by adherents of all traditions as their common enemy.[14]

Onuma Yasuaki confirms and extends Twiss's point. While acknowledging that the UDHR is "relatively West-centric," he is convinced that subsequent documents do not share this failing.

> The Vienna Declaration [on Human Rights of 1993] . . . was a product of elaborate negotiations accommodating not only differences in terms of foreign policies, but also conflicts involving diverse religious, cultural, and ethical views held by almost all nations composing the international society. Its intercivilizational legitimacy is strengthened relative to the Universal Declaration.

He concludes that international human rights documents "represent common normative standards based on the widest attainable consensus among nations with diverse perspectives." In his judgment as well, "taken as a whole, international human rights instruments can no longer be characterized as products of the West."[15]

The Vienna Declaration, to which Onuma refers as the product of a truly intercultural process of conferring, states explicitly,

> While the significance of national and regional particularities and various historical, cultural and religious backgrounds must be borne in mind, it is the duty of states, regardless of their political, economic and cultural systems, to promote and protect all human rights and fundamental freedoms.

The Bangkok Non-Governmental Declaration of Human Rights of 1993, another truly intercivilizational product, similarly declares,

> We affirm the basis of human rights which accord protection to all humanity. . . . While advocating cultural pluralism, those cultural practices which derogate from universally-accepted human rights, including women's rights, must not be tolerated.[16]

Thus, these two highly intercultural meetings, at which representatives from a great variety of countries and cultures gathered, have produced written testimonials strongly endorsing human rights as universal. They have actually gone beyond simply endorsing human rights as universal to declaring the unacceptability of any cultural practices that conflict with the rights and freedoms protected by human rights declarations. This is a very strong statement indeed.

Before we discuss the particularly Buddhist dimension of this issue, it will be helpful to gain a more precise understanding of the philosophical meaning of the phrase "human rights." The following analysis by Jack Donnelly clarifies the main points. "To claim that there are human rights is to claim that all human beings, simply because they are human, have rights [to such things as are claimed in the UDHR]. . . . Such rights are universal, held by all human beings. They are equal: One is or is not human, and thus has or does not have (the same) human rights, equally. And they are inalienable: One can no more lose these rights than one can stop being a human being, no matter how inhuman the treatment one may be forced to endure."[17] Thus, human rights assume the fundamental sameness and equality of all human beings. Human rights assume that there is something inherent in being human that qualifies every human being at all times and under all circumstances (inalienably) to deserve the treatments mandated in the articles of the UDHR. The UDHR and other documents frequently refer to this something as the "fundamental dignity and worth of the human person."

Donnelly goes on to point out that, although human rights are theoretically universal in their purview—that is, they seem philosophically to hold against all persons—in practice, human rights are understood to hold "primarily against the state and society of which one is a member." In other words, the primary purpose of human rights is to defend each human being against the greater power of the state and one's society as a whole. Secondarily, human rights require the state to provide certain services to each member of the state.

Twiss makes a useful distinction between the social-economic-political content of the human rights agenda and the specific philosophical language and concepts in which that agenda is expressed. The social-economic-political content, he says, simply represents "a practical moral consensus amongst diverse traditions . . . of the human importance of these values." It is a purely pragmatic agreement "grounded in shared historical experiences of what life can be like without these conditions." At an entirely different level, each participant to the agreement looks to its own moral tradition to find terms and concepts with which it can "justify its own participation in the consensus . . . as appropriate to its particular philosophical or religious vision of human nature, person and community." In the end, the area of moral consensus must be expressed in one set of terms, and human rights language has taken that role. Twiss insists, however, that we should see that language as "theory thin," that is, not carrying metaphysical baggage, but simply representing, in effect, a language of convenience for expressing a global moral consensus.[18]

With this distinction, we can make progress on our issue. It should be obvious that the social-economic-political content of the human rights agenda—the pragmatic consensus to which Twiss refers—is, for the greatest part (more on this later) quite compatible with Buddhist values. It is certainly beyond question that on the basis of Buddhist compassion alone, Buddhists would like to see a world in which all persons are safe from threats to their life, from physical harm of all kinds, a world in which their basic human needs are met and in which they have freedom of thought, conscience, and religion. There is no reason to think that Buddhists would hesitate to be party to the pragmatic international consensus that human beings should be treated humanely.

Even if we separate the two levels of justification, though, as Twiss proposes and as I concur that we should, all of our problems with Engaged Buddhists embracing human rights language are by no means resolved. The question from a Buddhist point of view is whether an appropriate way to reach for such a humane world involves the use of human rights language. A number of Buddhist intellectuals have concerns regarding the deeper philosophical implications of the human rights concept itself. What, then, are Buddhist intellectuals' concerns with the human rights concept? I will limit myself to a discussion of five of them.

The first family of concerns centers on the apparent individualism of the human rights concept. Thus, Craig Ihara believes that it "probably would be a mistake to introduce the notion of rights into Buddhist ethics." His concern? "[I]nvoking rights has the inevitable effect of emphasizing individuals and their status, thereby strengthening the illusion of self."[19] Ihara's concern, then, is with the metaphysical foundation of the human rights concept. Derek Jeffreys asks who, after all, is it that owns this alleged "right"? In light of the doctrine of *anātman*, after all, there is no self, no real person to own a human right. "The key difficulty for . . . a Buddhist human rights ethic is to define the rights-holder. Without a substance, who claims a right?"[20]

I consider this concern to be a red herring. Buddhist ethics function adequately without a substantial self in other contexts. For instance, the first precept states, "I undertake the precept to abstain from the taking of life."[21] Who is the one who undertakes the precepts? Whose life does one pledge not to take? A functional, not ultimately real, person is all that is needed here and for human rights. Moreover, as we have seen, human rights are about collective rights as well as individual rights.

Also evident in the Ihara passage is a concern with the consequences for the spiritual development of the person who takes the idea of his or her rights to heart. Peter Junger also expresses a concern on this point, stating, "[I]t is undoubtedly true that the virtuous man—the Brahmin—will respect the rights of others that are recognized by the local laws. . . . On the other hand, the virtuous man—the Brahmin—is not going to cling to his own rights." In support of his view, he quotes the *Dhammapada*, "He is free from the very basics of desire for this world or for the next, he is the unfettered one, the desireless one—this one I call a Brahmin."[22]

This concern seems to me more serious for Buddhist use of human rights language. It is, however, connected with the fifth issue we shall discuss below, that of the adversarial position implicit in human rights, which will occupy us throughout the remainder of this chapter, so I propose that we simply leave this question open for now as a challenge.

A second concern that arises when Buddhism is associated with human rights ideas has to do with particular rights included in the list of protections in the UDHR. Specifically, some question the right to ownership of property protected by the UDHR. The latter states,

> Article 17
> 1. Everyone has the right to own property alone as well as in association with others.
> 2. No one shall be arbitrarily deprived of his property.

What is the problem here? Junger writes,

> Although no Buddhist is likely to object to a legal system that permits one to possess a begging bowl and a set of robes, or even to possess land, the right to own property . . . should be looked upon with great skepticism, for

it is the contractarian ideology and its utilitarian offspring, with their emphasis on individuals blindly pursuing their own selfish interests, that are largely responsible for the modern destruction of traditional communities.[23]

There is another red herring herein. Obviously, traditional forms of Buddhism allow laypeople to possess much more than a begging bowl and robes. The Buddha taught that laypeople should have adequate wealth for their family and business and to be generous in sharing their wealth beyond this level of reasonable need.

On the other hand, the larger issue that Junger raises—the connection of property ownership to greed—is a serious one. A number of Engaged Buddhists do indeed very much wonder whether the developed world has the "right" to own as much of the property of the world as it does. They would question the skillfulness of a teaching that encouraged people to think only in terms of their property rights and not in terms of others' needs. For example, one of the Tiep Hien Precepts written by Thich Nhat Hanh states,

Do not accumulate wealth while millions are hungry. Do not take as the aim of your life fame, profit, wealth, or sensual pleasure. Live simply and share time, energy, and material resources with those who are in need.[24]

Similarly, Sulak frequently inveighs against "the religion of consumerism":

Consumerism is the personification of greed and people don't realize that one can die for greed just as one can die for nationalism. It drives a person to work too hard, to desire money and to consume. One is conditioned to think that without consumer goods one is nobody. 'I buy therefore I am' is the slogan of the modern age. We must understand consumerism as a new demonic religion and find a spiritual alternative.[25]

Nevertheless, although Engaged Buddhists such as Sulak and Nhat Hanh have these concerns, neither they nor any other Engaged Buddhist leader has ever challenged the idea of a right to property as a human right. We should bear in mind that, as the preamble of the UDHR states, the intention of the UDHR and of the particular rights that it proclaims is to ensure "freedom from fear and want" among all humankind. Thus, the right to own property is the right to own enough property to stave off fear and want and the security in knowing that that property will not be seized by an individual or group with greater power. In this respect, many Buddhists see the UDHR's protection of property rights as simply an affirmation of the second precept prohibiting "taking what is not given," that is, stealing. Thus, in his commentary on Article 3 of the UDHR ("Everyone has the right to life, liberty and security of person."), L. P. N. Perera writes,

> The right to life is recognized in the very first Precept that any Buddhist is expected to observe. In fact, the Five Precepts (*Pañca-sīla*) of Buddhism, broadly speaking, constitute an assertion not only of the right to life, but of the right to property too; and all the other human rights, explicitly or implicitly, seem to fall into one or the other of these two categories. Though we are not concerned with the latter right here, it will be appreciated that the right to property goes hand in hand with the right to life since property in certain forms is necessary for the very sustenance of life.[26]

Clearly, Perera regards the right to property as one of the most fundamental of human rights, inseparable from the right to life.

Moreover, the UDHR has important self-limiting language. Article 29 of the UDHR states, in part, "In the exercise of his rights and freedoms, everyone shall be subject only to such limitations as are determined by law solely for the purpose of securing due recognition and respect for the rights and freedoms of others." There are no absolute rights. As Donnelly points out, "Freedom of religion does not extend to human sacrifice. Freedom of association does not cover conspiracy to commit ordinary crimes."[27] The right to own property, then, must be balanced against other rights declared in the UDHR. Such other rights include a right to an adequate standard of living. Article 25 states, "Everyone has the right to a standard of living adequate for the health and well-being of himself and of his family, including food, clothing, housing and medical care and necessary social services." This article could be understood to imply that neocolonial practices depriving the Southern hemisphere of an adequate standard of living are unacceptable. The 1976 International Covenant on Economic, Social, and Cultural Rights clarified this point, partly at the urging of developing countries. It states, for example, "In no case may a people be deprived of its own means of subsistence" (Article 1)—incidentally introducing collective rights—and recognizes "the fundamental right of everyone to be free from hunger" (Article 11). In sum, although Buddhists might want to further nuance the UDHR language on property rights, there are sufficient limitations on its comprehensiveness to prevent insurmountable problems for Buddhists.

A third area that some believe is a concern regarding human rights has to do with its privileging of humanity. In the Buddhist view, although human beings are special inasmuch as the human birth is the "precious birth" within which one can make progress toward Buddhahood, it is still the case that humans are not rigidly separable from the larger category of sentient beings that includes the human alongside animals and a number of mythical beings such as gods, hungry ghosts, and denizens of the hells.

This concern, however, has been resolved by Engaged Buddhists. Actually, it was resolved before it became a concern. Engaged Buddhist leaders, from the start, articulated a concept of human rights that is not in conflict with the rights of nonhumans. Human rights in Engaged Buddhism are not conceived as separate from the rights of other beings. Ariyaratne writes, "Economic growth . . . has to take place with due acceptance of the rights of all forms of life to the resources of the planet, promoting equal and non-exploitative relationships between human beings and recognizing interdependence between human beings, the society and nature."[28] Ariyaratne has been able to act upon this principle more than other Engaged Buddhists by virtue of the kind of organization that he founded and heads, one that has focused for decades on the development of a less developed country, Sri Lanka. Endeavoring to guide the development of Sri Lanka along the lines of Buddhist values, Ariyaratne has conscientiously avoided sacrificing the interests of nonhuman beings for the sake of development that favors humans. Of course, being highly aware of interdependence, Ariyaratne knows very well that development that harmed other species or the environment would not benefit humans in the long run. But at the same time, as the above passage shows, inasmuch as we are all sentient beings, he sees no justification for privileging humans over other species. He has consistently put protection of the environment first.

The Dalai Lama is also an ardent environmentalist who does not see the welfare of human and nonhuman life as separate categories. "If an individual has a sense of responsibility for humanity, he or she will naturally take care of the environment." His Holiness promotes respect for the environment and nonhuman species from two perspectives. The first is pragmatic. In light of our dependence on the web of interdependent life, he writes, "the threat of nuclear weapons and the ability to damage our environment through, for example, deforestation, pollution, and ozone layer depletion, are quite alarming." His second approach is to observe that caring for other species and the environment is a natural expression of benevolence. "Compassion and altruism require not only that we respect human beings, but also that we respect, take care of, and refrain from interfering with other species and the environment."[29]

On this subject, we may safely take Ariyaratne and the Dalai Lama as representative of Engaged Buddhists as a whole. Coming from a worldview stressing interdependence, compassion, and human membership in the larger category of sentient beings, Engaged Buddhists consistently advocate protections for the environment and other species. They simply do not see any reason why advocating human rights should entail any loss for the welfare of other species or the environment as a whole. This is, in fact, a contribution of Buddhism to global thinking about human rights.

The fourth issue, seen very frequently, is that Buddhist ethics are based upon the idea of responsibilities, not rights. Sulak, whom we have seen very much endorses the idea of human rights, raises this issue. "[T]he classical Buddhist texts do not refer to rights, human or otherwise, but rather to duties or responsibilities. The duties of the *Sangha* [monastics] are outlined in the rule or *Vinaya*, those of rulers in the Dasarajadhamma, whereas guidelines for laypeople are found at various places in the Buddhist canon such as the *Sigolavada Sutta*, the Five Precepts, the Noble Eightfold Path and the Jataka Tales."[30] One sees this kind of remark frequently simply because it is correct; the language of the classical Buddhist texts on ethics is the language of responsibility. The question is whether this poses a problem for Buddhists adopting human rights ideas and language. In fact, Sulak raises this issue only to argue against it. He quotes Burmese Buddhist scholar and monk Venerable U Rewata Dhamma, "In the early, organic, societies the Buddha was addressing, [these] responsibilities were assumed to be adequate guidelines for human behaviour, with no need to identify the corresponding rights. In modern, fragmented societies, however, where the fulfillment of responsibilities cannot be guaranteed by the immediate community, the corresponding rights are specified and protected by States and International Organisations."[31]

Although critics might see this view as an unjustifiable hearkening back to an idyllic golden age of the past, it is correct that the Buddha lived in a state and society that allowed him to pursue religious seeking and teaching without hindrance and he had no reason to feel a need for protections from the state. Donnelly claims that it was because modern states and capitalism first appeared in Europe that ideas of human rights first developed there. It follows, he says, that, because "contemporary Asian individuals, families, and societies face the same threats from modern markets and states that Western societies do," they now "therefore need the same protections of human rights."[32]

Burma is a good example of a state in which, by virtue of a tremendous change in the nature of the state itself, Burmese people need human rights protections today that were not important, or even conceivable, before the advent of the colonial period. Venerable U Rewata Dhamma argues that in the modern state, human rights are needed. "The depiction of rights as simply a Western invention fails to understand the relationship of rights to responsibilities and ethical norms. . . . [T]he central values of all societies are very much the same. All ethical systems encourage people to love each other, and discourage killing, violence and so on. The universality and inseparability of human rights may therefore be understood as reflecting the universality and inseparability of inter-responsibility emerging from Dhamma."[33] Here Venerable U Rewata Dhamma implicitly makes Twiss's distinction between two levels of justification, asserting that the content of human rights declarations is recognized not only in Buddhism, but universally. He seems to have in mind by "human rights" not something like the political rights of the UDHR, but, rather, something akin to a right to life and probably other rights corresponding to the basic ethical teachings of Buddhism. His view seems to be that the Dhamma points to a society of "inter-responsibility" in which I am responsible not to kill you and you are responsible not to kill me. The main change in his view is that now, because of the fragmentation of society, colonialism, and the unprecedented power of the modern state, in countries like Cambodia and Burma people need to be "protected by States and International Organisations."

There are a number of issues raised in Venerable U Rewata Dhamma's views that will require considerable further attention. His view of society as a realm of "inter-responsibility" suggests a society of trustable interrelationships. What are the implications of this understanding of society? What is the significance of his equating the content of human rights with Buddhist ethics, apparently overlooking the specifically political rights? These matters will be major themes for the remainder of this chapter and are also linked to our fifth, and final, issue.

A fifth concern about associating Buddhism with ideas of human rights has to do with the adversarial nature of the latter. I believe that this is the most important of all the concerns regarding Buddhism and human rights. Taitetsu Unno asserts that "the concept of rights, as demanding one's due, arose as part of the adversarial legacy of the West. In East Asia, on the other hand, the consensual model of society prevailed, ruling out any assertions of self against recognized forms of authority, whether secular or religious."[34] Buddhists in many, perhaps all, Buddhist countries traditionally avoid confrontation. It is a virtue to know one's place in the greater whole, to make one's contribution to the greater whole, to be grateful for what the group gives to the individual. This takes us back to the discussion in chapter 4 on the relation between the individual and society. We have seen that the Buddhist idea of the interdependence of individual and society creates some ambiguity when it becomes necessary to define a proper balance between the needs of each. We should not be surprised if that ambiguity revisits us when considering Buddhist responses to the idea of human rights.

The present Kalon Tripa ("prime minister") of the Tibetan government in exile, Samdhong Rinpoche, expressed his views on several of these issues while discussing human rights in an interview with the author in 2000.[35] Regarding the UDHR, he said, "I don't find any one of those rights is contrary to Buddhist teaching. But the Buddhist way of looking at it is this: our emphasis is not to protect one's own rights, but to protect others' rights." [Question: Doesn't that come to the same thing?] "It is the other side of the same coin, but the emphasis is different; it starts from responsibility, not rights."

He went on, "His Holiness made several moral declaration drafts; they always included respect for the universal human rights, all the rights recognized by the world organizations." But there are different ideas of particular rights from country to country, he pointed out. "Rights would be a little different in a free Tibetan society [compared to the United States]. For example, we would not have the freedom to bear arms, like the United States. But this is not a 'universal human right.' We would, though, have freedom of religion, the political freedoms, freedom of speech, and so forth." But with regard to freedom of speech, "anything harmful to the group has to be limited, forbidden by law. So if someone takes a suicidal religious ideology or something, this must not be allowed. The individual's right does not override civic or society's right. The larger group is more important—this is quite clear in both Theravada and Mahayana."

Individual and society are interdependent, he went on. There must be a balance between them. Furthermore, "a society's rights must be balanced against all humankind, all sentient beings, the entire planet. Each is trumped by the level above: the individual by the community or state, the community or state by all humankind, humankind by all sentient beings."

In these remarks, the Rinpoche comments on three of the five issues discussed above. His closing remarks are an example of the Buddhist avoidance of anthropocentrism, even when endorsing human rights. Human rights cannot "trump" the rights, if you will, of other sentient beings or of the planet (and all its inhabitants). This is a given. Even all of humankind as a whole must cede to all sentient beings and to the planet. The Rinpoche also gives his views on the issues involved in the ambiguity of the balance between individual and society, that is, the issues of responsibilities versus rights and the adversarial versus consensual approach to social order. For the Rinpoche there is nothing ambiguous about it: the larger category—society—"trumps" the smaller one—the individual; the individual needs to cede to society. Clearly his thinking is much like Buddhadasa's on this matter: "the larger group is more important—this is quite clear." It is also much like U Rewata Dhamma's notion of inter-responsibility: each individual has a responsibility to everyone—that should be our focus. Nonetheless, the Rinpoche unequivocally endorses the universal human rights.

There is a significant issue hidden in these matters of responsibilities versus rights, adversarial versus consensual approaches. The human rights agenda is all about power. Historically, the concept of human rights did develop in European philosophy as an effort to empower the individual in the face of the growing power of the newly developing nation-state. Here we get into the real issue: what is it to "have" a "right"? We shall see that there is a crucial point here concerning power.

Donnelly has discussed this question, writing,

"Right" in English has two principal (moral and political) senses: "rectitude" and "entitlement." In the most general sense of rectitude, we speak of something *being* the right thing to do, indicating conformity with a standard of action. Entitlement is a narrower sense of "right." When one *has* a right, she is entitled to something and therefore armed with claims that have a special force. The focus is on the relationship between right-holder and duty-bearer, rather than duty-bearer and standard of rectitude.

If Anne has a right to x with respect to Bob, it is not simply desirable, good, or even merely right that Anne enjoy x. She is *entitled* to it. Should Bob fail to discharge his obligations, beyond acting improperly and harming Anne he violates her rights. This makes him subject to special claims and sanctions that she controls.[36]

Here we see in what way the conceptual structure of a right is unlike the conceptual structure of the morality of something like guidance by the Five Precepts. Although in both cases one is "doing right" to avoid, for example, attempting to take the life of another human, only in the case of "having" a "right" am I entitled to take action of a specified kind against one who attempts to deprive me of my life. In short, having a right is a legal matter that entitles me to a form of redress when my right is violated and to certain protections to prevent my right being violated. A religion such as Buddhism, inasmuch as it is not a legal system, is not in any position to do other than teach morality. It is not, that is, in a position to compel or to enforce. Thus, those who say that Buddhist morality is about responsibility, not about rights, are in effect making a category mistake. Buddhism is a religion, not a legal system.

It is precisely here, though, that we see what human rights are all about: they are about power—an adjustment in the power relations between more powerful and less powerful groups, individuals and institutions. The enactment of human rights treaties and declarations is the bringing into existence by a kind of performative statement[37] of a new form of power, put into the hands of ordinary people by consensus of the global community. Donnelly continues, "Anne is not a mere beneficiary of Bob's obligation. She is actively in charge of the relationship, as suggested by the language of 'exercising' rights. Anne may assert her right to x in order to try to assure that Bob discharges his obligation. If he fails to do so, she may press further claims against Bob (or excuse him), largely at her own discretion. Beyond benefiting their holders, rights empower them."[38] Therefore, when the Dalai Lama, as he frequently does, claims that the People's Republic of China is violating the human rights of the Tibetan people, he is saying that what China is doing is wrong, but he is also reminding the international community of their publicly professed commitment to the protection of human rights, such as the self-determination and freedom of religion being violated by China in Tibet, and inviting them to intervene on behalf of the people of Tibet. He is reaching for one of the few forms of power available to him.

We have at last arrived at the heart of the place where, I believe, Buddhist intellectuals have trouble with the concept of human rights: power. The very idea of Anne "exercising" her right with respect to Bob, of saying no, of negating his will in an uncompromising way seems to smack too much of self-assertion, of aggression, of confrontation, of adversarial relations, of me versus you, me versus them. This seems to separate those who are interdependent, to weaken the complex web of relationships that constitute society, without which we cannot live. It seems as well—as the first objection held—to strengthen the delusional individual ego by a self-aggrandizing reach for power.

But note that the Dalai Lama is reaching for that power *on behalf of* the people of Tibet. This is in no way a question of individualism. This is first and foremost a matter of compassion, of attempting to prevent widespread and profound harm to an entire people. As the Rinpoche said, the focus is on protecting the rights of others. This, in fact, is the way in which Tibetans use human rights language— on behalf of the entire community. And let us remember that the international human rights agenda includes not just individual rights, but also collective rights. China is violating not only the rights of individual Tibetans to freedom of religion, freedom of opinion and expression, and the right to have a government based on the will of the people, but also the collective rights of the Tibetan people as a whole "to live in freedom, peace and security as distinct peoples" (Draft Declaration on the Rights of Indigenous Peoples). Indeed, it seems impossible to distinguish the individual and collective rights violations in this case. The collective nature of this particular cry for human rights, one would think, should ease the concerns of Buddhist intellectuals.

But what if it were a matter purely of individual rights, a matter just of Anne and Bob? From a Buddhist perspective, if it is just Anne telling Bob "no," perhaps— let us get the whole mistrusted scenario out—suing Bob in court for violating her rights—is this wrong? Is it destructive of community and strengthening of ego?

To consider this question, we should reflect on the use of human rights language in another Buddhist country that has energetically grasped human rights language as part of its national campaign, Cambodia. Cambodia, of course, is an entirely different scenario than Tibet. With the Khmer Rouge and the Vietnamese gone, Cambodia's problem is no longer to defend a people against an outside group. With the loss of public order and Buddhist-based morality that is the legacy of the Khmer Rouge era, Cambodia is now a society struggling with amorality and lawlessness. Cambodia's problem is to defend a people against themselves. It is a situation in which it is difficult to trust anyone, in which the social fabric that Buddhists so strongly emphasize is already in tatters, a society in which the individuals constituting society, the Annes and Bobs, do not see themselves as being in relation to each other, as mutually dependent, but as unpredictable mutual threats. In this situation—at the urging, granted, of Western powers, Western nongovernmental organizations, and Western-educated Cambodians—the Cambodian Buddhist community has embraced the teaching of human rights as a necessary component of the country's moral reconstruction.

The Cambodian situation provides an interesting window on the issue of the relationship between human rights and Asian values. Charles Taylor shows how the presumed dichotomy between confrontation over individual rights and assumed social harmony has been drawn too starkly in this debate:

> One of the key points in the critique of a too exclusive focus on rights is that this neglects the crucial importance of political trust. Dictatorships, as Tocqueville pointed out, try to destroy trust between citizens, but free societies vitally depend on it. The price of freedom is a strong common commitment to the political formula that binds us, because without the commitment the formula would have to be aggressively enforced and this threatens freedom. What will very quickly dissolve the commitment for each and every one of us is the sense that others no longer share it or are willing to act on it. The common allegiance is nourished on trust.[39]

This point is well taken and helps us realize that, even in a society like the United States, in which ideas of human rights are present with their full complement of notions of empowerment and adversarial relations, a web of interdependent interpersonal relations that one can implicitly trust is already assumed. We insist upon our rights within the context of a community in which we understand what we expect of each other and assume with confidence that, in the vast majority of cases, those expectations will be fulfilled. Even in the United States, the world's leader in litigation, cases of conflict over rights are a miniscule fraction of the daily interpersonal interactions that flow smoothly on the basis of understood, assumed, and trusted patterns of interrelationship.[40] We notice the problems, not the smooth functioning of the web that is always in the background.

It may be that in pre–Khmer Rouge Cambodia ideas of human rights were not needed. Perhaps the consciousness of the web of social interdependence, the relationships that make life work, was sufficiently clear and present in people's minds to do well without human rights ideas. But in the unprecedented situation of Cambodia after the fall of the Khmer Rouge, when that consciousness became shattered and replaced by fear and mistrust, it seems that that web became a difficult thing to retrieve or recreate. In that situation, when there is no web of trust, no reliance upon mutual dependence, what is the shortest way back to a tolerable society in which one can reasonably assume decent behavior from one's neighbor? Certainly one cannot begin to develop a web of assumed trust in a climate in which random attacks occur too frequently and where institutional corruption makes a mockery of the rule of law. Are human rights a way to restrain antisocial behavior so that trust can begin to develop and the web of mutual dependence begin to be taken for granted? Whether it is seems a debatable point, but it is the path that Cambodia has taken.

In an unpublished paper, John Marston documents the process by which human rights ideas came to be known in Cambodia.[41] Human rights ideas were first planted in Cambodian minds in the refugee camps by the international organizations, including the United Nations, that ran those camps. These ideas took hold because "the situation of refugee camps provokes discussion of human rights—the right of free movement, the right to maintain one's own identity."[42] Buddhist monks soon became involved in the effort to teach and promote human rights ideas among the Cambodian people. The more creative and intellectual among them actively sought ways of linking the idea of human rights with traditional Buddhist teachings. But although the United Nations certainly actively promoted the promulgation of human rights ideas in Cambodia, Marston emphasizes that this was a dialogical, two-way process.

The U.N.'s promotion of human rights in Cambodia has never been a simple one-way street. One of the most well-known Cambodian human rights activists now working in the country, Kassie Neou, recalls how during the negotiations leading to the Paris Agreements . . . he actively lobbied for the peace plan to include a human rights component. [Buddhist monk] Yos Hut emphasizes the *dialogue* with [Dennis] McNamara [then head of United Nations Border Relief Operations] about Buddhism and human rights. That is to say, (Western-educated) Cambodians themselves played a role in the shaping of U.N. policy. And as U.N. programs on human rights have been implemented, they have succeeded or failed in relation to the degree they filled grass-roots needs and the goals of individual Cambodians.[43]

Buddhist monks became one of the key groups to whom ideas of human rights were taught, because they could then spread those ideas in their sermons (as they were requested to do). This was possible because high-ranking monks, including the Venerable Maha Ghosananda, the Venerable Hok Sovann, and the Venerable Prak Thon, all said that human rights were "consistent with Buddhist doctrine." "They said it was the same as *sel pram* [the Five Lay Precepts]. They didn't want people to think that human rights was politics; it was consistent with Buddhist dharma."[44] Translations were made of key human rights documents, and training manuals were made comparing these documents with Buddhist ideas. The promotion of the idea of the compatibility of human rights with Buddhist ideas has reached the point at which, Marston relates, "when I ask ranking monks in Phnom Penh and rural areas about the connection between human rights and Buddhism, they clearly recognize it as a topic about which a monk should be knowledgeable and are very quick to respond with a set of standard ideas about the relationship between human rights and Buddhist precepts."

Fascinatingly, Marston notes that a key element in the concept of human rights as understood internationally seems to be missing in the Cambodian hearing of that concept. "Cambodian intellectuals are right to suggest that, based on moral principles, it is possible to show how human rights relates to Buddhist principles and traditional Cambodian culture. This is not to say, however, that human rights, as it is conceived internationally, is merely morality, as much Cambodian discourse seems to suggest. To see human rights this way is to ignore the way that the principle of "rights" relates to law and the claims that can legitimately be made in a system of law." In other words, the very point we discussed above that distinguishes human rights from morality, the idea that human rights gives a person a basis for a legal claim against another person or group, may not be being successfully communicated in Cambodia.

Marston goes on to quote Caroline Hughes in corroboration of this point. "Arguably," Hughes states, "human rights and Buddhism become fused since, in the eyes of most respondents, the anarchy responsible for human rights abuse in Cambodia can be overcome by the propagation of an authoritative moral code." Human rights offer one such code, one with international cachet. Buddhism offers another, one with traditional authority. "Conflating the two creates a discourse which connects the grassroots to the international community" and, advocates hope, may both facilitate the introduction of international help for Cambodia's problems and appeal to traditional-minded Cambodians. This conflation of the two discourses, however, only goes so far. Hughes continues, "Discipline, professionalism, and adherence to imposed norms of behavior are emphasized, at the expense of deeper forms of democracy or individual freedom facilitated through empowered community forums of discussion and action. A harmonious relationship between a centralized and hierarchical government apparatus and Cambodian citizens, sharing a mutual respect and rightful conduct, is viewed as the appropriate goal. Frequently this goal is framed in terms of visions of an idealized past."[45]

Let us return to the question raised earlier. Are human rights standards a way back to a tolerable society in a situation in which dependence upon the web of social interconnections has been shattered? It seems that in Cambodia, as of yet, there is little understanding of the distinctiveness of human rights as a form of popular empowerment. Human rights have entered Cambodian society arm-in-arm with an effort to revive traditional Theravada Buddhist moral values and have become almost indistinguishable from the latter. If this is the case, the main contribution of the introduction of human rights ideas into Cambodia has been to supplement the authoritative status of Buddhist morality. It may be that the idea of empowerment has not been received because the idea of taking an adversarial position does not fit the Cambodian picture of a moral society. Adversarial relations may be associated in Cambodia with the Khmer Rouge era and with the current post–Khmer Rouge anarchic era—both scenarios that Cambodians are eager to replace with moral order. So far it seems that moral order cannot be separated in the Cambodian mind from harmonious, hierarchical, nonadversarial relations within a web of mutual dependence. Millennia-old ways of thinking do not change readily, even with such interventions as the Khmer Rouge cataclysm and the invasion of international norms and language.

Consider the three countries where Buddhists have made human rights a cornerstone of their national campaigns, Tibet, Burma, and Cambodia. All three are countries so far into conflictual situations that perhaps there was no need to take up an adversarial stance—that is, no volition necessary to move into such a posture—just a recognition that one already was in such a position, like it or not. Perhaps there is a threshold of conflict beyond which Asian Buddhists consciously or unconsciously recognize that the web of trusted mutual dependence is not in place and gradually lose their reluctance to take up the adversarial stance, grasping human rights language in an effort to achieve redress—much, indeed, as human rights language is intended to be used.

That such might be the case may be surmised from a very different, and much less conflictual, case, Thailand. In Thailand, as Soraj Hongladarom reports, "The concept of human rights, as expressed in the UN Declaration is . . . regarded as foreign, and the Thai word for human rights—*Sitthi Manussayachon*—still rings an unfamiliar sound. For most Thais, the word simply conjures up the image of some-one who disregard[s] the traditional pattern of compromise and harmonization of social relations; someone, that is, who is quite out of touch with the traditional Thai mores." Here is a case of a society with "Asian values" of harmony and com-promise in which adversarial human rights have no place. Nonetheless, at times of intense conflict, it seems that Thais begin to regard the concept of human rights as more useful or appropriate: "However, the mores themselves are changing. As the country is surging toward industrialization, and as the people are ever estranged from the traditional way of living, more Thais are beginning to realize the need for human rights. This is well attested by the Black May incident of 1993, when scores of Thais lost their lives fighting for democracy against the army. The discourse of Thai people is beginning to presuppose the basic premises of human rights, even though these are not spelled out explicitly."[46] It seems that, in the Thai case as well, the more conflictual their actual situation becomes, the more they begin to incorporate the use of human rights ideas—even though, as in Cambodia, these may be very incompletely understood.

Let us move on and consider particular ways in which attempts have been made to reconcile Buddhism and human rights language. Taylor makes a useful proposal for understanding what is involved in human rights language coming to be embraced by very different cultures, such as Buddhist cultures.

> What would it mean to come to a genuine, unforced international con-sensus on human rights? I suppose it would be something like what Rawls describes in his *Political Liberalism* as an "overlapping consensus." That is, different groups, countries, religious communities, and civilizations, al-

though holding incompatible fundamental views on theology, metaphysics, human nature, and so on, would come to an agreement on certain norms that ought to govern human behavior. Each would have its own way of justifying this from out of its profound background conception. We would agree on the norms while disagreeing on why they were the right norms, and we would be content to live in this consensus, undisturbed by the differences of profound underlying belief.[47]

Taylor thus agrees with Twiss that we should distinguish between what Twiss calls two levels of justification: on one level, an international "practical moral consensus" that certain behaviors are necessary and some must be prohibited and, on a second level, within each tradition, "its own set of moral categories as appropriate to its particular philosophical or religious vision." Taylor points out that the embracing of a new international form of language, such as human rights, "will be the easier to effect the more it can be presented as being in continuity with the most important traditions and reference points, properly understood."[48]

When scholars such as Damien Keown and I have cited ideas in classical Buddhist philosophy that seemed to suggest something like a philosophical connection between Buddhist thought and the idea of human rights, we were trying to establish the fundamental compatibility or "continuity," as suggested by Taylor, of Buddhist thought and values with the content of the human rights moral agenda—the pragmatic consensus on behavior. As this chapter has shown, this is not to say that those efforts established continuity between Buddhism and the deeper levels of the human rights concept, including its empowerment and adversarial stance. The extent to which these aspects of the human rights concept will be heard in various Asian countries remains an open question.

That granted, it seems useful at this time to summarize some of the major points of continuity noted by scholars and by activists over the last several years between classic Buddhist thought and the moral content, the "practical moral consensus," of the human rights agenda. The following are major Buddhist ideas seen as continuous with the moral content of the human rights agenda. They are certainly not mutually exclusive, but mutually supportive.

THE FIVE LAY PRECEPTS

As we have seen, Cambodian Buddhists themselves are claiming a link between the Five Lay Precepts and human rights. A Cambodian human rights training manual directly links the precepts and human rights, as follows:

1. Not killing living things is to respect the right to life.
2. Not to steal the belongings of others is to respect the right of property.
3. Not to commit sexual offenses is to respect the rights of individuals and the rights of society.
4. Not to drink intoxicating beverages is to respect the right of individual security and respect the right of security within society.
5. Not to lie or defame is to respect the right of human dignity.[49]

Although some of these links may seem poorly worded or poorly conceived, one can nonetheless see here what was discussed above as the effort to make of the human rights agenda a support for traditional Buddhist morality.

Scholars who have linked human rights and the Five Lay Precepts include Perera, Keown, and the present author. Perera wrote an entire book (*Buddhism and Human Rights: A Buddhist Commentary on the Universal Declaration of Human Rights*) in which he examines each article of the UDHR in turn and finds citations from Buddhist scripture and examples of Buddhist practice supportive of the content of each. For example, in dealing with the right to property, he states, "It is little realized that the second precept of the Buddhist *Pañca-sīla* . . . dealing, as it does, with theft, becomes meaningful only if the property rights of every individual are fully recognized."[50] Although the precepts are not the only resource upon which Perera draws, he does assume that their contents, among other things in Buddhist tradition, establish continuity between Buddhism and human rights ideas.

Keown links the precepts and human rights as follows: "In the context of the precepts . . . the right-holder is the one who suffers from the breach of Dharmic duty when the precepts are broken. In the case of the first precept this would be the person who was unjustly killed. The right the victim has may therefore be defined as a negative claim-right upon the aggressor, namely the right not to be killed. In simple terms we might say that the victim has a right to life which the aggressor has a duty to respect."[51] Keown implicitly makes the distinction between two levels of justification of human rights when he writes, "I suggest, then, that the apparent differences [sic] between the moral teachings of Buddhism and human rights charters is one of form rather than substance. . . . These rights are the extrapolation of what is due under Dharma; they have not been 'imported' into Buddhism but were implicitly present."[52]

In my own thinking on this subject, I have written of the key to linking Buddhist precepts and human rights as the idea of a Good society from a Buddhist perspective.

The foundation of Buddhist social ethics can be located most firmly in the five lay precepts. Therein we see that Buddhists have never traditionally spoken of rights, but have emphasized responsibilities, or obligations, in a sense. . . .

Philosophically, the precepts imply that that society will be Good in which its members do not harm each other, steal from each other, lie to each other, etc. This in turn implies that a member of a Good society should have a reasonable expectation not to be harmed, stolen from, etc. Now one may or may not want to call such a thing a "right," but it is certainly closing in on that ground in a practical sense, if not in the full conceptual sense. This is especially true since . . . from a Buddhist point of view, society *should* contribute to the end of suffering and the nurturance of awakening in all. Since the Good society brings into being conditions conducive to these ends, the individual is fully justified in claiming a kind of right to live in such a society. However, since society and individual are deeply interactive and mutually constructive, the individual likewise has a responsibility to contribute to the construction of such a society.[53]

These words perhaps recall Venerable U Rewata Dhamma's idea of "inter-responsibility." I still stand by these words, though I recognize more fully now how difficult it is for many Asian Buddhists to take up the degree of adversarial stance necessary to claim or exercise such a "right" to live in a Good society.

THE PRECIOUSNESS OF HUMAN BIRTH AND HUMAN ENLIGHTENABILITY

The idea of human rights is premised in international documents upon recognition of the inherent dignity of human being. In Buddhism a similar concept is the preciousness of a human birth. Keown, Suu Kyi, and I (as we saw above) have all commented on human rights in connection with this idea.

Keown identifies the core of human rights in the idea of human dignity and identifies the Third and Fourth Noble Truths as the source of Buddhist affirmation of human dignity. He writes, "[T]he most promising approach [to linking human rights and Buddhism] will be one which locates human rights and dignity within a comprehensive account of human goodness, and which sees basic rights and freedoms as integrally related to human flourishing and self-realization. This is because the source of human dignity in Buddhism lies nowhere else than in the literally infinite capacity of human nature for participation in goodness."[54]

HUMAN EQUALITY

Keown, Payutto, and I have all remarked on the continuity between Buddhist ideas of human equality and human rights. Logically, the idea of human equality is a necessary, though not a sufficient, element in the development of human rights thinking. Keown writes,

> [A] justification for the rejection of hierarchical social structures is not hard to find in Buddhism—one need look only at the Buddha's critique of caste. Buddhism also holds, in the doctrine of not-self, that all individuals are equal in the most profound sense. Like the Christian doctrine that all men are created equal before God this would appear to be fertile ground for a doctrine of natural rights.[55]

Linking human equality and the preciousness of the human birth, I have written,

> [W]hile in Buddhism a person is not an "individual" in the Western sense, s/he nonetheless possesses great value as one who may attain Buddhahood. . . . [T]his traditional Buddhist idea may be used by Buddhists to justify concern with human rights. . . .
>
> Some of the early teachings indicative of this idea are the following. (1) The Buddha taught all who would listen, without imposing restrictions by social class, gender, education, or other differentiating characteristics (this was, of course, highly unusual in his place and time). (2) Persons of all backgrounds were, in fact, confirmed as having attained the fruits of liberation during the Buddha's lifetime. (3) Most significantly, the Buddha's teachings strongly emphasized the rarity and preciousness of a human birth, urging everyone to take advantage of their human birth, to practice Buddhism and attain release, since release could not be had from any of the other five destinies.[56]

The view, mentioned above, that society *should* contribute to the end of suffering and the nurturance of awakening in all, a view found in early Buddhism (for example, in the *dasarājadhamma* and in Asoka's example) and heavily reemphasized in Engaged Buddhism, is based upon the preciousness of the human life as an opportunity for enlightenment. Once one believes that it is important to take very good care of each and every human life, it is not a far step to human rights—that is, their moral content.

NONVIOLENCE

In studying Buddhist writings, Taylor has come to the conclusion that human rights in the Buddhist case are more a consequence of the fundamental value of nonviolence than they are themselves a foundational value. He sees nonviolence as calling for "a respect for the autonomy of each person, demanding in effect a minimal use of coercion in human affairs." This founding of human rights in non-violence allows Buddhist and Western thinking to "converge . . . on certain norms of action," while the underlying philosophy and rhetoric remain quite different. For Taylor, this leads to a Buddhist posture free of "the politics of anger" as is familiar in Western approaches to justice and human rights.[57]

FREEDOM AS ESSENTIAL TO BUDDHISM

Saneh Chamarik has written an important paper linking human rights to human freedom, which he takes as essential to Buddhism. Chamarik writes, "There is no need at all to search for a place of human rights in the Buddhist tradition. Free-dom is indeed the essence of Buddhism." He develops this notion by referring to the Buddha's advice to the Kalamas (to make decisions on what spiritual path to follow by relying upon their own experiential knowledge, not upon anyone or any-thing external to themselves) and the dying words of the Buddha ("Be islands unto yourselves, Ananda. Be a refuge to yourselves; do not take any other refuge. . . . Work out your own salvation, with diligence.") These ideas emphasize self-reliance in achieving the task of the human life: working toward enlightenment. "In the Buddhist view, then, the individual is not merely a means. One can sense a subtle meaning of equality here. Although men may not be born 'free,' they are equal in dignity and rights, that is to say, dignity and rights to their own salvation or free-dom."[58] Payutto has written a preamble confirming and extending these ideas; we will examine it below.

PHRA PAYUTTO

Two Engaged Buddhist intellectuals, Phra Payutto and His Holiness the Dalai Lama, have written especially carefully and thoughtfully about the idea of human rights and their work deserves particular attention. We will begin with Payutto.

In his 1971 magnum opus *Buddhadhamma*, Payutto refers to human rights several times—not making a case for them on the basis of Buddhist values and ideas, but assuming the concept of human rights and using it. For example, he writes, "Everyone has equal rights by nature to achieve the fruits of success even though each person has different abilities"; "Lord Buddha gave rights to women . . ."; and "no matter what caste people were born into, they could be ordained and all have equal rights."[59]

In 1982, he takes up the task of making a Buddhist case for human rights. He writes: "Man is the best of trainable or educable beings. He has the potentiality of self-perfection by which a life of freedom and happiness can be realized. In order to attain this perfection, man has to develop himself physically, morally, psycho-spiritually and intellectually. . . . [T]he law of the Dharma . . . entails that every individual should be left free, if not provided with the opportunity, to develop himself so that his potentiality can unfold itself and work its way toward perfection." To be left alone to pursue self-development, then, is a must. Ideally, Payutto continues, all conditions should be made to support the individual's effort at self-development. Thus, "freedom of self-development and the encouragement of opportunities for it" are a "foundation of . . . Buddhist ethics." "This is to say, in other words, that every individual has the right to self-development. . . . [The Buddha] teaches the goal of freedom that is to be reached by means of freedom and a happy means that leads to a happy end."[60]

We can see that for Payutto certain rights—namely, freedom of thought, conscience, and religion—rights that are central to the path of self-development, will be the most important. This is very interesting when one considers the history of Buddhism in China and Vietnam, where one thing that recurrently brought monks to protest government behavior was repression of the Buddhist religion. While those monks, of course, did not protest in the name of human rights, they did seem to regard freedom of religion as an uncompromisable absolute, and they did put themselves in an adversarial and confrontational posture on its behalf, sometimes going to the length of sacrificing themselves to strengthen their demands. Although rights such as freedom of thought, conscience, and religion seem most essential, Payutto seems to suggest that one could develop a full list of human rights—including self-determination, freedom from want, and so forth—on the basis of the idea that they are important supports for the pursuit of spiritual self-development. Indeed, to the extent that "self-development" (self-perfection on the path to Buddhahood) is the very raison d'etre of Buddhism, we may have here something close to a Buddhist natural law foundation for human rights.

Payutto goes so far as to advocate, in certain circumstances, "struggle" to reach for the happy means and happy end that Buddhism promises.

If the right to self-development is denied or restricted, it is right to struggle for it. If help and favourable conditions are not provided for it, it is good to make exertion towards the encouragement of the same. However, there are some words of caution. That every human being has the right to self-development and, thus, to freedom and happiness is an imperative of the ethics which is based on the law of the Dharma. . . . If he is to struggle, he should do it for the sake of the Dharma, that is, for the good and for the righteous, out of love and compassion, not for personal gains or from any selfish motives, not out of greed or hatred. . . . Otherwise, the struggle to secure the human rights for some can become an act of appropriating the human rights of others.[61]

This is a striking passage. It seems to be saying something remarkably akin to the UDHR. If one is actively prevented from exercising a fundamental right—for Payutto, one involved in self-development—one not only is morally justified in struggling for it, one *should* struggle for it. That sounds like an endorsement of taking up an adversarial position on behalf of a basic freedom that is being denied—that is, a liberty. Such fundamental freedoms directly connected with self-development one presumes would have to include the UDHR's rights to life and liberty, to freedom of thought, conscience, religion, and opinion. It would seem to also be necessary to self-development to guarantee freedom of expression, peaceful assembly and association, and participation in the cultural life of the community. Cases such as the Tibetan demonstrate that the basic political freedoms can be necessary to secure the freedoms more directly associated with self-development. Even the right to own property seems a necessary right for the purpose of self-development when one considers China's ransacking of monasteries in China and Tibet, together with their libraries and ritual implements.

In a different category from these necessary liberties are the claims on others —namely, the state—to make certain things available to the individual. Some of these also seem necessary to self-development. They include, in the language of the UDHR, rights to things that the state is supposed to provide, such as an adequate standard of living and an education. According to Payutto, if one is not being given something to which one has a claim on behalf of self-development, one is justified to "make exertion" to "encourage" the development of these things. This seems to imply not an adversarial stance of struggle, but an approach more of working with, of building upon the established web of relations to gain the necessary goods.

Payutto's cautionary note on struggling only on behalf of the Dharma and not for selfish reasons is reminiscent of certain typically Buddhist concerns. One's struggle should not devolve, I take it, into anger and violence. One should not struggle—that is, enter into conflict—over anything other than self-development and things necessary to self-development. Of course, the UDHR places limits on the exercise of one's rights as well, defining these limits as the place where a person's actions impinge upon the rights and freedoms of others. To what extent those limits would coincide with the limits that Payutto has in mind would remain to be seen, but certainly there is room for differences in judgment here. There are significant differences even now between countries as to where these limits should be placed without endangering the fundamental universality of human rights.

We can see in these quotations that Payutto's "self-development" stands in the place of the "human dignity" presupposed by the UDHR and other international human rights documents. Each is the fundamental premise, assumed not proven, that justifies all the rights that follow. And even though Payutto himself never says such a thing—and even expressly denies such a thing in a subsequent statement, as we shall see shortly—I would argue that we have here a kind of natural law foundation for human rights in Buddhism. Such a case would run as follows: humans are by nature inherently an extremely precious form of life ("the best of educable beings"), the purpose of which is self-development in the direction of perfection (or Buddhahood). "By the law of Dharma," "every individual should be left free, if not provided with the opportunity, to develop himself so that his potentiality can unfold itself and work its way toward perfection." This is the duty of society, to which humans individually and collectively have a right. When the liberty to pursue self-development is denied by the state, individuals, and collections of individuals have the right to struggle to attain that liberty. When the state fails to provide important resources supportive of self-development, individuals and collections of individuals should work together with appropriate agencies to make such resources available.

The latter invitation to work together with others to gain necessary resources is not a right. It seems to me, however, that the invitation to struggle against any who interfere with one's process of self-development makes the freedoms related to self-development into rights. Moreover, inasmuch as those rights are based upon the nature of a human being as understood in Buddhism and upon the law of Dharma, these rights are based in Buddhist natural law. The claims, then, would not be rights, but the basic liberties would be inasmuch as, in Chamarik's words, "freedom is indeed the essence of Buddhism."

The above passage, so apparently supportive to human rights ideas, was written by Payutto in 1982. In 1992, Payutto gave a speech titled "The Making of a Democracy" to a group of Thai people in New York, shortly after serious political disturbances in Bangkok, and in 1993 Payutto gave a speech to the Parliament of the World's Religions in Chicago; in both these speeches, his comments on human rights are more restrained. Let us turn to them.[62]

It seems that in the 1992 and 1993 speeches Payutto wanted to clarify two points with respect to rights. First, he wanted to more carefully balance rights and responsibilities. Second, he wanted to emphasize the conventional and provisional nature of rights. In 1992 he said,

> [S]ometimes we tend to give so much attention to our rights and liberties that we forget that there are duties required of us. Rights must be balanced by duties. The people of a democracy have rights, and they also have duties; having obtained their rights, they must perform their duties. . . .
>
> Rights must arise with duties. . . . It is the duty of a democratic government to create an awareness of the importance of duties, so that the people understand that rights obtained are to be offset by duties performed. People should ask themselves what needs to be done in exchange for the rights they are to obtain, and think more of what they can do or give than what they can get. This attitude is exemplified in the famous statement by President John F. Kennedy—"Ask not what your country can do for you—ask what you can do for your country."
>
> When rights are coupled with duties there is a balance between getting and giving, between receiving and relinquishing. When this kind of balance arises we have the Middle Way which leads to good democracy. . . .
>
> All people, as citizens of the community, have a right to speak on political matters. However, we should not think only of exercising our rights, but also reflect whether what we are about to say is truly vital or beneficial to the community. . . .
>
> The more freedom there is, the more is a sense of responsibility necessitated. If liberty is coupled with a sense of responsibility, a balance—a Middle Way—will result, ensuring the creation of a true democracy.[63]

This is clear, and reasonable, enough. In fact, though he does not go into details, Payutto does a good job here of balancing the poles of the dichotomy that has exercised us throughout this chapter: individual liberty versus what one owes to the social web. As Taylor reminded us above, even in the most rights-oriented society on Earth, within the web of interdependent societal give and take, the smooth flowing of relationships far surpasses conflictual claims of rights. Payutto's Middle Way proposes that ideally, in the Good society, we will be mindful of both our rights and our responsibilities. In the United States, we tend to be more and more forgetful of the latter, as Payutto subtly reminds us with the Kennedy quotation. He is certainly correct that, if we forget our responsibilities, we will lose our freedoms. Perhaps it is equally true that in many Buddhist countries people are forgetful—or have never known—of their rights. Note that Payutto assumes an apparently universal right to free political speech. Thus, even though he is adding an emphasis on responsibilities here that was not evident in his 1982 writing, he has by no means abandoned human rights. What we see is indeed a very balanced, very Buddhist, Middle Way approach that seeks to reconcile what is good in both the emphasis on liberty of the human rights approach and the emphasis on responsibility of the communitarian social web approach.

Payutto's 1993 speech, given to an international audience, is quite negative with respect to human rights. He declares that he sees human rights as a purely conventional and provisional measure of coping with a world in conflict:

> If we look into the social situation deeply we will see that the reason that such values as human rights . . . are so important in this age is because we do live in such an age of contention, and our thinking is so divisive and factional. While the importance and esteem of concepts such as human rights . . . must be acknowledged, we must also recognize that their importance is based on a world still under the influence of divisive ways of thinking. . . . Human rights are our guarantee of not destroying each other while we are still under the influence of such divisive thinking.[64]

Here he acknowledges the importance of human rights and even states that we should esteem them, but it is a very grudging esteem. Whereas the 1992 speech balanced individuality and rights with the social web and responsibilities in a fairly neutral way, here Payutto longs to abandon the former and commit fully to the latter. The world's problem is that we do not give the social web its due; we engage in divisive thinking—that is, we think of ourselves as separate from others and from society—and contention is the result. Human rights are very important in such a world—and here we see a corroboration of our observation that, as conflict rises in Buddhist countries, there is a greater tendency to embrace human rights ideas—but such a world, ideally, should not exist in the first place.

"The concept of human rights," Payutto declares, "has three major flaws."

Firstly, the concept itself is a result of division, struggle and contention. The idea of human rights has been established to ensure self-preservation and protection of mutual interests. Human rights are usually obtained by demand.

Not only are human rights the product of contention, we see in the last sentence here that they further contribute to contention. In this way, they are far from ideal.

> Secondly, human rights are a convention, purely human inventions which do not exist as a natural condition. They are not "natural rights." Being a human invention, they are not firmly founded on truth. They must be supported by laws and they must be accepted by all parties in order to work. If human rights are to be lasting and firm they must be connected to natural reality and to do this human mentality must be developed to a stage where people are prepared to honor human rights.[65]

As indicated above, I believe that in 1982 Payutto was well on his way to seeing human rights, at least those related to self-development, as natural rights. Here, however, he expressly rejects such an idea. Why? It seems, again, that the very fact of the contentiousness inherent in human rights, their adversarial nature, is out of step, for Payutto, with "truth," that is, the web of interdependence. If I understand him correctly, the evidence for this is that they require force (laws) in order to work. If humankind developed its mentality such that we all automatically respected what we now call each other's rights (in other words, if we did not have the impulse to harm or oppress others), then we could say that human rights were in harmony with truth, that is, reality.

> [Third,] human rights . . . are merely conventions for social behavior. They do not delve into the question of mental motivation. . . . While we must acknowledge the demands of human rights activists, we must also analyze their quality of mind before we can clearly understand the situation. . . . [M]any demands for human rights . . . are often based on or influenced by aversion, resentment or fear. As long as such feelings are there, it will be very difficult to obtain a truly good result from human rights activities, because the basic feeling behind them is not truly harmonious. When human rights activities are motivated by unskillful drives, the resulting behavior will be too aggressive to obtain the required result.[66]

Once again, it seems that human rights are correct in moral content ("we must acknowledge the demands of human rights activists"), but what Payutto cannot accept is the adversarial relationship that they presume and the (from a Buddhist perspective) negative factors that frequently, even normally, are evoked by such a posture and become mixed in the motivation—aversion, resentment, or fear. Any structures that feed the latter can only be regarded as deleterious.

What, in the end, shall we conclude regarding Payutto's views on human rights? We should note that the writing that most strongly endorses rights was intended for a purely Thai audience at a time (1982) when human rights was a largely unknown idea among Thais; the speech for an audience of Thais in New York—right at the time when many Thais were beginning to exercise their rights—took an "in-between," balanced approach that assumed human rights but stressed the importance of exercising them with responsibility; and the 1993 speech to an international audience at the Parliament of the World's Religions—a very globalizing moment—is by far the most negative toward the concept of human rights. Did these times and audiences influence his words, such that those who most needed to hear about rights received the strongest endorsement of rights, whereas those who already assumed the correctness of a rights approach heard a corrective message? This would be possible if his "true" view is represented by the 1992 speech balancing rights and responsibilities in a Middle Way. On the other hand, perhaps his views have simply evolved over time, such that the latest speech represents his most mature and considered view. In either case, we can see in Payutto, I believe, that Buddhist position that endorses the moral content of the internationally recognized human rights, but is ambivalent at best about the adversarial and legalistic elements of the very concept of a right.[67]

THE DALAI LAMA

The Dalai Lama regularly speaks of both rights and responsibilities. Our focus here will be on his views on human rights and the interplay between rights and responsibilities.

The Dalai Lama's 1993 speech at the Non-Governmental Organizations United Nations World Conference on Human Rights, in Vienna, gave a succinct statement of his unequivocal support for human rights. "The acceptance of universally binding standards of Human Rights as laid down in the Universal Declaration of Human Rights and in the International Covenants of Human Rights is essential in today's shrinking world. Respect for fundamental human rights should not remain an ideal to be achieved but a requisite foundation for every human society."[68] It would hardly be possible to be more straightforward in one's endorsement of universal human rights than that.

His Holiness gives both a brief philosophical and a pragmatic justification for his endorsement of human rights:

> No matter what country or continent we come from we are all basically the same human beings. We have the common human needs and concerns. We all seek happiness and try to avoid suffering regardless of our race, religion, sex or political status. Human beings, indeed all sentient beings, have the right to pursue happiness and live in peace and in freedom. As free human beings we can use our unique intelligence to try to understand ourselves and our world. But if we are prevented from using our creative potential, we are deprived of one of the basic characteristics of a human being. It is very often the most gifted, dedicated and creative members of our society who become victims of human rights abuses. Thus the political, social, cultural and economic developments of a society are obstructed by the violations of human rights. Therefore, the protection of these rights and freedoms are of immense importance both for the individuals affected and for the development of the society as a whole.[69]

The philosophical case is this: in an implicit variation on the natural law perspective discussed in chapter 4, rights here explicitly follow from nature. All humans seek happiness and avoid pain. We can do no other. That is our nature. In the natural law perspective discussed above, it was held that human social arrangements should adapt themselves to the nature of reality/nature in such a way as to be conducive to freeing humans from suffering. It follows that governments should not interfere with this human imperative, that is, they have no justification for doing so. In short, humans have a right to freely pursue happiness.

Pragmatically, His Holiness points out the importance to society of allowing the "most gifted, dedicated and creative" members of society—those who tend to get into trouble in autocratic regimes—to freely speak and act. No one, and no state, likes to be criticized, and yet this is the way that improvement often is made. This argument is very similar to the argument that we saw Payutto make in chapter 4 on behalf of liberty:

> Liberty . . . is the ability to contribute personal potential to overall social growth. Everybody has their potential and abilities, but they cannot be expressed without freedom. Without liberty, people cannot voice their views or make use of their intelligence. Society in turn derives no benefit from their potential. Undemocratic governments tend to close off or limit op-

portunities for people to use their potential, and so they do not make the most of their human resources. In a democracy, people's abilities and intelligence are allowed to participate freely in social development, and this is one of the strengths of the democratic system.[70]

This remark is from Payutto's 1992 speech. He, the Dalai Lama, and Suu Kyi (see chapter 4), bearing in mind the interdependence of individual and society, all recognize that society cannot flourish if the individual is stifled. Thus, in their view it is in the interest of society, as well as the individual, for individual freedom to be maximized.

His Holiness explicitly takes on the issue of universality by responding to the "Asian values" challenge and the challenge of cultural diversity:

> Recently some Asian governments have contended that the standards of human rights laid down in the Universal Declaration of Human Rights are those advocated by the West and cannot be applied to Asia and other parts of the Third World because of differences in culture and differences in social and economic development. I do not share this view and I am convinced that the majority of Asian people do not support this view either, for it is the inherent nature of all human beings to yearn for freedom, equality and dignity, and they have an equal [right] to achieve that. . . . Diversity and traditions can never justify the violations of human rights. Thus discrimination of persons from a different race, of women, and of weaker sections of society may be traditional in some regions, but if they are inconsistent with universally recognized human rights, these forms of behavior must change. The universal principles of equality of all human beings must take precedence.[71]

Like Suu Kyi and Sulak, the Dalai Lama uncompromisingly affirms the necessity for full protection of human rights without the slightest compromise for cultural diversity. Human beings are by nature the same—all inherently seek freedom, equality, and dignity—so diversity of culture should make no difference. The Dalai Lama's view thus verges on a natural law view in which universal human nature makes imperative the fundamental human rights. His view is reminiscent of Donnelly's statement, "Within these limits, all is possible. Outside of them, little should be allowed."[72] But the Dalai Lama does not stop here. "[S]ome governments still consider the fundamental human rights of its citizens an internal matter of the state. They do not accept that the fate of a people in any country is the legitimate concern of the entire human family. . . . It is not only our right as members of the global human family to protest when our brothers and sisters are being treated brutally, but it is also our duty to do whatever we can to help them."[73] This is another striking statement, obviously pertinent to Tibet's situation with China, but clearly not limited to that context, in which we are invited to see human rights concerns as trumping not only cultural difference but also sovereignty and are invited to take action on behalf of anyone, anywhere suffering brutal treatment. This could suggest that the foreign policies of nations should be based upon human rights, as well as the actions of individuals. But not all of the Dalai Lama's comments pertain to Tibet's interests. "[T]here still remains a major gulf at the heart of the human family. By this I am referring to the North-South divide. If we are serious in our commitment to the fundamental principles of equality, principles which, I believe, lie at the heart of the concept of human rights, today's economic disparity can no longer be ignored. . . . We have a responsibility to find ways to achieve a more equitable distribution of world's resources."[74] A statement like this seems to spring from the Dalai Lama's compassion for the suffering of others and for the concern that the vast North-South economic inequities have the potential to breed tremendous violence.

His Holiness goes on: "It is natural and just for nations, peoples and individuals to demand respect for their rights and freedoms and to struggle to end repression, racism, economic exploitation, military occupation, and various forms of colonialism and alien domination. Governments should actively support such demands instead of only paying lip service to them."[75] After all we have heard of "Asian values" and fitting in harmoniously with the web of interdependence, it is startling to see this language of "demand" from an eminent Buddhist leader. Clearly, there is no hesitation about occupying the adversarial position here! Or is it adversarial? The Dalai Lama and other Tibetans frequently remark that it is bad for the Chinese that they are occupying Tibet and thus it is for both the Tibetans' and the Chinese' sake that the Tibetans oppose China's occupation of Tibet. The same would apply to opposing any violation of a fundamental human right. Thus, what appears to be adversarial is, in the Tibetan view, not adversarial at all.

The Dalai Lama concludes this address with his characteristic remarks on universal responsibility:

> As we approach the end of the Twentieth Century, we find that the world is becoming one community. We are being drawn together by the grave problems of overpopulation, dwindling natural resources, and an environ-

mental crisis that threaten the very foundation of our existence on this planet. Human rights, environmental protection and great social and economic equality, are all interrelated. I believe that to meet the challenges of our times, human beings will have to develop a greater sense of universal responsibility. Each of us must learn to work not just for one self, one's own family or one's nation, but for the benefit of all humankind. Universal responsibility is the key to human survival. It is the best foundation for world peace.[76]

Thus, the Dalai Lama combines total commitment to human rights with total commitment to social responsibility. With him it is clearly not a matter of either/or, but a matter of complete dedication to both/and. He clearly has no notion of any conflict between the two approaches. In fact, the Tibetan government in exile makes its case on behalf of Tibet mostly on the basis of human rights arguments, while His Holiness's most famous, and constantly repeated, contribution to international thinking about ethics is his idea of universal responsibility. This is a full commitment to both approaches. How, then, does he connect rights and responsibilities in his own thinking? Let us turn to his 1999 book *Ethics for the New Millennium* for insight into this matter.

As in 1993, in 1999 the Dalai Lama continues to maintain that the human desire for happiness, as part of our nature, is the foundation of regarding the freedom to pursue happiness as a human right.

> Our every intended action, in a sense our whole life . . . can be seen as our answer to the great question which confronts us all: "How am I to be happy?"
>
> . . . The desire or inclination to be happy and to avoid suffering knows no boundaries. It is in our nature. As such, it needs no justification and is validated by the simple fact that we naturally and correctly want this. . . .
>
> . . . [L]ike ourselves, all others desire to be happy and to avoid suffering. Given that this is a natural disposition, shared by all, it follows that each individual has a right to pursue this goal.[77]

As in his 1993 work, it is human nature to desire happiness. In light of the naturalness and universality of the human drive to achieve happiness, there can be no justification for interfering with this drive (unless, as we shall see, one is interfering with others' pursuit of happiness). Hence, our pursuit of happiness is an inalienable human right.

The right to pursue happiness, the Dalai Lama makes clear, is concerned with more than the pursuit of mundane happiness. He puts the human concern to overcome mundane suffering firmly within the purview of Shakyamuni Buddha's interest in eliminating suffering as such, at its root.

> When you realize that it *is* possible to eliminate the root that gives rise to suffering, that awareness will increase your determination to identify and reflect on suffering at all different levels, and that will inspire you to seek liberation. . . .
>
> [I]t is important to see that all sentient beings do not want suffering and do want happiness. Everyone has the right to be happy, to overcome suffering.[78]

Mundane suffering and the broader *duḥkha*, the dis-ease of the human condition as such, he seems to be saying, form a continuum; both are comprehended in Shakyamuni's work to eliminate suffering by its root. In this sense, the universal desire to be happy and to overcome suffering could be seen as the work of the Buddha nature within us, the natural functioning of which is our very dissatisfaction with mundane, deluded life and its flip side, the magnetic draw we feel toward something that can satisfy our dis-ease—enlightenment itself.

This being our nature, why not speak of a "right" to seek both mundane and spiritual happiness? If my analysis is correct, the Dalai Lama's view would be very similar to Payutto's 1982 view, both of which I see as expressing an implicit Buddhist natural law foundation for those human rights related to "self-development," spiritual self-realization, or the attainment of mundane and spiritual happiness. This would seem to be the way in which an Engaged Mahayana Buddhist "right" to freedom of religion is generated, a call to governments to protect something essential to every human being. Indeed, from a Buddhist perspective, this may be the most fundamental, natural, and ineluctable of all rights we claim as human beings. And, as we have seen, many other rights are necessary in support of this most basic right.

Whereas many Buddhists infer human rights from a traditional Buddhist understanding of moral responsibilities (as in the Cambodian interpretation of the Five Lay Precepts), the Dalai Lama actually infers ethical responsibilities from human rights: "I have observed that we all naturally desire happiness and not to suffer. I have suggested, furthermore, that these are rights, from which in my opinion we can infer that an ethical act is one which does not harm others' experience or expectation of happiness."[79] Here we move from nature (human nature seeks happiness and freedom from suffering) to rights (the good that human nature inherently and universally seeks no power is justified in impeding) to responsibility (all of us have an ethical duty to avoid impeding or harming another's pursuit of happiness). For the Dalai Lama, responsibility is based upon a specific right, the equal right everyone has to be happy and free from suffering. We have a clear duty—a moral imperative—not to interfere with others' pursuit of happiness, which is their fundamental right.

Beyond the level of our duty to respect others' rights, however, we may wish to do what we can to further others' happiness. Here we leave the realm of moral imperatives, but not, for the Dalai Lama, the realm of what we *should* do. This leads us to His Holiness's idea of universal responsibility. Let us take another look at a quotation seen before.

> I am convinced that it is essential that we cultivate a sense of what I call universal responsibility. . . . When I say that on the basis of concern for others' well-being we can, and should, develop a sense of universal responsibility. . . [w]hat is entailed . . . is . . . a reorientation of our heart and mind away from self and toward others. To develop a sense of universal responsibility—of the universal dimension of our every act and of the equal right of all others to happiness and not to suffer—is to develop an attitude of mind whereby, when we see an opportunity to benefit others, we will take it in preference to merely looking after our own narrow interests.[80]

What is universal responsibility, in the understanding of the Dalai Lama? Emotionally, it grows out of concern for others, or compassion. As this concern grows, it develops into a preference for doing something that will benefit others over acts that merely benefit oneself. Ultimately, we can see behind this preference four beliefs rooted in Buddhist thought, two of which are named here: an awareness of the "universal dimension of our every act" and of "the equal right of all others to happiness and not to suffer."

The "equal right of all others to happiness" is based upon human sameness—the fact that all humans desire happiness and that there is no objective reason to privilege oneself or any other person or being over any other. It is true, His Holiness notes, that "the impact our actions have on our close ones will generally be much greater than on others, and therefore our responsibilities toward them are greater. Yet we need to recognize that, ultimately, there are no grounds for discriminating in their favor."[81]

The basic Buddhist worldview of interdependence has two implications relevant to universal responsibility. First, because we live in a vast web of interconnectedness, "our every action, our every deed, word, and thought, no matter how slight or inconsequential it may seem, has an implication not only for ourselves but for all others, too."[82] That is, it is because of interconnectedness that our actions create a ripple effect that results in a "universal dimension in our every act." Second, a corollary of interdependence is also relevant to universal responsibility: the fact that "my" interest and well-being are inseparable from the interest and well-being of others means that not only can "my" interest not trump "your" interest, but also that no individual's interest can trump any other individual's interest. What remains is to act in the interest of all.

The fourth idea behind universal responsibility, frequently mentioned by His Holiness, is the relative numbers involved. This is most succinctly stated in his 1993 address. "To encourage myself in this altruistic attitude, I sometimes find it helpful to imagine myself standing as a single individual on one side, facing a huge gathering of all other human beings on the other side. Then I ask myself, 'Whose interests are more important?' To me it is quite clear that however important I may feel I am, I am just one individual while others are infinite in number and importance."[83] It is this awareness of the relative numbers involved that finally takes us from regarding all others as equal and inseparable from ourselves to the point of full-bodied altruism: giving preference to the welfare of others over one's own welfare. For His Holiness, this may ultimately get to the point at which one is ready to sacrifice oneself for the sake of others.

> We are just one individual among infinite others. No matter how important we are, we are just one sentient being, one single self, while others are infinite. But there is a close relationship of interdependence. Our suffering or happiness is very much related with others. That is also reality. Under these circumstances, if, in order to save one finger the other nine fingers are sacrificed, that is foolish. But if, in order to save nine fingers, one finger is sacrificed, it may be worth it. So you see the importance of others' rights and your own rights, and others' welfare and your own welfare.[84]

It should be obvious that the state of awareness under discussion here cannot be a merely intellectual understanding if it is expected to move us sufficiently to choose altruism over self-benefit. That is to say, we are here in the territory of the bodhi-sattva. As Śāntideva says in his *Bodhicaryāvatāra,*

> I should dispel the suffering of others because it is suffering like my own suffering. I should help others too because of their nature as beings, which is like my own being.
>
> When happiness is liked by me and others equally, what is so special about me that I strive after happiness only for myself?
>
> When fear and suffering are disliked by me and others equally, what is so special about me that I protect myself and not the other? . . .
>
> Without exception, no sufferings belong to anyone. They must be warded off simply because they are suffering. Why is any limitation put on this?[85]

The Dalai Lama makes it clear that the world will not be saved by respecting human rights. It is "universal responsibility [that] is the key to human survival." The respect of human rights is a necessary, but by no means sufficient, element in a world that works and supports human, and other, life. Although human rights are essential, they simply prevent harm. Compassion, or universal responsibility, far surpasses the reach of human rights in its ability to actively improve the world.[86]

In the end, then, how does His Holiness reconcile his championing of both human rights and universal responsibility? We have seen that many Buddhist intellectuals have said or implied that human rights and responsibility to others represent, respectively, self-concerned individualism and altruistic compassion. Do these two values, then, not point in opposite, irreconcilable directions? By no means.

What we see here is nothing but the familiar tripartite developmental ideal: "Not to do any evil, to cultivate good, to purify one's mind, this is the Teaching of the Buddhas." What we see in His Holiness's thought is the advocacy of a single continuum of behavior. From the point of view of the practitioner, "not to do any evil" embraces respecting others' human rights (and much more, of course). But the practitioner should go on and "cultivate good" that incorporates "purifying one's mind" (or, for Mahayana, "saving all beings"); that is, one practices universal responsibility, which is simply an expression of compassion, up to the point of bodhisattvahood. From this perspective, respecting human rights and practicing universal responsibility are a single continuum of behavior to be undertaken by the Buddhist practitioner.

From the perspective of the one on the receiving end of the practitioner's behavior respecting human rights and practicing universal responsibility, there is also a continuum, a continuum of expectation. If the social web of mutual dependence is in place at all, the very minimum we should be able to expect of each other is that our human rights should be respected. We should be able to expect as a norm that aggressive, antisocial behavior, and behavior that interferes with our efforts to achieve self-realization, will be both scarce and entirely unacceptable to human society. Beyond this, we should expect less frequent, but occasional, acts of caring and gratuitous kindness from others. This also is the norm.

But what about that problem that has so exercised us in this chapter, the apparent adversarial nature of human rights? This does not seem to bother the Dalai Lama, or the Tibetan leadership for that matter, one bit. He, and they, "demand" respect for human rights in Tibet. Is this surprising? There are two considerations that justify their attitude. First, as we have seen, the Tibetans do not see themselves as taking up an adversarial attitude. Their struggle and fate is interdependent with the struggle and fate of the Chinese. They wish the latter well. They believe that it is very much in the interest of the Chinese themselves that they stop committing the human rights violations that they are perpetrating in Tibet. These violations are earning them terrible karma, which will result in great suffering in the future. To act on their good wishes toward the Chinese, the Tibetans need to do everything they can (nonviolently) to stop the Chinese from acting against their own long-term interests by violating the Tibetans' human rights. So it is for the Chinese as well as for the Tibetans that the Tibetan leadership demands that the Chinese respect the Tibetans' human rights. By demanding their human rights of the Chinese, it seems that the Dalai Lama and the Tibetan leadership have followed to their end the implications of the nonadversarial stance.

In addition, if it is the case, as Payutto and the Dalai Lama seem to imply, that self-development, or one's progress along the path toward enlightenment, is the essence of what it is to be a human being and if it is also the case that one's fundamental human rights are necessary to that process of self-development—if, in short, human rights are natural rights based in the kind of beings we are within the law of Dharma—then does it not follow out of respect for one's own human imperative to progress toward enlightenment that one has a duty to struggle (nonviolently) for one's own human rights? Is this not necessitated by the imperative to do no evil and cultivate good? Is this not also the correct view if one views oneself and others dispassionately as same and equal—if one would act to protect the human rights of others, *should* one not act to protect one's own human rights just the same, for the sake of Dharma and self-development? It is never good to let the oppressor or the brutal one harm another. Is it not the case by the same token that it is also never good to *let* others or oneself be oppressed, brutalized, or impeded in one's progress on the path to enlightenment without making some (nonviolent) effort to protect what is of such great value—a human life with the potential of Buddhahood? Energy is a factor of enlightenment. The Buddha did say, "Work out your own salvation with diligence." Such considerations I see in the background of the Dalai Lama's espousing of both human rights and universal responsibility.

The Dalai Lama concludes his *Ethics for the New Millennium* with a comment on human rights, love, and compassion: "This, then, is my true religion, my simple faith. . . . Our own heart, our own mind, is the temple. The doctrine is compassion. Love for others and respect for their rights and dignity, no matter who or what they are: ultimately these are all we need."[87] Here, as his book closes, the Dalai Lama places respect for human rights together with love and compassion at the very core of his vision of what is needful for a happy and ethical life.

6   Nonviolence and Its Limits

Most Engaged Buddhists are principled adherents of nonviolence. That is, they adhere to nonviolence on principle in the belief that nonviolence is an inherent good that should not be sacrificed in the interest of achieving some other end, however important. The major traditional source of such principled Buddhist nonviolence is the first precept inviting abstention from the taking of life. In addition, such Buddhist virtues as *ahiṁsā* (nonharmfulness), compassion, and loving kindness are well understood in Buddhist countries to be marks of personal morality as well as religious and cultural ideals. Right Thought, the second component of the Noble Eightfold Path, is a condition that, among other things, is free from thoughts of violence.

Nonviolence, it would seem, should be a straightforward matter among Engaged Buddhists—but it is not. In this chapter, we will examine nonviolence as one of the core values of Engaged Buddhism and the creativity and insight with which Engaged Buddhist leaders apply it to the contemporary world. We will also look at various dilemmas that Engaged Buddhist nonviolence occasions as well as several ways in which its limits are tested.

PRINCIPLED NONVIOLENCE

MAHA GHOSANANDA

Maha Ghosananda, of Cambodia, has initiated walks for peace, known as Dhammayietra. The Dhammayietra movement grew out of an experience of profound suffering. Maha Ghosananda frequently prays, "The suffering of Cambodia has been deep. / From this suffering comes Great Compassion."[1] Maha Ghosananda believes that suffering of such magnitude as the Cambodian Holocaust leads to a gut-level revulsion from violence that cuts through all other considerations. In a Cambodia still divided into warring camps, Maha Ghosananda called the Dhammayietra the "army of the Buddha" and an "army for peace" that would "shoot the people with bullets of loving kindness." He declared that "nonviolence is the primary precept of Cambodian history, culture, and religion."[2]

Maha Ghosananda and the Dhammayietra have been a major force for peace and reconciliation in Cambodia in the post–Khmer Rouge years. The first, in 1992, accompanied the first refugees to return home from refugee camps. The second, held the following year immediately before the first national elections in Cambodian history, helped create an atmosphere that removed people's fear and made the elections possible.[3] Since then, the Dhammayietra has proceeded annually, entering areas where hostilities continued and taking on other issues such as the environment. In addition, Maha Ghosananda has himself been involved in working for dialogue and reconciliation between Cambodia's mutually antagonistic parties.

There have been remarkably few acts of revenge in Cambodia against the Khmer Rouge. The Cambodian people seem to have taken to heart the Buddhist teaching of karma—that if they take revenge on the Khmer Rouge, they will merely invite future retaliation against themselves or their children, and they just want the killing to stop. Maha Ghosananda has emphasized this theme since his first entry into the refugee camps on the Thai-Cambodian border, preaching on the *Dhammapada* text, "Hatred is never overcome by hatred; it is overcome by nonhatred. This is an eternal law." He also preaches directly about karma and ending the cycle of violence.

I do not question that loving one's oppressors—Cambodians loving the Khmer Rouge—may be the most difficult attitude to achieve. But it is a law of the universe that retaliation, hatred, and revenge only continue the cycle and never stop it. Reconciliation does not mean that we surrender rights and conditions, but rather that we use love in all of our negotiations. It means that we see ourselves in the opponent—for what is the opponent but a being in ignorance, and we ourselves are also ignorant of many things. Therefore, only loving kindness and right mindfulness can free us.[4]

Maha Ghosananda embodies many of the themes we will see in this chapter as principles of Engaged Buddhist nonviolence: focusing on stopping the killing as the first priority; remaining mindful of karma; being motivated by compassion and loving kindness; refusing to utterly separate oneself from and reject the enemy; and taking up a nonviolence that is active rather than passive and does not mean "surrendering rights and conditions."

A. T. ARIYARATNE

Ariyaratne is another of the principled nonviolent Engaged Buddhist leaders. Best known for his development work, in recent years the pursuit of an end to the violence in Sri Lanka has become one of Ariyaratne's principal goals. Whereas the Sarvodaya Shanti Sena (Peace Brigades) Movement was initiated in 1978, three further initiatives were recently launched: the People's Peace Initiative; the peace center, Vishva Niketan ("Universal Abode"); and the Sarvodaya People's Peace Plan.

Funds for the peace center Vishva Niketan have come from Ariyaratne's receipt of the Niwano Peace Award (1994) and the Gandhi Peace Prize (1997), along with donations. The following will give an idea of its purposes and the programs that are intended for it: "Vishva Niketan asserts human rights as the basis of peace and justice in every community of the world. It promotes inter-faith, inter-racial, inter-political and inter-state understanding. It sponsors actions that promote co-operation between communities and religious denominations, providing a neutral ground for the resolution of disputes arising within communities as well as those on a larger scale between countries."[5] More concretely, anticipated programs include training a "peace corps in activities and functions relating to peace building, crisis intervention and non-violent dispute resolution"; offering "dialogues, meditational sessions, educational and service camps, seminars and conferences" to promote understanding across lines of religious, racial, and communal divisions; and supporting research on peace and the publication of works on peace.

The People's Peace Initiative held its first event on August 29, 1999, with a massive peace walk and meditation in Colombo that drew 170,000 people. Since then, many other large peace walks and meditations have been held throughout Sri Lanka. The goal of this initiative is to get one million people to participate in such peace walks and meditations. Involving one million people in peace meditations, in turn, has two objectives: the development of personal peace and of collective peace. "When an individual lacks inner peace domestic harmony is affected. When domestic harmony is lost, peace among neighbours too thins out. In this manner when inner peace of an individual is lost, the family, neighbourhood, country and the world too start losing [their] peaceful atmosphere. Persons and groups lacking peace of mind hang on to nationality, language, religion, politics, ethnic groups, high status, low positions, etc. and engage themselves in anti-society acts of crime, terrorism and war."[6] Here peace is directly constructed by the inner transformation of the individual practicing peace meditation. It is expected that the peace thus constructed will be expressed in peaceful action that will make family, neighborhood, and, ultimately, country and world more peaceful. Thus, the more meditators become involved, the more peace is created.

A second idea at work in the People's Peace Initiative—less harmonious with modern, scientific, and Western ways of thinking, but directly expressed in ancient Buddhist texts and practices as well as this modern movement—is the idea of radiating out peace to one's community during the meditation practice itself. At the mass peace meditations, after an hour of meditation on the breath, meditation on loving kindness and vipassana meditation, the meditators are directed in their last meditation period to "direct the last five minutes of your meditation to spread in all directions the spiritual energy amassed by all of us wishing for peace for all."[7] It is expected that those who do not meditate will be transformed by those who do meditate and who radiate their state of consciousness toward the nonmeditators.

> [The] People's Peace Initiative aims at creating peace within the "psycho-sphere" through meditational practices. By extending loving-kindness to all beings while meditating (metta meditation), [a] "field of peace expands in one's mind, synchronizing with others. As the field of peace is gradually filling thousands of inner selves, negative sentiments that feed the war come to cease. The optimum impact will be that war becomes unthinkable.". . .
>
> The first task is, therefore, to get a million people to participate in this spiritual awakening process for peace within and outside. Secondly, 200,000 of them will regularly radiate spiritual energies in an hour-long meditation every morning and evening. Thirdly, 500 persons will commit themselves to be spiritual guides and promoters of this mass spiritual awakening process. Only when building up of a spiritual infrastructure is completed, non-violent direct action programmes will be advanced and implemented.[8]

Here one is radiating loving kindness (mettā) not only as part of one's own program of self-transformation, nor merely as an expression of one's wishing well toward others, but in the expectation that radiating loving kindness will have a causative effect in transforming the state of mind of nonmeditators and, consequently, their behavior.

In both Vishva Niketan and the People's Peace Initiative, violence (primarily the violence in Sri Lanka and secondarily violence anywhere in the world) is itself identified as the problem, the goal is identified as a state of peace, and the means by which the state of peace will be brought into being are themselves the embodiment of peace, that is, peace meditations and peace programs. Recently, among methods to bring peace into being, peace meditations have assumed a prominent place in Ariyaratne's work. He clearly believes that a necessary foundation for successful peace work is a sufficiently widespread mental condition of readiness for peace. "We believe that the only way to achieve peace is to cultivate individual and collective inner peace."[9]

Building upon the success of the People's Peace Initiative, Sarvodaya and Ariyaratne introduced the Sarvodaya People's Peace Plan early in 2001.[10] This plan explicitly states in its opening statement that violence is the problem and peace the solution: The problem is not LTTE [Tamil Tigers] or the Government. The problem is VIOLENCE and the conditions that nurture and support it. The Sarvodaya goal is to eliminate war and violence from our consciousness: TO MAKE WAR UNTHINKABLE.[11]

In his analysis of the situation in Sri Lanka, Ariyaratne ranges his Sarvodaya "army" against those of the government and the Tamil Tigers:

There are three "armies" in Sri Lanka right now:

- The largest armed group is the 175,000 member Sri Lankan military.
- The smallest force is the highly motivated Liberation Tigers of Tamil Eelam or LTTE. . . .
- The third force consists of Sarvodaya's staff and volunteers, numbering close to 100,000, along with over 215,000 people from all walks of life who have already attended a Sarvodaya Peace Meditation. This group is backed by an infrastructure of millions of Sri Lankans who have participated in Sarvodaya's development activities over the years. Sarvodaya is mobilizing and activating this nonviolent group to achieve lasting peace on the island. In Meditation Programmes and other peace activities to follow, more and more will join.[12]

Ariyaratne is convinced that the nature of the civil war in Sri Lanka is such that it cannot be won by the military forces of either the government or the Tamil Tigers. "History shows that ethnic conflicts can go on for decades, even centuries. This is because ethnic war (a war based in large part on ethnicity) is inherently unwinnable. Even if the parties stop shooting, the war will go on in other forms. Ethnic war can only be transcended. Curing the conditions that lead to conflict can transcend ethnic conflict. If the fuel for ethnic conflict is lack and deprivation, the real solution for ethnic peace is a sustainable, spiritually balanced island that works for all." Note that, after dismissing the possibility of either side "winning" the war, Ariyaratne moves into an analysis of the problem in terms of the Four Noble Truths, an approach that he took with great success in his development work. Implicit in the above paragraph is the following analysis: Noble Truth 1, the problem: the war in Sri Lanka. Noble Truth 2, the cause: lack and deprivation. Elsewhere, he adds, "In order to transcend war, we must transform our economy. Poverty breeds violence. The biggest force driving the war is the continued poverty that haunts our island."[13] Noble Truth 3, cessation of the problem: a state of peace, "a sustainable, spiritually balanced island that works for all." Noble Truth 4, the way to cessation of the problem: Sarvodaya peace and development programs.

Ariyaratne has a classically Buddhist view of how to stop war: remove the causes of war. "This arising, that arises. . . . This ceasing, that ceases."[14] Remove the fuel and the fire goes out. How does Ariyaratne envision the violence ending? "Because of Sarvodaya's work in the spiritual, psychological, and development fields, the war grinds to a halt as the foundations for violent conflict are removed."[15] No one "wins." When the conditions supporting the violence are eliminated, the war stops of itself.

How, more concretely, is this envisioned to happen? The Sarvodaya Peace Programme has five steps, the first of which is: "Step One: ALL PARTIES CEASE VIOLENCE RIGHT NOW, with no preconditions, limits or terms."[16] This is highly reminiscent of the approach taken by the Unified Buddhist Church of Vietnam and Thich Nhat Hanh during the war in Vietnam; in that case also, the Buddhists urged a "Third Way" favoring neither North nor South and called for a general ceasefire, leaving discovery of a political solution for the second step. The most urgent step was felt to be stopping the violence, the killing, and the sowing of further seeds of hatred and violence through present acts of hatred and violence.

A difficulty here is that violence is self-perpetuating; those who have been harmed generally feel the urge to retaliate. Of course, the Sri Lankan case is entirely different from the Vietnamese case in that the former is free of the presence of global superpowers that simply overwhelm any grassroots peace efforts. Even so, how does a nonviolent group get the combatants to lay down their arms? Sarvodaya, again, thinks in terms of removing the conditions supporting the violence, chiefly, here, popular support for violent acts on the part of both the Sri Lankan government and the Tamil Tigers. If that support could be removed, in the Sarvodaya thinking, the acts of violence would slowly cease for lack of fuel. Sarvodaya's effort to drain popular support from the violence on both sides is already well underway with its Peace Meditation program. This is part of a larger program to make violence unacceptable in the hearts and minds of the Sri Lankan people.

Thus, the specific program urged by Sarvodaya as "Step One: ALL PARTIES CEASE VIOLENCE RIGHT NOW," is

- First, eliminate violence from our own hearts and actions through participation in Peace Meditations. Educate the media to support this effort rather than ridicule it.
- Second, ask everyone you know to stop violence and stop supporting violence.
- Third, speak against violence and for peace at every opportunity. Build confidence in all people that we can transcend war.[17]

In other words, this is an effort to build a culture of peace.

The Sarvodaya leadership is well aware that if they succeed in building a culture of peace in Sri Lanka resulting in an end to immediate hostilities, they and the Sri Lankan people will need to take further steps in order for the ceasefire to be permanent. In other words, they will need to remove the deep causes of the conflict, principally ethnic tensions and poverty. The remaining four steps of the five-step Sarvodaya Peace Programme address this need.

"Step Two: All parties work toward healing, reconciliation and inclusivity for all communities." Specifically, Sri Lankans should "work for healing and reconciliation by bringing together all Sri Lankans, at the village level, regardless of race, ethnicity or religion." Sarvodaya has built such an approach into its village-based development program from the beginning.

"Step Three: All parties acknowledge the past pain, despair and suffering that fuels anger and violence. All parties work to end all current and future pain and suffering. . . . First, acknowledge your own pain in your own heart, through the Peace Meditation. Also, acknowledge the pain you have caused others. Second, work to acknowledge and heal past pain and suffering through inter-community work in your village, town or city." The first of these practices is part of the recent Peace Meditation initiative. The second has been part of Sarvodaya's village-based development work all along.

"Step Four: All parties end the economic, social and spiritual conditions that lead to violence (especially in the Dry Zones)." This, in a nutshell, is the basic idea of the Sarvodaya development program, as is reflected in the further directive, "work for the satisfaction of the 'Ten Basic

Needs' for all Sri Lankans." (The Ten Basic Needs have been identified by Sarvodaya as the ten needs that must be satisfied in all communities; they are the basic Sarvodaya goals: a clean and beautiful environment; a clean and adequate supply of water; basic clothing requirements; a balanced diet; a simple house to live in; basic health care; simple communications facilities; basic energy requirements; total education; satisfaction of cultural needs; and satisfaction of spiritual needs.)

And, last, "Step Five: All parties engage in a national conversation on envisioning a future that works for all." Sarvodaya aspires to fundamentally restructure Sri Lankan society and government, to "use the national conversations as the basis for a new, inclusive Constitution."[18]

Ariyaratne did not begin his activist career as a peacemaker; for decades his expertise has been in the area of development. The development work itself, however, has been profoundly nonviolent because of the ground-up nature of the organizing and decision-making processes. Sarvodaya has pioneered the shramadana camp, in which members of a village gather together, ordinarily in the presence of Buddhist monks and Sarvodaya organizers, discuss together the needs of the village, and decide by consensus what projects to take on. As the village decides to go forward with the Sarvodaya process, groups who typically say little in public—such as children, youth, and women—are formally including in oversight committees. This approach avoids the imposition of decisions from above and empowers both individuals and communities as a whole to identify their own needs and take care of them. Although the movement is inspired by Buddhist ideas, Ariyaratne has taken pains to ensure that all Sri Lanka's religious and ethnic groups are equally welcomed, included, respected, and empowered to act on their own behalf. At this point, Sarvodaya constitutes a grassroots network that encompasses half the villages in Sri Lanka, all trained in consensus decision making and all with an enhanced sense of self-reliance. If violence is understood as an extreme form of power over another person or group, this kind of empowerment of both individuals and communities enhances nonviolence at its roots. It has been on the basis of this profoundly nonviolent "development" work (development understood as psychological, spiritual and social, as well as economic), sustained over decades and embracing millions of Sri Lankans, that Ariyaratne and his movement were in an excellent position to respond as the Tamil-Sinhalese violence grew. Ariyaratne himself is well aware of this: "This is the Sarvodaya path to justice and peace through a participatory democracy that evolves from the bottom up. This kind of unorthodox total approach to peacebuilding demands lots of sacrifice and patience, and it is time-consuming. However, when we look at the unique position Sarvodaya holds today in the peacebuilding task of our society, after 41 years of continuous work carried out in over 10,000 villages, we can conclude that there is no shorter path to transform our society from a psychology of killing and threats to kill to one that is life-enhancing and spiritually fulfilling."[19]

At this writing there is a cease-fire in Sri Lanka. Sarvodaya is attempting to solidify and build upon this beginning by continuing their program. On March 15, 2002, crowds of close to 650,000 people gathered in Anuradhapura at the invitation of Sarvodaya to meditate for peace. According to observers, "the gathering may well have been the largest meditation event ever held in the world." At the same time, Sarvodaya launched its "1,000 Village Link-Up" program matching villages in Tamil and Muslim areas in the North and East with villages in the South. At the peace gathering, representatives from the villages exchanged symbolic gifts and lists of potential projects of shramadana (gifts of labor).[20] Ten thousand people from the South volunteered to live and work in Tamil-Muslim areas from March 2002 to the end of the year, giving their time, their labor, material requirements for projects (the rehabilitation of houses, wells, tanks, schools, toilets and places of religious worship), and their friendship in the effort to build a lasting peace. This stunning outpouring of committed work for peace on the part of so many thousands is the latest expression of decades of Sarvodaya's empowering and nonviolent work and a manifestation of the wisdom of the means fitting the end.

THICH NHAT HANH AND THE VIETNAMESE STRUGGLE MOVEMENT

Another famous case of principled nonviolence in Engaged Buddhism is the courageous nonviolence of the Struggle Movement Buddhists during the war in Vietnam. Although Nhat Hanh was the principal ideologue of this movement, nonviolence was put into practice by the many Vietnamese monastics and laypeople involved in the Vietnamese Struggle Movement, or Third Way, under extremely challenging conditions during the war years. This is one of the rare instances of a group maintaining strict nonviolence over a period of years in the midst of war, as the bullets, bombs, and chemical weapons are flying, as millions of one's people are being killed, in a war being fought by no less than the world's greatest superpower. Moreover, the self-identified "Third Way" refused to side with either the North or the South, claiming not to be against anyone, but to be on the side of life. Their reward was often to be attacked by both sides on the principle of "if you're not with us, you're against us."

The Vietnamese Struggle Movement was creative and courageous in engaging in many kinds of nonviolent acts to try to bring the violence to an end. Those actions included noncooperation with the government, including strikes, boycotts, and refusal to participate in the war; aid and protection of deserters and draft resisters; street protests and mass rallies against governments seen as too keen on engaging in war and uninterested in exploring negotiated political solutions; composing and popularizing antiwar songs, poems, plays, and stories; publicized fasting; placing family altars in the street in the path of approaching tanks; and shaving heads (to look like monks and nuns) in protest of government actions.[21]

The Struggle Movement claimed to represent the majority of the South Vietnamese people in its effort to bring the war to an end and probably did. This movement did succeed in bringing down a number of South Vietnamese governments perceived by the public as favoring the war too strongly. Indeed, in 1966 the Struggle Movement briefly seemed on the verge of winning the struggle with the government of South Vietnam, with large segments of the police, civil servants, and the army—both troops and some generals—said to be in "total sympathy" with the Struggle Movement. At this time, the army in Hue and Danang refused to cooperate with efforts to crush the Struggle Movement, and the Saigon government was forced to back down and promise free elections and an end to the military government. Soon, however, Saigon troops, with strong American backing, were brought in to rout the Struggle Movement.[22]

Features particularly representative of the ethical foundation of this movement—evident in the writings of Nhat Hanh—include principled nonviolence, nondualism, understanding the role of karma, and the imperative to act. As an illustration of his principled nonviolence, we may cite Nhat Hanh's comment, "I always put peace and human life above everything." He went on to say that peace in Vietnam was more important than the survival of Buddhism, and the survival of the Vietnamese people was more important than the survival of the Vietnamese nation.[23]

Nondualistic awareness, or nonseparation from all parties, was expressed in the refusal to side *against* anyone, to be only on the side of life. As an antiwar song based on a poem of Nhat Hanh put it,

Our enemy has the name of hatred
Our enemy has the name of inhumanity
Our enemy has the name of anger
Our enemy has the name of ideology

Our enemy wears the mask of freedom
Our enemy is dressed in lies
Our enemy bears empty words
Our enemy is the effort to divide us.
Our enemy is not man.
If we kill man, with whom shall we live?[24]

In the Vietnam War, in which family members might find themselves on both sides of the battlefield, it was particularly easy to see that the person one was killing was his brother, not just metaphorically, but literally. The same principle applied to the combatant sides in the war. Nhat Hanh wrote, "During the war in Vietnam we young Buddhists . . . were able to understand the suffering of both sides, the Communists and the anti-Communists. We tried to be open to both, to understand this side and to understand that side, to be one with them. That is why we did not take a side, even though the whole world took sides. We tried to tell people our perception of the situation: that we wanted to stop the fighting, but the bombs were so loud."[25] Nondualism also meant that the goal was peace and reconciliation, not one side winning over the other. "We wanted reconciliation, we did not want a victory."[26] As the above poem shows, at the end of the war, all parties need and want to live together.

Nonseparation from all parties was also closely linked to understanding the role of karma, or cause and effect, in bringing all involved to their present position of violent conflict. Nhat Hanh wrote, "Try to see that every person involved in the conflict is a victim. . . . See that the situation is possible because of the clinging to ideologies and to an unjust world economic system which is upheld by every person through ignorance or through lack of resolve to change it. See that two sides in a conflict are not really opposing, but two aspects of the same reality. See that the most essential thing is life and that killing or oppressing one another will not solve anything."[27] Nhat Hanh saw the Vietnam War as an ideological war in which the soldiers on the battlefield, both Vietnamese and American, were swept up alike in karmic causes much larger than they. The ideology that brought them to that place, and the vast economic and political systems with which it was interwoven, was their common enemy, but overcoming it did not require taking lives. The combatants were not really each other's enemy.

The imperative to act comes down to the inability to bear the suffering of others, the feeling of the necessity of getting up and doing something to help when confronted with suffering. Nhat Hanh said that, during the war, witnessing the suffering caused by the bombing and the oppressive government, "hurts us too much.

We have to react." In Cambodia also, he said, the bombing "hurt" so much that the monks went out to demonstrate.[28] This is an emotional and visceral process, but not one devoid of wisdom. As we saw in chapter 3, Buddhist ethics do not presume a separation between reason and emotion. In this case, we see a compassion which is emotional, but at the same time, as Nhat Hanh understands it, is the fruit of that experiential wisdom that does not create a wall of separation between self and other, but allows itself to feel their interconnection. Just as one would act to remove the source of one's own pain—pulling a thorn out of one's skin—so, if one no longer felt separation between oneself and another, would one act to remove the cause of suffering in another: as an instinctual, natural, almost inevitable act.

Since the war years, Nhat Hanh has devoted his energy to developing and teaching Engaged Buddhist ideas in many countries, but particularly in the West. He has made probably the single greatest contribution of any Buddhist to global thinking about peacemaking with his insight that, to make peace, it is necessary to "be peace."

> [W]ithout being peace, we cannot do anything for peace. If we cannot smile, we cannot help other people to smile. If we are not peaceful, then we cannot contribute to the peace movement.
> I hope we can bring a new dimension to the peace movement. The peace movement is filled with anger and hatred. It cannot fulfill the path we expect from them. A fresh way of being peace, of doing peace is needed. . . . It would be wonderful if we could bring to the peace movement our contribution, our way of looking at things, that will diminish aggression and hatred. Peace work means, first of all, being peace.[29]

It may sound simplistic to speak of confronting war and violence with a smile and "being peace," but we should not be misled by Nhat Hanh's gift for putting sophisticated ideas into simple words. In the simple idea of being peace is contained a world of Engaged Buddhist philosophy, including the idea of approaching conflict free of an assumption of adversarial relations; a commitment to profound, principled nonviolence; an understanding of the web of interdependence as the fabric of our existence; and awareness of the great importance of motivation and attitude in shaping the nature and outcome of an action.

Alhough Nhat Hanh was the one to recognize "being peace" as an idea and put a name to it, other Engaged Buddhist leaders manifest the same spirit. For example, Maha Ghosananda says,

There is little we can do for peace in the world without peace in our minds. And so, when we begin to make peace, we begin with silence—meditation and prayer.

Peacemaking requires compassion. . . .

Peacemaking requires mindfulness. . . .

Peacemaking requires selflessness. . . .

Peacemaking requires wisdom. . . .

Peacemaking is the middle path of equanimity, non-duality, and non-attachment. . . .

Loving kindness is the only way to peace.[30]

And the Dalai Lama writes,

Anger cannot be overcome by anger. If a person shows anger to you and you respond with anger, the result is a disaster. In contrast, if you control anger and show the opposite attitude—compassion, tolerance, patience— then not only do you yourself remain in peace, but the other person's anger will gradually diminish. World problems also cannot be challenged by anger or hatred. They must be faced with compassion, love, and true kindness.[31]

THE DALAI LAMA

Like the Vietnamese example, the Tibetan case as well is a stunning example of the maintenance of nonviolence under the most difficult possible conditions. Often when people contemplate nonviolence, they propose that people should maintain nonviolence as a norm, but may need to turn to violence in self-defense, when all else fails. Tibet does not avail itself even of this in extremis clause. What could be a more difficult situation than being invaded by one's neighbor, losing one's independence and one's government, being occupied by that neighbor and then steadily having one's culture, religion, and way of life systematically dismantled in a process of cultural genocide, while anyone who resists or protests is imprisoned and tortured and perhaps as many as a million of one's countrymen and women die as a direct or indirect result of the occupation? Who would not fight back in such a situation? Yet, aside from an occasional and brief spasm of violence at moments of especially high stress, the Tibetan people do not.

The Dalai Lama is the head of the Tibetan government in exile, the inspiration of the Tibetan people, and Nobel Peace Prize laureate. It is under his guidance that the Tibetan liberation movement maintains its principled nonviolent approach. Although there are reports that Tibetan young people, born after the dismantling of Tibetan culture was under way, are impatient with the failure of His Holiness's nonviolent approach to achieve results and are contemplating a violent response to the Chinese, His Holiness still maintains adamantly that nonviolence is the only way. He often says that, although he understands that the Tibetan people are suffering greatly and that under such conditions an occasional flaring of violence will be inevitable, if violence ever becomes ongoing on the part of the Tibetans, he will feel that he has no choice but to resign. It is clear that nonviolence is a part of who the Dalai Lama is.

The Dalai Lama does not actually call for complete Tibetan independence (another sore point with some younger Tibetans), but for internal autonomy that would preserve Tibet's culture, religion, and way of life. We have seen that he always insists upon the human rights of the Tibetan people. His most famous peace proposal, to which the Chinese have never responded, is the Five Point Peace Plan:

1. Transformation of the whole of Tibet into a zone of peace.
2. Abandonment of China's population transfer policy that threatens the very existence of the Tibetans as a people.
3. Respect for the Tibetan people's fundamental human rights and democratic freedoms.
4. Restoration and protection of Tibet's natural environment and the abandonment of China's use of Tibet for the production of nuclear weapons and dumping of nuclear wastes.
5. Commencement of earnest negotiations on the future of Tibet and of relations between the Tibetan and Chinese peoples.[32]

In addition to the insistence upon the protection of human rights and of the environment (expressions of nonviolence toward humans and the natural world), notable in this document is its use of nonviolence as an asset. The first point expresses His Holiness's cherished idea of making Tibet into a fully demilitarized zone. Not only would this allow Tibet to express its cultural identity (which, as the Dalai Lama understands it, includes nonviolence), but it would also strategically contribute to the geopolitical situation a zone of peace between two great powers, India and China, reducing the chance of hostilities between them. His Holiness later extended this idea, and the fourth point above, with a suggestion that Tibet could also be made into a vast nature preserve. Again, not only would this allow Tibet to express its cultural identity and practice nonviolence by protecting the lives of many animals and plants (many species have become endangered since the Chinese occupation), as well as care for the Earth itself, but this idea would also benefit Tibet's neighbors by stopping the pollution (begun since the Chinese occupation) of the headwaters of many of the major rivers that originate in Tibet, the "rooftop of the world," and flow into other Asian countries. Unfortunately, none of these ideas has received consideration by the Chinese. Nonetheless, the Dalai Lama was awarded the Nobel Peace Prize in 1989 for his peace leadership.

Let us look at the ethical principles underlying the Dalai Lama's nonviolent approach to Tibet's conflict with China. Themes that he particularly emphasizes are interdependence, human equality, compassion and gratitude to the enemy, and the practicality of nonviolence.

Interdependence, while always a cosmological fact, has taken on new political meaning in the modern world. "Today the world is getting smaller and more interdependent. In ancient times problems were mostly local and therefore tackled at the local level. But now the situation is transformed and we have become very closely connected on the international level. One nation's problems can no longer be solved by itself completely."[33] The fact of interdependence is particularly clear in the case of global conflict situations. How can the conflict between Tibet and China be resolved—really resolved, not just suppressed—without satisfying both parties? This seems true by definition. A state of peace is not simply the absence of hostilities. As long as both parties exist, true peace depends upon their mutual satisfaction with their situation. Gandhi showed that people could learn to be dissatisfied with a condition in which they oppressed others; the Dalai Lama would like to do the same in Tibet.

The Dalai Lama often refers to human equality as human "sameness." "For my part, meeting innumerable others from all over the world and from every walk of life reminds me of our basic sameness as human beings. Indeed, the more I see of the world, the clearer it becomes that no matter what our situation, whether we are rich or poor, educated or not, of one race, gender, religion or another, we all desire to be happy and to avoid suffering. Our every intended action, in a sense our whole life . . . can be seen as our answer to the great question which confronts us all: 'How am I to be happy?'"[34] This statement occurs at the beginning of a recent book by the Dalai Lama on ethics. Similar statements occur at the beginning of many of his books and addresses. In many ways, it is the foundation of his approach. Taking a dispassionate, objective view of any conflict situation, one can see that both parties are trying to gain happiness for themselves. Often they are trying to do so in a distorted and very misguided way; nonetheless, that is their ultimate objective. His Holiness writes, "All of us want happiness. In cities, on farms, even in remote villages, everyone is quite busy. What is the purpose? Everyone is trying to create happiness. To do so is right. However, it is very important to follow a correct method in seeking happiness."[35] On this basis, as we saw in chapter 5, the Dalai Lama has concluded that we all have a fundamental human right, based in our nature as human beings, to the pursuit of happiness. We have a right to happiness, though not at the expense of others, and often we need guidance (whether we realize it or not) in our means of gaining happiness. It is clear, from the Tibetans' perspective, that the Chinese need guidance in their means of seeking happiness.

Gratitude and compassion to the enemy is one of the Dalai Lama's most unique and challenging teachings. "Even our enemy is very useful to us because, in order to practice compassion we need to practice tolerance, forgiveness, and patience, the antidotes to anger. In order to learn tolerance, forgiveness, and patience, we need someone to create some trouble. From this point of view, there is no need to feel anger toward the enemy or the person who creates the problem for us. In fact, we should feel gratitude for the opportunity he provides us." The Dalai Lama has often repeated words like this, which seem to speak out of his own individual life as a Buddhist practitioner to others as spiritual beings. Of course, these words do not mean that the actions of the Chinese in Tibet, or any act of violence or violation of human rights, is morally justifiable on these grounds. The Tibetans invariably refer to the Chinese actions in Tibet as wrong. But there are two considerations behind these words. First, given that the actions of the Chinese have happened, how should one, as a spiritual being, respond to those actions? How can one turn a bad situation to one's spiritual benefit? Second, and more politically, how can one train one's mind in order to respond most skillfully to the challenge of defending the Tibetan people, culture, and religion? As we shall see, the Dalai Lama believes that anger and hatred inevitably worsen a situation. That being the case, it is good to eliminate anger and replace it with a more useful emotion.

> In order to cultivate genuine patience toward our enemy, there are certain types of mental trainings. For instance, if you have been injured by gunfire, if you feel angry, you should analyze the situation and think, what is it that I am angry at? If I am angry at the thing that injured me, I should be angry at the direct cause of my injury, which is the bullet. If I should feel anger toward the ultimate cause of my injury, I should feel anger toward the anger within the person who shot at me. But that is not the case. I

don't feel angry at the bullet or the other person's anger, I feel angry at the person, who is just the medium. Under different circumstances, that person could change into a good friend.

. . . So, just as we see how destructive is the anger generated within us, how it destroys our peace of mind, mental balance, and so forth, so it is in the case of the anger generated within the enemy's mind. It affects his mind and his happiness.

Therefore, when someone dominated by anger harms you, instead of feeling angry toward him, you should feel a sense of compassion and pity because that person is suffering himself.[36]

Along this line, there is also the "Prayer of Words of Truth" composed by the Dalai Lama immediately after his flight to India. A prayer addressed to all Buddhas and bodhisattvas, it reads in part:

> Please look at the religious people of the Land of Snows,
> Ruthlessly conquered by the cruel tactics of evil invaders,
> And let the might of your compassion swiftly arise
> To stop the terrible flow of their blood and tears.
>
> The violent oppressors are also worthy of compassion.
> Crazed by demonic emotions, they do vicious deeds
> That bring total defeat to themselves as well as to others.
> Please grant them the insight into right and wrong,
> And bring them to know the glory of loving friendship.[37]

Here we see even more clearly why the Chinese need guidance in their efforts to gain happiness. From the Tibetan perspective, they are doing themselves terrible harm, causing themselves vast future suffering as the karmic consequence of their present actions. And we see again the fundamental sameness of all people: both the oppressed and the oppressors suffer; the suffering of all should cease. Indeed, that suffering is interdependent, caused for both the Tibetans and the Chinese by the actions of the Chinese. This is a paradigmatic instance of the nonadversarial element in Engaged Buddhist ethics.

Despite the thorough-goingness of the Dalai Lama's nonadversarial outlook, it is not the case that he always agrees with Nhat Hanh's "being peace" approach, which advocates always speaking in gentle and polite language. The Dalai Lama says, "If you are genuinely a humble and honest person and *act* that way, some people may take advantage of you. So in such a situation, it may be necessary to react. But we should react without bad feelings. Deep down, tolerance, compassion and patience must still be present."[38] That is, although one's intentions and state of mind should always be compassionate and nonadversarial, one should use skill in selecting one's language and behavior so that one's good will is not taken as an invitation to attack.

Aung San Suu Kyi agrees. She reports that language and behavior along the lines recommended by Nhat Hanh have not worked for her movement in Burma:

> We've learned from experience that the metta (loving kindness) approach is misinterpreted by the authorities. They see it as a weakness. . . . During my six years under house arrest . . . Uncle U Aung Shwe [the National League for Democracy, NLD, chairman] tried very hard to keep the NLD together as well as trying to establish a harmonious relationship with SLORC [the Burmese military government]. He never said anything to which they could object. During those six years the NLD behaved in such a gentlemanly way that some people accused it of sheer cowardice and the lack of will to act. And what was the result? They [SLORC] just came down heavier and heavier on the NLD.[39]

Gentle and polite language and behavior proved counterproductive in Burma. That is not to say that the NLD and Suu Kyi have given up on the metta approach, she says, but they have become more confrontational and pointedly critical in their language in dealing with the military dictators. In short, for the Dalai Lama and Suu Kyi, nonviolence and a nonadversarial attitude do not always mean the use of gentle speech and behavior.

It is necessary to consider the practicality of the Dalai Lama's approach. While the Tibetan case has thus far been unsuccessful, we should consider what would have been the result if the Tibetans had responded to the Chinese with sustained violence. How many more people would have died? Would there have been any chance of success? And on the other hand, we should recall that the Tibetan struggle is not over yet. The Tibetans take a very long-term view of their situation and realize that change could come with the next generation of Chinese leadership, or a hundred years later or even more. As long as they do not compromise themselves, they avoid doubling their injury by refraining from causing themselves harm (by injuring the Chinese), and they preserve Tibetan religion and culture in a morally intact form as an option that will be available to later generations (as long as they keep that religion and culture alive, which, indeed, is a problem).

Moreover, the Dalai Lama's own tremendous skill and charisma has successfully kept the Tibetan situation before the eyes of the international community, while many other oppressed and brutalized people languish in obscurity. As long as the Tibetan people maintain their nonviolent stance, they hold the moral high ground in the eyes of the world. China, of course, holds the high ground of power.

Recognizing that his nonviolent approach strikes many people as idealistic and impractical, the Dalai Lama frequently takes time to defend the practicality of his approach. In the first place, he sees violence as ineffective:

> Chairman Mao once said that political power comes from the barrel of a gun. Of course it is true that violence can achieve certain short-term objectives, but it cannot obtain long-lasting ends. If we look at history, we find that in time, humanity's love of peace, justice, and freedom always triumphs over cruelty and oppression. This is why I am such a fervent believer in non-violence. Violence begets violence. And violence means only one thing: suffering. Theoretically, it is possible to conceive of a situation where the only way to prevent large-scale conflict is through armed intervention at an early stage. But the problem with this argument is that it is very difficult, if not impossible, to predict the outcome of violence. Nor can we be sure of its justness at the outset. This only becomes clear when we have the benefit of hindsight. The only certainty is that where there is violence, there is always and inevitably suffering.[40]

Violence begets violence. This is an ancient Buddhist view, based upon the idea of karma, held by many Buddhists, Engaged or otherwise, and well expressed in the *Dhammapada* verse, "Hatred is never appeased by hatred in this world; it is appeased by non-hatred. This is an eternal Law."[41] Violence means suffering, and suffering is what Buddhism is intended to eliminate, according to the Four Noble Truths. How can it be a constructive response to any situation to add further suffering to the suffering that is already present? Moreover, what can violence actually achieve? The Dalai Lama has written,

> Some people will say that while the Dalai Lama's devotion to non-violence is praiseworthy, it is not really practical. Actually, it is far more naive to suppose that the human-created problems which lead to violence can ever be solved through conflict.
>
> . . . Here we need to make a distinction between peace as a mere absence of war and peace as a state of tranquility founded on the deep sense

of security that arises from mutual understanding, tolerance of others' point of view, and respect for their rights.[42]

The Dalai Lama points out here that violence is a secondary effect of a primary problem. How do we expect that we can solve the primary problem by applying more violence to it? This is why he always calls for dialogue in order to resolve problems, including the Tibet-China problem. One can use violence to repress problems, but the problem remains. A state of peace is one in which the problem is resolved.

In addition, drawing perhaps upon the Buddhist observation of the web of interdependence as the basic reality of life, the Dalai Lama views violence as an aberration within the basic given of the web of human sociality.

> When the media focuses too closely on the negative aspects of human nature, there is a danger that we become persuaded that violence and aggression are its principal characteristics. This is a mistake, I believe. The fact that violence is newsworthy suggests the very opposite. Good news is not remarked on precisely because there is so much of it. Consider that at any given moment there must be hundreds of millions of acts of kindness taking place around the world. Although there will undoubtedly be many acts of violence in progress at the same time, their number is surely very much less.[43]

From a Buddhist perspective, humans are fundamentally social; we rely upon the social web to survive. As we have seen repeatedly in this volume, many Buddhists emphasize that it is in line with reality to live harmoniously in the web of social being. That is the fundamental given, the norm, without which life as we know it is simply impossible.

Part of His Holiness's vision of the practicality of nonviolence is his belief in the power of truth. We quoted above from his poem, "Prayer of Words of Truth." José Cabézón points out that, in the Dalai Lama's work, truth "is frequently associated with the will of the people and pitted against the power and propaganda of government. Hence, when he states in his recent autobiography that 'no matter what governments do, the human spirit will always prevail,' he means in part that truth has a power mightier than institutional power and force."[44] Truth in this context, it seems to me, includes the fact that humankind is by nature social as well as humankind's inherent pull toward self-realization. A government that is violent or that erects barriers to self-realization is out of step with truth. Expressions of violence can never be more than temporary aberrations. This leads His Holiness to be fundamentally optimistic. Looking again at the quotation above, we see, "of course it is true that violence can achieve certain short-term objectives, but it cannot obtain long-lasting ends. If we look at history, we find that in time, humanity's love of peace, justice, and freedom always triumphs over cruelty and oppression. This is why I am such a fervent believer in non-violence." It is in society's nature, says His Holiness, to be peaceful and cooperative. It is in human nature, as we saw in chapter 5, to require certain fundamental freedoms, particularly to self-development.

The Burmese case, moreover, shows that, although the military can seize power and control the people for many years, they cannot meet the people's fundamental aspirations for justice, freedom, and human rights and must expend tremendous effort to control the people, an effort that cannot be sustained indefinitely. Suu Kyi even agrees with the Dalai Lama's idea of the power of truth:

> Alan Clements: Daw Suu, here in your country, speaking the truth is regarded as a punishable crime against the state, if that truth is unacceptable to the authorities. But why is "truth" so threatening?
> Aung San Suu Kyi: Because the power of truth is great indeed. And this is very frightening to some people. Truth is a powerful weapon. People may not think so but it is very powerful. And truth—like anything that is powerful—can be frightening or reassuring, depending on which side you are on. If you're on the side of truth, it's very reassuring—you have its protection. But if you're on the side of untruth—then it's very frightening.[45]

Here "truth" is simply truth in the normal sense of the word: the truth that the Burmese people do not want the military government that holds power, the truth that they want freedom, democracy, and human rights. This is indeed the greatest asset of Suu Kyi's movement, that they are on the side of these truths.

The Dalai Lama may never again sit at a table with the Chinese rulers, but he nevertheless believes that one day, in one form or another, they will have to meet the basic aspirations of the Tibetan people, and of the Chinese people as well. As Gandhi believed, so do the Dalai Lama and Suu Kyi believe that the power of truth and reality cannot be resisted indefinitely. Ultimately, they believe, those who hold power among humankind must bend to the power of reality, in this case, the reality of human society's need and tendency to function harmoniously and the reality of human individuals' inherent drive to make their way to self-realization.

Despite Chinese stonewalling and the failure of his approach to achieve its goals for the Tibetan people, the Dalai Lama remains an ardent advocate of non-violence. Although one might think that the tasks of looking after the needs of the Tibetan community in exile and campaigning internationally for Tibetan autonomy would be sufficient tasks for a lifetime, the Dalai Lama seems, in addition, to put a great deal of time and energy into preaching nonviolence in a universalist voice to the global community. He is, arguably, the most respected and important global preacher of nonviolence living today. His recent book, *Ethics for the New Millennium*, which preaches nonviolence, compassion, and universal responsibility to the English-speaking world, spent more than three months on the *New York Times* bestseller list.

PARTIAL NONVIOLENCE

In light of these examples of maintaining a principled nonviolent stance in the face of the most challenging imaginable circumstances—particularly the Tibetan and Vietnamese situations—it can be startling to realize that some Engaged Buddhists are less than 100 percent committed to nonviolence. Buddhadasa Bhikkhu, for example, for the most part speaks strongly on behalf of nonviolence.

> Armed conflict cannot solve the problems of the world. It leads to senseless and enormous cost of life.
> Today human beings are so cruel that they are willing to drop a bomb which they know can annihilate people by the thousands. Our ancestors would have surrendered or fled rather than bring about this kind of destruction of their fellow humans. . . . In a true human community . . . people take pity on the unfortunate, and rectify wrongs by means other than taking life.[46]

Even so, Buddhadasa follows those statements with a surprising comment.

> No matter what kind of activity we carry out—be it politics, economics, or, indeed, even war—if done morally it will maintain the natural, harmonious balance of all things, and will be consistent with the original plan of nature. It is absolutely correct to fight for the preservation of dhamma in the world, but it is wrong to fight for anything other than that. Indeed, we should be happy to sacrifice our lives in fighting to preserve dhamma for . . . all humanity.[47]

We saw in chapter 4 that Buddhadasa espouses revolution in cases where the ruler does not rule in a manner consistent with the *dasarājadhamma*. Here it is clear that he does believe that violence would be justified in such a case or in other cases of threat to the Dhamma. How this is consistent with his earlier remark is not clear.

Buddhadasa's statement is especially surprising in light of the fact that the established national ideology in modern Thailand is represented by the slogan, "Nation, King, and Religion." This ideology has effectively merged the three elements such that they are widely viewed as three components of a single entity. Thus the state, when in autocratic hands, can claim that even something like highly justifiable criticism of current rulers is an attack on nation, king, and the Buddhist religion or that any threat to the country is a threat to Buddhism. Conservative elements in Thailand (including within the Sangha) therefore can justify a variety of aggressive or violent acts on the part of the state by saying that the state is acting to protect the Dhamma. This is a highly slippery slope.

PRAGMATIC NONVIOLENCE

Suu Kyi leads the nonviolent movement for democracy and human rights in Burma. She makes it clear, however, that she chooses nonviolence not on principle, but because she regards it as the best choice in her situation. In other words, her nonviolence is pragmatic rather than principled. This view differentiates her from the other Engaged Buddhists, whose nonviolence is principled.

Why, then, does she choose nonviolence? First, with insight that is simultaneously pragmatic and very Buddhist, she recognizes that violence perpetuates itself. "Military coups, which have happened enough in Burma, are violent ways of changing situations and I do not want to encourage and to perpetuate this tradition of bringing about change through violence. Because I'm afraid that if we achieve democracy in this way we will never be able to get rid of the idea that you bring about necessary changes through violence."[48] Those who want the violence to end should begin with themselves, by ceasing to react violently to violence. Change can be brought about by using violence, but nonviolence cannot be initiated by using violence. If one wants to initiate a state in which nonviolent change is the norm, one should use nonviolent means to bring that state into being. She and the NLD "have chosen the way of non-violence simply because we think it's politically better for the country in the long run to establish that you can bring about change without the use of arms."[49]

Second, "We've chosen non-violence because it is the best way to protect the people."[50] Here again, Suu Kyi expresses a very pragmatic and very Buddhist perspective: it is best to protect as many lives as possible. Suu Kyi explains, "In this day and age we can use non-violent political means to achieve our ends. But if you have a choice and feel that you have an equal chance of succeeding, I think you certainly ought to choose the non-violent way, because it means that fewer people will be hurt."[51] Unlike some of the other Engaged Buddhists, Suu Kyi is not willing to give up success for the sake of nonviolence. If success is possible with nonviolence, however, that is clearly preferable, because many lives will be saved.

Why, then, does Suu Kyi regard this choice for nonviolence as pragmatic only, rather than principled? First and foremost, she has respect and affection for many Burmese who have resorted to violence, chief among them, her father, Burmese students, and the army.

> I think that in the context of Burma today, non-violent means are the best way to achieve our goal. But I certainly do not condemn those who fight the "just fight," as it were. My father did, and I admire him greatly for it.[52]
>
> We [the NLD] have always said that we will never disown those students and others who have taken up violence. We know that their aim is the same as ours. They want democracy and they think the best way to go about it is through armed struggle. And we do not say that we have the monopoly on the right methods of achieving what we want. Also, we cannot guarantee their security. We can't say, "Follow us in the way of non-violence and you'll be protected," or that we'll get there without any casualties. That's a promise we can't make.[53]

It is interesting to note that one of the reasons for avoiding principled nonviolence is concern over the potential loss of life of those, such as students, whom they might cause to follow the path of nonviolence. Above we saw that one of the reasons for choosing nonviolence was to protect life as much as possible. Thus, an underlying principle in these considerations is the very Buddhist principle of protecting life as much as possible.

> [W]hen I was ten or eleven I wanted to enter the army. In those days the army was an institution which we thought of as very honourable because it was the institution founded by my father. And everyone referred to my father as *Bogyoke*, which means General, so I wanted to be a general too because I thought this was the best way to serve one's country, just like my father had done. . . . So this is why I can say with absolute truth that I have great affection for the army—I'm not making it up.[54]

Thus, Suu Kyi has a personal connection to the army through her father, who founded it as an instrument to gain Burma's independence; naturally, she regarded it as an honorable institution, and that sentiment has remained with her, despite the brutal use to which the current rulers of Burma have put the army. How would she envision the institution of the army if she were to become the leader of a democratic Burma?

> [A]s I see it, the main responsibility of the army is to protect and defend the people. If we lived in a world where it was not necessary to defend ourselves, there would be no need for armies. But I do not envisage that in the near future the world would be such that we can afford to be without protection. I would like to think of the army as a force of protection rather than a force of destruction.
>
> And there's always the question of *cetena* [*cetanā*, right intention]. The *cetena* of the army should be right.[55]

In fact, Suu Kyi seems to look forward to the possibility of transforming the moral standing of the army. She states that after democracy is achieved the army "will be a better and more honourable army and one that will be loved by the people. That is what you want an army to be. When my father founded the army he meant it to be an honourable one that was loved and trusted by the people. The kind of army we want is an army in which the soldiers themselves will be much happier."[56]

THE LIMITS OF NONVIOLENCE

Suu Kyi's comments on an honorable army in a future, democratic Burma usher in the topic of the limits of nonviolence. Whereas she has spoken straightforwardly on the subject, few other Engaged Buddhist leaders have publicly expressed themselves on these matters. We turn now to three contexts in which the limits of nonviolence are tested by Engaged Buddhists.

KILLING IN DEFENSE OF LIFE

It has been the tradition in Buddhist countries of Southeast Asia to regard the existence of an army and the defensive use of military violence as a perhaps regrettable but necessary aspect of a ruler's responsibility. An infrequently cited Pali text, the *Cakkavatti Sīhanāda Sutta* of the *Dīgha Nikāya*, seems to give legitimacy to the military in a Buddhist state. In it, the Buddha is recorded as giving the following advice to the one who aspires to be a *cakravartin*: "Yourself depending on the Dhamma, honouring it, revering it, cherishing it, doing homage to it and venerating it, having the Dhamma as your badge and banner, acknowledging the Dhamma as your master, you should establish guard, ward and protection according to Dhamma for your own household, your troops, your nobles and vassals, for Brahmins and householders, town and country folk, ascetics and Brahmins, for beasts and birds."[57] Thus is justified the existence of a military force for the purpose of protection. It is noteworthy that this is to be done "according to Dhamma," which I take to mean in this context that the military should operate in some sense within the bounds of Buddhist morality (though the specifics of those limits are not given). The phrasing here implies that it is a duty of the king to protect those who look to him for protection.

There is also an infrequently cited Mahayana *sūtra*, the "Skill in Means (*Upāyakauśalya*) Sūtra," that condones killing in order to protect life. In this *sūtra*, the Buddha tells a story from one of his past lives when he was a ship's captain named "Great Compassionate." This captain had a dream, sent by the local deities, that alerted him to the fact that on board the ship was a man who was planning to kill the five hundred merchants on board to steal from them. He is aware that if the man kills the merchants he will fall into hell for a long time. Upon awakening, the captain considers how he might prevent this mass murder. He reflects that if he reports the man's intentions to the merchants they would kill him "with angry thoughts" in their minds and go to hell themselves. He finally decides that he must kill the man himself.

> [H]e thought, 'If I were to kill this person, I would likewise burn in the great hells for one hundred-thousand eons because of it. Yet I can bear to experience the pain of the great hells, that this person not slay these five hundred merchants and develop so much evil karma. I will kill this person myself.
>
> . . . Accordingly, the captain Great Compassionate protected those five hundred merchants and protected that person from going to the great hells by deliberately stabbing and slaying that person . . . with great compassion and skill in means.

The Buddha comments:

> For me, samsara was curtailed for one hundred-thousand eons because of that skill in means and great compassion. And the robber died to be reborn in a world of paradise.[58]

In addition to the fact that killing is approved in this *sūtra* as an example of the "skill in means" that a bodhisattva might have to use in order to prevent violence, it is notable that the ship's captain not only does not himself earn negative karma by virtue of killing, he actually earns karmic reward. The key is his state of mind: the fact that he acted out of compassion, for the welfare of others, willing to sacrifice his own welfare for the sake of others canceled his negative karma and replaced it with positive.

This *sūtra* is seldom discussed. Certainly no Engaged Buddhist teacher has ever used it to justify an act of killing another; however, it is chilling to learn that Aum Shinrikyo—infamous for its poison gas attack in the Tokyo subway—did use the very idea presented in this *sūtra* to justify their own murderous behavior. Maekawa Michiko reports that Aum members believed in "killing certain persons in order to prevent them from accumulating more bad *karma* that would have to be worked out in future lifetimes; hence, it was a compassionate act."[59] Clearly, this is not the kind of idea that a responsible person wants to get into the wrong hands (or mind).

I had a private discussion with a Tibetan lama and Engaged Buddhist about nonviolence in which he brought up this *sūtra*. He emphasized that only a very advanced bodhisattva—one who could equally choose to consume either a great delicacy or a vile heap of refuse with neither attraction nor revulsion—would be able to generate the state of mind that would be required in order to kill someone without a shred of anger but only out of pure compassion. He indicated that he had never known a person capable of such a thing. The Dalai Lama has said that he himself is "not fully developed in that kind of altruism" and rules out that approach both for himself and for anyone else insufficiently advanced.[60] Perhaps because of this kind of consideration, this *sūtra* is never used by Engaged Buddhists as a justification for killing another, though it does exist and well-educated Mahayana Buddhists are aware of it. Its teachings are mentioned, however, in East Asia in connection with the practice of self-immolation, as we shall see.

Despite the existence of the above texts, Buddhism has never had a doctrine of just war (which is not to say that Buddhist countries did not or do not go to war). Is it possible to lead a country without an army helping one to perform one's duty of protecting the people? Or is it a duty to have an army for defensive purposes? The *dasarājadhamma* (ten virtues of a king) do not include protecting the people; to the contrary, they include nonviolence. On the other hand, the *Cakkavatti-Sīhanāda Sutta* does seem to indicate that there is such a duty. When the great King Asoka declared his intention to stop engaging in war, India was vastly more powerful than any of its neighbors and no one dared to attack. A Buddhist ruler today would not have that luxury. In a world with violence of a kind and extent inconceivable in the Buddha's time, what is the duty of those who govern nations? Is there a tension between their duty to the nonviolent Dharma of the Buddha and their duty to the safety of their people? Classical Buddhism gives little help here.

With the exception of Buddhadasa, the Engaged Buddhists are quite consistent in their advocacy and use of nonviolence in their present struggles. Whether and how they would maintain their nonviolence if they were ever to come to power in a state is something that has been considered by those with aspirations to national rule. We have seen how Suu Kyi would handle the situation: she would have an army. She has straightforwardly faced her own potential role as head of state in a country with an army:

> Alan Clements: Can you imagine yourself as the leader of a free and democratic Burma, having to make a decision to use violence against humans, to use force that you know will kill people?
> Aung San Suu Kyi: All members of governments may have to do that under certain circumstances.
> Alan Clements: So the "skilful" use of weapons and violence as a politician comes with the territory, so to speak?
> Aung San Suu Kyi: It's an occupational hazard.[61]

Might this be a modern version of the traditional idea that the *cakravartin* must defend the people using military force if necessary?

The Tibetan leadership takes the opposite approach. Samdhong Rinpoche is a great advocate of nonviolence. He has said, "If I could condense the Buddha's teaching into one word, I would say the word 'nonviolence' best sums it up."[62] Acknowledging that there has never yet been a nonviolent Buddhist state, including Tibet, he nonetheless declares that his "dream" is to build a nonviolent society in an autonomous Tibet. Indeed, he believes that "peace, compassion, non-violence and spirituality" are the "fundamental characteristics" of Tibet and that the existence of Tibet, for which the Tibetan liberation movement struggles, can be justified only if the Tibet that comes into being manifests those characteristics.[63] In his outline of the future Tibet, he declares that "the polity of future Tibet will be committed to the three cardinal principles: truth, non-violence (*ahiṁsā*) and genuine democracy." He follows the Dalai Lama's policy in declaring that the future Tibet will be a "Zone of Ahimsa, implying a demilitarized region, having no . . . involvement in any kind of the production of arms." If they achieve autonomy without full independence of China, he declares that, "Tibet will evolve and maintain its own modalities about non-involvement in war or weaponry production and its trade or transportation."[64] It seems that anything short of full demilitarization of Tibet will be sufficient to prevent an agreement being reached with China. In short, as far as the Rinpoche and the present Tibetan leadership is concerned, there will be a nonviolent Tibet entirely free of militarism, or there will be no Tibet at all.

SELF-IMMOLATION

During the war in Vietnam, Thich Quang Duc revived a practice that had been in disuse in East Asia for several centuries: self-immolation. In 1963, at a downtown crossroads in Saigon, he sat in the lotus posture and, in a state of meditative control, burned himself to death in protest of the Diem regime's repression of the Buddhist religion. Many Vietnamese monks, nuns, and laypersons followed his example. What is the meaning of this action? Nhat Hanh has written more on this subject than any other. He explains, "By burning himself, Thich Quang Duc awakened the world to the suffering of the war and the persecution of the Buddhists. When someone stands up to violence in such a courageous way, a force for change is released. Every action for peace requires someone to exhibit the courage to challenge the violence and inspire love. Love and sacrifice always set up a chain reaction of love and sacrifice. . . . Thich Quang Duc's act expressed the unconditional willingness to suffer for the awakening of others."[65] In short, self-immolation in the context of the Vietnam War was an attempt to penetrate the layers of denial in the minds of those perpetrating the war in order to bring them to realize what war is. Like Gandhi's principle of accepting a beating without fighting back so that the one doing the beating will become incapable of continuing to inflict harm, self-immolation was an attempt to make those perpetrating the war sickened by their own actions and incapable of continuing to war or promote warring. There is a tradition of self-immolation in China and Vietnam that traces back to the *Lotus Sūtra*. The ancient intentions behind self-immolation included making an offering to the Buddha, imitating the bodhisattvas, and protesting oppression of the Dharma. Thus, when Quang Duc immolated himself, though it had been centuries since such an act had been performed, it was something that was culturally and religiously understood in Vietnam.

Whether self-immolation is violent and whether it is or can be a moral action in the Buddhist view is a controversial point. Certainly the *Vinaya* prohibits taking one's own life. On the other hand, the *Skill in Means Sūtra* justifies the taking of life to save lives as long as the intention is altruistic. In East Asia, this text is taken as justification not of taking others' lives, but of taking one's own life in order to save others. The point of interest to the self-immolators is this text's indication that the one who sacrifices himself for the sake of others (in the *sūtra*, the ship's captain is willing to accept massive negative karma and future suffering) escapes earning negative karma and in fact earns positive karma by virtue of that person's state of mind of compassion and self-sacrificing willingness to accept negative karma for the sake of others. This tipping of the karmic scales in a positive direction indicates that the act of taking a life under these circumstances is a morally good act. Thus, the Mahayana tradition is generally interpreted as taking a positive view of self-sacrifice, assuming that the individual's motivation is purely altruistic. The self-sacrificers see their taking of their own life as a negative act in and of itself, but when motivated by compassion and willing to suffer for the sake of others, as a morally good act. In Vietnam, the self-immolators were largely regarded as heroic bodhisattvas committing a sacred act. Elsewhere in the Buddhist world, many Theravada Buddhists look at self-immolation as something that is prohibited for Theravadins and regard it as a Mahayana matter. Some admire it. One Theravada Engaged Buddhist leader referred to it as *dāna-pāramitā*, the perfection of giving.

There is one more aspect to this issue, however, which is not usually taken into consideration. Nhat Hanh writes,

> We do not intend to say that self-immolation is good, or that it is bad. It is neither good nor bad. When you say something is good, you say that you *should* do that. But nobody can urge another to do such a thing. So such a discussion is not pursued in order to decide whether self-immolation is a good tactic in the nonviolent struggle or not. It is apart from all that. It is done to wake us up.[66]

Nhat Hanh, however, overlooks something here. The French existentialist philosopher Jean-Paul Sartre argues persuasively that every time we perform an action, the actions we choose are at the same time recommendations to others that they should perform the same action.

> When we say that man chooses his own self, we mean that every one of us does likewise; but we also mean that in making this choice he also chooses all men. In fact, in creating the man that we want to be, there is not a single one of our acts which does not at the same time create an image of man as we think he ought to be. To choose to be this or that is to affirm at the same time the value of what we choose. . . .

For every man, everything happens as if all mankind had its eyes fixed on him and were guiding itself by what he does.[67]

For Sartre, our every action is a recommendation of that action to others, a recommendation far more sincere than many of our verbal recommendations. This seems to me to be correct. Whenever we do something, we are saying with our action, "I believe this is a good act." This in itself is a powerful, though indirect, recommendation to others to consider doing the same thing. This recommending effect is, of course, intensified when the action receives tremendous public attention and is either approved or tacitly condoned by the institution of which the actor is an exemplar and which is itself the acknowledged guardian of the people's ethical values (as is the case when a Buddhist commits self-immolation).

Let us recall the Buddhist view of self-immolation. The action itself is violent and contrary to the Buddhist precepts. What makes this action good, if anything, is the motivation behind the action. A crucial point overlooked by the Buddhist commentators is that others cannot see our motivation; they can only see our action. Once an action is performed, in effect publicly available, there is no way to stop others from imitating that action, even though their motivation may be quite different from the motivation of a bodhisattva. Quang Duc was a role model for all those who followed, and continue to follow, in his footsteps. He presumably never imagined, much less intended, such a thing, but once his action existed as a public act, it was as if he had recommended to the world: this is something possible that you might do.

This point is particularly important for Engaged Buddhist ethics inasmuch as these ethics, while by no means ignoring personal ethics, put relatively greater weight on the social aspects of ethics than traditional Buddhist ethics. Thus, it is not enough in Engaged Buddhist ethics to consider one's personal motivation in acting, whether one is earning good or bad karma by one's action and whether this action is helping one to progress toward liberation. In Engaged Buddhist ethics, it is more important than ever to consider in addition whether other beings are benefited by one's action, whether one's action makes the world a place more conducive to happiness and liberation. In other words, the consequentialist measure of the morality of an action weighs more heavily in Engaged Buddhism than in earlier forms.

From this perspective, condoning self-immolation by Buddhist leaders and institutions is problematic for Engaged Buddhist ethics. When one considers the legacy of Buddhist contributions to global ethical and political thinking in the twentieth century, the value of at least one Buddhist contribution is not clear—self-immolation. Whereas Quang Duc immolated himself to wake others up, today many self-immolators—copying the form but not the motivation of the Buddhist self-immolators—burn themselves to put pressure on those whose policies they oppose. In recent years, young Indian men of high caste status have burned themselves to death in outraged protest at universities that saved places for "scheduled caste" members while turning away Brahmin applicants. Kathy Change, an American social activist, burned herself to death on the campus of the University of Pennsylvania. She had been incoherent and no one understood what she was so upset about that she would do such a thing.[68] There have been many others, committed by persons of a great variety of motivations. Do Engaged Buddhists want to offer the act of self-immolation to the world if this kind of thing is one of the consequences?

In the end, self-immolation is an act that tests the limits of Engaged Buddhist nonviolence, limits of definition—Is the act violent, or not?—and limits of action—Is self-sacrifice an act of heroic giving, or is it a reprehensible act of killing? It is in fact both: a person is killed and yet it is an awe-inspiring act of heroic self-sacrifice.

VISUALIZING WORLD PEACE

The Engaged Buddhist Utopia is a world at peace. Do the Engaged Buddhists have any suggestions for approaching that goal? Today some Engaged Buddhist thinkers are starting to speak and write on the subject. Let us look at their remarks. The Dalai Lama writes in his *Ethics for the New Millennium*:

> [G]enuine world peace requires that we . . . begin to dismantle the military establishments that we have built. We cannot hope to enjoy peace in its fullest sense while it remains possible for a few individuals to exercise military power and impose their will on others. . . .
>
> Clearly we cannot hope to achieve military disestablishment overnight. Desirable as it may be, unilateral disarmament would be exceedingly difficult to achieve. . . . [C]learly it is too much to hope for the elimination of all weapons. After all, even our fists can be used as weapons. And there will always be groups of troublemakers and fanatics who will cause disturbance for others. Therefore, we must allow that, as long as there are human beings, there will have to be ways of dealing with miscreants.[69]

This is a very helpful and realistic start that hearkens back to the Buddha's assumption in the *Dīgha Nikāya* that there will be an organized force for self-defense in the state. It seems in the Buddha's remarks, as well as in the Dalai Lama's, to be a matter of common sense. These remarks are also reminiscent of Gandhi's view that in a world of *hiṁsā* (harm-causing or violence) *ahiṁsā* is an ideal that one never perfects, though one should always try to practice it more and more completely. There will always be fanatics and troublemakers from whom people (and other sentient beings) will need to be protected.

The question is how. It is clear that the Dalai Lama believes that our efforts to protect ourselves—the militarization of the planet and the stockpiling of weapons of mass destruction—have become less a means of protection than a threat to our security. He goes on to list steps that should be taken to move us in the right direction, including building on previous international agreements reducing weapons proliferation, the gradual dismantling of the arms industry, urging individuals to cease to work building armaments, and perhaps emulation of Costa Rica, the world's only proclaimed disarmed state.[70]

In a more visionary, but potentially controversial, passage the Dalai Lama also looks forward to the gradual erosion of the system of nation-states as a contribution to the reduction of intercommunal conflict. He points out that, in the case of the European Union, national borders and their need for national armies are being replaced by a regional association within which there are no borders and no need for standing armies. Because this group no longer needs to worry about multiple national defenses (including defense from each other), but only a single regional defense, their overall amount of militarization is reduced.[71] In the Dalai Lama's vision, such a development could ultimately lead in the direction of a world without armies. He envisions a scenario in which the world would evolve from national armies to regional security forces and eventually to a single "globally administered police force." The purpose of this force would be to protect human life and human rights anywhere in the world and to protect "against the appropriation of power by violent means." It would be under the control of the international community and could be called into action either by that community or by any community that felt itself to be under threat.[72]

It is true that if there were no nation-states, there would be no need for national armies. Two concerns, however, come immediately to mind. First, what is the difference between an army and an international police force? What forms of power or force would this police force use? Second, how could it be possible to guarantee that this international police force would not become itself an oppressor, and one with no power to contain it? For many, the Dalai Lama's vision of a world without armies could be just an alternative nightmare.

The Dalai Lama defends his idea by pointing out that we already have United Nations troops used as peacekeepers. He urges that that body be reformed and further developed. He also advocates the idea of establishing what he calls "zones of peace," demilitarized zones in potential trouble spots to acts as buffers between parties, not only in Tibet (between India and China), but also in the Sino-Russian borderlands and Germany. Finally, to empower individuals and give them a voice, he suggests the establishment of a "World Council of the People" to be made up of people from all walks of life, without political power and not officially representing anyone, but with the moral authority to "represent the conscience of the world."[73]

Sulak Sivaraksa agrees with the Dalai Lama that, although there may always be a need to use force to protect innocent people, the demilitarization of the world is nevertheless of critical and urgent importance. "A peaceful society may need certain weapons to defend itself or channel its internal conflicts, but society's parasitic dependence on the war process is clearly wrong. Economic peace conversion (turning tank factories into tractor factories, or Star Wars projects into space colonization projects) should be a common aspiration of citizens everywhere."[74] Again we see the assumption that it is only common sense to have means of self-defense coupled with the conviction that it is necessary to demilitarize.

Sulak also agrees with the Dalai Lama on the necessity of expanding and transforming the role of the United Nations, though his vision is somewhat different. He would like to see the United Nations made both more authoritative and more representative of the people of the world by transforming it into "a true world parliament elected directly by a world citizenry," rather than a body that represents the interests of the nation-states. He envisions this body then playing a greater role in international conflict resolution and global disarmament, and would look for it to "administer a strengthened international judiciary system and a permanent peacekeeping force recruited independently of existing armies.[75] Though he does not go as far as the Dalai Lama (he does not envision the end of national armies), Sulak does agree that the United Nations should take over the resolution of international conflicts. Like the Dalai Lama, he is searching for a way to transfer power from nation-states to individuals. As Sulak puts it, "Contemporary Buddhist internationalism envisions institutions that are configured to represent the interests of human beings rather than nation-states."[76]

Thus, both the Dalai Lama and Sulak Sivaraksa represent the sentiments of contemporary Buddhist internationalism. In the latter one can detect a general suspicion of the nation-state as a body that divides humanity, promoting separation and conflict by privileging the interests of its own people over all others, and that is thus out of step with the natural law of interdependence. Engaged Buddhists in general prefer to commit to bodies that promote cooperation and concern about the welfare of all without privileging a particular nationality, ethnic group, and so forth. Hence, their wish to see effective international bodies evolve.

We should not make too much of these speculative remarks from the Dalai Lama and Sulak. These are provocative suggestions that were no doubt intended to stimulate more thought and discussion in Buddhist, and other, communities. Indeed, these suggestions are not essentially different from current speculations by non-Buddhist pacifists.

CONCLUDING THOUGHTS

This chapter has demonstrated that Engaged Buddhist nonviolence is not as clear a principle for social ethics as one might have assumed. The incompleteness of Engaged Buddhist thinking on nonviolence is the heir of the incompleteness of classical Buddhist thinking on nonviolence outside of the context of personal ethics. This is the heart of the problem: nonviolence as part of a personal ethic has been fairly well worked out in classical Buddhism, whereas nonviolence as part of a social ethic was left ambiguous and given only slight attention. From a Buddhist perspective, one practices Buddhism, among other things, to become a person who is more and more incapable of committing ever-subtler forms of violence. Although this is clear, it does not help very much in the development of the kind of worked-out social ethic that Engaged Buddhism needs. It is not the same *kind* of thing for a state, for example, to say, "We will not commit violence," as it is for an individual to say, "I will not commit violence." For one thing, there will almost always be individuals within a purportedly nonviolent state who, as individuals, believe in the use of violence.

We may ask whether on Engaged Buddhist philosophical principles it is not also the *duty* of a people's leader to defend them. Nhat Hanh's rewritten first precept states, "I am determined not to kill, not to let others kill, and not to condone any act of killing in the world, in my thinking, and in my way of life." If one looks at just the "not to let others kill" part, one can see this element of moral imperative attached to protecting human life, that form of life which is so precious. If one kills in order not to kill, however, not only does one violate the first precept, one also steps onto a slippery slope that leads from killing to prevent imminent killing, through killing to prevent threatened killing, to the world as we know it with vast armies and vast wealth devoted to the technology of killing. How does one resolve this dilemma?

The first step is to see that it *is* a dilemma, that the personal ethic of nonviolence does not translate neatly into a social ethic of nonviolence, that the Buddhist view of the preciousness of life and Buddhist respect for human rights (the first of which is the right to life) point in the direction of needing to find a way to protect each precious human life in a world in which, as the Dalai Lama rightly says, there will always be fanatics and troublemakers ready to harm others. At the same time, as soon as one admits any exception to the prohibition against killing, one begins the slide down the slippery slope. The world has reached a point where our militarization may be the death of us. All Engaged Buddhists agree that we must find another way. It is indeed a dilemma for which there is no easy solution. Perhaps the most difficult aspect of the dilemma is that Buddhism, Engaged and otherwise, does endeavor to transform people in such a way that they become more and more incapable of committing an act of violence. This is the point at which the contradiction is direct. Engaged Buddhism does encourage all people, certainly including laypeople, to engage in this kind of transformative process. Who, then, will join the army—the least developed segment of society? This is surely not the kind of army that Suu Kyi envisages, whom the people could love and respect.

Nhat Hanh speaks to this dilemma in a passage we have seen before. Pointing out that it is impossible to be entirely nonviolent, he proposes that the ethically good thing to do is to strive to become ever more nonviolent. Once we accept this, we realize that it is incorrect to think of the world as composed of two camps, the violent military and the nonviolent civilians. "Anyone can practice some nonviolence, even army generals. They may, for example, conduct their operations in ways that avoid killing innocent people."[77] Does the fact that perfect nonviolence is impossible get Engaged Buddhists off the hook and make a Buddhist army more palatable? Surely everyone would agree that an army that avoided killing innocent people is better than one that sets no limits on its behavior. Does this point in the direction of Buddhists needing a doctrine of just war? Buddhist countries having militaries with only defensive capabilities? Or is that unthinkable?

Some Engaged Buddhists may find themselves someday in the position of leading a country. Suu Kyi has been elected the leader of Burma and, if given the opportunity, would serve as the leader of a democratic Burma. The Dalai Lama has led the effort to construct a democratic structure of government for Tibet, should it ever gain self-rule, and though he has said he himself would not rule, he and his associates are writing the rules that a future Buddhist leader would likely follow. Ariyaratne has steadily built an alternative form of self-governance on the grassroots village level in Sri Lanka, which he would like to see replace the present government structure. (He states, "My dream is to get 16,000 villages in Sri Lanka to build a truly alternative system without calling it alternative, and then one day to declare our freedom."[78]) All of these are movements that, if successful, could put Engaged Buddhists (whether the current leader or a successor) in positions of national governance. How would Engaged Buddhists handle the matter of self-defense? We have heard from Suu Kyi, who would have an army and strive to make it a highly honorable and ethical force. Ariyaratne has put in place Peace Brigades trained in nonviolent techniques to maintain order. The Dalai Lama would make of Tibet a zone of peace free of the necessity of a national army. These visions intend very different institutions, to be sure, as is only right for their very different situations, but they are all attempts to remain faithful to Buddhist nonviolence — more fully in some cases than others — while accepting the responsibilities of possible governance.

It is sobering to acknowledge, however, that Engaged Buddhist pacifists do have difficulty responding to the violence of the early twenty-first century. In the wake of the terrorist attacks on the United States of September 11, 2001, the comments of Engaged Buddhist leaders tended to deplore the attacks and implore the United States to be restrained in its response but had very little to offer in the way of constructive suggestions of what the United States should do. Most constructive suggestions tended to fall into two categories. First, the suggestion was made that the United States should allow international organizations to handle the situation. This comment reflects both revulsion at the destructive power of the United States military that is typical of Engaged Buddhists and the turn toward an international solution that we saw above in the Dalai Lama and Sulak. In fact adequate international organizations to handle this kind of thing do not exist at present; perhaps Engaged Buddhists will want to make the development of such international institutions a priority. If someone ultimately must use force to restrain violent attacks, however, it is difficult to see what the ultimate advantage is in transferring that responsibility from one group to another — the world would still contain the same amount of violence.

The second kind of suggestion made after September 11 encouraged the United States and its people to seek to understand the underlying causes of the attack (largely understood by Engaged Buddhists to lie in numerous American international economic and political actions in the twentieth century) and to make changes that would remove the conditions that could lead to future such attacks. This kind of advice reflects classic Buddhist cause-and-effect thinking of the kind reflected in Ariyaratne's approach to ending the violence in Sri Lanka. It does make an important contribution, crucial in fact to the future of U.S. relations with the rest of the world. Following such advice and acting on what was discovered could prevent future violence. This suggestion does not, however, help the United States know what to do now, either to catch those responsible or to prevent further imminent attacks by the same or related groups—both of which require the use of some force.

The problems that Engaged Buddhists face with respect to the application of nonviolence are by no means unique to Buddhism. It is well known that pacifism's strength exists before and after violence—that is, in prevention and in reconciliation and healing. To prevent a war from occurring—which pacifism *can* do—is a great good, though it does not win headlines. To heal a country when the war is over and reconcile former foes is another essential task to which pacifists are well suited and generals most ill suited. Pacifism's weakest moment is in the midst of war—pacifists' well-intentioned efforts to stop a war in progress seem irrelevant, as a rule, to those engaged in combat who are concentrated on winning, as even Shakyamuni Buddha discovered when he failed to stop an imminent war.

Since September 11, 2001, Buddhist groups in America have spent many hours in anguished and intense debates on these issues without yet finding any clear answers. However difficult, these debates are essential. Though Buddhist nonviolence dates from the time of the Buddha, this is a conversation that is really just beginning.

7 Justice/Reconciliation

Engaged Buddhists regularly speak about social issues in the international forum, where Western ethical language dominates. I have observed that some terms of this Western discourse are more readily embraced by Buddhist activists than others. "Justice" language, in particular, is much less common among Engaged Buddhists than "human rights" language. The use of human rights language among Engaged Buddhists is both extensive (found in many different Buddhist countries and Engaged Buddhist movements and leaders) and intensive (this language is not just occasionally used, but is also the cornerstone of political rhetoric in some cases, such as in the Tibetan, Burmese, and Cambodian examples). In contrast, one hears comparatively little justice language among Engaged Buddhists in their discourse on social and political issues. A few Engaged Buddhist leaders do seem to be fundamentally oriented to thinking in terms of justice—for example, B. R. Ambedkar and Sulak Sivaraksa.[1] Others, such as Thich Nhat Hanh, use justice language occasionally,[2] whereas still others seem not to use it at all. Why are Engaged Buddhists, as a whole, so much less ready to embrace and use justice language than human rights language?

We will discuss separately the ideas of political, economic, and criminal justice. We will find that, by and large, Engaged Buddhists are least willing to use justice language in the context of global political conflict. They are much more willing to speak of economic justice, as we shall see. Of criminal justice they have thus far had little to say, but we will explore this area as best we can with the few comments that we have.

POLITICAL JUSTICE

Several questions will be considered in the course of this inquiry. First, can a Buddhist theory of social justice be found in traditional Buddhist ideas? The Buddhist karma theory is a justice theory, but it is traditionally understood to lead away from concerns for social engineering. Next, can karma and social justice work be reconciled? What, if anything, is lost if Buddhist ethical theory does not have a concept of social justice? Finally, are traditional Buddhist values, such as the concern to eliminate suffering, adequate to analyze the issues and justify the social change that Engaged Buddhists seek and to construct the Good society that they are beginning to envision, or is a concept of social justice necessary to those ends?

At the outset, we should clarify what is meant by "justice." Peter A. Angeles's *Dictionary of Philosophy* gives the following definition:

> 1. Fairness. Equitableness. 2. Correct treatment. Merited reward or punishment. 3. Rectitude. Correctness and impartiality in the application of principles of rightness and of sound judgment. 4. The embodiment of the virtues (ideals, values, principles) of a society. 5. The establishment of a harmony between one's right and the rights of others (society, the public, government, or individuals).[3]

Of these meanings, I need to say a few words on the first three, which seem to be most relevant to our inquiry.

There is, in the concept of justice, concern about the following: (1) Fairness. Philosophically, this term is associated with impartiality—a fair outcome is one that an impartial and competent person—such as a judge in a court of law—would recognize to be the right one. (2) Moral rectitude or rightness. The concept of moral rightness immediately raises the issue of whether there is such a thing as an objective right and wrong in Buddhist ethical thought. Finally, (3) merited reward or punishment. Legally, this value is present in the maxim that the guilty should be punished and the innocent should go free. In international political discourse, this idea manifests itself in the idea that wrongdoers (such as those who invade another country) should receive loss or punishment, whereas the morally right (such as those who lose their freedom or their land) should receive gain, vindication, or victory.

Let us begin with the second of these ideas, justice as moral rectitude or rightness. The idea of justice, as used in international political discourse, clearly rests upon the assumption of an objective moral right and wrong. Does such an idea exist in Buddhist ethical thought?

Buddhism does have a theory of natural justice in the concept of karma. That the concept of karma must imply a concept of objective right and wrong was made clear, as we saw in chapter 3, by Bruce Reichenbach, in his study of karma:

> [T]he law of karma is a special application of the law of universal causation, an application which uses the metaphysics of causation both to explain a moral phenomenon and to vindicate the moral order by applying universal justice to human moral actions. . . . This vindication accords with the fact

that the law of karma presupposes an objective ethic. It affirms that intentions and actions can be objectively determined to be right and wrong, so that the proper or just consequences can result or be apportioned.[4]

I find this persuasive. In Buddhism karma is always presented as an utterly just system, in the sense of justice as fairness. It was very important to the Buddha to distinguish Buddhism from moral nihilism by presenting Buddhism as teaching that the universe is a place in which appropriate consequences follow from one's actions, in this lifetime or a future one. Thus, the universe is portrayed as a place of justice, of merited consequences. In this sense, Buddhism does teach that there is an objective standard of good and bad, right and wrong, in the universe. Moreover, without God or any other being making a choice or judgment as to what consequence should ensue from a given behavior, the mechanisms or processes of justice are as objective and impartial as can be conceived.

Buddhadasa Bhikkhu refers to this very objectivity and impartiality as constituting the justice of *kamma* and other aspects of the Dhamma:

> In this world it is sometimes the case that "might is right," or that expediency is right, or that the evidence given by a witness is made the basis for rightness and justice. But if the witness is lying or mistaken regarding the accuracy of the evidence, then the supposed justice based on it is totally deceptive. Real justice can be based only on dhamma. . . . [J]ustice based on dhamma is totally independent of human error. It is absolute. Examples are the law of *kamma* and laws of impermanence (*anicca*), suffering (*dukkha*), and not-self (*anatta*). The truths of suffering, the cause of suffering, the cessation of suffering, and the way leading to the cessation of suffering: these are absolute and totally just. They favor no one; no one has any special privileges in regard to them. They are laws of nature and they apply absolutely.[5]

Similarly, when asked about justice, Sulak, who is one of the Buddhist activists who more readily uses justice language, said that his basic idea of justice is that "there is something above the law."[6] The idea that there is something above the law is a very concise statement of the idea that there is an absolute right and wrong, that justice is more than mere cultural mores or social contract.

If karma is a concept of natural justice, what are its implications for social action? It is quite true that the Buddhist sense of karma as natural justice does remove to some degree, perhaps a great degree, the sense of urgency and necessity to intervene in a situation that was perceived as unfair or harmful. I had a discussion on this topic with Sulak. Contrary to my expectations for such an active activist, Sulak said, "Justice in Buddhism is this: whatever you do, *kamma* [karma] justice will be done. Also, the wrongdoer suffers already, so we should be compassionate to him." He added that this view is both a strength and a weakness for Buddhism: "Of course, if you don't believe in a next life, it does not work at all, but also with this view, you may forgive too quickly. In the case of the Khmer Rouge, for example, it is necessary for the leaders to be tried."[7]

I asked, "Why, if you believe this, do you work so hard at all your different social projects, protests, etc.?"

Sulak replied, "The law of *kamma* works more appropriately if people put in good thinking and good action. If the poor are empowered now, you get the results sooner rather than in the future. You need good conditioning. You have to counter bad conditioning. The point is to apply conditioning.

"People who are impatient cannot understand. You have to see cause and effect. Once you start, you see more and more clearly. Selfish motives can be enlarged. People are against the pipeline [between Burma and Thailand] because it's in their backyard, but then they become concerned about human rights in Burma. They are ordinary people who now fight for human rights."[8]

It seems for Sulak, then, that it is quite true that, because karma takes care of things that humans do not there is less necessity for human intervention. All the same, though, it is still useful for activists to intervene energetically in social affairs in order to, more or less, help karma along. In other words, everything does work out eventually—wrongdoers get their due and justice is served—but in the meantime, a great deal of avoidable suffering has occurred. To prevent avoidable suffering, action should be taken now—the Khmer Rouge leaders should be tried, a pipeline that shores up the brutal regime in Burma blocked. In this understanding, Engaged Buddhist work in society may be seen as complementary to the natural justice of karma and motivated by compassion in a context in which karma may work justice very, very slowly. Moreover, inasmuch as karma is not fate but a system of cause and effect, activists such as Sulak see karma as a system within which activists can and should work, applying the right kind of conditioning, or causes, to get the desired effects.

Let us turn now to the first meaning of justice mentioned earlier, fairness or impartiality. It is clear that Buddhism has always embraced impartiality as an important virtue. First, Buddhism recognizes impartiality as an attribute of wisdom. Prayudh Payutto writes, "The attitude that results from the possession of mindfulness and clear comprehension . . . [is] one of neutrality, objectivity, and freedom, a state unfettered by unwholesome tendencies that can be linked to desire or disappointment."[9] Traditionally, many meditations are continued up to the point where one can observe one's responses to all kinds of people and see that one's responses are identical to all of them. Classically, this is the case in the meditations on the four *Brahmavihāra*, or Sublime States.[10]

Let us summarize where we stand with respect to our three proposed meanings of "justice" in terms of some of the classic Buddhist concepts upon which Engaged Buddhists draw. First, we have seen that fairness or impartiality is a well-recognized virtue that is expected in the advanced practitioner of Buddhism. Second, we have seen that there is a concept of objective right and wrong in Buddhism assumed by the concept of karma. Third, we have seen that karma itself is a form of natural justice that delivers merited reward and punishment, but that, because it often works slowly, there may be appropriate opportunity or even need for Buddhists to engage in social action as an expression of compassion.

We turn now to examine some Engaged Buddhist discussions of the concept of justice. In light of my thesis that Engaged Buddhists rarely use justice language, the reader might think that such discussions would not occur. Indeed, they do not very often. Occasionally, however, often when prompted by a Westerner, justice language may be used, but interpreted in a Buddhist manner.

Let us begin with the entirety of a comment by Sulak, a part of which we saw earlier. Having observed that Sulak sometimes does use justice language, I asked him what he meant by "justice." The term, Sulak replied, means "that there is something above the law. Likewise, justice must be interpreted with compassion and mercy. Whatever you do, you must always bear in mind the Four Noble Truths: the basic framework is suffering and overcoming suffering."[11]

This captures quite nicely the fundamental ideas present in many Engaged Buddhists' view of social ethics. Justice language, it would seem here, is not sufficient. A more Buddhist way of thinking holds the following themes in close association. First, there is a right and wrong (something above the law), but — and note that this comes immediately — this right and wrong cannot justify harming others. Justice must be interpreted with compassion and mercy, nonnegotiable Buddhist values that, it is implied here, may sometimes be in conflict with rhetoric of justice. If there is a conflict, it seems, we should hang on to compassion and mercy and let ideas of justice go. Why? Because the basic framework for thinking about human relations, human social life, is the Four Noble Truths, the fundamental aim of which is to eliminate suffering. The means should fit the end. If the goal of Buddhism is to eliminate suffering, one should not act in such a way as to increase suffering in service of some end conceived as "justice."

Samdhong Rinpoche further confirms this Buddhist reconfiguration of justice rhetoric in the direction of nonviolence. When directly asked to speak on the subject of nonviolence and social justice, he said, "Justice, or social justice, may be called a synonym with nonviolence. Mahatma Gandhi counseled that truth and nonviolence are two sides of the one coin. It can also be said that nonviolence and social justice are also the two sides of one coin. Social justice is not possible unless and until you establish a nonviolent society. And you cannot establish a nonviolent society unless and until you believe in truth and you act in accordance with it."[12] In other words, wherever there is violence, there is not justice.

A few days after he gave this talk, when I had the opportunity to interview the Rinpoche, I asked him about the concept of justice. He said, "I don't know the Western concept of justice. In Buddhism no one has the right to do some injustice." When asked, "What do you mean by 'injustice'?" he replied, "Harm to any living being."[13] Here injustice and harm to any living being are simply equated.

Similarly, after the attacks of September 11, 2001, Nhat Hanh was asked what kind of response there should be to the terrorist attacks. His interviewer asked, "What is the 'right action' to take with regard to responding to terrorist attacks? Should we seek justice through military action? Through judicial processes? Is military action and/or retaliation justified if it can prevent future innocents form being killed?" Nhat Hanh responded, "All violence is injustice."[14]

Thus, nonviolence is at least a necessary condition for justice, if one must use the term. That it may not be a sufficient condition for justice is suggested by Samdhong Rinpoche's reference above to the synonymy between social justice, nonviolence, and truth. For Buddhists this truth will be *Dhamma*, in other words, what is.

Likewise, the Rinpoche made it clear that nonviolence does not mean passivity and endorsed Gandhi's *satyagraha* approach, glossing it as "insistence upon truth." That nonviolence does not mean passivity is well understood by all the Engaged Buddhists, some of whom, like Aung San Suu Kyi, must struggle to teach more traditional Buddhists the necessity of taking action. "Non-violence means positive action. You have to work for whatever you want. You don't just sit there doing nothing and hope to get what you want. It just means that the methods you use are not violent ones. Some people think that non-violence is passiveness. It's not so."[15] Another window into Buddhist thinking on the concept of justice came during the visit of the Peace Council, an interfaith peace team in which Buddhists are well represented, to Jerusalem in May 2000. After several days of hearing both Israeli and Palestinian leaders speaking of the suffering and injustice each suffers at the hands of the other, it became clear that the Buddhist members of the Peace

Council, despite, as might be expected, feelings of sympathy and compassion for the suffering on both sides, to a person were feeling increasingly out of harmony with the message that they were hearing from both sides. And, indeed, from the point of view of the Buddhists present, they were hearing the same message from both sides.

Here is what, from a Buddhist perspective, was heard over and over from both the Israeli and Palestinian leaders: This crime was committed against us. We will never forget. There can be no peace without justice — no peace without justice *first*.

This was heard by the Buddhists present as the voice of victimhood, of righteous — that is, justified — anger, of the memory that is central to the identity of a people and passed on from generation to generation, the memory that says: I will never forget what you have done to me and my people. Chatsumarn Kabilsingh, at that time a Buddhist laywoman and scholar from Thailand (now the bhikkhuni Dhammananda), spoke for the other Buddhists when she said that she could not understand, in her heart, what the Israelis and Palestinians were saying. She saw them as "nourishing their suffering," whereas her training is "to let go of it."[16]

Again, after the Peace Council had been in Jerusalem and hearing statements from Israelis and Palestinians for several days, Geshe Sopa, a Tibetan monk and scholar, spoke words that were stunning for the temporal and spatial locations in which he spoke them and the groups to whom he addressed them. Here is a summary of what he said to the dean of Hebrew Union College on Holocaust Memorial Day, right after a very emotional program remembering the Nazi Holocaust and its victims.

> The Tibetans were invaded by the Chinese and suffered greatly, losing their homes and many lives. Why did the Chinese attack Tibet? It was a karmic result. We believe that this is due to karma, our collective karma. Sometime in our past lives we as a group did something terrible to the Chinese; our suffering now at the hands of the Chinese is the result.
>
> Think about karma. You might think: maybe in the past I was one of those German soldiers. That person earned bad karma. Someone else had karma that led him to be born as a Jew and be killed. With general karma, if a group in the past together killed an enemy, that group would later be reborn and be killed together.
>
> The main thing is to have compassion for mistakes made from an egocentric viewpoint, from ignorance. Sometimes you have a wrong view that fills you with hatred and you do something out of hatred that earns

you negative karma. That must be subject to our compassion, our love. The Chinese are now earning terrible karma for what they are doing to us. We must feel compassion for *all* who are suffering, on both sides. We don't look at the Chinese as evil, but try to find a peaceful solution and make them happy and peaceful.[17]

Very similar words were spoken by Geshe Sopa a few days later to the director of the Deheishe Camp for Palestinian refugees.

On both occasions, Geshe Sopa's words were met with a rather stunned silence. Indeed, this encounter between, on the one side, both the Israeli and Palestinian views, and on the other side Buddhist views, was the starkest example of incommensurability that I have ever witnessed. Neither the Israeli-Palestinian side (which, again, from the Buddhist perspective seemed to be a single point of view) nor the Buddhist side could really understand what the other was talking about.

Here are some things that the Buddhists present on this occasion rejected in Israeli-Palestinian discourse on justice in their situation of conflict. First, they rejected the identity politics of victimhood, of purposely cultivating memories of one's own suffering and the wrong-done-to-me associated with it. They rejected identifying oneself and one's group with that suffering and that victimhood. Buddhists are taught to let go of suffering and move on. They are taught to consider what actions of their own contributed to their present situation.

Second, they rejected the anger and one-sidedness of this victim politics, the "righteous" or supposedly justified anger supported by the idea that right is entirely on my side and wrong entirely on the other side. From the Buddhist perspective these one-sided ideas of right and wrong were held in the face of the obvious fact that there is plenty of right and wrong on both sides. Geshe Sopa spoke of scientifically and historically unknowable wrong deeds that he nonetheless is confident were committed by the Tibetans in past lives—thus evening out the account of bad on both sides of the China-Tibet conflict, whereas the Buddhists perceived both the Israelis and Palestinians as unwilling even to admit to wrongs well known to have been committed by present actors. Although Geshe Sopa spoke for himself, it was clear that all the Buddhists perceived the Israelis and Palestinians as failing to see the interdependence of the two sides, the truth on the other side, and the shortcomings of their own side.

Third, the Buddhists present rejected the insistence they heard upon attaining justice before there could be peace. That is, they rejected allowing the insistence upon attaining justice *first* to become a block to finding a mutually acceptable resolution. Indeed, because the Buddhists perceived "justice" being conceived by the Israelis and Palestinians in one-sided terms, it was clear to the Buddhists that such insistence upon two different one-sided versions of "justice" entirely precluded the possibility of reaching a mutually acceptable resolution. Thus, both the Israelis and Palestinians could feel morally justified in their insistence upon justice, but peace could never be achieved. This inability to reach a condition of peace, or livable harmony, from these starting points in supposed "justice" was in itself a sufficient demonstration to the Buddhists present that these conceptions of "justice" were fundamentally flawed.

Fourth, and finally, the Buddhists of course rejected allowing ideas of justice to justify acts of revenge or retribution, "an eye for an eye" thinking. To the Buddhists, no preceding act on the other's part can ever justify a misdeed (that is, an act of violence) on my or our part. Violent acts motivated by misguided ideas of retributive justice simply earn me/us bad karma and make the present problem that much more difficult to resolve. As Venerable Dhammananda said on the occasion of the Peace Council's visit to Northern Ireland, "'I lost my son, therefore you must lose your son.' This is the wrong idea of justice. We must look for an understanding of justice that uplifts humanity."[18]

These are the kinds of ideas, emotions, and attitudes that Engaged Buddhists of my acquaintance associate with Western rhetoric of "justice."[19] All four of these ideas are rejected by these Buddhists when they encounter them in the speech and action of others. I surmise that it is a fundamental disharmony with these kinds of ideas that has prevented the widespread adoption of "justice" language by Engaged Buddhists.

A separate piece of evidence supporting this understanding comes from a report on a 1994 UNESCO forum that was meeting to draft the Declaration on the Role of Religion in the Promotion of a Culture of Peace. The report cites the following exchange, which Pataraporn Sirikanchana, professor of Buddhist studies at Thammasat University in Bangkok, initiated:

> I don't think we should say that there can be peace only where there is justice. I don't understand peace in that way. For a Buddhist, peace is not a result. It is a state of being.
>
> A monsignor from Rome representing the Pontifical Council for Justice and Peace, looked at her incredulous, "Of course peace requires justice. How can there be peace where people are suffering under injustice?"
>
> She tried to explain, "For us, the word 'justice' implies making a judg-

ment about what is just. My idea about what is just may be different from your idea, so how can we find peace in that way?"

After an awkward pause, most of the others turned away and began to discuss another part of the text.[20]

Pataraporn Sirikanchana expresses the same Buddhist preference for peace over "justice" with the conviction that ideas of justice may stand in the way of peace; the same puzzled silence greets her.

THE ENGAGED BUDDHIST ALTERNATIVE

I would like to look now at a question raised at the beginning of this chapter: Are traditional Buddhist values adequate to analyze the issues and justify the social change that Engaged Buddhists seek and to construct the good society that they are beginning to envision, or is a concept of social justice necessary to those ends? Let us consider this question by examining the "People's Peace Plan" for Sri Lanka currently proffered by Ariyaratne and the Sarvodaya Shramadana. Nowhere in Sarvodaya's peace plan does justice language appear. This is not to say, however, that there is no analysis of the causes of the Sri Lankan conflict or of the need to redress those problems. On the contrary, these points are strongly emphasized. Such an analysis, however, does not require justice language; instead, as we have seen, the analysis of the conflict and its causes was implicitly made in language of the Four Noble Truths. Let us review that analysis.

Noble Truth 1, the problem: "The problem is not LTTE [Tamil Tigers] or the Government. The problem is VIOLENCE and the conditions that nurture and support it." Noble Truth 2, the cause: poverty and ethnic conflict. Noble Truth 3, the goal: The goal is a state of peace, "a sustainable, spiritually balanced island that works for all." Noble Truth 4, the way to cessation of the problem: Sarvodaya peace and development programs. Ariyaratne's view is a classically Buddhist view of how to stop war: remove the causes of war. Remove the fuel, and the fire goes out. No one "wins." When the conditions supporting the violence are eliminated, the war stops of itself. Justice language is not necessary in this analysis; cause and effect language is adequate.

In addition, justice language is perhaps seen as inappropriate. "Neither the government nor LTTE can bring peace. Neither of them is entirely blameless in this conflict, in its start or its continuation. Sarvodaya is the largest national organization with 'clean hands' that can lead all sides to peace."[21] If Western justice language is perceived to be associated with one-sided claims to having right on one's side and wrong on the other side, here is a statement rejecting such a notion in the case of Sri Lanka's civil war; it is explicitly stated in the document that both the government and the Tamil Tiger sides played a role in initiating and sustaining violence. Here also are echoes of Samdhong Rinpoche's assertion that nonviolence is justice. Where is "blame"? Wherever violent acts have been done. Thousands have died on both sides, leading to further acts of violence in retaliation. Only those who are "blameless" (read *nonviolent*), a nonviolent organization like Sarvodaya, can appropriately claim to be a vehicle to peace; only nonviolent means can engender a state of peace, understood as "a sustainable, spiritually balanced island that works for all."[22] A state of peace is not and cannot by its very nature be one-sided: the island must work for all. Identifying the problem as violence, rather than injustice, in step 1 of the analysis of course ensures that the envisioned answer will be a state of peace, but that, in turn, ensures that step 4, the effort to realize the goal, will be envisioned as an effort to meet and balance the needs of all, rather than as a struggle between two opposing forces, both claiming that "right" is on their side.

As a result of all these factors, we can see that the justice paradigm, as discussed above, does not fit the work for peace of Ariyaratne in Sri Lanka. Instead, we can see that Ariyaratne is working within what we might call a reconciliation paradigm. In this paradigm, the goals are (1) a speedy end to all violence; (2) the needs of all parties being met; (3) a win-win outcome for both (or all) parties involved; and (4) an ongoing condition of friendly and cooperative relationship. Behind these goals are corresponding elements of Engaged Buddhist philosophy: (1) nonviolence and compassion; (2) objectivity, or the equal right of all to happiness; compassion and loving kindness; (3) awareness of interdependence; and (4) interdependence and the norm of cooperative human sociality. This paradigm fits the work of the other Engaged Buddhists as well. It was clearly the paradigm within which the Buddhists visiting Jerusalem were thinking as they viewed the Israeli-Palestinian conflict and the reason why they felt so alienated from the justice paradigm at work there.

Thinking within the reconciliation paradigm can certainly be seen in the actions and attitude of the Vietnamese Struggle Movement discussed in chapter 6. That movement made it a central and conscious principle to avoid taking sides in order to be on the same side as all parties. The goals were an end to the killing and the reconciliation of the warring parties. Reconciliation certainly presumed avoiding taking sides. "[I]f we align ourselves with one side or the other, we will lose our chance to work for peace. Reconciliation is to understand both sides, to go to one side and describe the suffering being endured by the other side, and then to go to the other side and describe the suffering being endured by the first side. Doing only that will be a great help for peace."[23] Although the Vietnamese Struggle Movement never got far enough to discuss all parties' needs being met, they did consistently call for a negotiated political resolution to the conflict, rather than a military resolution; certainly a military resolution represents a one-sided win, whereas negotiation is based on the premise of identifying acceptable outcomes that all can accept.

In chapter 4, we looked at one aspect of Nhat Hanh's famous poem "Please Call Me by My True Names." This poem, and Nhat Hanh's commentary on it, may be the single best source for understanding the Engaged Buddhist reconciliation paradigm and its difference from the justice paradigm. Again, it reads, in part:

I am the mayfly metamorphosing on the surface of the river,
and I am the bird which, when spring comes, arrives in time to eat the
    mayfly.

I am the frog swimming happily in the clear water of a pond,
and I am also the grass-snake who approaching in silence, feeds itself on
    the frog.

I am the child in Uganda, all skin and bones, my legs as thin as bamboo
    sticks,
and I am the arms merchant, selling deadly weapons to Uganda.

I am the 12-year old girl, refugee on a small boat, who throws herself into
    the ocean after being raped by a sea pirate,
and I am the pirate, my heart not yet capable of seeing and loving.[24]

What is so striking here is the lack of negative judgment of the arms merchant and the pirate. They both are put in the same category as the bird and the snake, the actions of neither of which elicit negative judgment from anyone. How can this be? And, especially, how can this be if this is supposed to represent a form of morality? To one raised on the justice paradigm it is initially impossible to reconcile morality with this absence of moral judgment.

There are two elements here that are pertinent to the reconciliation paradigm and its difference from the justice paradigm. The first is cause and effect, as discussed in chapter 4. Everyone does what they do for a reason. It may be a very misguided reason, but it is a reason. In Buddhist terms, these reasons are conditions of the action. As Nhat Hanh writes, "I saw that if I had been born in the village of the pirate and raised in the same conditions as he was, I am now the pirate.... I saw that many babies are born along the Gulf of Siam, hundreds every day, and if we educators, social workers, politicians, and others do not do something about the situation, in 25 years a number of them will become sea pirates. That is certain."[25] Sociology is a science. We do know that certain social conditions produce certain outcomes. One who keeps that awareness in the foreground is going to tend to be much more interested in changing the causes and conditions to prevent undesirable outcomes or criminal activity. From a sociological point of view, once the causes are present in a population of a certain size, one can be sure that a certain amount of criminal behavior will be produced—not necessarily in this or that particular individual, but somewhere within the population. This does reduce the degree of responsibility or guilt of the individual, though it does not eliminate it entirely.

The second element pertinent to the reconciliation paradigm is nonseparation. Nhat Hanh writes, "I" am the mayfly and the bird, "I" am the frog and the snake, the child and the arms merchant, the refugee and the pirate. Nonseparation is present here on at least two levels. "I" am the arms merchant and the pirate. The kind of separation that is necessary in the justice paradigm between a good "me" who can sit in judgment on a bad "you" does not exist here. There is no separation between judge and judged, and therefore there is no judgment: as Nhat Hanh says, I cannot dismiss myself as so utterly worthless, simply "bad" and to be rejected. In addition, as Nhat Hanh's commentary makes clear, in his view we are all partially to blame for producing and tolerating the conditions of poverty and hopelessness that contribute to the creation of criminals. Even if we want to give the lion's share of responsibility to the arms merchant or the pirate, inasmuch as we share some responsibility for the situation, we cannot entirely separate ourselves from it.

This poem discusses behavior on the individual level, but the same points apply to societies and countries as well. Let us take again the example of Israel and Palestine. The cause and effect are plain. The Jewish people were decimated by the Holocaust. With the foundation of modern Israel, they vowed "never again." Today they feel themselves surrounded by hostile neighbors who threaten their right to exist. Their fear and security consciousness cause them to keep a tight grip on the Palestinians and to react powerfully to any attack. On the other side, many Palestinian people lost their homes and live in refugee camps. Their children are brought up to understand that they suffered a great injustice that they must never

JUSTICE/RECONCILIATION • 215

accept. The children see their parents regularly humiliated by Israeli soldiers and nothing but a future of hopelessness for themselves. They express their anger in violent actions. From one point of view, there is plenty of room for blame in this: everyone is doing something they should not be doing. But from another point of view, it is all very understandable. If "I" had been born in their circumstances, I would probably do the very same thing. What is the use in blaming anyone? As Geshe Sopa said, "The main thing is to have compassion for mistakes made from an egocentric viewpoint, from ignorance." The only helpful thing is to end the violence and suffering, to resolve the situation by trying to meet everyone's real needs. This is the reconciliation paradigm.

Of course not all Engaged Buddhists avoid the use of justice language entirely. Even those who sometimes do speak of justice in the political context, however, are operating within the reconciliation paradigm rather than the justice paradigm. Suu Kyi is a good example of this. Although she usually speaks of her movement as one that seeks democracy and human rights for Burma, justice is occasionally mentioned. That is, usually when speaking freely or given an open question, she uses rhetoric of democracy and human rights:

> Aung San Suu Kyi: I think that monks and nuns, like everybody else, have a duty to promote what is good and desirable. And I do think they could be more effective. In fact, they should help as far as they can. I do believe in "engaged Buddhism," to use a modern term.
> Alan Clements: How might they be more effective?
> Aung San Suu Kyi: Simply by preaching democratic principles, by encouraging everybody to work for democracy and human rights, and by trying to persuade the authorities to begin dialogue.[26]

On rare occasions, she employs justice rhetoric: "I don't think [the Burmese] people will go on for ever accepting injustice."[27]

What is Suu Kyi's position with respect to our two paradigms of justice and reconciliation? In fact, although she occasionally uses the word "justice," she is fully within the reconciliation paradigm.

First, she wishes no ill toward her opponents, the military rulers of Burma (SLORC).

> I think here they [SLORC] underestimate both the people and us as a movement for democracy. Obviously, there is some hatred among the

people, especially among those who have suffered. However, we are confident that we can control this hatred. But there is no hate among the leaders of the NLD. The authorities find this difficult to understand.[28]

Second, she constantly calls for dialogue with SLORC.

[I]f we got to the dialogue table, the first thing I would like to say is, "You tell us what you have to say." I would like to listen to them first. Why are you so angry with us? What is it that you object to?[29]

Third, once democracy comes to Burma, she sees a truth and reconciliation process, as opposed to a criminal justice process, as the best way to respond to what we might call the justice issues of the people's suffering during the SLORC regime.

Alan Clements: What about the victims who . . . feel violated and made resentful by the atrocities committed towards them?

Aung San Suu Kyi: Of course. Of course. This is why we are talking about the connection of truth and reconciliation. I think that first of all, their sufferings have to be acknowledged. You can't just wipe away the past. If you try, there will always be this ocean of festering resentment within those who have truly suffered. They will feel . . . as though they've undergone torture for nothing; as though their sons and fathers had died for nothing. Those people must have the satisfaction of knowing that their sufferings have not been in vain, and this very fact, that there's an admission of the injustice done, will take away a lot of the resentment. . . . There will always be people who can never forgive. But we must always try to. In Chile they had a Council for Truth and Reconciliation and there's one now in South Africa, under Archbishop Desmond Tutu. I very much believe in it. The admission of injustice, to a certain extent, will prevent it from happening again. People will realize that if you do such things, they get known. You can't hide them.
. . . [S]omething must be done to satisfy the victims and the families of those victims.[30]

This very interesting passage contains language of justice but a paradigm of reconciliation. The central difficulty with the reconciliation paradigm is put in the foreground here: people who have suffered greatly need *something* to be able to move on with their lives. This, for some, is the strength of the justice paradigm:

people who have committed crimes need not only to be held accountable but to suffer in some way in recompense for the suffering they caused others. Notice that we are not talking here about a question of safety from future harm but of satisfaction in seeing the one who has caused harm being held accountable and suffering in some way.

The reconciliation paradigm has not entirely resolved this issue of how to respond to the suffering that has occurred, but it has been greatly helped by the development of truth and reconciliation commissions. It is interesting that Suu Kyi talks about the *connection between* truth and reconciliation. In other words, reconciliation is the goal. In this case, that seems to mean first and primarily an internal reconciliation that allows one to accept what has happened and move on with one's life. Secondarily, it seems to refer to reconciliation with the perpetrators of harm, or in other words forgiveness of them, but it is immediately accepted as a matter of fact that this full level of reconciliation cannot always, perhaps not even usually, be reached—though if it could, the personal reconciliation would be more complete as well.

The role of truth in this process is crucial. Herein hinges the difference between the justice and reconciliation paradigms. Those who have suffered need *something*, but what is it that they need? Suu Kyi is correct in pointing out that it does not work to tell people simply to forget what they have suffered; people are unable to do so, and their feelings of resentment, anger and misery will fester and grow. History has shown that such resentments, if not resolved in some way, are simply handed down to the next generation (Yugoslavia is one example). But what, again, is it that people need in order to resolve their ongoing suffering after experiencing great trauma? The justice paradigm holds that what they need is retribution, to see the perpetrators of harm suffer in turn. The reconciliation paradigm believes that what is needed is truth and acknowledgment of the wrongness of what was done. People need to tell their story and be heard, they need to hear the truth, they need someone to accept responsibility, and they need some kind of reparations. They also need public acknowledgment, by an authoritative and respected group or individual, that what they suffered was wrong. This is what Suu Kyi means by an admission of the injustice done.

In this context, Suu Kyi's talk of justice clearly does not mean punishment of the offender. It means public, official acknowledgment that moral wrong was done (in Burma, this amounts to SLORC's violation of most of the Five Lay Precepts, the moral floor beyond which one should not fall). What will happen to the offender is a totally separate subject that countries with truth and reconciliation commissions have handled in different ways according to their circumstances. As long as the situation has changed in such a way that the one who has suffered harm feels safe from future harm — a key requirement — what happens to the offender is not the main point. Some offenders may be set free and suffer no punitive consequences. Others may be imprisoned, made to give service, and so forth. What counts is whether the truth and acknowledgment have been sufficient to give satisfaction, a degree of inner peace, to the one who has suffered. Notice that, whatever the outcome, the perpetrator has been made to state publicly what she, or he did. They have been made to face their own wrongdoing. There is accountability not only to the one directly harmed, but also to the entire society. The perpetrator knows that everyone knows what they have done. This is a very different situation from "getting away with it," in which there is no public accountability.

To conclude this section on political justice/reconciliation, Engaged Buddhists are sometimes regarded as if they are so thoroughly under the influence of Western concepts and thought patterns that they are the victims of Western cultural imperialism. Very much to the contrary, my observation is that Engaged Buddhists are Buddhists first and foremost. As intelligent contributors to intercultural discussions, they have to be conversant with the dominant, Western terminology. The choice that is evident in the language of many Engaged Buddhist leaders to use human rights language but avoid justice language, however, demonstrates their consistent practice of choosing language that they find to be harmonious with the nonnegotiable Buddhist values to which they are committed.

ECONOMIC JUSTICE

All the Engaged Buddhists on record on the subject embrace the basic idea of economic justice — regardless of whether they use the term. That is, they all believe that there should be a sufficiently adequate distribution of the wealth of the world so that no one's wealth is inadequate to meet their basic needs. Because humans are equal in rights in the view of Engaged Buddhists, there is no justification for the vast disparities in wealth that exist between individuals or between regions of the world. There should be no exploitation of one part of the world's population and resources by another part.

The usually soft-spoken Dalai Lama becomes quite passionate, and speaks for the other Engaged Buddhists, on this subject. Hearing that the number of billionaires in America was multiplying, he remarked, "This I consider to be completely immoral. It is also a potential source of problems. While millions do not even have the basic necessities of life — adequate food, shelter, education, and medical facilities — the inequity of wealth distribution is a scandal." It is not so much the wealth per se, he notes, that is immoral; if everyone's needs were met, "then perhaps a luxurious lifestyle would be tenable." But of course it is not like that. In this world, some "throw surplus food away while others close by—our fellow humans, inno- cent children among them—are reduced to scavenging among rubbish, and many starve." He concludes that in this kind of world, the luxurious life of the rich is "unworthy" and "spoiling." Like Buddhadasa, he points out, "as human beings we have only one stomach. There is a limit to the amount we can eat." Amassing more than we can use and letting it go to waste is wrong. Being rich itself, however, is not immoral. On the contrary, it is "a tremendous opportunity to benefit others. What a waste when that opportunity is squandered on self-indulgence."[31]

The Dalai Lama and other Engaged Buddhists share a number of concerns. To have vastly more than one can use while others starve is "completely immoral," for several reasons. Not to relieve the intense suffering of others when one has the means to do so is entirely lacking in compassion, loving kindness, and generosity. To be so blatantly greedy and selfish harms oneself and others. It is blind to the sameness of all human beings—our equal right to happiness. It squanders an op- portunity for self-development, for the giving that would make others and oneself happy. And it is "a potential source of problems," that is, resentment, anger and violence.

Ariyaratne is very familiar with a world in which "the poor man still can- not find one liter of water to drink while these others [in affluent countries] have thousands of liters in which to swim." He declares that the superpowers "have no moral right to spend $900 billion a year for armaments when 900 million people are starving." When money of this magnitude "is completely diverted for the de- struction of people," the result is that "the economies of the poor people are shat- tered."[32] If the superpowers "have no moral right" to spend money in this way, it is because human beings are equal and have an equal right to life and to a decent life. Similarly, Samdhong Rinpoche, in *Tibet: A Future Vision*, states that "all persons have a right to a decent standard of living for themselves and their families" and that therefore in a future autonomous Tibet "efforts will be directed to minimize the gap between the rich and the poor, the educated and the uneducated, the city dwellers and the residents of villages and the older and the younger generations, in all possible manner."[33]

In a similar vein, Nhat Hanh makes economic justice into one of his Tiep Hien precepts: "Do not accumulate wealth while millions are hungry. Do not take as the aim of your life fame, profit, wealth, or sensual pleasure. Live simply and share time, energy, and material resources with those who are in need."[34] Nhat Hanh interprets and broadens the second of the Five Lay Precepts, in which traditionally an individual undertakes not to steal, to have it embrace economic justice. Nhat Hanh rewrites the second precept to include the lines "I am determined not to steal and not to possess anything that should belong to others. I will respect the property of others, but I will prevent others from profiting from human suffering or the suffering of other species on Earth."[35] He comments that this second precept, not stealing, is closely interrelated with the first, not killing: "When we meditate on the Second Precept, we see that stealing, in the forms of exploitation, social injustice, and oppression, are acts of killing—killing slowly by exploitation, by maintaining social injustice, and by political and economic oppression. Therefore, the Second Precept has much to do with the precept of not killing."[36] Thus, the precept is transformed from an exclusively personal ethic (I will not steal/individuals should not steal) to include a social ethic (societies should not steal, either). When societies steal, because of their size and economic power, the result can easily be starvation or death for those from whom they steal.

Commenting also on the second precept, Sulak writes,

> We must . . . take responsibility for the theft implicit in our economic systems. . . .
> The establishment of a just international economic order is a necessary and interdependent part of building a peaceful world. Violence in all its forms—imperialist, civil, and inter-personal—is underpinned by collective drives for economic resources and political power.[37]

Again, the first (no killing, no harming) and second (no stealing) precepts are seen to be highly interdependent when viewed from a societal and intersocietal perspective. Because nonharming is one of the core Buddhist values, it becomes clearer why there is such unanimity among Engaged Buddhist thinkers in favor of economic justice. Within social ethics, economic justice is a necessary part of nonharming.

To probe Engaged Buddhist ideas on economic justice more deeply, we must turn to the work of Ariyaratne. It is incontestable that Ariyaratne has done more by far to forward Buddhist thinking and, especially, practice on economic issues than any other Engaged Buddhist. This section on economic justice will therefore focus on his thought and work.

The fact that most of the Engaged Buddhist leaders are from the Third World no doubt plays a role in their having such strong convictions and speaking in such a unified voice on the subject of economic justice. Speaking from the perspective of Sri Lanka, Ariyaratne states that only an "insignificant minority" are benefiting from economic globalization, whereas "the poor are becoming poorer, and the numbers of the poor are increasing." This, he says is the case "in all the developing countries." He therefore calls for changes in international trade in order to end the "injustice" of the current international economic order and see that people's basic needs are met.[38]

With regard to foreign debt, Ariyaratne points out that the international banks set the rules in such a way that the developing countries cannot win: "You see, right from the beginning, at the time we were given the money, it was inherent in the system that we were not in a position of earning and paying it back." The only solution, for Ariyaratne, is to "tell the banks, 'we are not going to pay our debt'" and face the consequences.[39]

Not only is the entire international economic system unjust, in Ariyaratne's view, but even the established way of talking and thinking about that system is unjust. "The 'basic need' is our first economic objective, not growth, not increasing the per capita income. This talk about growth and no-growth is nonsense when there is no value attached to the whole thing. You should not ask the question, 'How much has the economy grown?' You should ask, 'How many people are now getting a balanced meal?'"[40] "To eradicate hunger," it is necessary to reject the dominant kind of economic theory.

Sulak develops this view, stating that noneconomic values are not taken into account when trade issues are under discussion. Whether "economic activity promotes satisfaction or despair is afforded no consideration." "As a Buddhist, I cannot consider economic efficiency as the ultimate value for a social order. I am constrained to evaluate a system of social organization in terms of its capacity to address human suffering, to promote distributive justice and allow for individuals within society to realize their full potential."[41] Thus, economics is value laden, but the dominant economic theories and measures overlook the values that are most important: human suffering and well-being, the distribution of goods to meet the basic needs of all, and the particularly Buddhist concern that social and economic structures support human self-realization.

Because he finds that the established economic theories and practices do not serve the needs of the poor, Ariyaratne has devoted his life to creating a new approach, building from the ground up, that is, starting from human beings' basic needs. Sarvodaya has identified ten basic needs for human communities. They are

1. A clean and beautiful environment (both physical and psychological)
2. A clean and adequate supply of water
3. Simple requirements of clothing

4. Balanced food requirements
5. A simple house to live in
6. Basic health care
7. Simple communication facilities
8. Minimum energy requirements
9. Total education
10. Cultural and spiritual needs[42]

Notable in this list of needs is the first, a clean and beautiful environment. Its inclusion on a list of basic needs indicates a major difference between Engaged Buddhist ideas of economic justice and dominant Western ideas of the same: economic justice for humankind—which we could paraphrase as meeting the basic needs of every person—is not permitted to be in a competitive or adversarial relationship with justice, if you will, for the environment—which we could paraphrase as meeting the basic needs of other plant and animal species and of the Earth and its component parts as well—if only by leaving them alone!

Phra Payutto agrees with Ariyaratne's perspective: "To be ethically sound, economic activity must take place in a way that is not harmful to the individual, society or the natural environment. If ethical values were factored into economic analysis, a cheap but nourishing meal would certainly be accorded more value than a bottle of whiskey."[43] Payutto here agrees with Ariyaratne not only in including protection of the environment as a factor in economic justice, but also in decrying the poverty of economic measures that cannot distinguish between something of real value—nourishing food—and something of negative worth—whiskey.

In light of Ariyaratne's focus on meeting the ten basic needs, one might suppose that he would be an advocate of full employment, of decent jobs with decent wages for all who seek them. This is not his approach. Jobs and wages are components of the modern marketplace, and Ariyaratne is thinking outside that framework. "Employment," he says, "is not considered by Sarvodaya as a basic human need." Employment is a means of satisfying needs. He believes in "full engagement" rather than full employment. Such engagement is intended not only to meet basic needs, but also to provide "an opportunity to be industrious, to co-operate for common benefit, learn skills and understand problems and exercise their minds to seek solutions."[44]

In other words, humans need to have their basic needs met, and they need to be engaged in meaningful activity. There is no need to assume that roles like employer and employee or an exchange of cash will have anything to do with these processes.

Another unique and important feature of Ariyaratne's approach to economic justice, satisfying basic needs, is that it should be approached in the context of the overall health of the individual and community. As can be seen in the ten basic needs, the effort to meet basic economic needs should be accompanied by an effort to meet basic educational, cultural, and spiritual needs as well. For Ariyaratne, poverty does not exist in isolation. Because of interdependence, it is interactive with educational, psychological, sociological, and cultural factors. Therefore, poverty cannot be overcome with an exclusively economic approach but requires a holistic approach that addresses all these factors at once. In addition, Ariyaratne, like all the Engaged Buddhists, sees humankind as fundamentally spiritual beings. Economic justice is for the purpose of supporting humankind's reach for ultimate self-realization, for awakening or Buddhahood. For both these reasons, Ariyaratne's approach to gaining economic justice includes within the very fabric of the economic work careful attention to other dimensions of human and community development: economic development utilizes self-reliance and cooperation; any harm to any being or to the environment in the name of development is prohibited; and power in decision making must be decentralized and returned to the people. In other words, it is very clear to Ariyaratne that economics are value laden, and he is very clear what his values are.

Within that larger goal of supporting our reach for Buddhahood, for Ariyaratne the purely economic goal is likewise Buddhist: "As we live amidst poverty in Asia our priority should be not to create a small minority of affluent people but to liberate the majority of people who are poor from that state of poverty. Buddha showed us a Middle Way to liberate ourselves from the sufferings in this cycle of births and deaths, discarding both self-mortification and self-indulgence. The best course of action in the Buddhist spirit we can follow is to have as our aim a no-poverty and no-affluence society."[45] The Buddha taught the Middle Way between the extremes of asceticism and hedonism. Ariyaratne interprets this as pointing to a Good society as one without either extreme need or extreme indulgence. He makes the very Buddhist distinction between needs, which must be met, and greed, which the society has no need to attempt to satisfy. Other than advocating that Third World countries refuse to repay their debt to the international banks, however, his theory does not address what to do about greed, beyond encouraging Buddhist practice and devotion to the community.

Payutto also sees economics through the lens of the Middle Way: "Consumption . . . which is attuned to the Middle Way, must be balanced to an amount appropriate to the attainment of well-being rather than the satisfaction of desires. Thus, in contrast to the classical economic equation of maximum consumption leading to maximum satisfaction, we have moderate, or wise consumption, leading to well-being."[46] The presumption that "more is better" is simply incompatible with Buddhist values. Siddhartha Gautama left home precisely because more was not better, and, on the basis of that act, the Middle Way was founded.

The Dalai Lama decries the "culture of excessive materialism" that is the source of damage to the natural environment and of harm to others, especially the poor and the weak. Whereas the rich, for example, can move to avoid pollution, the poor cannot. We leave a polluted world as our legacy for our descendants. For these reasons, he believes that, "the culture of perpetual economic growth needs to be questioned." In his view, "it fosters discontent, and with this comes a great number of problems, both social and environmental." While Europe is comfortable, people elsewhere starve. "And where there are imbalances as profound as these, there are bound to be negative consequences for all."[47] The theory of perpetual economic growth, being out of tune with the Middle Way, is fundamentally harmful and unsustainable. Thus, for Engaged Buddhists the distinction between need and greed goes right to the heart of the issue of economic justice and the Middle Way points the way out of the mess we are making.

In sum, Engaged Buddhists embrace the idea of economic justice with great unanimity. There is nothing to prevent them from doing so, because economic justice, unlike political justice, has no notion of retribution attached to it and no one-sidedness in its perspective. On the contrary, economic justice is about human equality, fairness, and sharing, all of which are foundational Buddhist values. Because it is about meeting people's real needs, it is easy to see it as an expression of compassion. It also seems to be in tune with natural law. As both Buddhadasa (chapter 3) and the Dalai Lama remarked, each one of us only has one stomach. Beyond a certain level, excess consumption and amassing of wealth can become grotesquely out of step with nature. The harm to the natural world that results from excess consumption is a direct demonstration of this unnaturalness. Likewise, the imbalance that leaves so many millions starving and impoverished while others have far more than they can use shows that something is fundamentally wrong with the order of things. All of this makes concern about economic justice a natural for Engaged Buddhism.

CRIMINAL JUSTICE

As we turn to the area of criminal justice, let us return to a question raised at the beginning of the chapter. Can Engaged Buddhists construct the Good society that they are beginning to envision on the basis of purely Buddhist values, or is a concept of justice, in this case criminal justice, necessary to that end? What would an Engaged Buddhist theory of criminal justice look like?

Engaged Buddhists generally have not written about this issue. Nevertheless, we can gain some insight into it by looking at the following exchange taken from an interview I had with Samdhong Rinpoche.[48]

> Samdhong Rinpoche: I don't know the Western concept of justice. In Buddhism no one has the right to do some injustice.
> Sallie King: What do you mean by "injustice"?
> Samdhong Rinpoche: Harm to any living being. If you have done that, then there is a procedure of punishment, of regretting. We do have the theory of punishment, the objective of punishment, the way of punishing, and then also how to redress the person who has been the victim.
> Sallie King: Why punish?
> Samdhong Rinpoche: To punish means to impose certain things on account of a wrong action, to impose unpleasant things—this is clearly prescribed in the *Vinaya*. In the *Vinaya*, there are ten kinds of punishment. These punishments are a reminder to let the wrongdoer regret his action and affirm not to repeat it. In the *Vinaya*, the punishment includes asking a monk to sit at the lowest level for a period (below his juniors), to clean the kitchen and vihara; the most severe punishment is that all the monks will not speak to him—this is imposed if they see that he has not repented his deed. Punishment is a training to transform a person.
>
> There are four basic points to recover from an evil deed: If you have done a horrible thing, you (1) must take refuge in the Three Gems; (2) feel very sorry, repent; (3) have the strong determination not to repeat your deed; and (4) do something positive to recover from what you have done and earn some merit. If you have done all these four things, then you don't experience further karmic results from your deed. Two and four can be imposed from without, by society.

Asked about the purpose of punishment within a criminal justice system, the Rinpoche replied, "As aims, protecting society comes first, protecting the individual comes second. There are aims to create fear in other people's minds to prevent the same crime being committed by others, and to help the individual understand that what he did was wrong and that he should change. A very horrible criminal will be kept separate from others in order not to infect them."

There is a great deal of interest in these remarks. A criminal justice system is necessary, we can infer, in a state based upon Buddhist principles. The purposes of such a criminal justice system would be, first, to protect society and individuals from any harm and, second, to transform the wrongdoer. As we have seen, the state has a duty to protect its citizens. There are, however, at least two ways to conceive this duty. In the justice paradigm, the relationship between the state and the wrongdoer is adversarial. The court is set up with two opposing sides, prosecution and defense. The prosecution intends to show that the accused is guilty and seeks to exact the maximum punishment. The defense aims to prove the defendant's innocence and thereby eliminate the consequence of punishment. In the Rinpoche's remarks, however, there is no adversarial relationship. While seeking to protect society and individuals (as in the justice paradigm), the state that followed the Rinpoche's approach would also be seeking the welfare of the wrongdoer by applying means that would help him or her to understand the wrongness of his or her deeds and to be transformed in such a way as not to repeat them. This Buddhist form of criminal justice, in short, is not retributive, but rehabilitative.

These two forms of criminal justice are well recognized. Retributive justice is "justice whose principle aim is revenge and/or vindictiveness as indicated in the statement 'An eye for an eye and a tooth for a tooth.'" Corrective/rehabilitative justice is "justice whose aim, for example, is not punishment for the sake of punishment or for revenge but for the purpose of changing the character and the environment of the offender so that similar actions will not occur again."[49]

In his Buddhist commentary on the Universal Declaration of Human Rights, L. P. N. Perera concurs with this placement of Buddhist criminal justice within the norms of rehabilitative justice rather than retributive. He writes, "Buddhism would accept the necessity of punishment as a corrective measure for an erring individual with the objective of rehabilitating him or her within acceptable norms, and not as a lawful retaliatory measure for an offence committed or even simply as an expression of outraged feelings."[50]

It is clear that justification of punishment for punishment's sake is contrary to Buddhist views concerning compassion and karma. Punishment can have a place in a Buddhist state on the basis of these same values if one understands its purpose in terms of corrective and rehabilitative justice. It would seem, however, that there would be some careful judgment involved in assigning the correct kind and degree of punishment to simultaneously fulfill the deterrent effect of punishment, which the Rinpoche recognized, to induce the wrongdoer to repent the wrong-doing, which the Rinpoche mentions can be imposed from without by the state, and to condition and support inner transformation in the wrongdoer.

It is also worth noting that the Rinpoche mentions doing "something posi-tive to recover from what you have done and earn some merit." Although the root concern here is the traditional idea of minimizing the negative karmic effects that will follow from one's wrongful act, the idea of doing something positive suggests that one need not conceive of state-imposed consequences to wrongful acts ex-clusively in terms of punishment. It would seem that within a Buddhist criminal justice system there would be a place for atonement, that is, making amends or reparation for the injury or wrong one has committed. In such a system, one would be required to repair or make up for the damage one had caused as far as possible. Such approaches can in some cases play a role in helping the wrongdoer to trans-form and in healing the one who has been harmed. Obviously, for those considered to be continuing threats, society's and individuals' needs for protection from harm would override other objectives and could preclude an atonement approach.

I did not ask the Rinpoche about capital punishment; however, I have never yet heard of an Engaged Buddhist who defended capital punishment. There is a good reason for this. Sulak said, "I am opposed to capital punishment. People have to have a chance. I like it that Western Buddhists are teaching meditation in pris-ons."[51] As long as one's aim includes transformation or rehabilitation of the wrong-doer, capital punishment can have no place. People "have to have a chance" to transform themselves.

Wondering whether there is anything that needs to be done in a society based upon Buddhist principles, that could not be done without a concept like the West-ern concept of justice, I put two cases of actual events in contemporary American society before Samdhong Rinpoche. These are both cases in which harm has been done but is now over and we can presume that similar harm from the same wrong-doer will not occur in the future. The justice paradigm would indicate that when a wrong has been committed justice has been offended and, therefore, the wrong-doer should be tried for the crime committed and punished if found guilty. The idea of "offending justice" seems too abstract for Buddhism, yet how would one conceive of the justification of pursuing the wrongdoer, assuming that protecting others from harm was not at issue?

> Sallie King: There was a case of a father committing incest with his step-
>   daughter. The mother found out about it and the family entered into
>   mediation. In the course of a lengthy mediation process, the step-

daughter grew up and left home. Nothing was ever done to the father. What is your view of this situation? Is it enough that the stepdaughter is now safe from further harm by the father?

Samdhong Rinpoche: The father should be punished so that he would understand that what he did was wrong and so that other people would be shown that this was wrong.

Sallie King: Are you familiar with the O. J. Simpson case? (I briefly explained that in this highly publicized case many people were convinced that Simpson had been guilty of two murders, but had been found not guilty and set free.)

Samdhong Rinpoche: This would be the same.

In these cases, although one could not appeal to protecting society or individuals as justification for apprehending and punishing a wrongdoer, one would still not need to appeal to justice. For the Rinpoche, the state should apprehend and punish such a wrongdoer for two reasons: to help the wrongdoer, for his own sake, to realize that what he did was wrong and to help convince him of the necessity of changing; and for the sake of society, to publicly demonstrate to everyone that these actions are wrong. Thus, a concept of justice as such is not required, though a concept of right and wrong, or moral limits beyond which one must not fall, is required. Such a concept, as we saw above, is presumed in the idea of karma in Buddhist thought.

CONCLUDING THOUGHTS

Looking back over Engaged Buddhist views in the three areas of political, economic, and criminal justice, a continuity of perspective is apparent. In all three, we can see important underlying common principles and values—namely, compassion; a nonadversarial posture; and an awareness of interconnectedness, whether between individual and society, between human communities, or between humankind and the natural world. There is an overriding wish to ameliorate suffering, a consistent search for win-win outcomes that benefit everyone, and a great desire to reconcile any elements of the web of interbeing that have fallen into adversarial relations. It is a great challenge, at least in the political and criminal justice areas, to find the best ways and create the best institutions to apply these principles. Much may be done, however, with time, more thought, and practical experimentation. In the area of economic justice, it seems that what is needed is mostly the will to change.

8   Conclusion

The courage and accomplishments, the genius and creativity, of the present generation of Engaged Buddhists are impressive and inspiring by any measure. The Engaged Buddhists are best known for helping to reduce the suffering of millions of people, but we should not neglect their pioneering of a new way of thinking about how one engages the problems and needs of the world. When the present generation of activists is gone, future generations will draw upon their ethical thought, as well as their example, as they respond to the new challenges that time will bring.

The Engaged Buddhists stand on the ground of traditional Buddhist ideas and values. They have adjusted those ideas under two influences: first and foremost, the practical challenge of the situations of conflict, poverty, and suffering in which they find themselves and, second, the influence of the modern Western and international ideas with which they are in dialogue. In this way, the Engaged Buddhists are creating a unique approach to social ethics, an approach that is innovative in both the Buddhist and the global contexts.

I believe that the Engaged Buddhists' insights into ethics, as well as their innovative practices, have much to offer the global community. At the same time, as a philosophical school and a social engagement movement in its infancy, there is much that requires further consideration. I hope that Engaged Buddhism will attract another generation of intellectuals and activists, as there are a number of issues that will require a great deal of thought for this movement to achieve its potential. In this chapter, I will consider both the most important contributions that the Engaged Buddhists have made and some of the issues that stand out as requiring further attention. I hope that the latter will be seen as a contribution to the ongoing development of Engaged Buddhist thought, and not as a criticism.

ENGAGED BUDDHIST CONTRIBUTIONS TO GLOBAL ETHICAL THOUGHT AND TO THE PRACTICE OF SOCIAL ACTIVISM

First, the ethical theory of Engaged Buddhism is a sui generis theory that is best understood in its own terms. This ethical theory has a number of important features capable of freeing dominant Western ethical thought from a number of straitjackets that have limited its development. In Engaged Buddhist ethical theory, human beings are approached holistically. Reason and emotion are regarded as interactive, and both play an important role in the ethical life. In this sense, Engaged Buddhist ethical theory addresses human beings as they are.

Engaged Buddhist ethical theory recognizes human moral growth as a central fact of the ethical life and constructs its theory on that basis. It provides a vision of properly developed reason and emotion and applies training that begins from where one is and helps one to move on a trajectory toward the ideal.

Engaged Buddhist ethical theory avoids both ethical relativism and rigid rule following. It maintains ethical objectivity with clear minimum standards that make clear what behaviors are unacceptable; however, it also maintains open-ended moral ideals or virtues that make flexibility possible as one responds to the particularity of each unique situation. The open-ended moral ideals also constitute a standing invitation to each individual to achieve ever higher moral standards.

Second, Engaged Buddhism succeeds in communicating a morality that is relatively free of judgmentalism. Although there is right and wrong, the idea of morality being developmental frees Engaged Buddhist ethical theory of the need to be condemnatory. There is no human soul that can "be" good or evil. A person is where she is morally and developmentally for a host of reasons. From this perspective, blame is simply irrelevant. The worst of us need to be restrained, but each of us needs to be addressed where we are and to be surrounded by wholesome influences that will encourage us to move to ever more ethically developed levels.

Third, although Thich Nhat Hanh gets credit for coining the term, all the Engaged Buddhists embody the idea of "being peace." This is the quintessentially Buddhist idea that one's state of being influences everything that one does. Considered from a cause-and-effect perspective, the end is prefigured in the means. Thus, Aung San Suu Kyi, because she wants the future Burma to be a nonviolent state, rejects the idea of using violence to bring that state into being. Peace activists, says Nhat Hanh, should always "be peace" as they work to bring peace into the world. This idea has had a great influence on non-Buddhist peace activists, who had not considered the matter before. "Being peace" also has a side benefit — intentionally nurturing peace within oneself can help prevent burnout, a chronic problem among Western social activists.

Fourth, the nonadversarial perspective of Engaged Buddhist ethics is one of its most important features. Although nonadversariality is also found in Gandhian and some Christian social activism, Engaged Buddhists may have explored the theory and practice of nonadversarial relations on a larger scale and in a greater variety of conflict situations than anyone else. More than any other major group, they seem to be carrying forward the torch that Gandhi lit. There is a legacy of experience and practical wisdom here that deserves the widest attention.

Fifth, one of the great potential contributions of Engaged Buddhism is its perspective on international conflict situations. Engaged Buddhist views challenge the international community to rethink the relationship between peace and "justice." Coming from a culture without justice language, they are able to see how often retribution is implicit in many groups' demands for "justice" and how the desire for retribution can prolong a conflict. In this light, they oppose the dominant idea of "no peace without justice," an idea that in practice often becomes a slogan used to obstruct movement toward peace, and urge groups in conflict to place a higher priority on preserving every human life. They largely do without "justice" as a tool for analyzing social conflicts and replace it with a dispassionate analysis in terms of cause and effect. They also do without "justice" as a goal, replacing it with a goal conceived as freedom from suffering for all involved or as a harmonious society that works for everyone.

The Engaged Buddhist view in this area represents a very different approach to the way conflict is conceptualized. It is little known in international circles and difficult for people steeped in "justice" thinking to understand. These ideas also deserve wide circulation and trial.

Sixth, the Engaged Buddhists have achieved inspiring greatness in maintaining nonviolence under the worst provocations. They have also been highly creative in applying it. Their stories are too little known and even less understood and again deserve widespread attention.

Seventh, and finally, the Engaged Buddhists have, more than any other major group of Buddhists, succeeded in modernizing Buddhist thought and in making it available to the global community of social activists and thinking people. People who would never consider reading other Buddhist books avidly read the Dalai Lama and Nhat Hanh. They have been extremely successful in crossing the cultural gap and communicating an authentic Buddhist perspective in a way that can be understood and appreciated in the non-Buddhist world.

ISSUES IN ENGAGED BUDDHISM
THAT REQUIRE FURTHER THOUGHT

In this section, I will take a step back from the Engaged Buddhists themselves and allow myself to make my own suggestions regarding four issues in Engaged Buddhist social ethics that require further thought. We have seen throughout this book the many ambiguities that follow from the Engaged Buddhist understanding of the relationship between individual and society. Of the four issues I will discuss, the first three are all manifestations of this ambiguity. The fourth, nonviolence, is simply a very difficult ideal.

PERSONAL OR INSTITUTIONAL CHANGE

As a group, the Engaged Buddhists have not resolved in their own thinking whether desirable social change can be achieved by changing the human mind alone or whether it is necessary to direct efforts toward making structural and institutional changes in society as well. A number of them emphasize mental change to the exclusion of institutional change.

Maha Ghosananda says, "The wise ones know that the root causes and conditions of all conflicts are in the mind," and "the world is created by the mind. If we can control feeling, then we can control the mind. If we can control the mind, then we can rule the world."[1] Cheng Yen, the least political of the Engaged Buddhists, particularly emphasizes internal change. Her web site states, "Improvements in society do not come from society itself but from its members. It is through personal growth that profound changes can be possible on the greater level of society. The Master sees the individual as the crucial agent for change."[2] These kinds of comments represent the wing of the Engaged Buddhist movement that emphasizes personal change, to the exclusion of institutional societal change, as the correct response to the problems of society. This kind of thinking represents a strength of Engaged Buddhism—pointing out how important to social issues the attitudes and mental states of the members of society are. One wonders, however, whether it represents a sufficient analysis of what is needed.

Shortly after the September 11, 2001, attacks, Venerable Cheng Yen commented, "All hatred comes from the mind! If everyone's hearts carried love and righteousness, the airplanes would not have crashed into the towers. With a tranquil mind, one would have realized the roots of injustice and hatred, and would not have turned love and rationality into hatred, allowing this disaster to happen."[3] This statement is true. Because one cannot force potential terrorists to meditate and transform themselves, though, what should one do if one wants to prevent such things from happening in the future? The personal change approach is not adequate in a situation of this kind.

Sulak Sivaraksa is the strongest and most consistent advocate of institutional change among the Engaged Buddhists. He argues that an exclusive focus on the mental realm is not Buddhist. Because a "fundamental tenet of Buddhist doctrine is the co-arising of mind and matter," we cannot ignore the material dimension of life. The world is a complex place in which the psychological, the economic, the political, and the military are interwoven. Therefore, "merely tinkering with one link in the complex circle of causation does not stop the process that leads to violence and warfare. Rather, the practice of Buddhism strives to address each aspect of the process in a holistic way."[4] Sulak is arguing primarily with other Buddhists here! Clearly, he is on solid ground in his reference to Buddhist philosophical principles. Consequently there is no reason for a focus on the mental realm to dominate Engaged Buddhism; certainly it should not dominate to the exclusion of all else.

A. T. Ariyaratne has done the most among the Engaged Buddhists to actually create new social institutions. Like Sulak very aware of interdependence, he has a great deal of practical insight into the interplay of personal and societal change and consistently works at both the individual and the societal level simultaneously, as the Sarvodaya slogan demonstrates: "We build the road and the road builds us."

Engaged Buddhism has made an important contribution to global peace activism by highlighting the role played by the mind in constructing conflict and emphasizing the importance of each person working on his or her own mental and emotional state as an element of peace work. All Engaged Buddhists include internal, personal change as a part of peace work. In doing so, they draw upon a traditional strength of Buddhism. Buddhists have a highly sophisticated two-and-a-half-millennia-old tradition of understanding and transforming the inner workings of the human being. There is no doubt that this traditional Buddhist strength makes a significant contribution to peace work. The question is whether it is sufficient to *constitute* peace work.

This problem is a manifestation of the difficulties for Engaged Buddhist practice created by the ambiguous interrelationship of individual and society in Engaged Buddhist theory. Nhat Hanh writes, "To transform our situation is also to transform our minds. To transform our minds is also to transform our situation, because the situation is mind, and mind is situation."[5] Because individual and society are fundamentally interrelated, in what direction does this interrelationship point us when we want to make a change in society? Some draw from this interrelationship the conclusion that social problems can be solved by changes on the individual level, whereas others believe that changes on both the individual and social level are necessary. Both inferences can be justified in terms of the interdependence of individual and society. But surely the approach of working for change on both the individual and the societal level is by far the more adequate response to the complex issues before modern societies, and therefore the more powerful. Surely, if one can justify working for social change on Buddhist grounds, one can justify working on social institutions as well as individuals. What is needed is only the will to further develop Buddhist social ethics and their application to social problems. Ariyaratne has been tremendously successful and thoroughly Buddhist in his work. He shows the way forward on this issue.

RIGHTS AND RESPONSIBILITIES, INDIVIDUALISM AND COMMUNITARIANISM

The Engaged Buddhists are correct when they point out that society is constructed of individuals while the individual is constructed of elements of society. They are correct in seeing that no real line can be drawn between the two. Inasmuch as individual and society are interdependent, all societies must work out how much freedom they want to give the individual and how much they want the individual to put society's needs first.

Societies around the world form a continuum from those that emphasize freedom for the individual, on one side, to those that stress communitarian values, on the other. In the United States, we have moved quite far on this continuum in the direction of hyper-individualism. Buddhists are by no means the only ones who perceive American society in particular as being too individualistic; many American social analysts contend that we need to find a way to inject into our culture a greater sense of responsibility to society.

The perception of American society as hyper-individualistic is one of the major grounds for concern that human rights are too individualistic and too adversarial. But why blame human rights? I recall taking my daughter to an excellent preschool program when she was a toddler. I was stunned when, the very first week, she brought home papers indicating that the theme of their activities that week had been, "I'm me. I'm special." What do we expect when this is what we teach our children, when these are the thoughts we plant in their minds from the time they can understand language? There were no occasions later in the year when that stress on individuality was balanced by a week's theme stressing the importance of the group. Contrast this with schools in some Asian countries where all the children are expected from day one to provide daily service to the group, by having a work period where all pitch in together to clean the room for the whole group. If these kinds of messages are given in many ways, day after day, no wonder American children grow up highly individualistic, while many Asian children have a greater sense of responsibility to the group.

The Burmese and Tibetan examples demonstrate very clearly that "everyone but everyone should be entitled to human rights." People who live lives of severe oppression and restriction have lost essential elements of what is necessary to live a life that can be considered human. No one chooses to live in such a way. If one cries out against such a life, should one be blamed for destroying society? Certainly not. Those who have taken away the liberty and well-being of others are the ones who have tattered the net of social interbeing, the net within which millions of cooperative and harmonious actions spontaneously occur every day. They bear the responsibility of destroying that net and replacing it with a net in which there is still interaction, but fewer of those interactions are spontaneously cooperative and harmonious and many more are compelled, fearful, and resentful. If the only way that one can regain one's ability to be free of fear, to practice one's religion, to meet with others, to express one's opinion is to verbally or in action demand one's human rights, then one who does so is not the one responsible for destroying the net of social cooperation—such a person is taking an action that ultimately may help to repair that net. It is in many cases, certainly in the Tibetan and Burmese cases, entirely inaccurate to think of human rights as promoting excessive individualism. Those struggling for human rights in those countries are risking their individual life and liberty for the sake of the collective rights of all the people of their country. Their actions are the self-sacrificing actions of a bodhisattva. Are their actions adversarial? The Tibetans insist that they are not—to stop the Chinese from harming the Tibetans is good for the Chinese as well as for the Tibetans. We may add that it is good for all humankind when tyrannical behavior is ended—it frees that many more people to flourish, contributing their potential to all humankind; it demonstrates to future would-be dictators wherever they may be that tyranny does not succeed for long.

A struggle against tyranny is adversarial only insofar as it says "no" to certain actions. The Tibetans show how such a struggle follows the Gandhian rule "hate the deed, not the doer." The human beings who compose the Chinese government are not opposed; their actions are. Adversariality is the wrong way to conceive human rights struggles from the perspective of interrelated humankind as well—these are struggles that serve humankind as such. Are human rights adversarial, then? Not the way the Engaged Buddhists use them. Let us lay that concern to rest.

When one contemplates the continuum from highly individualistic societies to communitarian societies, Phra Payutto's 1992 suggestion to think in terms of a Middle Path seems to this observer to express an appropriate goal for an Engaged Buddhist society. When a society moves too far in the direction of individualism, society as a whole can suffer, as when private corporations are allowed to profit by polluting the environment (harming most individuals as well as society as a whole). When a society moves too far in the direction of communitarianism, the individual can suffer, as when individual initiative, thinking, and creativity are squelched, which harms society as well. Surely the "correct" place to occupy—in Buddhadasa Bhikkhu's sense of "correct," that is, the place that most naturally fits the nature of human being—is somewhere in the Middle. Suu Kyi and Payutto both speak in terms of embracing human rights while maintaining a culture of greater compassion and sense of social responsibility than is typical of some Western countries. Probably most, if not all, Engaged Buddhists would sympathize with them in this. The Dalai Lama sees no conflict between human rights and social responsibility. There is no reason why human rights should not be a cornerstone of an Engaged Buddhist society's constitution. There are so many ways in which a society can nurture communitarian values—schools can, in their daily routines, train students to highly value the good of the group; clubs, religious organizations, scouting programs, and other organizations can promote an ideal of service to humankind or to all life and such service heroes can be nationally celebrated.

But we are not looking for a communitarian society; we are looking for a Middle Way society that finds the "correct" balance between individualism and communitarianism, rights and responsibilities. Why cannot the individual's free thinking that may often criticize and challenge society be promoted alongside a (secularized) bodhisattva ideal of service to all? Though we may think of the former as characteristic of an individualistic society and the latter as characteristic of a communitarian society, the intellectual's critical thought and the bodhisattva's service to others are not ideals that inherently conflict with each other. Indeed, many Engaged Buddhist leaders embody both ideals: Aung San Suu Kyi, Buddhadasa Bhikkhu, A. T. Ariyaratne, Sulak Sivaraksa, Thich Nhat Hanh, and the Dalai Lama all embody both ideals to one degree or another.

It seems, then, that the Engaged Buddhists can achieve the kind of society they want within the basic framework of democracy and human rights as it has developed in the West. Let us then imagine an Engaged Buddhist society as a democracy with human rights. Many of the Engaged Buddhists have stated plainly that that is what they want. Let us take that as a given. The creative challenge for a future Engaged Buddhist society will be to construct not political institutions, but social institutions that embody the correct balance between individualist and communitarian values. They will want social institutions that promote critical thought and individual initiative (both Buddhist values) as well as concern for the welfare of others and the ability to work together with others. It seems that to achieve that balance they will be drawing not upon the advice of political scientists, but upon the advice of anthropologists, sociologists, and educators familiar with the practices of many countries.

CRIMINAL JUSTICE

Engaged Buddhists have not yet begun to work out the details of a criminal justice system that would embody the implications of their philosophy. How would a criminal justice system work that recognized the responsibility of the actor for his or her action but also recognized the major contributing role of society in supporting that action?

We have seen that, although Engaged Buddhist leaders are repelled by the idea of retribution in connection with justice, there is some correspondence between Buddhist ideas and the idea of corrective or rehabilitative justice. Another concept of justice in which Engaged Buddhists might have interest is the idea of restorative justice currently being explored by progressive Western thinkers and with parallels in the justice practices of many traditional societies.

In *Changing Lenses*, Howard Zehr introduces and advocates for the idea of restorative justice. He begins by contrasting restorative justice with retributive.

Retributive Justice
Crime is a violation of the state, defined by lawbreaking and guilt. Justice determines blame and administers pain in a contest between the offender and the state directed by systematic rules.

Restorative Justice
Crime is a violation of people and relationships. It creates obligations to make things right. Justice involves the victim, the offender, and the community in a search for solutions which promote repair, reconciliation, and reassurance.[6]

There is much here of potential interest to Engaged Buddhists. Restorative justice is much less abstract than retributive justice. Its focus is on harm to people and relationships rather than the state and its laws. It is nonadversarial, aiming not to inflict harm on the wrongdoer but to make things right. It takes account of interdependence by involving all parties—victim, wrongdoer, and community—in that effort to make things right. Its ultimate goals are to end harm doing, to repair harm done, and to reconcile.

The idea of making things right leads restorative justice to experiment with atonement practices. As we have seen, there is a place in Buddhism as well for doing "something positive to recover what you have done." We saw that such an approach can help the wrongdoer to transform and contribute to healing the one who has been harmed. Instead of *balancing* harm done to the victim by inflicting harm (punishment) on the wrongdoer, restorative justice aims to *repair* everyone's harm.

Restorative justice also speaks to the dilemma, considered in chapter 4, faced by Engaged Buddhists regarding the placement of responsibility for wrongdoing on the individual wrongdoer or society. Restorative justice regards the dominant form of justice in the West as overly individualistic. Zehr states that Western concepts of guilt are based on "a belief in the individual as a free moral agent. If someone commits a crime, she has done so willfully. Punishment is thus deserved because it is freely chosen. Individuals are personally and individually accountable. Guilt is individual." Although maintaining belief in human freedom and personal accountability is essential, Zehr asserts that alone it "fails to take into account the context of behavior. Although each of us is responsible for the choices we make, the social and psychological context in which we find ourselves certainly influences our actual and potential choices." In the end, "our individualistic concept of guilt ignores the context."[7]

This kind of thinking speaks to the concern of Engaged Buddhists such as Nhat Hanh, who are troubled by the blaming of the individual wrongdoer alone, without taking into account the larger picture of the many karmic conditions that played a role in a person or persons committing criminal or violent acts. Maha Ghosananda, defending his willingness to work with the Khmer Rouge, wrote that, in them, "the seed of goodness may have died because warmth was lacking for its growth. It perished from coldness in a world without compassion."[8]

In restorative justice, it is not that a concern with individual responsibility needs to be replaced with a sole focus on the important role of societal influence but that the two need to be balanced. Restorative justice is aware that many wrongdoers have themselves been wounded by childhood abuse, poverty, racism, and the like. It seeks to balance healing of the wounds in the wrongdoer with insistence upon accountability, which is a necessary element in that healing. Thus, "offenders too need healing. They must be accountable for their behavior, of course. They cannot be 'let off the hook.' Yet this accountability can itself be a step toward change and healing. And their other needs must receive attention."[9] This speaks nicely to the dilemma considered in chapter 4, the degree to which we should hold society or the individual responsible for wrongdoing. It seemed clear that from an Engaged Buddhist perspective, in some way we need to hold both responsible, but it was unclear how this might work in practice. The answer suggested here seems a good starting place: society is responsible for its part and needs to reform itself where appropriate, and the individual is responsible for his or her part and must be held accountable for his or her individual acts but in such a way that that accountability exists as one element within the larger context of helping the individual toward reform.

Finally, says Zehr, "the community also needs healing. Crime undermines a community's sense of wholeness, and that injury needs to be addressed."[10] Here we come full circle. The community needs healing from crime, but at the same time it is partially responsible for crime, to the extent that it tolerates poverty, racism, known child abuse, or any other horrific act. To heal what is wrong in the society will help to prevent the crime from which society needs healing. Buddhists will appreciate the understanding of interdependence that permeates restorative justice.

Lest this seem too lenient, the reader should be aware that restorative justice is actually related to the victims' rights movements and strongly emphasizes transforming the justice system for the sake of victims. Persons who have suffered violence or other harm are seen as needing to understand as fully as possible what has happened, to feel safe, to be supported by the community, to be empowered, as far as possible to have what was lost be restored, and to heal. Restorative justice advocates believe that the current justice system actually meets only a small measure of these needs when it finds the wrongdoer guilty and punishes him or her. Hence, there is no need for an overtly adversarial criminal justice system in order to meet the needs of crime victims. Instead, restorative justice makes meeting the real needs of the victims its first priority. Such needs do include the ongoing safety of the community; certainly a wrongdoer who was believed to be an ongoing threat would need to be restrained. From an Engaged Buddhist perspective, of course, this still would not take us to an adversarial situation, because it is in the wrongdoer's own interest to be prevented from doing further harm.

Restorative justice is a theory in its infancy. With its nonadversarial perspective, its rehabilitative values, and its acknowledgement of a degree of interdependence between individual and society, there is much in restorative justice ideas, I believe, that could interest Engaged Buddhists.

NONVIOLENCE

To fight or not to fight? Buddhist countries have always had armies, and those armies have often fought wars. Although Buddhist personal ethics clearly point in the direction of nonviolence, in practice that has never stopped Buddhists from serving in the armies of Buddhist countries. Of course, the nonviolent teaching of Jesus has not stopped Christian countries from warfare, either. There is, however, one significant difference between the Buddhist and the Christian cases. Whereas the Christian church has obliged the rulers of Christian countries by developing a prominent and much-used "just war" theory, with the exception of Sri Lanka (where the chronicle Mahāvaṃsa does open the door to such thinking), no major Buddhist intellectual has ever developed a Buddhist just war theory.[11] In practice, there has been in Buddhist countries the kind of understanding that we saw in the Cakkavatti Sīhanāda Sutta: an assumption that it is the duty of a ruler to protect the people (and animals, according to the text) of his country, supplemented by the idea that it is good to protect Buddhism and Buddhist institutions. Despite this, a just war theory did not develop. This seems to point to a situation in which there is a major gap in traditional Buddhist social ethics. Buddhist countries have engaged in war, and the Buddhist church has supported the state in this, but an ethic justifying this practice has not been worked out.

When issues of Buddhism and war come up, Buddhists love to cite the example of the great King Asoka (circa 270–232 B.C.E.). Before his conversion to Buddhism, Asoka was by no means averse to the use of war as a tool of statecraft. According to his thirteenth Rock Edict, in the eighth year of his reign, Asoka conquered the neighboring country of Kalinga. He was moved to profound remorse over the large number of persons captured and taken away, the scores killed, the number who died of causes related to the war, and the grief and affliction of the friends and relatives of those dead and captured.[12] This remorse caused him to embrace Buddhism, give up war, and progressively move away from violence altogether, giving up hunting and becoming a vegetarian.

Asoka is taken as the paradigmatic example of a king who embodies the moral principles of Buddhism, indeed, as the historical example most closely approaching the cakravartin ideal, the ideal Buddhist monarch who rules by Dharma, by Buddhist principles. It is important to note, however, that in his Rock Edict, Asoka makes it clear that his firm intention to avoid taking life has a limit. He publicly announces to the "[peoples in the remote sections of the conquered territory] . . . that he exercises the power to punish, despite his repentance, in order to induce them to desist from their crimes and escape execution."[13] In other words, he tells them that he will not passively tolerate violent deeds on their part, but will retaliate with deadly force to ensure the peace of the empire. That is, although Asoka gave up offensive war, he puts his neighbors on notice that he will engage in defensive warfare.

Although there is no question that Asoka was a great king, and although it was extremely significant for a man of his time and power to give up offensive warfare, his example does not help very much with the issue Engaged Buddhists raise today. None of them advocates use of war for offensive purposes; who does in the modern world? The question raised by the Engaged Buddhists is whether a Buddhist should use war and violence defensively and, if so, how this action could be justified in terms of Buddhist values. This is a much tougher question and Asoka does not help us with it.

It seems to me that there are four options before the Buddhist world at this time for resolving, or not resolving, the challenge of Buddhist use of military force raised by the Engaged Buddhists. First, Buddhists might continue as now with unthinking and unreserved engagement in military life. Traditionally, most Buddhists have been happy with this approach. It is not satisfactory, however, from an Engaged Buddhist perspective, which is, in dramatic ways, encouraging Buddhists to do better. The examples of the Tibetans, the Vietnamese, and the Burmese hold up a mirror to the rest of the Buddhist world, challenging them to think about their own acceptance of the military option. To continue with the status quo is simply to ignore all the contradictions between militarism and Buddhist principles, leaving Buddhist social ethics seriously underdeveloped in an area of central importance. It is to ignore the possibility of applying Buddhism to this issue.

Second, Buddhists might try to develop some sort of just war theory. Although the mere suggestion of such a thing is to many Buddhists unthinkable, such an effort would not be entirely without scriptural roots, as we have seen. The few comments of the Buddha recorded on the subject (for example, the *Cakkavatti Sīhanāda Sutta*) indicate that he assumed the existence within the state of a military body for purposes of defense of the people and animals of the state. The *Upāyakauśalya Sūtra* of the Mahayana affirms, albeit in less down-to-earth terms, the importance of preventing violent crime and defending the innocent. These few textual passages fit the popular *lokiya/lokuttara* distinction in Buddhism, the "two wheels" of Dhamma, according to which there are two spheres, the mundane and the transmundane, with somewhat different rules appropriate to each sphere. Buddhists could also point to the role of intention in determining karmic outcomes—a soldier's act of killing in order to defend his country is karmically different from a murder committed in a jealous rage—and awareness of degrees of violence—as Nhat Hanh showed, it is morally better for a general to conduct a war in such a way that innocent civilians are not killed. To develop a just war theory would also fit the actual example of Buddhist states, none of which has ever done without an army and in each of which the ruler was expected to keep the land peaceful for the practice of Buddhism. The general attitude of people in Buddhist countries seems to be that an army is unfortunate, but necessary.

Such a potential Buddhist just war theory, if it came to be, would probably look a great deal like the just war theories of other traditions. Obviously, just war theories are painfully open to slippery slope applications and hypocrisy. At a time when our militarization may be the death of us all, few thoughtful Buddhists are enthusiastic about playing this game.

On the other hand, of the various Engaged Buddhist leaders we have discussed, perhaps Suu Kyi might be pleased with such a development. Perhaps under the kind of Engaged Buddhist leadership that she advocates a Burmese army would, like the Swiss, be trained and equipped in such a way that only defensive action would be possible. Perhaps, like the Canadian armed forces, it would play a significant role in international peacekeeping. Perhaps, like the Swedes, Burmese foreign policy would actively seek to minimize the need for use of the military even though they maintain one. A Swedish government publication states,

> Seeking means to prevent violent conflict has long been a cornerstone of
> Swedish policy both on the domestic front and in the international arena.
> This policy, the fruit of long, cumulative experience, has not only led to
> greater economic well-being and social harmony in our country but also to
> peaceful relations with the outside world. Swedish foreign policy is based
> on the conviction that we contribute, through international co-operation,
> to the establishment of common norms for international relations and
> human rights—and thereby to greater security. For a small, militarily
> non-aligned state, safeguarding international law and international co-
> operation are especially important concerns.[14]

Policies like this seem appropriate for the Engaged Buddhists as well.

Third, Buddhists may want to hold fast to principled nonviolence and give up the idea that Buddhism is compatible with national rule. Perhaps nonviolence and national rule are simply incompatible. Here personal ethics and social ethics meet head on. Although any individual may refuse to use violence in self-defense, it seems clear that for a head of state to refuse to use violence in defense of the country is another matter entirely. Buddhist personal ethics do not translate neatly into a social ethic. There will no doubt be individuals within the state who have not embraced principled nonviolence; they expect their rulers to take steps to protect them.

Compare the case of early Quakers in William Penn's Pennsylvania. Quakers, including Penn, were and are principled pacifists, and in colonial Pennsylvania they actually held power for a time. While in power, they had to contend with issues of war and the military. The historical record shows that at least one of these issues was resolved successfully. "Penn's colony had no army and yet maintained peace with its native [American] neighbors for 70 years, a record unmatched in American colonial history."[15] This was possible because, unlike other colonists, Penn and the Quaker colonists maintained unequivocally friendly, truthful, and fair relationships with the Native Americans. This successful record, however, was not to last. Although the Quaker party was in the majority for the first several decades of the establishment of the Pennsylvania Assembly, they found themselves in an awkward situation each time the assembly was asked to support a war of someone else's instigation, either financially or by supplying combatants. For a time, the Quakers balanced the contradiction between their peace testimony and their desire to be in power by compromising—for example, by voting funds to the queen for her to use for unspecified purposes when she had requested funds for war. Such acts provided only a very thin veneer of appearing to remain in accord with the Quaker Peace Testimony. Ultimately, it became impossible to compromise on demands for defense funds in the French and Indian War. With Quakers' clear reluctance to support that war (both on nonviolence and justice principles), they were largely voted out of office by a Pennsylvania electorate that had become majority non-Quaker and that was not sympathetic to pacifism. Quakers never again held a majority in the Pennsylvania Assembly.[16]

What does this case teach us? The Quaker example is an interesting example of a group that tried very hard to maintain their principled nonviolence while holding public office, even endeavoring not to support wars regarded by the public as defensive, and ultimately found that principled nonviolence and the holding of public office was an impossible combination to maintain. Quaker peace witness was forced to the periphery of political life—which is not to say that it became an insignificant thing, as it has periodically had tremendous influence—but it has not proven possible for Quakers, despite their political concern and involvement, to maintain a place at or near the center of institutional governance.

Perhaps the contradictions between nonviolence and the responsibilities of governance will prove too great for most, or all, Engaged Buddhists. Certainly there are some Engaged Buddhists who do not aspire to govern, but only to guide from the periphery. These Buddhists fit into the traditional Buddhist role of advisors to rulers, though with modern democratic forms of government, that advisory role has been transformed into guidance of the people as a whole, as those in whom power ultimately rests. Some have made major contributions from the periphery. Vietnamese Buddhists in the "Struggle Movement" during the war were for a time able to persuade divisions of the army not to support the South Vietnamese rulers. Maha Ghosananda has made critical contributions to the post–Khmer Rouge pacification of Cambodia. Sulak served as a very public moral critic of the military regime when it was in power. Recently, Nhat Hanh (who argued during the war that Vietnamese Buddhists should *not* form a political party and *not* hold power) insisted that his American followers do *something* to try to stop the United States from going to war in Iraq. It is clear that Engaged Buddhists can play a significant role in the military life of their countries with contributions like these that do not require holding office.

Fourth, the last option is for Buddhists to maintain their principled nonviolence without giving up the aspiration to national rule, that is, to pioneer ways to have national rule without a military. Certain Engaged Buddhist leaders not in power, but with some hope that they or their heirs someday will be, currently advocate this approach. The Dalai Lama, for example, has proposed making of Tibet a zone of peace free of any militarization whatsoever. The intention of this proposal is not only to free Tibet of all military presence but also to decrease the likelihood of military violence between India and China by establishing a demilitarized buffer between them. In the Sarvodaya Shramadana movement of Sri Lanka, Ariyaratne has put in place peace brigades trained in nonviolent techniques to maintain order. Very soon the Nonviolent Peaceforce—an international, civilian, nonviolent peacemaking body—will begin work in Sri Lanka. Samdhong Rinpoche gave the keynote address at the inaugural meeting of the Nonviolent Peaceforce, speaking of it as "very necessary and relevant."[17] Many Engaged Buddhists see these kinds of approaches as natural for them.

Most people dismiss principled nonviolence as unrealistic in the extreme. Of course, they have good reason. What do the Engaged Buddhists who have maintained principled nonviolence in acute struggles have to show for their efforts? In Vietnam, they utterly lost. In Tibet, the Chinese are as entrenched as anyone ever could be. In Burma, military dictators continue to rule. One cannot point to a single victory of Engaged Buddhist nonviolence against a military power. Although one admires the idealism of the nonviolent Engaged Buddhists, one still wishes that they would have some victories. Results count.

Or do they? Of the struggle in Vietnam Nhat Hanh has written,

Despite the results—many years of war followed by years of oppression and human rights abuse—I cannot say that our struggle was a failure. The conditions for success in terms of a political victory were not present. But the success of a nonviolent struggle can be measured only in terms of the love and nonviolence attained, not whether a political victory was achieved. In our struggle in Vietnam, we did our best to remain true to our principles.

We never lost sight that the essence of our struggle was love itself, and that was a real contribution to humanity."[18]

I think it is unarguable that the Vietnamese Buddhist Struggle Movement was a real and magnificent contribution to humanity. But if we agree with this, must we also agree that it does not matter whether victory is achieved?

I have made a case elsewhere in this volume for the view that Engaged Buddhist ethics embrace many strands of ethical thinking, including deontology, virtue ethics, and consequentialism. I also hold that Engaged Buddhist ethics tend to be relatively more consequentialist than traditional Buddhist ethics. If that is the case, results do count.

Within the value system of Engaged Buddhism, results count for several reasons. First, Engaged Buddhism is pragmatic. Suffering is real, not an illusion. The point of Buddhism really is to eliminate real suffering. Second, the key motivation of Engaged Buddhist ethics is compassion. If one really is concerned to relieve the people's suffering, one needs not only to do the morally right thing, but also, simultaneously, to try one's best to protect the people. Third, if we take to heart the Engaged Buddhist ethical view that it is imperative to act, that it is not good enough simply to avoid evil, that we must *do good* as well, we will understand that it is not good enough for us simply to avoid killing others; we must also prevent others from killing, as Nhat Hanh's proactive reading of the precepts spells out clearly. An ethic that is nonviolent for individualistic reasons—to keep one's own hands clean, to avoid karmic retribution to oneself, or even to develop one's own character—is not an Engaged Buddhist ethic. Therefore, if one wants to practice nonviolence, one must also want to succeed—for the sake of compassion to end or prevent the suffering of the people.

Although the Engaged Buddhists have made great contributions in nonviolent theory and practice, I suspect that a crucial shortcoming in their approach has been their neglect of considerations of power. The reader may have noticed that the word "power" has not appeared in these pages in the words of the Engaged Buddhists themselves. This is not coincidental. A theory that emphasizes the web of interdependence, the importance of harmony, the goal of reconciliation, win-win solutions, and—perhaps especially—the nonadversarial approach is not conducive to the contemplation of power. Power issues suggest adversariality. Engaged Buddhist thinking does not naturally tend to move in that direction.

Engaged Buddhists do, however, frequently use the word "struggle." The Burmese and the Tibetans are well aware that they are involved in struggles, as were the Vietnamese during their "Struggle Movement." Perhaps their awareness that they are involved in struggles could open the door to an acceptance of facing the power issues involved in those struggles.

A way of thinking about power that might prove congenial to Engaged Buddhists is that advocated by scholar and nonviolent activist Gene Sharp.[19] Sharp has devoted a lifetime to studying nonviolence and power from a secular and pragmatic point of view. Although he recognizes that people often practice nonviolence for religious reasons, he declares issues of motivation to be irrelevant and focuses exclusively on the study of what can make nonviolence successful as a form of political action—even in such "hard" cases as overthrowing dictators and preventing foreign invasions from succeeding.

There is nothing in the way that Sharp talks about power that should put off Engaged Buddhists. His basic premise is the old premise of political science: In order to govern, rulers require the consent of the ruled. While a ruler may gain that consent through coercion and violence, it is still the case that if he were to lose the consent of the governed, he would fall. One dictator, by himself, cannot rule; he does not have sufficient power. One dictator plus a circle of cronies cannot rule; they lack sufficient power. They require the assistance of many people, including the army, the police, the civil service, and those who run transportation, banking, communications, and so forth. And they require the passive acceptance of their rule by the people. This is the Achilles heel of a dictatorship.

Sharp lists 198 methods of nonviolent action that can challenge this power arrangement, among which noncooperation plays a large role, in the form of strikes, slowdowns, economic boycotts and shutdowns, intentional "mistakes," and other such actions. If a society gets to the point at which the critical support system of a dictator—the army or the police—no longer cooperates, that dictator will no longer be able to function. Shortly before the 1992–1993 American war in Iraq, Sharp was asked what he would do about Saddam Hussein. Adamantly opposed to dictatorship, and equally committed to nonviolence, he replied, "What would most likely oust Hussein is noncooperation. He and his entourage at the top of the pyramid can't function if the bottom of the pyramid doesn't function. If soldiers don't obey orders, if communication shorts out, if the transportation system suddenly does not work, then nothing happens after dictators give orders."[20] In the past, there have been many successes with nonviolent action, some of them spectacular—in India, Poland, and the Philippines, for example—but there have also been many failures. Sharp argues that this is because most nonviolent action has been spontaneous and unplanned. Why should a nonviolent campaign be any less carefully planned than a military campaign, if it wants to succeed? Sharp is convinced that with careful advance study of what does and does not work in nonviolent action, and with careful strategic planning for each particular nonviolent campaign, the success rate of nonviolent action can be dramatically improved, though not guaranteed.

How this approach differs from the approach of some of the Engaged Buddhists can be seen if we consider the place of negotiation in each. We have seen that both Suu Kyi and the Dalai Lama frequently speak about their desire to negotiate with their political opponents, with the expectation that those negotiations will resolve the situation. Sharp, however, is very critical of the idea of negotiation with one's opponent. If negotiations imply compromise, he argues, they are inappropriate in situations such as those facing Burma and Tibet. "When the issues at stake are fundamental, affecting religious principles, issues of human freedom, or the whole future development of the society, negotiations do not provide a way of reaching a mutually satisfactory solution. On some basic issues there should be no compromise."[21] Moreover, dictators have often used sham negotiations to improve their own position or to harm their opponents. Most important, the idea that negotiations, in and of themselves, resolve anything is, he says, naïve. One may be sure that the dictators are thinking strictly in terms of power. If they give anything up, it will be because they have been forced to give it up due to changes in the power balance between themselves and "the democrats." If they are not forced by such a power change, they will not give anything up. "[T]he content of a negotiated agreement is largely determined by the power capacity of each side."[22] Sharp's approach is to increase the power of the people and reduce the power of the dictators so that the latter will have no choice but to yield.

I believe that such strategic thinking about power relations has largely been a missing element in Engaged Buddhist thinking about nonviolent action. Perhaps this will change. Indeed, recently the Burmese and the Tibetans have in fact begun to work with Sharp.[23] I do not mean to imply that this collaboration will solve all the Burmese and Tibetan problems. Thinking in terms of power relations seems as if it could be a very helpful element in many Engaged Buddhist struggles if they wish to succeed while maintaining their nonviolent principles; certainly results — success — matter very much to the Tibetans and the Burmese.

Nevertheless, although I believe that strategic thinking about power relations could be useful for Engaged Buddhists, this belief requires one qualification. In the last few years, reports have been coming out of China indicating that many Chinese people are developing a very positive view of Tibet as a land of purity and spirituality, even a kind of Shangri-la. With spirituality and idealism at low ebb in Chinese culture, many Chinese are left with a sense of emptiness and meaninglessness. It is not uncommon for such people to look to Tibet to fill that spiritual void. If this trend continues to grow, and more and more Chinese people come to see Tibet as a place with spiritual treasures to be preserved, it is just possible that popular attitudes might pressure future Chinese leaders to deal with Tibet and Tibetan culture in a way that respects it and allows it to be itself, especially in the cultural and spiritual domains. If this were to occur, then the Dalai Lama's approach will have worked. That approach rests largely on maintaining the purity of Tibetan Buddhist ideals in order to attract allies and win over their opponents. The only kind of power it takes into consideration is the power of truth. In the case of Tibet, one might well suspect that this kind of power is the only kind of power that ever stood a chance, however slim, in a struggle with China.

One last idea of Sharp's must be mentioned, as it also seems to have much to offer the Engaged Buddhists—civilian-based defense.[24] Simply put, his idea is that, if the population of a country could be trained in advance in complete non-cooperation with an invading army, the army could enter the borders of a country, but could not "seize" it. Such an approach, though with an untrained population, was used with some success against the French and Belgian occupation of the German Ruhr in 1923. If Engaged Buddhists ever were to come to power, the idea of a civilian-based defense holds out a hope: if one could succeed in protecting the people while maintaining one's nonviolence, one would have resolved the challenge raised for Engaged Buddhists by the Cakkavatti Sīhanāda Sutta—the assumption that a ruler will protect his or her people—without having given up one's ethical principles.

Eschewing idealistic ethical and religious language, Sharp promotes his ideas and methods as practical, first and foremost. Ideas of this kind, which take power considerations as fundamental and aim to make nonviolence a realistic and practical alternative to violence, could well be combined with Engaged Buddhist moral and spiritual values. Such a combination not only would not damage Engaged Buddhist ethical standards, but also could enhance those standards, because if the people's suffering is important, if compassion is important, then nonviolently enhancing one's power to succeed is important.

CONCLUSION

In closing, let us return to one of the questions with which this book began. Is there such a thing as "Engaged Buddhism"? Is there sufficient unity and coherence among the individual leaders and movements we have discussed to justify regarding them as multiple manifestations of a single school of thought? I think there is. Several points draw them together.

Engaged Buddhists' core values include benevolence (compassion, loving kindness, and giving); the necessity of putting Buddhist values into practice with active service on behalf of all beings; self-development on the path to enlightenment; and progressive altruism. Their picture of the Buddhist path is one in which self-development and service to others are inseparable. They believe that society and the individual are interdependent and mutually constructive. In political theory, they are beginning to envision a democracy that has human rights as well as communitarian values and a greater sense of social responsibility than Western democracies. In economic theory, their first priority is for the basic needs of every person to be met. They support social institutions that promote humanitarian values, self-development, cooperation, nonharmfulness, and benevolence. Harm to the environment is completely unjustifiable, in their view. Nonviolence is a priority among them; they are engaged in creatively testing nonviolence in practice and taking it as far as it can go. They consistently look for ways to heal the web of interbeing when adversariality intrudes, promoting harmony and reconciliation. These fundamental values, beliefs, and goals seem more than enough to unify Engaged Buddhism.

Let us close with the words of the *Mettā Sutta*, expressing as it does the ethos of all the Engaged Buddhists: "Just as a mother would protect her only child, even at the risk of her own life, so let one cultivate a boundless heart toward all beings. Let one's thoughts of love pervade the whole world—above, below, and across, without any obstruction, without any hatred, without any enmity."[25]

Notes

Chapter 1: Introduction

1. Yu-ing Ching, *Master of Love and Mercy: Cheng Yen* (Nevada City, Calif.: Blue Dolphin, 1995), pp. 81–82.

2. Ibid., pp. 65–66.

3. Cheng Yen, "Performing Good Deeds Is More Important Than Shunning Evil Ones," *Inspirational Extracts*, May 1, 2001. http://www.tzuchi.org/global; accessed June 7, 2002.

4. Cheng Yen, quoted in Yu-ing Ching, p. 66.

5. Ibid.

6. Christopher S. Queen and Sallie B. King, eds., *Engaged Buddhism: Buddhist Liberation Movements in Asia* (Albany: State University of New York Press, 1996).

7. Donald K. Swearer, "Introduction," in *Me and Mine: Selected Essays of Bhikkhu Buddhadāsa* (Albany: State University of New York Press, 1989), p. 2.

8. I would like to express my thanks to C. Julia Huang for sharing with me several articles on Tzu Chi in press at the time of writing. Interested readers are referred to her article, "The Buddhist Tzu-Chi Foundation of Taiwan," in Christopher S. Queen, Charles Prebish, and Damien Keown, eds., *Action Dharma: New Studies in Engaged Buddhism* (London: RoutledgeCurzon), 2003.

9. Grant A. Olson, "Introduction," in Phra Prayudh Payutto, *Buddhadhamma: Natural Laws and Values for Life*, trans. Grant A. Olson (Albany: State University of New York Press, 1995), p. 9.

10. Bruce Evans, "Contributions of Venerable Prayudh to Buddhism and Society," in *Socially Engaged Buddhism for the New Millennium: Essays in Honor of the Ven. Phra Dhammapitaka (Bhikkhu P. A. Payutto) on His 60th Birthday Anniversary*, ed. Sulak Sivaraksa (Bangkok: Sathirakoses-Nagapradipa Foundation and Foundation for Children, 1999), p. 9.

11. Ibid.

Chapter 2: Building from Tradition

1. A. T. Ariyaratne, "Sarvodaya Shramadana's Approach to Peacebuilding," in *Buddhist Peacework: Creating Cultures of Peace*, ed. David W. Chappell (Boston: Wisdom Publications, 1999), p. 70.

2. Dalai Lama, *Ethics for the New Millennium* (New York: Riverhead Books, 1999), pp. 41, 47.

3. Ibid., pp. 161–162.

4. Thich Nhat Hanh, *Being Peace* (Berkeley, Calif.: Parallax Press, 1987), pp. 45–47.

5. Maha Ghosananda, *Step by Step: Meditations on Wisdom and Compassion* (Berkeley, Calif.: Parallax Press, 1992), p. 27. The reference is to *Dhammapada*, vv. 3–5.

6. Dith Pran, in a private conversation at James Madison University, Harrisonburg, Virginia, in October 1995. Quotations are from notes made immediately after the conversation and are not precise.

7. Dalai Lama, *Ethics*, p. 202.

8. Sulak Sivaraksa, "Buddhism and Contemporary International Trends," in *Inner Peace, World Peace: Essays on Buddhism and Nonviolence*, ed. Kenneth Kraft (Albany: State University of New York Press, 1992), p. 127.

9. Buddhadasa Bhikkhu, *Heartwood of the Bodhi Tree: The Buddha's Teaching on Voidness.* (Boston: Wisdom Publications, 1994), p. 17.

10. Ariyaratne, "The Non Violent Struggle for Economic and Social Justice." Address to the Sixth International Conference of the Society for Buddhist Christian Studies, Tacoma, Washington, August 2000 (Ratmalana, Sri Lanka: Sarvodaya Vishva Lekha, 2000), p. 5.

11. See Joanna Macy, *Dharma and Development: Religion as Resource in the Sarvodaya Self-Help Movement*, rev. ed. (West Hartford, Conn.: Kumarian Press, 1985), p. 34.

12. On Ambedkar, see Christopher S. Queen, "Dr. Ambedkar and the Hermeneutics of Buddhist Liberation," in *Engaged Buddhism: Buddhist Liberation Movements in Asia*, ed. Christopher S. Queen and Sallie B. King (Albany: State University of New York Press, 1996), esp. pp. 55–63.

13. Nhat Hanh, *Being Peace*, pp. 45–46.

14. Ghosananda, *Step by Step*, p. 64.

15. Aung San Suu Kyi, *The Voice of Hope: Conversations with Alan Clements* (New York: Penguin, 1997), p. 135.

16. Ibid., p. 143.

17. Sulak, *Global Healing: Essays and Interviews on Structural Violence, Social Development and Spiritual Transformation* (Bangkok: Thai Inter-Religious Commission for Development and Sathirakoses-Nagapradipa Foundation, 1999), p. 71.

18. Ariyaratne, "The Non Violent Struggle," pp. 4–5.

19. Nhat Hanh, *Being Peace*, p. 9.

20. Sulak, "Buddhism and Human Rights in Siam," in *Socially Engaged Buddhism for the New Millennium: Essays in honor of the Ven. Phra Dhammapitaka (Bhikkhu P. A. Payutto) on His 60th Birthday Anniversary*, ed. Sulak Sivaraksa (Bangkok: Sathirakoses-Nagapradipa Foundation and Foundation for Children, 1999), pp. 198-199.

21. Suu Kyi, p. 134.

22. Ibid., p. 8.

23. Ibid., p. 122.

24. Ibid., pp. 17-18.

25. Dalai Lama, *Ethics*, pp. 22-23.

26. Ibid., pp. 64-68.

27. Ibid., p. 77.

28. Venerable Shih Cheng-Yen, "A New Millennium of Goodness, Beauty, and Truth," in *Buddhist Peacework*, ed. Chappell, p. 49.

29. http://www.tzuchi.org/global/master/themaster/briefintro.html; accessed June 7, 2002.

30. Cheng Yen, "The Spiritual Foundation of Tzu Chi," *Inspirational Extracts*, December 5, 2001. http://www.tzuchi.org/global; accessed June 7, 2002.

31. Cheng Yen, "We Are an Extraordinary Organization of Bodhisattvas," *Inspirational Extracts*, May 18, 2001. http://www.tzuchi.org/global; accessed June 7, 2002.

32. Daisaku Ikeda, "The SGI's Peace Movement," in *Buddhist Peacework*, ed. Chappell, pp. 136-137.

33. Dalai Lama, *Ethics*, p. 237.

34. Nhat Hanh, *Being Peace*, pp. 9, 45.

35. Nhat Hanh, "Ahimsa: The Path of Harmlessness," in *Buddhist Peacework*, ed. Chappell, pp. 161-162.

36. Dalai Lama, *Ethics*, p. 81.

37. Ariyaratne, "The Non Violent Struggle," p. 3.

38. Hammalawa Saddhatissa, *Buddhist Ethics* (London: Wisdom Publications reprint, 1987), p. 73.

39. http://www.plumvillage.org/DharmaDoors/MindfulnessTraining/mindfulness_train ings.htm; accessed February 1, 2002. See also Nhat Hanh, *For a Future To Be Possible: Commentaries on the Five Wonderful Precepts* (Berkeley, Calif.: Parallax Press, 1993).

40. Sulak, in *Inner Peace, World Peace*, ed. Kraft, pp. 129-133, and *A Socially Engaged Bud-*

dhism (Bangkok, Thailand: Thai Inter-Religious Commission for Development, 1988), pp. 66–68. The wording of the two accounts differs, but I have combined excerpts from both.

41. C. Julia Huang, "The Buddhist Tzu-Chi Foundation of Taiwan," in *Action Dharma: New Studies in Engaged Buddhism*, ed. Christopher S. Queen, Charles Prebish, and Damien Keown (London and New York: RoutledgeCurzon, 2003), n. 19, p. 151. Second bracketed addition mine.

42. Nhat Hanh, *Being Peace*, p. 88.

43. One version of these vows, as recited at the Rochester Zen Center in Rochester, New York is

> All beings, without number, I vow to liberate
> Endless, blind passions, I vow to uproot
> Dharma gates, beyond measure, I vow to penetrate
> The great Way of Buddha, I vow to attain.

44. www.tzuchi.org/global/master/themaster/briefintro.html; accessed June 7, 2002.

45. Nhat Hanh, *Being Peace*, p. 67.

46. Nhat Hanh, "Ahimsa," pp. 162–163.

47. Macy, *Dharma and Development*, pp. 38–39.

48. Ariyaratne, "Sarvodaya Peace Meditation Programme: Introduction and Guide to Participants," (1999), p. 11; and "Peoples' Peace Initiative: A Progress Report, August 1999–February 2000," (2000), p. 1. Also see http://Sarvodaya.org/PeaceInitiative/MeditationProgram.htm; accessed June 7, 2002.

49. Huang, *Action Dharma* pp. 140–141.

50. Dalai Lama, *Kindness, Clarity, and Insight*, trans. and ed. Jeffrey Hopkins, coed. Elizabeth Napper (Ithaca, N.Y.: Snow Lion, 1984), pp. 34–35.

51. Ibid., p. 111.

52. Ibid.

53. Dalai Lama, *Ethics*, p. 113.

54. Yu-ing Ching, *Master of Love and Mercy: Cheng Yen* (Nevada City, Calif.: Blue Dolphin, 1995), p. 6.

55. Shih Cheng-Yen, in *Buddhist Peacework*, ed. Chappell, pp. 49, 51.

56. Macy, *Dharma and Development*, pp. 38, 56.

57. Nhat Hanh, *Being Peace*, pp. 113–114.

58. Yeshua Moser-Puangsuwan, "The Buddha in the Battlefield: Maha Ghosananda Bhik-

khu and the Dhammayietra Army of Peace," in *Nonviolence for the Third Millennium*, ed. G. Simon Harak (Macon, Ga.: Mercer University Press, 2000), p. 129.

59. Ariyaratne, "Sarvodaya Shramadana's Approach to Peacebuilding," pp. 71, 75.

60. Dhammachari Lokamitra, "The Dhamma Revolution in India: Peacemaking Begins with the Eradication of the Caste System," in *Buddhist Peacework*, ed. Chappell, p. 32 and n. 9, p. 36.

61. http://www.tzuchi.org/global/master/themaster/briefintro.html; accessed June 7, 2002.

62. Cheng Yen, "The Full Moon," *Inspirational Extracts*, November 1, 2001. http://www.tzuchi.org/global; accessed June 7, 2002.

63. Ibid; see also Cheng Yen, "We Are an Extraordinary Organization of Bodhisattvas," *Inspirational Extracts*, May 18, 2001; accessed June 7, 2002.

64. Lokamitra, pp. 34–35.

65. *The Dhammapada*, trans. John Ross Carter and Mahinda Palihawadana (Oxford: Oxford University Press, 1987), p. 25 (*Dhammapada* verse 130).

66. *Mettā Sutta, Sutta-Nipāta*, trans. H. Saddhatissa (London: Curzon Press, 1985), p. 16.

Chapter 3: Engaged Buddhist Ethical Theory

1. A. Padmasiri de Silva, "Buddhist Ethics," in *A Companion to Ethics*, ed. Peter Singer (Oxford: Blackwell, 1991 and 1993), pp. 58–68.

2. James Whitehill, "Buddhist Ethics in Western Context: The Virtues Approach," *Journal of Buddhist Ethics* 1 (1994) (http://jbe.gold.ac.uk/a/white1.html); accessed May 30, 1996. Damien Keown, *The Nature of Buddhist Ethics* (Basingstoke, U.K.: Palgrave, 1992, 2001), chap. 8.

3. Dalai Lama, *Ethics for the New Millennium* (New York: Riverhead Books, 1999), pp. 28–30.

4. Stephen Buckle, "Natural Law," in *A Companion to Ethics*, ed. Singer, p. 162.

5. Buddhadasa Bhikkhu, "Everyday Language and Dhamma Language," in *Me and Mine: Selected Essays of Bhikkhu Buddhadasa*, ed. Donald K. Swearer (Albany: State University of New York Press, 1989), p. 128.

6. Phra Praydh Payutto, *Buddhadhamma: Natural Laws and Values for Life*, trans. Grant A. Olson (Albany: State University of New York Press, 1995), p. 77. The Buddha is quoted from *Saṁyuttanikāya*, vol. 2, no. 45 (hereafter given as "S.II.25").

7. Maha Ghosananda, *Step by Step: Meditations on Wisdom and Compassion*, ed. Jane Sharada Mahoney and Philip Edmonds (Berkeley, Calif.: Parallax Press, 1992), p. 36.

8. Payutto, p. 48.

9. Ibid., p. 247.

10. Buddhadasa, "The Value of Morality," in Me and Mine, p. 159.

11. Ibid.

12. Ibid., p. 164.

13. Dalai Lama, Dimensions of Spirituality (Boston: Wisdom Publications, 1995), pp. 8–9.

14. Bruce R. Reichenbach, The Law of Karma: A Philosophical Study (Honolulu: University of Hawai'i Press, 1990), p. 2.

15. A. T. Ariyaratne, quoted in Catherine Ingram, In the Footsteps of Gandhi: Conversations with Spiritual Social Activists (Berkeley, Calif.: Parallax Press, 1990), p. 132.

16. Payutto, p. 248.

17. Buddhadasa, "The Value of Morality," p. 161.

18. Buddhadasa, "Dictatorial Dhammic Socialism," in Me and Mine, p. 186.

19. Payutto, pp. 72–74.

20. Buddhadasa, "Benefiting the World," in Me and Mine, p. 198.

21. Buddhadasa, "Democratic Socialism," in Me and Mine, p. 174.

22. Buddhadasa, "Dictatorial Dhammic Socialism," in Me and Mine, p. 187.

23. Mark Johnson, Moral Imagination: Implications of Cognitive Science for Ethics (Chicago: University of Chicago Press, 1993), p. 59.

24. Hammalawa Saddhatissa, Buddhist Ethics (London: Wisdom Publications reprint, 1987), p. 73.

25. Ibid., p. 76.

26. Mettā Sutta, Sutta-Nipāta 1.8, trans. H. Saddhatissa (London: Curzon Press, 1985, 1987), p. 16.

27. Thich Nhat Hanh, Love in Action: Writings on Nonviolent Social Change (Berkeley, Calif.: Parallax Press, 1993), p. 65.

28. Buddhadasa Bhikkhu, Heartwood of the Bodhi Tree: The Buddha's Teaching on Voidness, ed. Santikaro Bhikkhu, trans. Dhammavicayo (Boston: Wisdom Publications, 1994), pp. 40–41.

29. Payutto, p. 246.

30. See Saddhatissa, pp. 87ff; Peter Harvey, An Introduction to Buddhist Ethics: Foundations, Values and Issues (Cambridge: Cambridge University Press, 2000), p. 68; and Sulak Sivaraksa, ed., A Socially Engaged Buddhism for the New Millennium: Essays in Honor of the Ven. Phra Dhammapitaka (Bhikkhu P. A. Payutto) on His 60th Birthday Anniversary (Bang-

kok: Sathirakoses-Nagapradipa Foundation and Foundation for Children, 1999), (Bangkok: Thai Inter-Religious Commission for Development, 1988), p. 59.

31. Maha Ghosananda, pp. 66–67.

32. Dalai Lama, from *Worlds in Harmony*, cited in Arnold Kotler, ed., *Engaged Buddhist Reader* (Berkeley, Calif.: Parallax Press, 1996), pp. 130–131.

33. Payutto, pp. 135–136.

34. Johnson, p. 105. He cites John Dewey, *Theory of the Moral Life* (New York: Holt, Rinehart, and Winston, 1960), p. 141. Emphases removed from the first quotation.

35. Payutto, p. 246.

36. Dalai Lama, *Ethics*, pp. 27–28.

37. Ibid., p. 150.

38. Ibid.

39. Johnson, pp. 8–9. I am indebted to my reading of this book for many of the insights into Buddhist ethics recorded in this section of the chapter.

40. Ibid.

41. Dalai Lama, *Ethics*, pp. 152–153.

42. Payutto, p. 285, note 118.

43. James Whitehill, "Buddhist Ethics in Western Context: The Virtues Approach," *Journal of Buddhist Ethics* 1 (1994): 3, 5. I omit in the first part of the quotation Whitehill's remark that virtue ethics are character-based rather than principle-driven or act-focused. Obviously, I see elements of both virtue ethics and the incorporation of principles in Engaged Buddhist ethics.

44. Dalai Lama, *Ethics*, pp. 30, 32.

45. Ibid., p. 30.

46. Ibid., p. 150.

47. Ibid.

48. Ibid., pp. 112–113.

49. Ariyaratne, "Sarvodaya Shramadana's Approach to Peacebuilding," in *Buddhist Peacework*, ed. David W. Chappell (Boston: Wisdom Publications, 1999), p. 77.

50. Nhat Hanh, *Being Peace*, (Berkeley, Calif.: Parallax Press, 1987), p. 74.

51. Payutto, pp. 198, 199.

52. Ibid., p. 224; ellipses in Payutto. Payutto quotes *Itivuttaka* 9–10.

53. Ibid., pp. 223, 224.

54. Ibid., pp. 255–256.

55. Ibid., p. 256.

56. Ibid., p. 248.

57. Ibid., p. 37.

58. Sulak, "Buddhism and Human Rights in Siam," in A *Socially Engaged Buddhism*, p. 200.

59. Buddhadasa Bhikkhu, *Heartwood of the Bodhi Tree*, pp. 15, 17.

60. Sulak, A *Socially Engaged Buddhism*, pp. 75–76.

61. Dalai Lama, *Ethics*, pp. 30–32.

62. Ibid., pp. 73–74.

63. Ibid., pp. 72–73.

64. Ibid., pp. 148–149.

65. Nhat Hanh, *Being Peace*, p. 14.

66. Ibid., pp. 91–92.

67. Maha Ghosananda, *Step by Step: Meditations on Wisdom and Compassion*, ed. Jane Sharada Mahoney and Philip Edmonds (Berkeley, Calif.: Parallax Press, 1993), pp. 34–35.

68. Dalai Lama, *Ethics*, p. 47.

69. Daniel Berrigan and Thich Nhat Hanh, *The Raft Is Not the Shore: Conversations toward a Buddhist-Christian Awareness* (Boston: Beacon Press, 1975), p. 99.

70. http://www.tzuchi.org/global/master/themaster/briefintro.html; accessed June 7, 2002.

71. Dalai Lama, *Ethics*, pp. 55, 61–62.

72. Maha Ghosananda, pp. 56–57.

73. Ibid., p. 62.

74. Aung San Suu Kyi, *The Voice of Hope: Conversations with Alan Clements* (London and New York: Penguin Books, 1997), p. 135.

75. Maha Ghosananda, p. 54.

76. Ibid., pp. 68–69.

77. Nhat Hanh, *Being Peace*, p. 69.

78. Ibid., p. 70.

79. Nhat Hanh, *Touching Peace: Practicing the Art of Mindful Living* (Berkeley, Calif.: Parallax Press, 1992), pp. 77–78.

80. Dalai Lama, *Kindness, Clarity and Insight*, trans. and ed. Jeffrey Hopkins, coed. Elizabeth Napper (Ithaca, N.Y.: Snow Lion, 1984), p. 63.

81. Dalai Lama, *Ethics*, p. 102.

82. Dalai Lama, *The Principle of Universal Responsibility* (New York: Potala Publications, n.d.), p. 5.

83. Suu Kyi, p. 121.

84. B. R. Ambedkar address to the All-India Depressed Classes Conference in 1942, Dhananjay Keer, *Dr. Ambedkar: Life and Mission*, 3rd ed. (Bombay: Popular Prakasahan, 1971), p. 351; cited in Christopher S. Queen, "Dr. Ambedkar and the Hermeneutics of Buddhist Liberation," in *Engaged Buddhism: Buddhist Liberation Movements in Asia*, ed. Christopher S. Queen and Sallie B. King (Albany: State University of New York Press, 1996), pp. 62–63.

85. Ambedkar, "Report of the Fourth Conference of the World Fellowship of Buddhists, Kathmandu, Nepal," quoted in D. C. Ahir, *Dr. Ambedkar on Buddhism* (Bombay: Siddharth Publications, 1982), p. 105, cited by Dhammachari Lokamitra, in *Buddhist Peacework*, ed. Chappell, pp. 30–31.

86. Daisaku Ikeda, "The SGI's Peace Movement," in *Buddhist Peacework*, ed. Chappell, p. 130.

87. Santikaro Bhikkhu, "Buddhadasa Bhikkhu: Life and Society through the Natural Eyes of Voidness," in *Engaged Buddhism*, ed. Queen and King, pp. 156–157.

88. Ambedkar, *The Buddha and His Dhamma*, 3rd ed. (Bombay: Siddharth Publications, 1984), pp. 254–255 (sects. IV.I.13–15); cited in Chris Queen, "Dr. Ambedkar and the Hermeneutics of Buddhist Liberation," in *Engaged Buddhism*, ed. Queen and King, 59.

89. Payutto, pp. 85–86, 165.

90. Dalai Lama, "The Principle of Universal Responsibility."

91. Thich Nhat Hanh, *Being Peace*, p. 89.

92. Ibid., pp. 89–90.

93. Cited in Buddhadasa Bhikkhu, *Heartwood of the Bodhi Tree*, p. 14.

94. http://www.tzuchi.org/global/services/index.html; accessed June 7, 2002.

95. Cheng Yen, "Performing Good Deeds Is More Important Than Shunning Evil Ones," *Inspirational Extracts*, May 1, 2001. http://www.tzuchi.org/global; accessed June 7, 2002.

96. Ikeda, p. 133.

97. Cited in Joanna Macy, *Dharma and Development: Religion as Resource in the Sarvodaya Self-Help Movement*, rev. ed. (West Hartford, Conn.: Kumarian Press), p. 39.

98. Suu Kyi, p. 17.

99. Ibid., p. 7.

100. Ibid., pp. 124–125.

101. Buddhadasa Bhikkhu, "Me-and-Mine," in *Me and Mine*, p. 83.

102. Cited in Macy, *Dharma and Development*, p. 68.

103. Maha Ghosananda, p. 63.

Chapter 4: Individual and Society

1. Aung San Suu Kyi, *The Voice of Hope: Conversations with Alan Clements* (London and New York: Penguin Books, 1997), p. 148.

2. Maha Ghosananda, *Step By Step: Meditations on Wisdom and Compassion* (Berkeley, Calif.: Parallax Press, 1992), p. 58.

3. Dalai Lama, *Ethics for the New Millennium* (New York: Riverhead Books, 1999), pp. 87–89.

4. Phra Prayudh Payutto, *Buddhadhamma: Natural Laws and Values for Life*, trans. Grant A. Olson (Albany: State University Press of New York, 1995), p. 42.

5. Ibid.

6. Ibid., p. 44.

7. Ibid., p. 45.

8. Ibid.

9. L. P. N. Perera, *Buddhism and Human Rights: A Buddhist Commentary on the Universal Declaration of Human Rights* (Colombo, Sri Lanka: Karunaratne and Sons, 1991), pp. 23–24.

10. Cheng Yen, "Applying the Spirit of Lotus Sutra," *Inspirational Extracts* November 5, 2001. http://www.tzuchi.org/global; accessed June 7, 2002.

11. A. T. Ariyaratne, "Sarvodaya Shramadana's Approach to Peacebuilding," in *Buddhist Peacework: Creating Cultures of Peace*, ed. David W. Chappell (Boston: Wisdom Publications, 1999), p. 71.

12. Dalai Lama, *Ethics*, p. 4.

13. Buddhadasa Bhikkhu, *Heartwood of the Bodhi Tree: The Buddha's Teaching on Voidness* (Boston: Wisdom Publications, 1994), pp. 11–12.

14. Thich Nhat Hanh, *Touching Peace: Practicing the Art of Mindful Living* (Berkeley, Calif.: Parallax Press, 1992), p.89.

15. Dalai Lama, *Ethics*, p. 47.

16. Payutto, *Buddhadhamma*, p. 259.

17. Ibid., pp. 259–260.

18. Nhat Hanh, *Being Peace* (Berkeley, Calif.: Parallax Press, 1987), pp. 45–47.

19. Sulak Sivaraksa, *A Socially Engaged Buddhism* (Bangkok: Thai Inter-Religious Commission for Development, 1988), p. 76.

20. Dalai Lama, *Worlds in Harmony* (Berkeley, Calif.: Parallax Press, 1992), pp. 131–139; cited in Arnold Kotler, ed., *Engaged Buddhist Reader* (Berkeley, Calif.: Parallax Press, 1996), p. 127.

21. Ibid., p. 130.

22. Dalai Lama, *Ethics*, pp. 162–163.

23. Ibid., p. 169.

24. Payutto, *Buddhadhamma*, p. 147. The Buddha is quoted from *Aṅguttaranikāya*, vol. 1, no. 173.

25. Ibid., p. 150. The scripture quoted is *Aṅguttaranikāya*, vol. 1, no. 249.

26. Ibid., p. 186.

27. Ibid., pp. 189–190. Quoting *Saṁyuttanikāya*, vol. 5, nos. 29–30.

28. Ibid., pp. 226–227.

29. Dalai Lama, *Ethics*, p. 107.

30. Nhat Hanh, *Being Peace*, pp. 63–64.

31. Ibid., p. 62.

32. Dalai Lama, *Ethics*, pp. 162–163.

33. Dhammachari Lokamitra, "The Dhamma Revolution in India: Peacemaking Begins with the Eradication of the Caste System," in *Buddhist Peacework*, ed. Chappell, pp. 30–34.

34. Joanna Macy, *Dharma and Development: Religion as Resource in the Sarvodaya Self-Help Movement*, rev. ed. (West Hartford, Conn.: Kumarian Press, 1985), p. 38.

35. Ariyaratne, in *Buddhist Peacework*, ed. Chappell, p. 72. Emphasis added.

36. Ariyaratne, "The Non Violent Struggle for Economic and Social Justice," talk presented to the 6th International Conference of the Society for Buddhist-Christian Studies, Tacoma, Washington, August 2000, p. 28.

37. Buddhadasa Bhikkhu, "A Dictatorial Dhammic Socialism," in *Me and Mine: Selected Essays of Bhikkhu Buddhadasa*, ed. Donald K. Swearer (Albany: State University of New York Press, 1989), p. 192.

38. Payutto, *Buddhadhamma*, p. 237.

39. Buddhadasa, "Toward the Truth of Buddhism," *Me and Mine*, p. 66.

40. Payutto, *Buddhadhamma*, pp. 223-224.

41. Ibid., p. 227.

42. Suu Kyi, pp. 40, 91-93.

43. Buddhadasa, "A Dictatorial Dhammic Socialism," in *Me and Mine*, pp. 184-185.

44. P. A. Payutto, *Buddhist Solutions for the Twenty-First Century*, trans. Bruce Evans (Bangkok: Buddhadhamma Foundation, n.d.), p. 12.

45. Ibid., p. 4.

46. Ibid., p. 6.

47. Suu Kyi, p. 137.

48. Payutto, *Buddhist Solutions*, p. 20.

49. Ibid., pp. 24-25.

50. Ibid., pp. 21, 22.

51. Suu Kyi, pp. 157-158.

52. Payutto, *Buddhist Solutions*, p. 11.

53. Or even the provocatively, but misleadingly, named "dictatorial dhammic socialism."

54. Buddhadasa, "Dictatorial Dhammic Socialism," in *Me and Mine*, p. 184.

55. Although the written political views of Buddhadasa are more conservative than those of Payutto, in their impact on Thai political life, Payutto has been the more conservative of the two. This may be due partially to differences in personality and way of life, though their views on the proper role of a monk also play a role. Buddhadasa broke with the Thai Buddhist establishment as a young man and lived the rest of his life physically and socially as an outsider to that establishment. Payutto has been eminently successful within that establishment, not only as a scholar, but also as an administrator. The cornerstone of Buddhadasa's spirituality has been the "void" or nonattached mind (*cit-wang*). To borrow a phrase from the modern business lexicon, this has allowed him consistently to "think outside the box" of established Buddhist interpretations and to be uniquely creative in applying Buddhism to the modern world. Payutto, the most eminent scholar of his time, speaks with a scholar's voice, consistently grounding his statements in quotations from scriptures. Buddhadasa liked to bait and provoke others as a kind of skillful means to try to get others to

see things in a fresh way, to think deeply on matters on which the established understanding had shut off thought. This role as provocateur frequently extended to the realm of politics. Payutto is concerned for the Sangha to be apolitical and tends to criticize the most politically engaged elements of the Sangha, which makes him appear to support the status quo. When he makes statements with political implications, they tend to be couched in very traditional terms. As a consequence of these traits, Buddhadasa has been much more influential in the development of social and political criticism in Thailand than Payutto. (My thanks to Donald Swearer for discussing these matters with me. Any errors in interpretation are my responsibility alone.)

56. The reader may note that the concern addressed in this section of the paper is similar to the concern addressed by such "Critical Buddhism" thinkers as Hakamaya Noriaki, who seeks to identify the source in Buddhist philosophy of certain ethical lapses in East Asian Buddhist institutional and individual behavior. Hakamaya believes the idea of *wa* (harmony) in Japanese Buddhist thought bears responsibility for an oppressive political rhetoric mandating harmony with the demands of authoritarian regimes and rigid social norms. I suggest, in light of the conclusions of this paper, that the idea of harmony need not necessarily lead to such oppressive results, *particularly* if it is properly contextualized—as it was *not* in Japan—with other Buddhist ideas, such as critical thinking, the *dasarājadhamma*, the mutuality of interdependence between ruler and ruled, and the fundamental emptiness of all social institutions. (See Jamie Hubbard and Paul L. Swanson, eds., *Pruning the Bodhi Tree: The Storm over Critical Buddhism* [Honolulu: University of Hawai'i Press, 1997]).

57. Sulak, "An Alternative Agenda for a Global Economy," *Seeds of Peace* 13, no. 1 (January–April 1997), pp. 15–16.

58. Ariyaratne, "The Non Violent Struggle for Economic and Social Justice," pp. 28–29.

59. Ariyaratne, "Introduction," in Macy, *Dharma and Development*, p. 15.

60. On *gram swaraj*, see George D. Bond, *Buddhism at Work: Community Development, Social Empowerment and the Sarvodaya Movement*. Foreword by Joanna Macy (Bloomfield, Conn.: Kumarian Press, 2004), pp. 103–110.

61. Ibid., p. 109.

62. Ibid.

63. Ariyaratne, *Buddhist Thought in Sarvodaya Practice* (Ratmalana, Sri Lanka: Sarvodaya Vishva Lekha, 1995), p. 13. Cited in Bond, *Buddhism at Work*, p. 109.

64. Bond, p. 111.

Chapter 5: Human Rights

1. Vishva Niketan, "Vishva Niketan, 'Universal Abode': A Dream Becoming a Reality" (Moratuwa, Sri Lanka: A. T. Ariyaratne Charitable Trust, n.d.), n.p.

2. Maha Ghosananda, *Step by Step: Meditations on Wisdom and Compassion* (Berkeley, Calif.: Parallax Press, 1992), p. 78.

3.   Sulak Sivaraksa, "Buddhism and Contemporary International Trends," in *Inner Peace, World Peace: Essays on Buddhism and Nonviolence*, ed. Kenneth Kraft (Albany: State University of New York Press, 1992), pp. 134–135.

4.   http://Tibet.com; accessed June 7, 2002.

5.   http://Tibet.com/Humanrights/index.html; accessed June 7, 2002.

6.   http://www.ned.org/grantees/cihr/civicorg.html, p. 4; accessed June 12, 2002.

7.   Aung San Suu Kyi, *Freedom from Fear and Other Writings* (New York: Penguin, 1991), pp. 173–174.

8.   On the three generations of human rights, see Sumner B. Twiss, "A Constructive Framework for Discussing Confucianism and Human Rights," in *Confucianism and Human Rights*, ed. Wm. Theodore de Bary and Tu Weiming (New York: Columbia University Press, 1998), p. 32.

9.   Joanne R. Bauer and Daniel A. Bell, "Introduction," in *The East Asian Challenge for Human Rights*, ed. Joanne R. Bauer and Daniel A. Bell (Cambridge: Cambridge University Press, 1999), pp. 5–6. Internal quotation from Lee Kuan Yew taken from the *International Herald Tribune*, November 9–10, 1991.

10.   Bauer and Bell, "Introduction," pp. 4, 6.

11.   Suu Kyi, *Freedom from Fear*, pp. 167, 174, 175.

12.   Quoted in ibid., p. 174.

13.   Twiss, "A Constructive Framework for Discussing Confucianism and Human Rights," pp. 30–31.

14.   Ibid.

15.   Onuma Yasuaki, "Toward an Intercivilizational Approach to Human Rights," in *The East Asian Challenge*, ed. Bauer and Bell, pp. 122–123.

16.   Quoted by Sulak Sivaraksa in his "Buddhism and Human Rights in Siam," in *Socially Engaged Buddhism for the New Millennium: Essays in Honor of the Ven. Phra Dhammapitaka (Bhikkhu P. A. Payutto) on His 60th Birthday Anniversary*, ed. Sulak Sivaraksa (Bangkok: Sathirakoses-Nagapradipa Foundation and Foundation for Children, 1999), p. 195.

17.   Jack Donnelly, "Human Rights and Asian Values: A Defense of 'Western' Universalism," in *The East Asian Challenge*, ed. Bauer and Bell, p. 61.

18.   Twiss, "A Constructive Framework for Discussing Confucianism and Human Rights," pp. 35–36, 37–38.

19.   Craig K. Ihara, "Why There Are No Rights in Buddhism: A Reply to Damien Keown," in *Buddhism and Human Rights*, ed. Damien V. Keown, Charles S. Prebish, and Wayne R. Husted (Richmond, U.K.: Curzon Press, 1998), p. 51.

20. Derek S. Jeffreys, "Does Buddhism Need Human Rights?" in *Action Dharma: New Studies in Engaged Buddhism*, ed. Christopher Queen, Charles Prebish, and Damien Keown (London: RoutledgeCurzon), 2003, p. 276.

21. Hammalawa Saddhatissa, *Buddhist Ethics: The Path to Nirvana* (London: Wisdom Publications, 1987), p. 73.

22. Peter D. Junger, "Why the Buddha Has No Rights," in *Buddhism and Human Rights*, ed. Keown, Prebish, and Husted, p.86.

23. Ibid., p. 83.

24. Thich Nhat Hanh, *Being Peace* (Berkeley, Calif.: Parallax Press, 1987), p. 92.

25. Sulak Sivaraksa, *Global Healing: Essays and Interviews on Structural Violence Social Development and Spiritual Transformation* (Bangkok: Thai Inter-Religious Commission for Development and Sathirakoses-Nagapradipa Foundation, 1999), p. 13.

26. L. P. N. Perera, *Buddhism and Human Rights: A Buddhist Commentary on the Universal Declaration of Human Rights* (Colombo, Sri Lanka: Karunaratne and Sons, 1991), p. 29.

27. Donnelly, "Human Rights and Asian Values," p. 77.

28. Ariyaratne, ""The Non Violent Struggle for Economic and Social Justice," printed copy of a presentation given to the 6th International Conference of the Society for Buddhist-Christian Studies, Tacoma, Washington, August 5–12, 2000, Sarvodaya Shramadana, 2000, p. 26.

29. Dalai Lama, *Worlds in Harmony* (Berkeley, Calif.: Parallax Press, 1992), pp. 3–10; quoted in Arnold Kotler, ed. *Engaged Buddhist Reader* (Berkeley, Calif.: Parallax Press, 1996), pp. 3–4.

30. Sulak Sivaraksa, "Buddhism and Human Rights in Siam," p. 196.

31. Venerable U Rewata Dhamma, "Dhamma, Ethics and Human Rights." Discourse delivered to the Asian Leaders Conference, Seoul, South Korea, December 1994, quoted in Sulak, "Buddhism and Human Rights in Siam."

32. Donnelly, "Human Rights and Asian Values," p. 69.

33. Venerable U Rewata Dhamma, in Sulak, "Buddhism and Human Rights in Siam," p. 196.

34. Taitetsu Unno, "Personal Rights and Contemporary Buddhism," in *Human Rights and the World's Religions*, ed. Leroy S. Rouner (South Bend, Ind.: University of Notre Dame Press, 1988), p. 129.

35. Interview with Samdhong Rinpoche, September 24, 2000, Cincinnati, Ohio. Samdhong Rinpoche is the former chairman of the Assembly of Tibetan People's Deputies and at the time of writing the Kalon Tripa, or chair, of the Kashag (cabinet) of the Tibetan government in exile. He is the first elected Kalon Tripa and functions as the Tibetan executive

chief. The quotations are taken from notes made at the time of the interview and should not be considered completely accurate.

36. Donnelly, "Human Rights and Asian Values," p. 61.

37. A performative statement is one that brings a new reality into being simply by stating (or writing) the words. For example, in a marriage ceremony, when the minister says, "I now pronounce you man and wife," a married couple has been brought into being by the act of saying so.

38. Donnelly, "Human Rights and Asian Values," p. 61.

39. Charles Taylor, "Conditions of an Unforced Consensus on Human Rights," in *The East Asian Challenge*, ed. Bauer and Bell, pp. 130–131.

40. This is not to say that there is not too much litigation in the United States—but this is an issue beyond the focus of this book!

41. The following information on human rights in Cambodia is taken from John Marston, "Buddhism and Human Rights NGOs in Cambodia." Paper presented at the American Academy of Religion, Denver, Colorado, November 11, 2001.

42. Quotation ascribed to the "current director of the Konrad Adenauer Foundation in Cambodia" by Marston.

43. Marston, "Buddhism and Human Rights NGOs in Cambodia." My additions in brackets.

44. The first quotation is from Marston. The second is Ou Bun Long, head of a Cambodian human rights NGO, quoted by Marston. The bracketed translation is Marston's.

45. Caroline Hughes, "Human Rights in Cambodia: International Intervention and the National Response" (Ph.D. dissertation, University of Hull, 1998), pp. 300–301, 306, cited by Marston, "Buddhism and Human Rights NGOs in Cambodia."

46. Soraj Hongladarom, "Buddhism and Human Rights in the Thoughts of Sulak Sivaraksa and Phra Dhammapidok (Prayudh Prayutto)," in *Buddhism and Human Rights*, ed. Keown, Prebish, and Husted, p. 97.

47. Taylor, p. 124.

48. Ibid., p. 140.

49. Marston, "Buddhism and Human Rights NGOs in Cambodia"; his translation of a 1996 training manual.

50. Perera, p. 74.

51. Damien Keown, "Are There Human Rights in Buddhism?" in *Buddhism and Human Rights*, ed. Keown, Prebish, and Husted, p. 32.

52. Ibid., p. 33.

53. Sallie B. King, "Human Rights in Contemporary Engaged Buddhism," in *Buddhist Theology: Critical Reflections by Contemporary Buddhist Scholars*, ed. Roger Jackson and John Makransky (Richmond, U.K.: Curzon Press, 2000), pp. 298, 299. See also King, "A Buddhist Perspective on a Global Ethic and Human Rights." *Journal of Dharma* 22, no. 2 (April–June 1995): 122–136.

54. Keown, p. 30.

55. Keown, p. 23.

56. King, "Human Rights in Contemporary Engaged Buddhism," in *Buddhist Theology*, ed. Jackson and Makransky, pp. 300–301.

57. Taylor, pp. 134, 135.

58. Saneh Chamarik, "Buddhism and Human Rights." Preamble by Phra Rajavaramuni [P. A. Payutto]. Paper no. 12 (ISBN 974-572-182-4). Bangkok, Thailand: Thai Khadi Research Institute, Thammasat University, 1982. pp. 5, 22, 23.

59. Phra Prayudh Payutto, *Buddhadhamma: Natural Laws and Values for Life*, trans. Grant A. Olson (Albany: State University of New York Press, 1995), pp. 42, 44, 45.

60. Payutto (Rajavaramuni), Preamble in Chamarik, "Buddhism and Human Rights."

61. Ibid.

62. Both speeches are contained in Payutto, *Buddhist Solutions for the Twenty-First Century*, trans. Bruce Evans (Bangkok: Buddhadhamma Foundation, n.d).

63. Ibid., pp. 8–9, 10–11.

64. Ibid., p. 70.

65. Ibid, p. 71.

66. Ibid.

67. I have had the benefit of reading a prepublication draft of "Does Buddhism Need Human Rights?" in *Action Dharma*, ed. Queen, Prebish, and Keown. My views differ substantially from those of Jeffreys.

68. His Holiness: The XIV Dalai Lama of Tibet, "Human Rights and Universal Responsibility," in *Buddhism and Human Rights*, ed. Keown, Prebish, and Husted, p. xviii.

69. Ibid., p. xvii.

70. P. A. Payutto, *Buddhist Solutions*, p. 6.

71. Dalai Lama, "Human Rights and Universal Responsibility," pp. xviii–xix.

72. Donnelly, "Human Rights and Asian Values," p. 87.

73. Dalai Lama, "Human Rights and Universal Responsibility," p. xix.

74. Ibid., p. xix.

75. Ibid., p. xx.

76. Ibid., p. xx.

77. Dalai Lama, *Ethics for the New Millennium* (New York: Riverhead Books, 1999), pp. 4-5, 28.

78. Ibid., p. 130.

79. Ibid., p. 49.

80. Ibid., pp. 162-163.

81. Ibid., p. 126.

82. Ibid., p. 41.

83. Dalai Lama, "Human Rights and Universal Responsibility," pp. xx-xxi.

84. Dalai Lama, *Worlds in Harmony* (Berkeley, Calif.: Parallax Press, 1992), pp. 131-139; cited in Kotler, *Engaged Buddhist Reader*, p. 130.

85. Śāntideva, *The Bodhicaryāvatāra*, trans. Kate Crosby and Andrew Skilton (Oxford: Oxford University Press, 1996), p. 96, 97.

86. Jay L. Garfield ably argues that in the thought of the Dalai Lama human rights and compassion are compatible but that compassion is more fundamental. See his "Human Rights and Compassion," in *Buddhism and Human Rights*, ed. Keown, Prebish, and Husted.

87. Dalai Lama, *Ethics*, p. 234.

Chapter 6: Nonviolence and Its Limits

1. Maha Ghosananda, *Step by Step: Meditations on Wisdom and Compassion*, ed. Jane Sharada Mahoney and Philip Edmonds (Berkeley, Calif.: Parallax Press, 1992), p. 28.

2. Ibid., pp. 77, 78.

3. First-hand accounts of these Dhammayietra can be found in *Nonviolence Today* online at www.uq.net.au/~zzdkeena/NvT/, issue 29 (November-December 1992) and issue 34 (September/October 1993); accessed June 7, 2002.

4. Maha Ghosananda, *Step by Step*, p. 69.

5. "Vishva Niketan 'Universal Abode': A Dream Becoming a Reality."

6. Sarvodaya Shramadana, "Sarvodaya Peace Meditation Programme Introduction and Guide to Participants," (Sarvodaya Shramadana, 1999), p. 5.

7. Ibid., p. 13.

8. Sarvodaya Shramadana, "People's Peace Initiative: A Progress Report August 1999–February 2000." (Sarvodaya Shramadana, 2000), pp. 3, 35.

9. "Peace Meditation Programme," p. 6.

10. The following information is taken from the Sarvodaya web page. "The Solution to Continuing War: An Overview of the Sarvodaya People's Peace Plan," http://www.sarvodaya.org/PeaceInitiative/ SarvodayaPeoplesPeacePlan.htm; accessed February 9, 2001.

11. Ibid., p. 1. All capitals in the original.

12. Ibid., pp. 2–3.

13. Ibid., p. 5.

14. *Majjhima Nikāya* (Pali Text Society trans.) III, p. 63; *Saṁyutta Nikāya* (Pali Text Society trans.) II, pp. 28, 95.

15. "The Solution to Continuing War," p. 5.

16. Ibid., p. 7. All capitals in the original.

17. Ibid., p. 7.

18. Ibid., pp. 7–8.

19. Ariyaratne, "Sarvodaya Shramadana's Approach to Peacebuilding," in *Buddhist Peacework: Creating Cultures of Peace*, ed. David W. Chappell (Boston: Wisdom Publications, 1999), p. 73.

20. Rick Brooks article on the Sarvodaya homepage, www.sarvodaya.org; accessed July 18, 2002. Also sarvodaya.org/PeaceInitiative/PeaceOperation2002/LetterTo Supporters.html; accessed July 7, 2002.

21. For more information, see Sallie B. King, "Thich Nhat Hanh and the Unified Buddhist Church," in *Engaged Buddhism: Buddhist Liberation Movements in Asia*, ed. Christopher S. Queen and Sallie B. King (Albany: State University of New York Press, 1996), pp. 321–363.

22. See ibid. Also see George McT. Kahin, *Intervention: How America Became Involved in Vietnam* (New York: Alfred A. Knopf, 1986), especially pp. 416–431; and Takashi Oka, "Buddhism as a Political Force," I–VI (Institute of Current World Affairs, *Newsletter*, TO 25–27, TO 34–35: July 17, 1966; July 21, 1966; July 29, 1966; August 4, 1966; May 29, 1967; May 30, 1967).

23. Daniel Berrigan and Thich Nhat Hanh, *The Raft Is Not the Shore: Conversations toward a Buddhist-Christian Awareness* (Boston: Beacon Press, 1975), p. 20.

24. Cited in James H. Forest, *The Unified Buddhist Church of Vietnam: Fifteen Years for Reconciliation* (Hof van Stony, Netherlands: International Fellowship of Reconciliation, 1978). p. 12.

25. Thich Nhat Hanh, *Being Peace*, ed. Arnold Kotler (Berkeley, Calif.: Parallax Press, 1987), p. 69.

26. Ibid.

27. Nhat Hanh, *The Miracle of Mindfulness: A Manual on Meditation*, rev. ed. Preface and translation by Mobi Ho. Afterword by James Forest. (Boston: Beacon Press, 1981), p. 95.

28. Nhat Hanh, in Berrigan and Hanh, *The Raft Is Not the Shore*, p. 99.

29. Nhat Hanh, *Being Peace*, pp. 79-80.

30. Maha Ghosananda, pp. 51-52.

31. Tenzin Gyatso, the XIVth Dalai Lama, "Hope for the Future," in *The Path of Compassion: Writings on Socially Engaged Buddhism*, rev. 2nd. ed., ed. Fred Eppsteiner (Berkeley, Calif.: Parallax Press, 1988), p. 5.

32. *Tibet Briefing* (New York: Office of Tibet, 1991), pp. 10-11.

33. Dalai Lama, *The Principle of Universal Responsibility* (New York: Potala Publications, n.d.), p. 2.

34. Dalai Lama, *Ethics for the New Millennium* (New York: Riverhead Books, 1999), p. 4.

35. Dalai Lama, "Hope for the Future," p. 4.

36. Dalai Lama, *Worlds in Harmony* (Berkeley, Calif.: Parallax Press, 1992), pp. 131-139; cited in Kotler, pp. 131-132.

37. Dalai Lama, *A Prayer of Words of Truth* (Dharamsala, India: Library of Tibetan Works and Archives, 1975), translated by Robert A. F. Thurman and cited in his "Tibet and the Monastic Army of Peace," in *Inner Peace, World Peace: Essays on Buddhism and Nonviolence*, ed. Kenneth Kraft (Albany: State University Press of New York, 1992), p. 87.

38. Dalai Lama, quoted in José I. Cabézon, *H.H. the Dalai Lama, The Bodhgaya Interviews* (Ithaca, N.Y.: Snow Lion, 1988), p. 32, cited in Cabézon, "Buddhist Principles in the Tibetan Liberation Movement," in *Engaged Buddhism*, ed. Queen and King, p. 304.

39. Aung San Suu Kyi, *The Voice of Hope: Conversations with Alan Clements* (New York: Penguin Books, 1997), pp. 143-144.

40. Dalai Lama, *Ethics*, p. 201.

41. Adapted by the present author from the translation by Walpola Rahula in his *What the Buddha Taught*, rev. 2nd. ed. (New York: Grove Press, 1974), p. 125.

42. Dalai Lama, *Ethics*, p. 202.

43. Ibid., p. 186.

44. José Ignacio Cabézon, "Buddhist Principles in the Tibetan Liberation Movement," in *Engaged Buddhism*, ed. Queen and King, pp. 307-308.

45. Suu Kyi, *The Voice of Hope*, p. 29.

46. Buddhadasa Bhikkhu, *Me and Mine: Selected Essays of Bhikkhu Buddhadasa*, ed. Donald K. Swearer. (Albany: State University of New York Press, 1989), pp. 198, 199.

47. Ibid., p. 203.

48. Suu Kyi, *The Voice of Hope*, p. 112.

49. Ibid., p. 113.

50. Ibid., p. 114.

51. Ibid., p. 114.

52. Ibid., p. 114.

53. Ibid., p. 113.

54. Ibid., p. 33.

55. Ibid., p. 21.

56. Ibid., p. 41.

57. Maurice Walsh, trans., *The Long Discourses of the Buddha: A Translation of the Dīgha Nikāya* (Boston: Wisdom Publications, 1987, 1995), pp. 396-397 (*Dīgha Nikāya* III.61).

58. *The Skill in Means (Upāyakauśalya) Sūtra*, translated by Mark Tatz (Delhi: Motilal Banarsidass, 1994), pp. 73-74.

59. Maekawa Michiko, "When Prophecy Fails: The Response of Aum Members to the Crisis," *Religion and Social Crisis in Japan*, ed. R. Kisala and M. Mullins (New York: Palgrave, 2001), p. 192. Cited in Charles Kimball, *When Religion Becomes Evil* (New York: Harper San Francisco, 2002), p. 82.

60. The Dalai Lama is quoted in Catherine Ingram, *In the Footsteps of Gandhi: Conversations with Spiritual Social Activists* (Berkeley, Calif.: Parallax Press, 1990), p. 13.

61. Suu Kyi, p. 159.

62. Samdhong Rinpoche, "Democracy in Exile: An Interview with Tibetan Leader Samdhong Rinpoche," *Tricycle*, No. 46 (Winter, 2002), p. 78.

63. Smdhong Rinpoche, *Tibet: A Future Vision* (New Delhi: Tibetan Parliamentary and Policy Research Centre, 1996), pp. 8-9.

64. Ibid., pp. 14, 41.

65. Nhat Hanh, *Love in Action: Writings on Nonviolent Social Change* (Berkeley, Calif.: Parallax Press, 1993), pp. 43-45.

66. Nhat Hanh, in Berrigan and Hanh, *The Raft Is Not the Shore*, p. 62.

67. Jean-Paul Sartre, *Existentialism*, trans. Bernard Frechtman (New York: Philosophical Library, 1947).

68. *Chronicle of Higher Education*, January 10, 1997, p. A61; and November 1, 1996, p. A8. Details of the latter supplied by friends of the present author who were familiar with the story.

69. Dalai Lama, *Ethics*, pp. 206–207.

70. Ibid., pp. 207–210.

71. Ibid., p. 211.

72. Ibid., p. 212.

73. Ibid., pp. 212–216.

74. Sulak in Kraft, p. 131.

75. Ibid., p. 135.

76. Ibid.

77. Nhat Hanh, *For a Future To Be Possible: Commentaries on the Five Wonderful Precepts* (Berkeley, Calif.: Parallax Press, 1993), pp. 16–17.

78. Ariyaratne, quoted in Ingram, *In the Footsteps of Gandhi*, p. 138.

Chapter 7: Justice/Reconciliation

1. For example, B. A. R. Paradkar quotes Ambedkar as saying, "So long as justice is not respected in the world there cannot be any peace. Buddhism and Buddhism alone can save the world." Paradkar, "The Religious Quest of Ambedkar," in *Ambedkar and the Neo-Buddhist Movement*, ed. T. W. Wilkinson and M. M. Thomas (Madras: Christian Literature Society, 1972), p. 64. Similarly, Dhananjay Keer quotes Ambedkar as saying, "My final word of advice to you is educate, agitate and organize; have faith in yourself. With justice on our side, I do not see how we can lose our battle." Dhananjay Keer, *Dr. Ambedkar Life and Mission* (Bombay: Popular Prakashan, 1990), p. 351. We will see some of Sulak's views below.

2. A basic teaching of Thich Nhat Hanh, the Fourteen Mindfulness Trainings, refers to justice four times (mindfulness trainings 9, 10, 11, and 13). See www.plumvillage.org, "Fourteen Mindfulness Trainings of the Order of Interbeing"; accessed June 7, 2002.

3. Peter A. Angeles, *A Dictionary of Philosophy* (London: Harper and Row, 1981), p. 140.

4. Bruce R. Reichenbach, *The Law of Karma: A Philosophical Study* (Honolulu: University of Hawai'i Press, 1990), p. 2.

5. Buddhadasa Bhikkhu, *Me and Mine: Selected Essays of Bhikkhu Buddhadasa*, trans. Donald K. Swearer (Albany: State University of New York Press, 1989), p. 77.

6. Interview with the author, August 9, 2000, Tacoma, Washington.

7. Ibid.

8. Ibid.

9. Phra Prayudh Payutto, *Buddhadhamma: Natural Law and Values for Life*, trans. Grant A. Olson (Albany: State University of New York Press, 1995), p. 265.

10. See Edward Conze, *Buddhist Meditation* (New York: Harper and Row, 1956), pp. 126–133.

11. Interview with the author, August 9, 2000, Tacoma, Washington.

12. Talk given at Gethsemani Abbey on September 20, 2000, at a retreat of the Peace Council. Quotations from the present author's notes and a transcript of the talk.

13. Samdhong Rinpoche, interview with the author, Gethsemani Abbey, September 24, 2000.

14. Thich Nhat Hanh, "What I Would Say to Osama bin Laden," in *From the Ashes: A Spiritual Response to the Attack on America*, collected by the editors of Beliefnet (n.p.: Rodale Inc. and Beliefnet Inc., 2001), p. 98.

15. Aung San Suu Kyi, *The Voice of Hope: Conversations with Alan Clements* (New York and London: Penguin Books, 1997), p. 7.

16. Jerusalem, May 3, 2000.

17. From notes taken by the author and reviewed by Geshe Sopa, , May 2–4, 2000, Jerusalem.

18. Comment in a Peace Council meeting, Belfast, Northern Ireland, June 19, 2003.

19. This analysis may appear to be unfairly comparing Buddhist ideals with "Western" realities. The reader is asked to bear in mind that the present passage is not a comparison of two ways of thought, in which case ideals would need to be compared to ideals and realities to realities, but a study of the rhetoric of Engaged Buddhists. The effort to understand the latter requires an analysis of Engaged Buddhists' perception of Western "justice" rhetoric as popularly used.

20. Daniel Gómez-Ibáñez, "Dialogue Is More Than Talk," *Benedictine Bridge* (Advent 1999): 10.

21. "The Solution to Continuing War: An Overview of the Sarvodaya People's Peace Plan," http://www.sarvodaya.org/PeaceInitiative/SarvodayaPeoples PeacePlan.htm; accessed February 9, 2001, p. 3.

22. Ibid., p. 4.

23. Nhat Hanh, *Being Peace* (Berkeley, Calif.: Parallax Press, 1987), p. 70.

24. Nhat Hanh, "Please Call Me By My True Names," in *Being Peace*, pp. 63–64.

25. Ibid., p. 62.

26. Suu Kyi, p. 8.

27. Ibid., p. 84.

28. Ibid., p. 5.

29. Ibid., p. 6.

30. Ibid., pp. 86–87.

31. Dalai Lama, *Ethics for the New Millennium* (New York: Riverhead Books, 1999), pp. 175–177.

32. Ariyaratne, interviewed by Catherine Ingram in Catherine Ingram, *In the Footsteps of Gandhi: Conversations with Spiritual Social Activists* (Berkeley, Calif.: Parallax Press, 1990), p.133, 134.

33. Samdhong Rinpoche, *Tibet: A Future Vision* (New Delhi: Tibetan Parliamentary and Policy Research Centre, 1996), p. 18.

34. Nhat Hanh, *Being Peace*, p. 92.

35. Nhat Hanh, *For a Future to Be Possible: Commentaries on the Five Wonderful Precepts* (Berkeley, Calif.: Parallax Press, 1993), p. 20.

36. Ibid., pp. 24–25.

37. Sulak, "How Society Can Practice the Precepts," in Nhat Hanh, *For a Future to Be Possible*, p. 111.

38. Ariyaratne, in Ingram, pp. 129–130.

39. Ibid., p. 134.

40. Ibid., p. 135.

41. Sulak, "An Alternative Agenda for a Global Economy," *Seeds of Peace* 13:1 (January–April, 1997), p. 15.

42. Ariyaratne, "The Non Violent Struggle for Economic and Social Justice," p. 18. (It should be noted that the title of this address is the topic on which Ariyaratne was requested to speak by the conference organizers. The word "justice" does not appear within the text itself.)

43. P. A. Payutto, *Buddhist Economics: A Middle Way for the Market Place*, 2nd rev. ed. (Bangkok: Buddhadhamma Foundation, 1992, 1994), p. 26.

44. Ariyaratne, "Non Violent Struggle," p. 19.

45. Ibid., p. 7.

46. Payutto, *Buddhist Economics*, p. 69.

47. Dalai Lama, *Ethics*, pp. 166–167.

48. Interview with the author at Gethsemani Abbey in Kentucky on September 24, 2000. The quotations are taken from careful notes made at the time of the interview, but cannot be considered exact.

49. Peter A. Angeles, *A Dictionary of Philosophy* (London: Harper and Row, 1981), p. 140.

50. L. P. N. Perera, *Buddhism and Human Rights: A Buddhist Commentary on the Universal Declaration of Human Rights* (Colombo, Sri Lanka: Karunaratne and Sons, 1991), p. 38.

51. Interview with the author, August 9, 2000, Tacoma, Washington.

Chapter 8: Conclusion

1. Maha Ghosananda, *Step by Step: Meditations on Wisdom and Compassion* (Berkeley, Calif.: Parallax Press, 1992), pp. 64, 41.

2. http://www.tzuchi.org/global/master/themaster/briefintro.html; accessed June 7, 2002.

3. Cheng Yen, "Love and Kindness Can End Violence," *Inspirational Extracts*, October 28, 2001. http://www.tzuchi.org/global; accessed June 7, 2002.

4. Sulak Sivaraksa, "Buddhism and Contemporary International Trends," in *Inner Peace, World Peace: Essays on Buddhism and Nonviolence*, ed. Kenneth Kraft (Albany: State University of New York Press, 1992), p. 127.

5. Thich Nhat Hanh, *Being Peace* (Berkeley, Calif.: Parallax Press, 1987), p. 74.

6. Howard Zehr, *Changing Lenses: A New Focus for Crime and Justice* (Scottsdale, Penn., and Waterloo, Ont.: Herald Press, 1990), p. 181.

7. Ibid., pp. 70–71.

8. Maha Ghosananda, *Step by Step: Meditations on Wisdom and Compassion* (Berkeley, Calif.: Parallax Press, 1992), p. 68.

9. Zehr, Changing Lenses p. 188.

10. Ibid.

11. One might argue that a Buddhist just war theory was developed in Japan during World War II, but in my view that was a case in which Japanese Buddhists mouthed Shinto-Confucian ideology to justify Japan's warfare. While that does not relieve Japanese Buddhists of their responsibility for supporting the war, the point is that this is not a case of using *Buddhist concepts* to justify war.

12. N. A. Nikam and Richard McKeon, ed. and trans., *The Edicts of Asoka* (Chicago: University of Chicago Press, 1959), p. 27–28.

13. Ibid., p. 28–29.

14. *Preventing Violent Conflict: A Swedish Action Plan* (Stockholm: Ministry for Foreign Affairs, 1999), p. 29 (ISBN 91-7496-132-2; ISSN 0284-6012).

15. Chuck Fager, "Some Quaker Reflections on Our Latest War," http://www.quakerhouse.org/elon-01.htm, accessed July 14, 2002, p. 1. There is much in this article to interest Engaged Buddhists.

16. See David E. W. Holden, *Friends Divided: Conflict and Division in the Society of Friends* (Richmond, Ind.: Friends United Press, 1988), pp. 37–43.

17. Samdhong Rinpoche, quoted at www.nonviolentpeaceforce.org; accessed January 13, 2003; cited from Nonviolent Peaceforce Press Release of November 30, 2002, Suraj Kund, India.

18. Nhat Hanh, *Love in Action: Writings on Nonviolent Social Change* (Berkeley: Parallax Press, 1993), p. 47.

19. Gene Sharp's magnum opus is his three-volume work, *The Politics of Nonviolent Action* (Boston: Porter Sargent, 1973).

20. Sharp, quoted in "Give Peace a Chance," *New York Times Magazine*, November 24, 2002 (n.p.). Reprint provided by the Albert Einstein Institution.

21. Sharp, *From Dictatorship to Democracy: A Conceptual Framework for Liberation* (Boston: Albert Einstein Institution, 1993), p. 10.

22. Ibid., p. 11.

23. Sharp has in recent years been working with prodemocracy Burmese activists, both in Thailand and in the Burmese jungle. His *From Dictatorship to Democracy: A Conceptual Framework for Liberation* was first published in Bangkok by the Committee for the Restoration of Democracy in Burma. He has led intensive workshops with Tibetan leaders and activists. One of his books has recently been translated into Tibetan with a foreword by the Dalai Lama. ("The Albert Einstein Institution," promotional brochure. See also www.aeinstein.org).

24. Sharp, *Civilian-Based Defense: A Post-Military Weapons System* (Princeton, N.J.: Princeton University Press, 1990).

25. As quoted by Maha Ghosananda, *Step by Step*, p. 27.

Bibliography

Angeles, Peter A. *A Dictionary of Philosophy.* London: Harper and Row, 1981.

Ariyaratne, A. T. "Sarvodaya Shramadana's Approach to Peacebuilding." *Buddhist Peacework: Creating Cultures of Peace,* pp. 69–77. Edited by David W. Chappell. Boston: Wisdom Publications, 1999.

———. "The Non Violent Struggle for Economic and Social Justice." Address to the Sixth International Conference of the Society for Buddhist Christian Studies, Tacoma, Washington, August 2000. Ratmalana, Sri Lanka: Sarvodaya Vishva Lekha, 2000.

Bauer, Joanne R., and Daniel A. Bell, eds. *The East Asian Challenge for Human Rights.* Cambridge: Cambridge University Press, 1999.

Berrigan, Daniel, and Thich Nhat Hanh. *The Raft Is Not the Shore: Conversations toward a Buddhist-Christian Awareness.* Boston: Beacon, 1975.

Bond, George D. *Buddhism at Work: Community Development, Social Empowerment and the Sarvodaya Movement.* Foreword by Joanna Macy. Bloomfield, Conn.: Kumarian Press, 2004.

Buckle, Stephen. "Natural Law." In *A Companion to Ethics,* pp. 161–174. Edited by Peter Singer. Oxford: Blackwell, 1991 and 1993.

Buddhadasa Bhikkhu. *Dhammic Socialism.* Edited and translated by Donald K. Swearer. Bangkok: Thai Inter-Religious Commission for Development, 1986.

———. *Me and Mine: Selected Essays of Bhikkhu Buddhadāsa.* Edited by Donald K. Swearer. Albany, N.Y.: SUNY Press, 1989.

———. *Heartwood of the Bodhi Tree: The Buddha's Teaching on Voidness.* Edited by Santikaro Bhikkhu. Translated by Dhammavicayo. Boston: Wisdom Publications, 1994.

Chamarik, Saneh. "Buddhism and Human Rights." Preamble by Phra Rajavaramuni [P. A. Payutto]. Paper no. 12. Bangkok, Thailand: Thai Khadi Research Institute, Thammasat University, 1982.

Chappell, David W., ed. *Buddhist Peacework: Creating Cultures of Peace.* Boston: Wisdom Publications, 1999.

Cheng Yen. *Inspirational Extracts,* May 1, 2001. http://www.tzuchi.org/global; accessed June 7, 2002.

Cheng-Yen, Venerable Shih. "A New Millennium of Goodness, Beauty, and Truth." In *Buddhist Peacework: Creating Cultures of Peace,* pp. 47–52. Edited by David W. Chappell. Boston: Wisdom Publications, 1999.

Ching, Yu-ing. *Master of Love and Mercy: Cheng Yen.* Nevada City, Calif.: Blue Dolphin, 1995.

Conze, Edward. *Buddhist Meditation*. New York: Harper and Row, 1956.

Dalai Lama. *Kindness, Clarity and Insight*. Translated and edited by Jeffrey Hopkins, coedited by Elizabeth Napper. Ithaca, N.Y.: Snow Lion, 1984.

———. *Worlds in Harmony*. Berkeley, Calif.: Parallax Press, 1992.

———. *Dimensions of Spirituality*. Boston: Wisdom Publications, 1995.

———. *The World of Tibetan Buddhism: An Overview of Its Philosophy and Practice*. Edited and translated by Geshe Thupten Jinpa. Boston: Wisdom Publications, 1995.

———. "Human Rights and Universal Responsibility." In *Buddhism and Human Rights*, pp. xvii–xxi. Edited by Damien V. Keown, Charles S. Prebish, and Wayne R. Husted. Richmond, U.K.: Curzon Press, 1998.

———. *Ethics for the New Millennium*. New York: Riverhead Books, 1999.

———. *The Principle of Universal Responsibility*. New York: Potala Publications, n.d.

de Bary, Wm. Theodore, and Tu Weiming, eds. *Confucianism and Human Rights*. New York: Columbia University Press, 1998.

de Silva, Padmasiri. "Buddhist Ethics." In *A Companion to Ethics*, pp. 58–68. Edited by Peter Singer. Oxford: Blackwell, 1991 and 1993.

Dhammapada, The. Translated by John Ross Carter and Mahinda Palihawadana. Oxford: Oxford University Press, 1987.

Eppsteiner, Fred. *The Path of Compassion: Writings on Socially Engaged Buddhism*, rev. 2nd ed. Berkeley, Calif.: Parallax Press, 1988.

Evans, Bruce. "Contributions of Venerable Prayudh to Buddhism and Society." In *Socially Engaged Buddhism for the New Millennium: Essays in Honor of the Ven. Phra Dhammapitaka (Bhikkhu P. A. Payutto) on His 60th Birthday Anniversary*, pp. 3–12. Edited by Sulak Sivaraksa. Bangkok: Sathirakoses-Nagapradipa Foundation and Foundation for Children, 1999.

Garfield, Jay L. "Human Rights and Compassion." In *Buddhism and Human Rights*, pp. 111–140. Edited by Damien V. Keown, Charles S. Prebish, and Wayne R. Husted. Richmond, U.K.: Curzon Press, 1998.

Ghosananda, Maha. *Step by Step: Meditations on Wisdom and Compassion*. Edited by Jane Sharada Mahoney and Philip Edmonds. Berkeley, Calif.: Parallax Press, 1992.

Gómez-Ibáñez, Daniel. "Dialogue Is More than Talk." *Benedictine Bridge* (Advent 1999): 10.

Hanh, Thich Nhat. *The Miracle of Mindfulness: A Manual on Meditation*, rev. ed. Preface and translation by Mobi Ho. Afterword by James Forest. Boston: Beacon Press, 1975, 1987.

———. *Being Peace*. Berkeley, Calif.: Parallax Press, 1987.

———. *Touching Peace: Practicing the Art of Mindful Living*. Berkeley, Calif.: Parallax Press, 1992.

———. *For a Future to Be Possible: Commentaries on the Five Wonderful Precepts*. Berkeley, Calif.: Parallax Press, 1993.

———. *Love in Action: Writings on Nonviolent Social Change*. Berkeley, Calif.: Parallax Press, 1993.

———. "What I Would Say to Osama bin Laden." In *From the Ashes: A Spiritual Response to the Attack on America*. Collected by the editors of Beliefnet. n.p: Rodale Inc. and Beliefnet Inc., 2001.

Harris, Ian, ed. *Buddhism and Politics in Twentieth Century Asia.* London: Pinter, 1999.

Harvey, Peter. *An Introduction to Buddhist Ethics: Foundations, Values and Issues.* Cambridge: Cambridge University Press, 2000.

Huang, C. Julia. "The Buddhist Tzu-Chi Foundation of Taiwan." In *Action Dharma: New Studies in Engaged Buddhism,* pp. 134–151. Edited by Christopher S. Queen, Charles Prebish, and Damien Keown. London and New York: RoutledgeCurzon, 2003.

Hughes, Caroline. "Human Rights in Cambodia: International Intervention and the National Response." Ph.D. dissertation, University of Hull, 1998.

Ingram, Catherine. *In the Footsteps of Gandhi: Conversations with Spiritual Social Activists.* Berkeley, Calif.: Parallax Press, 1990.

Johnson, Mark. *Moral Imagination: Implications of Cognitive Science for Ethics.* Chicago: University of Chicago Press, 1993.

Kahin, George McT. *Intervention: How America Became Involved in Vietnam.* New York: Alfred A. Knopf, 1986.

Kalupahana, David J. *Ethics in Early Buddhism.* Honolulu: University of Hawai'i Press, 1995.

Keer, Dhananjay. *Dr. Ambedkar Life and Mission.* Bombay: Popular Prakashan, 1990.

Keown, Damien. *The Nature of Buddhist Ethics.* Basingstoke, U.K.: Palgrave, 1992, 2001.

Keown, Damien V., Charles S. Prebish, and Wayne R. Husted, eds. *Buddhism and Human Rights.* Richmond, U.K.: Curzon Press, 1998.

King, Sallie B. "A Buddhist Perspective on a Global Ethic and Human Rights." *Journal of Dharma* 22, no. 2 (April–June 1995): 122–136.

———. "Human Rights in Contemporary Engaged Buddhism." In *Buddhist Theology: Critical Reflections by Contemporary Buddhist Scholars,* pp. 293–311. Edited by Roger Jackson and John Makransky. Richmond, U.K.: Curzon Press, 2000.

Kimball, Charles. *When Religion Becomes Evil.* New York: Harper San Francisco, 2002.

Kotler, Arnold, ed. *Engaged Buddhist Reader.* Berkeley, Calif.: Parallax Press, 1996.

Kraft, Kenneth, ed. *Inner Peace, World Peace: Essays on Buddhism and Nonviolence.* Albany, N.Y.: SUNY Press, 1992.

Macy, Joanna. *Dharma and Development: Religion as Resource in the Sarvodaya Self-Help Movement,* rev. ed. West Hartford, Conn.: Kumarian Press, 1985.

Marston, John. "Buddhism and Human Rights NGOs in Cambodia." Paper presented at the American Academy of Religion, November 11, 2001, Denver, Colorado.

Mettā Sutta, Sutta-Nipāta. Translated by H. Saddhatissa. London: Curzon Press, 1985.

Moser-Puangsuwan, Yeshua. "The Buddha in the Battlefield: Maha Ghosananda Bhikkhu and the Dhammayietra Army of Peace." In *Nonviolence for the Third Millennium,* pp. 121–136. Edited by G. Simon Harak. Macon, Ga.: Mercer University Press, 2000.

Nikam, N. A., and Richard McKeon, eds. and trans. *The Edicts of Asoka.* Chicago: University of Chicago Press, 1959.

Paradkar, B. A. R. "The Religious Quest of Ambedkar." In *Ambedkar and the Neo-Buddhist Movement,* pp. 33–70. Edited by T. W. Wilkinson and M. M. Thomas. Madras: Christian Literature Society, 1972.

Payutto, Phra Prayudh. *Good, Evil and Beyond: Dhamma in the Buddha's Teaching.* Translated by Bhikkhu Puriso. Bangkok: Buddhadhamma Foundation, 1993.

――. *Buddhist Economics: A Middle Way for the Market Place*, 2nd rev. ed. Bangkok: Buddhadhamma Foundation, 1992, 1994.

――. *Buddhadhamma: Natural Laws and Values for Life.* Translated by Grant A. Olson. Albany, N.Y.: SUNY Press, 1995.

――. *A Constitution for Living: Buddhist Principles for a Fruitful and Harmonious Life.* Translated by Bruce Evans. Bangkok: Buddhadhamma Foundation, 1996.

――. *Buddhist Solutions for the Twenty-First Century.* Translated by Bruce Evans. Bangkok: Buddhadhamma Foundation, n.d.

Perera, L. P. N. *Buddhism and Human Rights: A Buddhist Commentary on the Universal Declaration of Human Rights.* Colombo, Sri Lanka: Karunaratne and Sons, 1991.

Queen, Christopher S. "Dr. Ambedkar and the Hermeneutics of Buddhist Liberation." In *Engaged Buddhism: Buddhist Liberation Movements in Asia*, pp. 45–71. Edited by Christopher S. Queen and Sallie B. King. Albany, N.Y.: SUNY Press.

Queen, Christopher S., and King, Sallie B., eds. *Engaged Buddhism: Buddhist Liberation Movements in Asia.* Albany, N.Y.: SUNY Press, 1996.

Queen, Christopher S., Charles Prebish, and Damien Keown, eds. *Action Dharma: New Studies in Engaged Buddhism.* London: RoutledgeCurzon, 2003.

Reichenbach, Bruce R. *The Law of Karma: A Philosophical Study.* Honolulu: University of Hawai'i Press, 1990.

Saddhatissa, Hammalawa. *Buddhist Ethics: The Path to Nirvana.* London: George Allen & Unwin, 1970; reprint London: Wisdom Publications, 1987.

Samdhong Rinpoche, "Democracy in Exile: An Interview with Tibetan Leader Samdhong Rinpoche." *Tricycle* 46 (winter 2002): 76–79.

――. *Tibet: A Future Vision.* New Delhi: Tibetan Parliamentary and Policy Research Centre, 1996.

Śāntideva. *The Bodhicaryāvatāra.* Translated by Kate Crosby and Andrew Skilton. Oxford: Oxford University Press, 1996.

Sarvodaya Shramadana. "Sarvodaya Peace Meditation Programme: Introduction and Guide to Participants." Ratmalana, Sri Lanka: Sarvodaya Vishva Lekha, 1999.

――. "Peoples' Peace Initiative: A Progress Report, August 1999–February 2000." Ratmalana, Sri Lanka: Sarvodaya Vishva Lekha, 2000.

――. "The Solution to Continuing War: An Overview of the Sarvodaya People's Peace Plan," http://www.sarvodaya.org/PeaceInitiative/SarvodayaPeoplesPeacePlan.htm; accessed February 9, 2001.

Sharp, Gene. *The Politics of Nonviolent Action.* 3 vols. Boston: Porter Sargent, 1973.

――. *From Dictatorship to Democracy: A Conceptual Framework for Liberation.* Boston: Albert Einstein Institution, 1993.

Sivaraksa, Sulak. *A Socially Engaged Buddhism.* Bangkok: Thai Inter-Religious Commission for Development, 1988.

――. "An Alternative Agenda for a Global Economy." *Seeds of Peace* 13, no. 1 (January–April 1997): 15–16.

――. *Global Healing: Essays and Interviews on Structural Violence Social Development and Spiritual Transformation.* Bangkok: Thai Inter-Religious Commission for Development and Sathirakoses-Nagapradipa Foundation, 1999.

———, ed. *Socially Engaged Buddhism for the New Millennium: Essays in Honor of the Ven. Phra Dhammapitaka (Bhikkhu P. A. Payutto) On His 60th Birthday Anniversary.* Bangkok: Sathirakoses-Nagapradipa Foundation and Foundation for Children, 1999.

Suu Kyi, Aung San. *Freedom from Fear and Other Writings.* Edited by Michael Aris. New York: Penguin, 1991.

———. *The Voice of Hope: Conversations with Alan Clements.* With contributions by U Kyi Maung and U Tin U. New York: Penguin, 1997.

Unno, Taitetsu. "Personal Rights and Contemporary Buddhism." In *Human Rights and the World's Religions*, pp. 129–147. Edited by Leroy S. Rouner. South Bend, Ind.: University of Notre Dame Press, 1988.

Vishva Niketan. "Vishva Niketan, 'Universal Abode: A Dream Becoming a Reality." Moratuwa, Sri Lanka: A. T. Ariyatane Charitable Trust, n.d.

Whitehill, James. "Buddhist Ethics in Western Context: The Virtues Approach." *Journal of Buddhist Ethics* 1 (1994); http://jbe.gold.ac.uk/a/white1.html; accessed May 30, 1996.

Zehr, Howard. *Changing Lenses: A New Focus for Crime and Justice.* Scottsdale, Penn., and Waterloo, Ont.: Herald Press, 1990.

Index

practices, self-transformative, 27–41, 63.
See also self-transformation
pragmatism, 80–82
Pran, Dith, 16
precepts, ethical, 28–31, 41; consensus
on, 58; as moral guides, 58; new, 30–31;
Tiep Hien (Order of Interbeing) 31, 71,
81, 129, 219
Precepts, Five Lay, 28–30, 52–54, 58; Ariyaratne on, 28–29; breaking, 59–60; and
economic justice, 219–220; as ethical
principles, 55–56, 60; and human rights,
119, 130, 135, 139, 142–144; and natural
law, 58; and nonadversarial ethics, 75;
positive correlates of, 53–54
principles, ethical, 55–58, 59; positive and
negative poles of, 60
property, 128–130. *See also* economics
prototype, ethical, 56, 58–59, 61, 71
punishment, capital, 227

Quakerism, 242–243
Quang Duc, Thich, 192, 194, 195

reason: Buddhadasa on, 107; and emotion,
67–72; and ethics, 64–65, 70; and moral
choice, 97–98, 107–108; Payutto on, 64,
65, 107; Suu Kyi on, 108
reconciliation, 211–218, 228; Ariyaratne
on, 211–212; in Burma, 78; and justice,
237; Maha Ghosananda on, 74, 76, 165;
and nonviolence, 165, 174, 212; Suu Kyi
on, 74–75, 215–216; Thich Nhat Hanh
on, 76–77, 174, 212–214
reform: of Buddhism, 12; of Theravada
Buddhism, 8–9, 84, 86
Reichenbach, Bruce, 47–48, 203–204
relativism, ethical, 55, 57
religions, world, 2, 80
responsibility: Dalai Lama on, 14, 91, 94,
100–101, 156–163; and human rights,
121, 132–135, 144, 150–151, 156–163,
234–236; Ikeda on, 83; individual and
social, 99–104, 113–114, 237–239; to
oneself and others, 52; Payutto on, 111;

as response-*ability*, 53–54, 56; in Sarvodaya, 103; Sulak on, 113; Suu Kyi on,
111; in TBMSG, 102–103; Thich Nhat
Hanh on, 99–101; universal, 14, 94–95,
100, 156–163
revenge, 16, 165, 210
revolution, 106, 115–117. *See also* struggle
Rewata Dhamma, Venerable U, 132–133
rights, human, 126, 135; and adversariality,
133–142, 147–148, 156, 162–163; Ariyaratne on, 118, 131; and "Asian values,"
122–126, 137–141, 155, 156; Buddhist
concerns with, 127–137; in Burma, 119–
120, 123–124, 132; in Cambodia, 118,
119, 137–141, 142–143; collective, 121–
122, 130, 136; and communitarianism,
122–123, 134, 151–152; and compassion, 136, 156, 159, 161, 163; content
vs. language of, 126–127; Dalai Lama
on, 77, 95, 136, 153–163; and democracy, 119–120, 140; documents, 119–122,
124–126; and economics, 128–130, 131,
156–157; and environmentalism, 131,
134, 156–157; and Five Lay Precepts,
119, 130, 135, 139, 142–144; and four
Brahmavihara, 119; and freedom of religion, 121, 147–148, 158; and happiness,
157–159; and harmony, 122, 137–141,
156; and human birth, 123–124, 131,
144–145; and human enlightenability,
123–124, 144–146; and human equality,
145, 154–157, 159–160; and human freedom, 146–149, 150, 157; and human
nature, 146–147, 149, 154, 155, 157–
159; and individual, 119–120, 134; and
individualism, 122–123, 127–128, 161;
and interdependence, 134; Maha Ghosananda on, 118, 139; and natural law,
147, 149, 152, 154–155, 158–159; and
nonhuman rights, 131–132; and nonviolence, 119, 146, 166; and no self,
127–128, 145; Payutto on, 89, 146–
153, 154–155, 158, 162–163; Perera
on, 89; and power, 135–136, 140; and

174–175; unavoidable, 1–2. See also *duḥkha;* happiness
Suu Kyi, Aung San, 8, 9; on democracy, 111; on forgiveness, 20, 74; on human rights, 119–120, 123–124, 236; and imperative to act, 83–84; on justice, 215–216; on karma, 23, 84; on *mettā,* 23–24, 181; on nonviolence, 181, 186–188, 207; on political freedom, 110, 111; on power of truth, 184; on reconciliation, 74–75, 215–216

Taiwan, 1, 9, 39
Taylor, Charles, 137, 141–142, 146
TBMSG, 38, 40–41, 79
Thailand, 8–9, 10–11, 113, 186; human rights in, 141
theory, ethical: Western, 42–43, 51–52, 95–96
theory, political, 104–117
thinking, critical. See reason
Tibet, 9; government in exile of, 9, 157; human rights in, 118–119, 134; nonviolence in, 191–192; relations with China, 9, 77, 136, 148, 156, 162, 176–185, 208–209, 247–248. See also Dalai Lama; Samdhong Rinpoche
tradition, 12, 86, 155
Trailokya Bauddha Magasangha Sahayaka Gana. See TBMSG
transformation, of self and society, 32–34, 39, 63, 166–167. See also change, individual and social
Twiss, Sumner, 124–125, 126–127, 142
Tzu Chi, 1–2, 6, 9, 33–34; imperative to act in, 82; Ten Precepts, 30–31; work in, 39–40. See also Cheng Yen, Master

UDHR (United Nations Universal Declaration of Human Rights), 89, 120–122, 124, 134, 143, 148–149, 153, 155
understanding, and ethics, 64–65. See also reason

United Nations, 197, 210. See also UDHR
Unno, Taitetsu, 133
Untouchables, former. See Buddhists, new
utilitarianism, 94, 160

values, Asian, 122–126, 137–141, 155, 156
Vietnam, 11; nonviolent struggle in, 27–28, 76, 172–175; war in, 11, 73, 81, 169, 192
violence, 77, 182–183, 185–186; in Burma, 186; defensive, 188, 189–192, 195–196, 198–201; and *Dhammapada,* 16–17; and just war doctrine, 190, 199; and nation-state, 196–198; in Sri Lanka, 33, 167–171; Suu Kyi on, 186–188, 191. See also nonviolence; war
virtues: and moral principles, 60; as open-ended, 53–54, 56–57. See also ethics, virtue
Vishva Niketan, 118, 166
vows, bodhisattva, 31–32. See also bodhisattva

war, 239–242; causes of, 169–171; defensive, 188, 189–192, 240–242; just, 190, 240, 241–242, 275n.11; stopping, 169–172, 173, 201, 211. See also Vietnam; violence
Way, Middle, 150–151, 223–224
web. See interdependence
West, the: human rights in, 120, 122–126, 132, 135, 137; as influence on Engaged Buddhism, 1–4, 202, 218
Whitehill, James, 42, 60
will, free, 95, 98
wisdom, 64–66; and compassion, 70–71
work, 39–41
world-negation, 1–2

Yew, Lee Kuan, 122

Zehr, Howard, 237–239

About the Author

Sallie B. King is professor of Philosophy and Religion at James Madison University. She is co-editor of *Engaged Buddhism: Buddhist Liberation Movements in Asia* (State University of New York Press) and author of many books and articles on Buddhism, Engaged Buddhism, and the cross-cultural philosophy of religion.

Production Notes for King/*Being Benevolence*
Text and cover design by Elsa Carl. Text in Goudy Old Style and display
in Hiroshige
Text composition by Tseng Information Systems, Inc. in Buffalo TEX
Printing and binding by The Maple-Vail Book Manufacturing Group
Printed on 60 lb. Sebago Eggshell, 420 ppi

Breinigsville, PA USA
21 January 2010
231120BV00001B/59/P